MARKET-BASED MANAGEMENT

STRATEGIES FOR GROWING CUSTOMER VALUE AND PROFITABILITY

SECOND EDITION

Roger J. Best

Professor of Marketing
University of Oregon

1,3,4 (1)   6,7,8,11,12 (3)

5,14   (2)   9,10,15,16 (4)

~~6,11,12~~
~~9,12,15,16~~

Prentice Hall, Upper Saddle River, New Jersey 07458

Acquisitions Editor: Leah Johnson
Editorial Assistant: Rebecca Calvert
Managing Editor: Bruce Kaplan
Editor-in-Chief: Natalie E. Anderson
Marketing Manager: Shannon Moore
Production Editor: Tara Ruggiero
Permissions Coordinator: Monica Stipanov
Associate Managing Editor: John Roberts
Manufacturing Buyer: Diane Peirano
Manufacturing Supervisor: Arnold Vila
Senior Manufacturing Manager: Vincent Scelta
Senior Designer: Cheryl Asherman
Design Manager: Patricia Smythe
Interior Design: Jill Little
Cover Design: John Romer
Illustrator (Interior): ElectraGraphics, Inc.
Cover Illustration/Photo: Rob Colvin/Stock Art Inc.
Composition: Rainbow Graphics, LLC

Credits and acknowledgments for materials borrowed from other sources and reproduced, with permission, in this textbook appear on page 373.

Library of Congress Cataloging-in-Publication Data
Best, Roger J.
    Market-based management : strategies for growing customer value
and profitability / Roger J. Best. — 2nd ed.
      p.   cm.
    Includes bibliographical references and index.
    ISBN 0-13-014546-7
    1. Marketing—Management.   I. Title.
HF5415.13.B46   1999
658.8—dc21

                                     99-37126
                                        CIP

Prentice-Hall International (UK) Limited, London
Prentice-Hall of Australia Pty. Limited, Sydney
Prentice-Hall Canada, Inc., Toronto
Prentice-Hall Hispanoamericana, S.A., Mexico
Prentice-Hall of India Private Limited, New Delhi
Prentice-Hall of Japan, Inc., Tokyo
Pearson Education Asia Pte. Ltd., Singapore
Editora Prentice-Hall do Brasil, Ltda., Rio de Janeiro

Printed in the United States of America

10 9 8 7 6 5 4 3

To my wife, Robin, and my children, Mary and Oliver.

brief contents

Preface   xvii

Part I   Market-Based Management 3

Chapter 1 Market Orientation, Customer Satisfaction, and Profitability 5

Chapter 2 Market-Based Performance 27

Part II   Market Analysis 53

Chapter 3 Market Definition, Potential, and Demand 55

Chapter 4 Customer Analysis and Value Creation 79

Chapter 5 Market Segmentation and Segmentation Strategies 105

Chapter 6 Competitor Analysis and Competitive Position 126

Part III   Tactical Marketing Strategies 151

Chapter 7 Product Positioning and Product Strategies 153

Chapter 8 Market-Based Pricing and Pricing Strategies 175

Chapter 9 Marketing Channels and Sales Systems 196

Chapter 10 Marketing Communications and Customer Response 215

Part IV   Strategic Market Planning 239

Chapter 11 Portfolio Analysis and Strategic Market Plans 241

Chapter 12 Offensive Strategic Market Plans 261

Chapter 13 Defensive Strategic Market Plans 276

Part V   Market Planning, Implementation, and Performance 295

Chapter 14 Building a Marketing Plan 297

Chapter 15 Strategy Implementation and Performance Metrics 325

Chapter 16 Profit Impact of Market-Based Management 344

Glossary   365

Index   375

V

contents

Preface   *xvii*

Part I   Market-Based Management   3

Chapter 1   Market Orientation, Customer Satisfaction, and Profitability   5

LONG-RUN AND SHORT-RUN BENEFITS 5
How to Underwhelm Customers and Shareholders 6
Market Orientation and Customer Satisfaction 6
Customer Satisfaction: A Key Market Performance Metric 8
A Wide Angle View of Customer Satisfaction 9
Customer Dissatisfaction and Customer Exit 10
Customer Satisfaction and Profitability 11
Profit Impact of Customer Dissatisfaction 12
Profit Impact of Customer Retention 14
Customer Satisfaction and Customer Retention 15
Customer Retention and Customer Life Expectancy 15
The Lifetime Value of a Customer 16
Customer Abandonment and Customer Retention 18
BUILDING A MARKET ORIENTATION 18
Market Orientation and Marketing Knowledge 18
Market Orientation and Marketing Leadership 19
Market Orientation and Employee Satisfaction 20
SUMMARY 22
MARKET-BASED LOGIC AND STRATEGIC THINKING 22
APPLICATION PROBLEM: AIRCOMM 22
NOTES 23
APPENDIX 1.1—PRESENT VALUE TABLE 26

Chapter 2   Market-Based Performance   27

MARKET VS. FINANCIAL PERFORMANCE 27
A Market-Based Strategy 29
Market-Based Performance 29
MARKET-BASED PERFORMANCE METRICS 30
Internal vs. External Performance Metrics 30
In-Process vs. End-Result Performance Metrics 31
MARKETING PROFITABILITY 31
MARKET-BASED MEASURE OF PROFITABILITY 32

NET MARKETING CONTRIBUTION 33
    Net Marketing Contribution and Business Unit Profitability 36
MARKET-BASED MARKETING PROFITABILITY 37
MARKET-BASED STRATEGIES AND PROFITABLE GROWTH 39
    Strategies to Grow Market Demand 40
    Strategies to Increase Market Share 41
    Strategies to Increase Revenue per Customer 41
    Strategies to Lower Variable Cost 42
    Strategies to Increase Market Efficiency 42
MARKETING PRODUCTIVITY 43
MARKET-BASED ORGANIZATIONS 44
SUMMARY 47
MARKET-BASED LOGIC AND STRATEGIC THINKING 47
APPLICATION PROBLEM: DELL COMPUTER 48
NOTES 49

Part II Market Analysis 53

Chapter 3 Market Definition, Potential, and Demand 55

MARKET DEFINITION 55
    Market Vision 56
    Strategic Market Definition 57
    Vertical vs. Horizontal Market Opportunities 57
    Served Market Definition 58
MARKET POTENTIAL 59
    Untapped Market Opportunities 59
    Market Development Index 62
    Market Potential and Market Growth 62
    Rate of Market Development 63
    Accelerating Market Growth 64
MARKET DEMAND 66
PRODUCT LIFE CYCLE 67
MARKET SHARE AND SHARE POTENTIAL 68
    Share Development Tree 69
    Market Share Index 71
    Share Potential and Market Share Management 72
    Market Share Potential 73
    Share Development Index 73
UNIT VOLUME VECTOR 74
SUMMARY 75
APPLICATION PROBLEM: OREGON CHAI 76
MARKET-BASED LOGIC AND STRATEGIC THINKING 77
NOTES 77

Chapter 4 Customer Analysis and Value Creation 79

DISCOVERING CUSTOMER BENEFITS 79
  A Day in the Life of a Customer 80
  Empathic Design Process 80
  Staple Yourself to an Order 81
  Customer Benefits and Customer Value 82
ECONOMIC BENEFITS AND VALUE CREATION 83
  Low Price 84
  Acquisition Costs 84
  Usage Costs 84
  Maintenance Costs 85
  Ownership Costs 85
  Disposal Costs 86
PRICE-PERFORMANCE AND VALUE CREATION 87
  Relative Performance 87
  Relative Price 88
  Customer Value 89
  Value Map 89
PERCEIVED BENEFITS AND VALUE CREATION 90
  Product Benefits 90
  Service Benefits 91
  Company or Brand Benefits 92
  Overall Customer Benefits 93
  Perceived Cost of Purchase 93
  Perceived Customer Value 94
EMOTIONAL BENEFITS AND VALUE CREATION 95
  Emotional Benefits and Psychological Value 95
  Brand Personality and Value Creation 96
CUSTOMER TRADE-OFFS AND VALUE CREATION 97
  Customer Trade-Offs: Benefits vs. Price 97
  Positioning and Customer Value 100
SUMMARY 100
APPLICATION PROBLEM: ADVANTECH SOFTWARE 101
MARKET-BASED LOGIC AND STRATEGIC THINKING 102
NOTES 103
APPENDIX 4.1—TRADE-OFF ANALYSIS COMPUTATIONS 104

Chapter 5 Market Segmentation and Segmentation Strategies 105

CUSTOMER NEEDS AND MARKET SEGMENTATION 105
  Forces That Shape Consumer Market Needs 106
  Forces That Shape Business Market Needs 107
NEEDS-BASED MARKET SEGMENTATION 108
  The Demographic Trap 109
  Needs-Based Market Segments 110

Segment Identification 111
Segment Attractiveness 111
Segment Profitability 113
Segment Positioning 114
Segment Strategy Acid Test 116
Segment Marketing Mix Strategy 117
SEGMENTATION STRATEGIES 118
Mass Market Strategy 118
Large Segment Strategy 118
Adjacent Segment Strategies 119
Multisegment Strategies 120
Small Segment Strategy 120
Niche Segment Strategies 122
Mass Customization 122
SUMMARY 123
MARKET-BASED LOGIC AND STRATEGIC THINKING 123
APPLICATION PROBLEM: THE WEB DEPOT 124
NOTES 125

**Chapter 6 Competitor Analysis and Competitive
Position 126**

COMPETITION AND COMPETITIVE POSITION 126
INDUSTRY ANALYSIS 127
Barriers to Entry 127
Barriers to Exit 128
Customer Buying Power 128
Supplier Selling Power 129
Product Substitutes 129
Competitive Rivalry 129
Prisoner's Dilemma 130
COMPETITOR BENCHMARKING 130
Benchmark Competitors 131
Competitor Analysis 131
Competitor Intelligence 133
A Sample Competitor Analysis 133
Competitive Benchmarking 135
COMPETITIVE ADVANTAGE 136
COST ADVANTAGE 137
Variable Cost Advantage 137
Marketing Cost Advantage 139
Operating Cost Advantage 140
DIFFERENTIATION ADVANTAGE 141
Product Advantage 141
Service Advantage 141
Reputation Advantage 142
MARKETING ADVANTAGE 142
Channel Advantage 143

Sales Force Advantage 143
Brand Awareness 144
SUMMARY 144
APPLICATION PROBLEM: NEWVECTOR CONSULTING 145
MARKET-BASED LOGIC AND STRATEGIC THINKING 146
NOTES 147

Part III Tactical Marketing Strategies 151

Chapter 7 Product Positioning and Product Strategies 153
PRODUCT POSITIONING 154
PRODUCT POSITIONING AND MARKET SHARE 155
PRODUCT MANAGEMENT STRATEGIES 156
PRODUCT POSITIONING AND DIFFERENTIATION 157
Product Differentiation 158
Service Differentiation 160
Brand Differentiation 160
Low-Price Position 161
Lower Transaction Costs 162
PLUS-ONE PRODUCT POSITIONING 162
PRODUCT LINE POSITIONING 162
Product Line Development 163
Product Line Extensions 164
Umbrella Branding 164
Product Bundling 165
Product Unbundling 165
NEW PRODUCT DEVELOPMENT 166
New Product Sales 166
Commitment to Innovation 166
Development Process 167
SUMMARY 171
APPLICATION PROBLEM: APOLLO PRINTER 171
MARKET-BASED LOGIC AND STRATEGIC THINKING 172
NOTES 173

Chapter 8 Market-Based Pricing and Pricing Strategies 175
MARKET-BASED VS. COST-BASED PRICING 175
MARKET-BASED PRICING 176
Economic Value Pricing 177
Perceived Value Pricing 177
Segment Pricing 178
COST-BASED PRICING STRATEGIES 179
Commodity Pricing 179

Cost Leader Pricing 180
Competitive Bid Pricing 180
REFERENCE PRICE AND PRICE STRATEGY 181
Flagship Products 182
PRICE ELASTICITY AND PERFORMANCE 183
Inelastic Price Performance 183
Elastic Price Performance 185
Competitor Price Response 185
PRODUCT LINE PRICING 186
Pricing Substitute Products 186
Pricing Complementary Products 187
PROMOTION PRICING 187
Price Promotion Bundling Strategies 188
NEW PRODUCT PRICING 189
Skim Pricing 189
Penetration Pricing 190
PRICING STRATEGIES AND BREAK-EVEN ANALYSIS 191
Price and Break-Even Volume 191
Price and Break-Even Market Share 192
SUMMARY 193
APPLICATION PROBLEM: MICROSOFT WINDOWS 95 194
MARKET-BASED LOGIC AND STRATEGIC THINKING 194
NOTES 195

Chapter 9 Marketing Channels and Sales Systems 196
CHANNEL SYSTEMS 196
ALTERNATIVE CHANNEL SYSTEMS 197
Direct Channel Systems 199
Indirect Channel Systems 200
Two-Tier Marketing Channels 200
Mixed Channel Systems 201
Consumer Channel Systems 201
Business-to-Business Channel Systems 202
CHANNEL SYSTEMS THAT BUILD CUSTOMER VALUE 204
Delivering Product Benefits 204
Delivering Service Benefits 205
Building Brand Image 205
Building Company Benefits 205
Improving Cost Efficiency 206
CHANNEL SYSTEMS AND COMPETITIVE ADVANTAGE 207
Sales Force Advantage 208
Sales Productivity 209
Distribution Advantage 209
PROFIT IMPACT OF ALTERNATIVE CHANNEL SYSTEMS 210
APPLICATION PROBLEM: BLOCKBUSTER ENTERTAINMENT 212
SUMMARY 212

MARKET-BASED LOGIC AND STRATEGIC THINKING 213
NOTES 214

Chapter 10 Marketing Communications and Customer Response 215

MARKETING COMMUNICATIONS 216
MARKETING COMMUNICATIONS AND CUSTOMER
  RESPONSE 216
STRATEGIES TO INCREASE CUSTOMER RESPONSE 217
BUILDING CUSTOMER AWARENESS AND COMPREHENSION 219
  Media Selection and Customer Awareness 219
  Message Frequency and Customer Awareness 220
  Ad Copy and Customer Response 222
MESSAGE REINFORCEMENT 222
  Message Reinforcement and Pulsing 223
  Heavy-Up Message Frequency 223
STIMULATING CUSTOMER ACTION 223
PUSH VS. PULL COMMUNICATIONS STRATEGIES 224
PULL COMMUNICATIONS AND CUSTOMER RESPONSE 226
  Advertising Elasticity 226
  Advertising Carryover Effects 227
  Direct Marketing Promotions 228
  Promotional Price Elasticity 229
PUSH COMMUNICATIONS AND CUSTOMER RESPONSE 230
  Trade Promotions and Customer Response 230
  Forward Buying and Customer Response 231
  Market Infrastructure and Push Communications 231
SUMMARY 231
APPLICATION PROBLEM: GARDENBURGERS 234
MARKET-BASED LOGIC AND STRATEGIC THINKING 234
NOTES 235

Part IV Strategic Market Planning 239

Chapter 11 Portfolio Analysis and Strategic Market Plans 241

PRODUCT–MARKET DIVERSIFICATION 242
STRATEGIC MARKET PLANNING PROCESS 243
BUSINESS PERFORMANCE 244
MARKET ATTRACTIVENESS 245
COMPETITIVE ADVANTAGE 247
PORTFOLIO ANALYSIS AND STRATEGIC MARKET PLANS 248
  Offensive Strategic Market Plans and Performance Impact 250
  Defensive Strategic Market Plans and Performance Impact 251

TACTICAL MARKETING STRATEGY
  AND PERFORMANCE PLAN 252
    Tactical Marketing Strategy 252
    Performance Plan 253
SUMMARY 255
APPLICATION PROBLEM: FLX-100 256
MARKET-BASED LOGIC AND STRATEGIC THINKING 258
NOTES 259

Chapter 12 Offensive Strategic Market Plans 261
OFFENSIVE STRATEGIC MARKET PLANS 262
MARKET PENETRATION STRATEGIES 263
    Strategies to Grow Market Share 263
    Strategies to Grow Customer Purchase 265
    Strategies to Enter New Customer Segments 266
    Strategies to Grow Market Demand 267
NEW MARKET ENTRY STRATEGIES 268
    Related New Market Entry Strategies 269
    Diversified New Market Entry Growth Strategies 269
    Strategies to Enter New Emerging Markets 270
    Strategies to Develop New Market Potential 271
EVALUATING OFFENSIVE STRATEGIC MARKET PLANS 272
SUMMARY 272
APPLICATION PROBLEM: COMPAQ COMPUTER 273
MARKET-BASED LOGIC AND STRATEGIC THINKING 274
NOTES 274

Chapter 13 Defensive Strategic Market Plans 276
DEFENSIVE STRATEGIC MARKET PLANS 277
PROTECT MARKET STRATEGIES 278
    Protect Market Share 278
    Protecting Share in Growth Markets 279
    Protecting a High-Share Position 280
    Protecting a Follower Share Position 281
    Protecting a Niche Share Position 282
    Building Customer Retention 284
    Reduced Market Focus 285
EXIT MARKET STRATEGIES 286
    Harvest Price Strategy 286
    Harvest Resource Strategy 288
    Divest Market Strategies 289
SELECTING A DEFENSIVE STRATEGIC MARKET PLAN 290
SUMMARY 291
APPLICATION PROBLEM: AMAZON.COM 292
MARKET-BASED LOGIC AND STRATEGIC THINKING 292
NOTES 293

Part V Market Planning, Implementation, and Performance 295

Chapter 14 Building a Marketing Plan 297
CREATIVITY VS. STRUCTURE 298
BENEFITS OF BUILDING A MARKETING PLAN 298
   Identifying Opportunities 298
   Leveraging Core Capabilities 299
   Focused Marketing Strategy 299
   Resource Allocation 299
   Performance Roadmap 299
BUILDING A MARKETING PLAN: PROCESS AND LOGIC 300
   Step I: Situation Analysis 300
   Step II: SWOT Analysis and Key Performance Issues 303
   Step III: Strategic Market Plan 304
   Step IV: Tactical Marketing Strategy 305
   Step V: Marketing Budget 306
   Step VI: Performance Timeline 308
   Step VII: Performance Evaluation 309
SAMPLE MARKETING PLAN 309
   Step I: Situation Analysis 311
   Step II: SWOT Analysis 311
   Step III: Strategic Market Plan 312
   Step IV: Tactical Marketing Strategy 312
   Step V: Marketing Budget 313
   Step VI: Performance Timeline 313
   Step VII: Performance Evaluation 313
SUMMARY 314
APPLICATION PROBLEM: STERICYCLE, INC. 314
MARKET-BASED LOGIC AND STRATEGIC THINKING 315
NOTES 316

Stericycle Marketing Plan 317

Chapter 15 Strategy Implementation and Performance Metrics 325
FORCES THAT SHAPE SUCCESSFUL STRATEGY IMPLEMENTATION 325
   Owning the Marketing Plan 326
   Supporting the Marketing Plan 328
   Adapting the Marketing Plan 329
   Assessing Marketing Plan Implementation 331
MARKET METRICS AND FINANCIAL PERFORMANCE 332
PROCESS VS. END-RESULT MARKET METRICS 334
   Process Market Metrics 334
   End-Result Market Metrics 336
VARIANCE ANALYSIS OF A MARKETING PLAN 337

SUMMARY 340
APPLICATION PROBLEM: STERICYCLE, INC. 341
MARKET-BASED LOGIC AND STRATEGIC THINKING 342
NOTES 342

Chapter 16 Profit Impact of Market-Based Management 344

HOW TO OVERWHELM CUSTOMERS AND SHAREHOLDERS 344
CUSTOMER SATISFACTION AND PROFITABILITY 345
HOW MARKETING STRATEGIES AFFECT PROFITABILITY 347
    Customer Volume 347
    Margin per Customer 348
    Total Contribution 349
    Net Marketing Contribution 350
    Net Profit (before Taxes) 350
HOW MARKETING STRATEGIES AFFECT ASSETS 350
    Investment in Accounts Receivable 351
    Investment in Inventory 352
    Investment in Fixed Assets 352
RETURN MEASURES OF PROFITABILITY 353
MEASURES OF SHAREHOLDER VALUE 355
MARKET-BASED MANAGEMENT 357
SUMMARY 359
APPLICATION PROBLEM: STERICYCLE, INC. 360
MARKET-BASED LOGIC AND STRATEGIC THINKING 361
NOTES 362

Postlogue 363

Glossary 365

Credits 373

Index 375

preface

Based on positive feedback from students, professors, and those working in the field of marketing, I was encouraged to pursue a second edition of *Market-Based Management.* The strength of the book remains its focus on market orientation and the process and tools for building marketing strategies that deliver superior levels of customer value and profitability. A differentiating feature of this book is its focus on marketing profitability, and the role marketing strategies play in building the profits of a business. The best way to accomplish this is with a market-driven strategy that can attract, satisfy, and retain customers with a value that is superior to competing products or services.

The second edition builds on this theme in several ways. First, at the end of each chapter there is an Application Problem. These are comprehensive problems built around real companies such as Dell Computer, Gardenburger, Hewlett Packard, and Amazon.com. Each problem highlights a key concept presented in the chapter. Those interested can work the Application Problem and check their understanding by reviewing a discussion of the problem at www.prenhall.com/phbusiness. Other noteworthy features of the second edition include a separate chapter for Strategic Market Planning, a sample Marketing Plan, Glossary, and more examples of how well-known companies utilize the marketing tools presented to build marketing strategies that deliver profitable growth.

Market-based management is intuitively easy but deceptively difficult. The reason students and professionals like this book is because it is readable, and because it presents the tools and processes needed to actually build a market-driven strategy. The concepts, by themselves, are important and the backbone of market-based management. However, they are of limited value if they cannot be applied in a way that delivers superior customer value and profitability. Those in marketing need to take a greater level of responsibility for managing profits and the external performance of a business. This is an important benefit of this book. It is my hope that this book will help you in your understanding of, commitment to, and practice of market-based management.

Roger J. Best

Professor of Marketing

University of Oregon

acknowledgments

To steal ideas from one person is plagiarism. To steal ideas from many is research.

A book such as this is an assimilation of knowledge from many sources. It is an integration of perspectives intended for a particular audience. An author's added value is in the focus, integration, and presentation, but the basic knowledge is derived from many sources. I would like to acknowledge specific individuals whose knowledge contributed to the writing of this book.

First, I would like to acknowledge three individuals who shaped my career and greatly influenced the way I think about marketing: Don S. Tull (deceased), University of Oregon; Del I. Hawkins, Professor of Marketing, University of Oregon, and Charles M. Lillis, CEO, MediaOne Group. Each provided a great deal of insight into my thinking of marketing and eventually market-based management. From each, I have learned a great deal.

Second, I would like to acknowledge the individual feedback I received from Brian T. Engelland, Mississippi State University; Dave Jones, LaSalle University; Ruth Smith, Virginia Tech; and Joseph Belonax, Western Michigan, who provided reviews of this book prior to its revision. Their thoughtful reviews and suggestions for improvement are greatly appreciated and will enhance this second edition.

Finally, this book would not have been possible without the very thorough and dedicated support of Hal Sipe. His participation and contributions were critical to every aspect of the book and are greatly appreciated. I also owe a special thanks to my wife, Robin Best, and Marcia LeBlanc for their time and effort in proofreading this book and making it more readable.

about the author

Roger J. Best is Professor of Marketing at the University of Oregon. Dr. Best earned a Bachelor of Science in Electrical Engineering from California State Polytechnic University in 1968. Following graduation, he joined General Electric where he worked in both engineering and product management. In 1971, he received a patent for a product he invented while with GE. He completed his MBA at California State University–Hayward in 1972 and went on to complete his Ph.D. in Business at the University of Oregon in 1975.

Over the past 25 years, he has published many academic articles. In 1998, Dr. Best was awarded an Excellence in Teaching award by the American Marketing Association. He is also co-author of *Consumer Behavior: Implications for Marketing Strategy,* which is in its sixth edition. More recently, Dr. Best has developed the Marketing Excellence Survey, an assessment tool for measuring an individual's marketing knowledge and market orientation. He also developed a business simulation called BID-STRAT that requires business teams to develop global marketing strategies in high-tech industries.

Dr. Best also has worked with a variety of companies in both marketing consulting and management education over the past 25 years. These companies include: Dow Chemical, Eastman Kodak, ESCO Corporation, General Electric, James Hardie Industries, Lucas Industries, Pacific Western Pipe, Tektronix, US West, and Xerox. Dr. Best has also taught many executive management education programs at INSEAD in Fontainebleau, France.

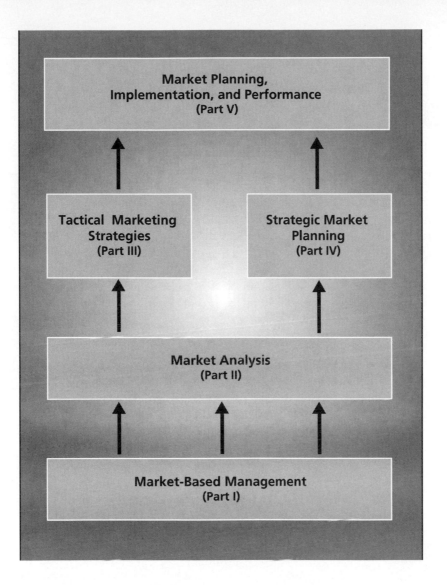

This model represents both the logic of market-based management and the organization of this textbook. The base, or bedrock, of a market-oriented business is market-based management, which is the focus of part I. Without a passion for customer satisfaction, on-going monitoring of competition, and a team approach to market-based management, there is little hope for long-term success in any market. Market analysis, the focus of part II, is an on-going activity that enables a market-based business to stay connected with the key inputs to market-based strategies, the customers, competitors, and changing market conditions.

As implied in this model, the inputs from parts I and II drive both short-run tactical marketing strategies (part III) and long-run strategic market planning (part IV). Naturally, marketing strategies do not happen by themselves. Carefully thought-out marketing plans and sufficiently resourced implementation programs are essential to deliver a desired level of market and financial performance (part V).

part I

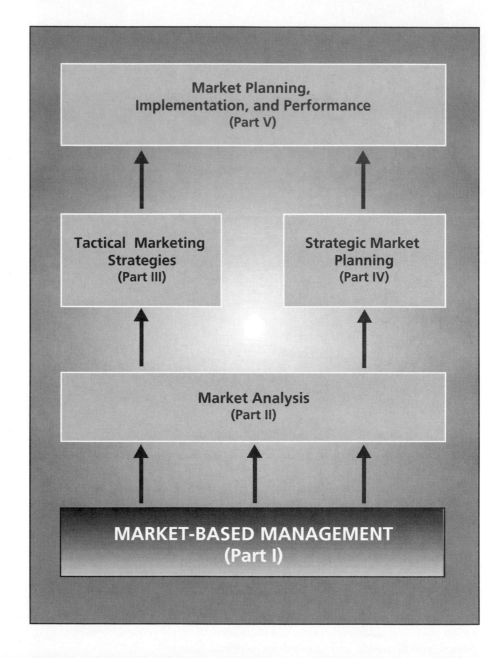

Market Planning,
Implementation, and Performance
(Part V)

Tactical Marketing
Strategies
(Part III)

Strategic Market
Planning
(Part IV)

Market Analysis
(Part II)

MARKET-BASED MANAGEMENT
(Part I)

Market-Based Management

A market-based business has a strong market orientation that cuts across the functions and employees of an organization. While those in marketing have the primary responsibility to lead marketing excellence, in a market-based business, all members of the organization have a strong market orientation. This means all members of the organization are sensitive to customers' needs, aware of competitors' moves, and work well across organizational boundaries toward a timely market-based customer solution. The payoff—market-based businesses with a strong market orientation are more profitable.

The purpose of part I is to make explicit the connectivity between market orientation, customer satisfaction, market-based management, and profitability. In chapter 1, we examine the fundamental components of market orientation and how each is related to customer satisfaction and retention. From this perspective, we will demonstrate the profit impact of a lifetime customer as well as the high cost of customer dissatisfaction. While a strong market orientation enhances a business's chances for long-run survival, short-run profits can also be increased with marketing efforts to increase customer satisfaction and retention.

A strong market orientation does not occur by mere proclamation. To attain a strong market orientation, a business needs to adopt a market-based management philosophy. This means implementing a process for tracking market performance and restructuring an organization around markets rather than products or factories and creating an employee culture that is responsive to customers and changing market conditions. Market-based management also requires businesses to measure profits at the market level and to track external, market-based performance metrics. These topics, and their relation to marketing strategies and profitable growth, are discussed in chapter 2.

chapter 1

Market Orientation, Customer Satisfaction, and Profitability

In today's globally competitive world, customers expect more, have more choices, and are less brand-loyal. Businesses such as IBM, Sears, and General Motors at one time seemed invincible in terms of their market domination. However, in each case, these companies have had to restructure (reengineer) their organizations to address changing customer needs and emerging competitive forces. In the long run, every business is at risk for survival. Although companies such as Dell Computer, Microsoft, and Wal-Mart were business heroes of the nineties, there is no guarantee that these same companies will continue to dominate over the next decade. The only thing that is constant . . . is *change*.

- Customers will continue to *change* in needs, demographics, lifestyle, and consumption behavior.
- Competitors will *change* as new technologies emerge and barriers to foreign competition shift.
- The environment in which businesses operate will continue to *change* as economic, political, social, and technological forces shift.

The companies that *survive* and *grow* will be the ones that *understand change* and are out in front leading, often creating, change. Others, slow to comprehend change, will follow with reactive strategies, while still others will disappear, not knowing that change has even occurred.

LONG-RUN AND SHORT-RUN BENEFITS

A sports reporter once asked Wayne Gretzky what made him a great hockey player. Gretzky's response was, "I skate to where the puck is going, not to where it is." In other words, Wayne Gretzky has a tremendous instinct for change. He is able to position himself as change is occurring in such a way that he can either score a goal or assist in scoring a goal. Businesses that can sense the direction of change, and position themselves to lead in the change, prosper and grow. Those that wait to read about it in the *Wall Street Journal* are hopelessly behind the play of the game and, at best, can only skate to catch up.

Businesses that are able to skate to where the puck is going have a strong (external) market orientation. They are constantly in tune with customers' needs, competitors' strategies, changing environmental conditions, and emerging technologies, and they seek ways to continuously improve the solution they bring to target customers. This process enables them to move with—and often lead—change.

One of the benefits of a strong market orientation is long-run survival. Western cultures have long been criticized for being extremely short-term in perspective. Consequently, long-run survival of a business may not be a strong management motive in developing a strong market orientation. Managers are often judged on the last quarter's results and not on what they are doing to ensure the long-run survival of the business. Likewise, shareholders can be more interested in immediate earnings than in the long-run survival of a business.

Although the long-run benefits of a strong market orientation are crucial to business survival and the economic health of a nation, the purpose of this chapter is to demonstrate the *short-run* benefits of a strong market orientation. Businesses with a strong market orientation not only outperform their competition in delivering higher levels of customer satisfaction, they also deliver higher profits in the short run. Businesses driven by a strong market orientation create greater customer value and, ultimately, greater shareholder value. But perhaps the best way to understand the marketing logic that links market orientation to customer and shareholder value is to examine the sequence of events that evolves when a business has little or no market orientation.

How to Underwhelm Customers and Shareholders

Businesses with a weak market orientation underwhelm both customers and shareholders. A business with a weak market orientation has only a superficial or poor understanding of customer needs and competition. Moving clockwise from the top in Figure 1.1, this poor understanding translates into an unfocused competitive position and a "me-too" customer value.[1] Customers are easily attracted to competitors who offer equal or greater customer value, which leads to high levels of customer turnover and market share instability. Efforts to hold off customer switching are expensive, as is the cost of acquiring new customers to replace lost customers.

The combination of market share instability and higher marketing costs results in sporadic business profits. In response, short-term sales tactics and accounting maneuvers are used to achieve short-run financial results. However, investors and Wall Street analysts are able to see through this facade, and shareholder value generally stagnates. Perhaps even worse, as shown in the scenario described in Figure 1.1, management is now under even greater pressure to produce short-run results. This means that there is not the time, the inclination, or the motivation to understand customer needs and to unravel competitors' strategies, and the circular performance displayed in Figure 1.1 continues.

Market Orientation and Customer Satisfaction

Contrary to the scenario presented in Figure 1.1, a market-oriented business has three management characteristics that make it unique:[2]

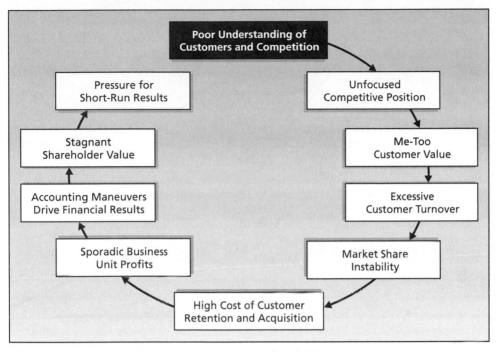

Figure 1.1 ◆ How to Underwhelm Customers and Shareholders

- **Customer Focus**: An obsession with understanding customer needs and delivering customer satisfaction.
- **Competitor Orientation**: Continuous recognition of competitors' sources of advantage, competitive position, and marketing strategies.
- **Team Approach**: Cross-functional teams dedicated to developing and delivering customer solutions.

A strong *customer focus* enables a business to stay in close contact with customer needs and satisfaction. Marketing strategies in these businesses are built around customer needs and other sources of customer satisfaction. The strength of a business's market orientation also relies on how well it *understands key competitors* and evolving competitive forces. This aspect of market orientation enables a business to track its relative competitiveness in such areas as pricing, product quality and availability, service quality, and customer satisfaction. Businesses with a strong market orientation also work well as a team *across functions,* thereby leveraging cross-functional skills and business activities that affect customer response and satisfaction.

The real benefit of a strong market orientation and higher levels of customer satisfaction is a higher level of customer retention.[3] Keeping good customers should be the *first priority* of market-based management. As shown in Figure 1.2, a business with a strong market orientation is in the best position to develop and implement strategies that deliver high levels of customer satisfaction and retention. In turn, customer satisfaction and retention drive customer revenue and the cost of doing business. Ultimately, they are key forces in shaping the profitability of a business.

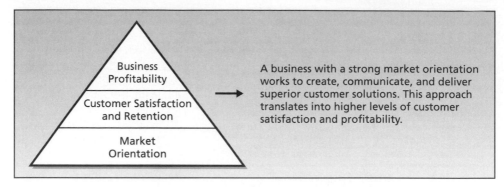

Figure 1.2 ◆ Market Orientation, Customer Satisfaction, and Profitability

Customer Satisfaction: A Key Market Performance Metric

While a market-based business will have several external metrics to track market performance, an essential performance metric is customer satisfaction. There are many marketing strategies that can be developed to attract customers, but it is the business that completely satisfies customers that gets to keep them. This viewpoint may sound philanthropic to those who do not accept the whole concept of market orientation and market-based management, but we will demonstrate in this chapter the tremendous leverage a business can create in growing profits from a base of very satisfied customers and proactive management of dissatisfied customers.

There are many ways to measure customer satisfaction. However, one common measure of customer satisfaction can be derived from customers' ratings of their overall satisfaction on a seven-point scale that ranges from 0 (very dissatisfied) to 6 (very satisfied), as shown below.

0	1	2	3	4	5	6
Very Dissatisfied	Moderately Dissatisfied	Slightly Dissatisfied	Neutral (Neither)	Slightly Satisfied	Moderately Satisfied	Very Satisfied

When this method of measuring customer satisfaction is applied to a sample of customers, we can compute an overall measure of customer satisfaction. Assume, for example, that an interview with 100 Xerox copier customers produced an average score of 4.32. An overall average of 4.32 does not tell us much and is not likely to get management's attention. To increase the sensitivity of this measure, we need to index it in a more meaningful way. By dividing the average score by the maximum score of six (very satisfied) and multiplying by 100, we can create an index that varies from 0 to 100. When this index is used, the overall average of 4.32 translates to a score of 72, where 100 would be the maximum. Management can quickly discern that the business has achieved a 72 level of customer satisfaction, whereas a 100 would be equivalent to 100 percent very satisfied customers.

Is an overall customer satisfaction score of 72 a good level of performance? That depends on what the business's overall score was in earlier measurements, its target objective, and the overall score given to a leading competitor. Let's assume that an overall score of 72 is an improvement over earlier average scores and that the average score of a leading competitor is 62. Those numbers would lead many businesses to feel pretty good about their level of performance and perhaps become complacent in their pursuit of customer satisfaction. Also, efforts to increase customer satisfaction cost time and money, and many managers may argue that the incremental benefit is not sufficient to justify the cost. That argument would *not* apply at Xerox, where customer satisfaction is a top corporate performance metric and priority.[4] To really understand customer satisfaction and to leverage its profit potential, we need to expand our view of customer satisfaction.

A Wide-Angle View of Customer Satisfaction

An average customer satisfaction score of 72 (where 100 is the maximum) may be viewed as acceptable, and even very good. However, *managing to the average* masks our understanding of customer satisfaction and opportunities for increased profits.[5]

If we expand our view of customer satisfaction by reporting the percentage for each category on our customer satisfaction scale, a more meaningful set of insights emerges. The average customer satisfaction score of 72 was derived from 74 percent who reported varying degrees of satisfaction, 10 percent who were indifferent or neutral, and 16 percent who reported varying degrees of dissatisfaction, as illustrated in Figure 1.3. The 10 percent who were neutral in their customer satisfaction are certainly vulnerable to competitor moves, but it is the 16 percent categorized as dissatisfied who are very serious candidates to exit as customers. Thus, our immediate concern should be our dissatisfied customers.

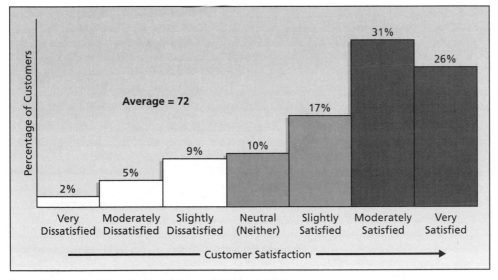

Figure 1.3 ◆ Customer Satisfaction: A Wide-Angle View

Customer Dissatisfaction and Customer Exit

Dissatisfied customers often do not complain to a manufacturer, but they do walk and they *do* talk.[6] Well-documented studies show that out of 100 dissatisfied customers, only four will complain to a business.[7] Of the 96 dissatisfied customers who do not complain, 91 will exit as customers, as shown in Figure 1.4. While market position is quietly eroded by exiting customers, attracting new customers is made more difficult because each dissatisfied customer will tell eight to 10 other people of his or her dissatisfaction.

The market impact is enormous. For example, assume that a business has captured 10 percent of a 2-million-customer market, or 200,000 customers. If 15 percent of those 200,000 customers were dissatisfied, this business would have 30,000 dissatisfied customers. The statistics presented in Figure 1.4 would indicate that the business would lose 92 percent of those dissatisfied customers—27,600 customers—each year. This percentage translates to a 1.4 point reduction in market share. To hold a 10 percent share of the market (customers), the business would have to attract 27,600 new customers. This, of course, is a very expensive way to hold market share.

But the situation is much worse.[8] Many dissatisfied customers become "terrorists"; they vent their dissatisfaction by telling others about it. Recall that each dissatisfied customer tells eight to 10 other people. This means that the 30,000 dissatisfied customers will communicate their dissatisfaction to approximately a quarter of a million other individuals. These may not all be potential customers, but this level of negative word-of-mouth communication makes new customer attraction much more difficult and more expensive.[9]

This kind of market behavior has led some businesses to develop programs to encourage dissatisfied customers to complain. For example, Domino's Pizza instituted a program in which their strategy was simply to encourage dissatisfied customers to complain rather than just leave.[10] Figure 1.5 illustrates that their efforts succeeded in getting 20

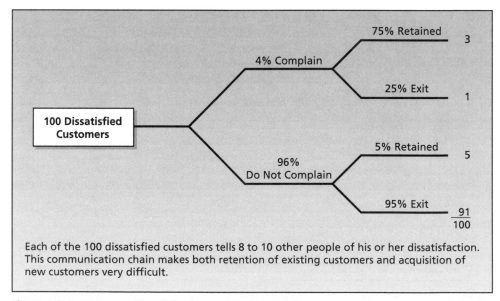

Each of the 100 dissatisfied customers tells 8 to 10 other people of his or her dissatisfaction. This communication chain makes both retention of existing customers and acquisition of new customers very difficult.

Figure 1.4 ◆ Customer Dissatisfaction and Customer Exit

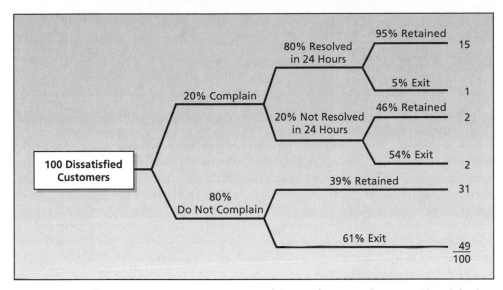

Figure 1.5 ◆ Efforts to Encourage Customer Complaints and Manage Customer Dissatisfaction

percent of their dissatisfied customers to complain. For those who complain, Domino's can resolve 80 percent of the problems in 24 hours. When complaints can be resolved quickly, 95 percent of those customers can be retained. When complaints cannot be resolved within 24 hours, the customer retention rate falls to 46 percent.

Not surprisingly, if customers do not complain, the odds of retention drop below 40 percent. Thus, while it may seem odd at first, one of the jobs of market-based management is not only to track customer satisfaction but also to *encourage dissatisfied customers to complain.* Only with the specific details of a customer complaint and the source of dissatisfaction can a business take corrective action.[11]

Companies such as AT&T proactively address potential customer dissatisfaction by encouraging customer complaints through full-page ads with toll-free telephone numbers. Their proactive marketing efforts have two important effects. First, their proactive services address problems as they occur, greatly reducing potential customer dissatisfaction and exit. Second, communicating their proactive services reinforces customer satisfaction by communicating the importance of their efforts to provide maximum customer satisfaction.[12]

Customer Satisfaction and Profitability

Customer satisfaction is an excellent market-based performance metric and barometer of future revenues and profits, as stated below.

> Customer satisfaction is a forward-looking indicator of business success that measures how well customers will respond to the company in the future. Other measures of market performance, such as sales and market share, are backward-looking measures of success. They tell how well the firm has done in the past, not how well it will do in the future.[13]

Thus, customer satisfaction is a good leading indicator of future operating performance. A business may have produced excellent financial results while underwhelming and disappointing a growing number of its customers. Because customers cannot always immediately switch to alternative solutions, customer dissatisfaction often precedes customer exit and reductions in sales and profitability. Thus, for many businesses, quarterly measures of customer satisfaction provide an excellent leading indicator of future performance. If customer satisfaction is on the decline, an early warning signal is given, providing the opportunity to correct a problem before real damage is done. Of course, if a business does not track customer satisfaction, it forgoes the opportunity to correct problems before declines in sales and profits result.

For example, a dissatisfied FedEx customer can move quickly to an alternative provider of overnight mail. That fact has led FedEx to develop a service quality index for every transaction in order to spot problems as they occur and to avoid the potential loss of customers. In the long run, it is more profitable to keep existing customers than to continually have to work to attract and develop new customers to replace exiting ones. FedEx has demonstrated that gains in customer satisfaction, driven by improvements in service quality, provide gains in revenue and lower cost.

Profit Impact of Customer Dissatisfaction

MBNA America is a Delaware-based credit card company that, in the early 1990s, became frustrated with customer dissatisfaction and defection. All 300 employees were brought together in an effort to understand and develop methods of delivering greater levels of customer satisfaction with the intent of keeping each and every customer. At the time, MBNA America had a 90 percent customer retention rate. After several years of dedicating themselves to improved customer satisfaction and retention, they raised customer retention to 95 percent. That may seem like a small difference, but the impact on their profits was a *sixteenfold* increase, and their industry ranking went from 38th to 4th.[14] Thus, their marketing efforts to satisfy and retain customers paid off in higher levels of profitability.

As demonstrated, most dissatisfied customers do not complain; they just walk away. To hold market share in a mature market, a business must replace those lost customers. Let's examine a business that is in a mature market with 200,000 customers and has a 75 percent rate of customer retention. Each year this business loses 50,000 customers and, to hold a customer base of 200,000, must replace those customers with 50,000 new customers. However, before we look at the profit impact of this level of customer satisfaction and retention, let's look at how this business got to a level of 75 percent customer retention. A closer look at customer satisfaction, complaint behavior, and customer retention enables us to build the *Customer Retention Tree* in Figure 1.6. As shown, the business is operating at a 70 percent level of customer satisfaction. Of the 30 percent who are dissatisfied, 24.9 percent are lost. Furthermore, the majority of dissatisfied customers who are lost do not complain to the business about the source of their dissatisfaction.

The customer profitability profile shown in Figure 1.7 reflects the information presented in Figure 1.6. It shows the average annual revenue, margin, and marketing expense per customer for retained customers, lost customers, and new customers. As shown, retained customers are the profit driver of this business, producing 80 percent of the sales revenue and 89 percent of the total contribution.

Lost customers are generally dissatisfied or neutral customers. Because they are not with the business for the whole year or are in the process of reducing their purchases

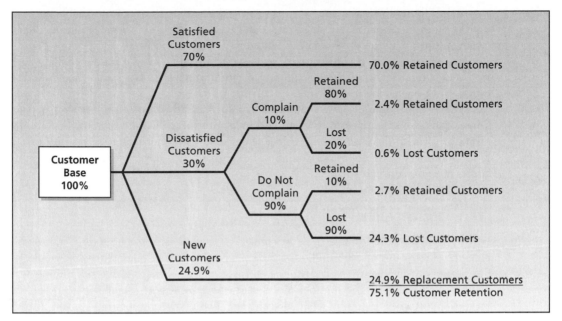

Figure 1.6 ◆ Customer Retention Tree

from the business, the annual revenue per customer is much lower. However, retaining dissatisfied customers is also expensive because they require the business to expend extra resources in an attempt to keep them. These extra efforts often mean extra work for the sales force, price concessions, adjustments to inventory or terms of sale, and more customer service. The net result of losing dissatisfied customers in this example is a negative *net marketing contribution* of $2.5 million per year. The net marketing contribution

Customer Performance	Retained Customers	Lost Customers	New Customers	Overall Performance
Number of Customers	150,000	50,000	50,000	250,000
Revenue per Customer	$800	$200	$400	
Sales Revenue (millions)	$120.0	$ 10.0	$ 20.0	$150.0
Variable Cost per Customer	$400	$150	$300	
Margin per Customer	$400	$ 50	$100	
Total Contribution (millions)	$ 60.0	$ 2.5	$ 5.0	$ 67.5
Marketing Expense per Customer	$ 60	$100	$300	
Total Marketing Expense (millions)	$ 9.0	$ 5.0	$ 15.0	$ 29.0
Net Marketing Contribution (millions)	$ 51.0	–$ 2.5	–$ 10.0	$ 38.5
Operating Expenses (millions)				$ 30.0
Net Profit before Taxes (millions)				$ 8.5
Return on Sales				5.67%

Figure 1.7 ◆ Profit Impact of 75 Percent Customer Retention

shown in Figure 1.7 is the total revenue received from customers less variable costs of producing those revenues less direct marketing expenses needed to serve this level of customer volume. This concept will be discussed in detail in chapter 2.

New customers are also less profitable. Advertising and sales promotion dollars have to be spent to generate sales leads and produce trial purchases. This raises the marketing expenses associated with attracting, qualifying, and serving new customers. New customers also generally buy less because they are in the evaluation stage and have not yet fully committed themselves to the business or its products. This lowers both the annual revenue and margin produced by each new customer. The net result in this example is that the business actually loses $10 million in net marketing contribution each year in its efforts to replace lost customers.

Profit Impact of Customer Retention

For the business situation presented in Figure 1.7, overall sales revenues of $150 million produce a net profit of $8.5 million, a 5.67 percent return on sales. But what would be the profit impact of improved customer satisfaction? Let's assume that $1 million was dedicated to reducing the number of dissatisfied customers so that 80 percent of the business's customers could be retained each year. The marketing logic and profit impact of this strategy can be summarized as follows:

> If the business can retain 80 percent of its customers each year instead of 75 percent, the business will reduce the cost associated with customer dissatisfaction and exit and will not have to spend as much on marketing efforts to attract new customers. Also, because retained customers produce a higher annual revenue and margin per customer than do lost or new customers, the total profits of the business should increase.

This effort would produce only a slight increase in sales revenues, as shown in Figure 1.8. However, there would be a tremendous improvement in marketing efficiency and

Customer Performance	Retained Customers	Lost Customers	New Customers	Overall Performance
Number of Customers	160,000	40,000	40,000	240,000
Revenue per Customer	$800	$200	$400	
Sales Revenue (millions)	$128.0	$ 8.0	$ 16.0	$152.0
Variable Cost per Customer	$400	$150	$300	
Margin per Customer	$400	$ 50	$100	
Total Contribution (millions)	$ 64.0	$ 2.0	$ 4.0	$ 70.0
Marketing Expense per Customer	$ 62.5	$100	$300	
Total Marketing Expense (millions)	$ 10.0	$ 4.0	$ 12.0	$ 26.0
Net Marketing Contribution (millions)	$ 54.0	–$ 2.0	–$ 8.0	$ 44.0
Operating Expenses (millions)				$ 30.0
Net Profit before Taxes (millions)				$ 14.0
Return on Sales				9.2%

Figure 1.8 ◆ **Profit Impact of Five Percent Improvement in Customer Retention**

profitability. Because retained customers are more profitable than new customers, the overall total contribution derived from retained customers would increase from $60 million to $64 million. The overall marketing expenses would go up because of the $1 million that was added to the business's marketing budget to achieve an 80 percent customer retention. The net result would be a $3 million improvement in net marketing contribution derived from retained customers.

More important, the net loss of managing dissatisfied customers who exit and the net loss associated with attracting new customers would be reduced by a total of $2.5 million in this example. The cumulative impact of increased customer satisfaction and retention is an increase of net profits from $8.5 to $14 million. This incremental gain in net profits is derived from a larger number of retained customers, the reduced cost of serving dissatisfied customers, and reduced expenses associated with acquiring new customers to maintain the same customer base. This is a 64 percent increase in net profits with essentially *no change in market share or sales revenue.*

One can readily see the enormous potential for increased profits and cash flow that centers around customer satisfaction and retention. For each additional customer that is retained, net profits increase. Inefficient costs associated with serving dissatisfied customers and the cost of acquiring new customers to replace them are reduced. Thus, there is tremendous financial leverage in satisfying and retaining customers.

Customer Satisfaction and Customer Retention

The relationship between customer satisfaction and customer retention is intuitively easy to discern. However, different competitive conditions modify this relationship.[15] For example, in less competitive markets, customers are more easily retained even with poor levels of customer satisfaction because there are few substitutes or switching costs are high. In markets where there are relatively few choices, such as phone service, water companies, or hospitals, customers may stay even when dissatisfied. In these types of markets, where choice is limited or switching costs are very high, higher levels of customer retention are achievable at relatively lower levels of customer satisfaction.

However, in highly competitive markets with many choices and low customer switching costs, even relatively high levels of customer satisfaction may not insure against customer defection. Grocery store, restaurant, and bank customers can switch quickly if not completely satisfied. While the time between purchase events is longer, personal computer, automobile, and consumer electronics customers can also easily move to another brand if not completely satisfied. In these markets, customer retention is much more difficult. And, as a result, it takes higher levels of customer satisfaction to retain customers from one purchase to the next.

Customer Retention and Customer Life Expectancy

Customer satisfaction and retention are important linkages to a market-based strategy and profitability. The ultimate objective of any given marketing strategy should be to attract, satisfy, and retain target customers. If a business can accomplish this objective with a competitive advantage in attractive markets, the business will produce above-average profits.

The customer is a critical component in the profitability equation but is completely overlooked in any financial analysis or annual reports. Customers are a *marketing asset* that businesses have yet to quantify in their accounting systems. Yet, the business that can attract, satisfy, and keep customers over their lifetime of purchases is in a powerful position to deliver superior levels of profitability. Businesses that lack a market orientation look at customers as *individual purchase transactions*. A market-based business looks at customers as *lifetime partners*.

The higher the rate of customer retention, the greater the profit impact for a given business. In the short run, we showed this to be true on the basis of increased profits from retained customers, reduced losses from lost customers, and a lower cost of attracting new customers in order to maintain a certain customer base. However, there is also a longer-term profit impact of higher levels of customer retention because a higher rate of retention lengthens the life of a customer relationship.

A business that has a 50 percent rate of customer retention has a fifty-fifty chance of retaining a customer from one year to the next. This fact translates into an average customer life of two years, as shown in Figure 1.9. The average life expectancy of a customer is equal to one divided by one minus the rate of customer retention.[16] Therefore, as customer retention increases, the customer's life expectancy increases. But, more important, customer life expectancy increases exponentially with customer retention, as illustrated in Figure 1.9.

For example, the average level of customer retention among health care providers is 80 percent.[17] This translates into an average customer life of five years. If a health care provider could manage to increase its customer retention to 90 percent, that increase would produce an average customer life of 10 years. Thus, the life expectancy of a customer grows exponentially as a business moves to higher levels of customer retention.

The Lifetime Value of a Customer

The Cadillac division of General Motors estimates that a Cadillac customer will spend approximately $350,000 over a lifetime on automotive purchases and maintenance. If Cadillac loses that customer early in this customer life cycle, it forgoes hundreds of thou-

Figure 1.9 ◆ Customer Life Expectancy and Customer Retention

sands of dollars in future cash flow. And, to replace that lost customer, Cadillac has to attract and develop a new customer, which is an expensive process. Thus, the cost of marketing efforts to ensure customer satisfaction is small in comparison with both the current and future benefits of customer purchases, as well as the cost of replacing customers if they become dissatisfied and leave. In general, it costs five times more to replace a customer than it costs to keep a customer.

Figure 1.10 illustrates the average profit per credit card customer generated over a five-year period. Acquiring and setting up accounts for new credit card customers nets an annual loss of $51 per customer. Newly acquired credit card customers are also slow to use their new cards; they produce an average profit of $30 the first year, $42 the second year, and $44 the third year. By year 5, the average profit obtained from a credit card customer is $55. Thus, the lifetime value of a credit card customer continues to grow. Of course, if a credit card company loses a customer after year 4 because of customer dissatisfaction, the process of replacing him or her is expensive. This cost in the first year following customer exit is $106 ($55 in lost profit from the exiting customer and the $51 loss associated with attracting a new customer to replace that customer).

In this example, the average customer life is five years. Working backward, we can estimate the customer retention to be 80 percent, as shown below.

$$\frac{\text{Customer}}{\text{Retention}} = 1 - \frac{1}{N} = 1 - \frac{1}{5} = 0.80 \text{ (or 80\%)}$$

To estimate the lifetime value of a customer at this rate of customer retention, we need to compute the *net present value* of the customer cash flow shown in Figure 1.10. The initial $51 that it cost to acquire this customer is gone immediately. However, it takes a year to achieve the first year's revenue of $30. The present value of $30 received a year in the future is less than $30 received immediately. In this example, the business has a discount rate of 10 percent. Therefore, the present value of $1 received after one year is $0.909 (the rate at which $1 is discounted for one year at 10 percent). Thus, $30 to be received one year later is $27.27 ($30 × 0.909). This discounting is performed for each year's receipts, and the values are totaled to arrive at the net present value of this cash flow. When each

Period	Cash Flow	Present Value of $1*	Present Value of Cash Flow
0	−$51	1.000	−$51.0
1	$30	0.909	$27.3
2	$42	0.826	$34.7
3	$44	0.751	$33.0
4	$49	0.683	$33.5
5	$55	0.621	$34.2
Net Present Value of Cash Flow			$111.7

* Appendix 1.1 provides a table of present values.

Figure 1.10 ◆ Customer Lifetime Value

year's cash flow is properly discounted, the net present value of the sum of these cash flows is equal to $111.70. This is what this customer is worth in today's dollars.

If customer life expectancy were only three years, the customer value (net present value) would be considerably smaller. Thus, the higher the rate of customer retention, the longer the average customer life expectancy and the greater the customer value.

Customer Abandonment and Customer Retention

AT&T identified 1.7 million customers as "spinners."[18] These are customers that switch carriers at least three times per year while looking for the best deal. Needless to say, this type of customer drives down retention and is one a business would like to avoid. One of the Baby Bell companies estimates that 3 percent of its customers are "movers and shakers." These customers sign up, use the company services, don't pay their bills, and move on. In this instance, there is only a negative cash flow, which hurts overall profitability.

Customer selection is an important aspect of managing to a higher level of customer retention and profitability.[19] Customer dissatisfaction is not the only cause of poor customer retention. Identifying customers who do not pay their bills, are too costly to serve, or tend to be "switchers" is an important part of managing customer retention.[20]

BUILDING A MARKET ORIENTATION

Businesses with a strong market orientation are in the best position to develop responsive marketing strategies that deliver high levels of customer satisfaction and retention. But how does a business build a strong market orientation? Why do some businesses have a strong market orientation and others cannot seem to develop one? There are three fundamental forces that drive the degree to which a business has a market orientation:

- **Marketing Knowledge:** The degree to which managers and employees have been educated and trained in the area of marketing directly affects the market orientation of a business.
- **Marketing Leadership:** The market orientation of a business starts at the top. If the senior management and key marketing managers of a business do not have a strong market orientation, it is difficult for a business to establish any level of marketing excellence.
- **Employee Satisfaction:** If employees are unhappy in their jobs and uninformed as to how they affect customers, the business's market orientation will never achieve even minimal effectiveness regardless of senior management speeches and market-based statements of mission and philosophy.

Market Orientation and Marketing Knowledge

A manager's marketing orientation is directly linked to a manager's marketing knowledge, as displayed in Figure 1.11. This graphic was built from a database of 8,000 managers in over 150 Fortune 500 businesses.[21] As shown, the higher one's level of marketing knowledge, the stronger that individual's market orientation. Further analysis of these 8,000 managers also found that marketing knowledge and market orientation could be

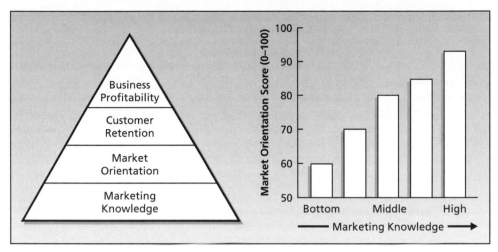

Figure 1.11 ◆ Marketing Knowledge and Market Orientation

directly linked to formal marketing education, participation in marketing training programs, and marketing experience.

While formal marketing education and training are absolutely essential for persons in marketing and higher-level positions of leadership, market orientation is also fundamental to every employee of the organization. For example, Disney spends four days training personnel who clean their theme parks.[22] They train what they call the "popcorn people" to be information guides because they are the first to be asked where something is located. These "popcorn people" are also trained to treat customers as guests and to consider themselves on stage. Naturally, the individual marketing orientation of these employees plays a key role in creating a Disney company market orientation that delivers high levels of customer satisfaction.

Market Orientation and Marketing Leadership

A marketing orientation audit of a mid-sized hi-tech company involved assessing marketing attitudes and practices at several layers of the business's management hierarchy. The following comments were given in response to the question "How often do you see customers?"

> **Company CEO:** I really don't have too much time for that. I have many financial issues, administrative tasks, and many meetings. So I leave it to my vice president of marketing.

> **Vice President of Marketing:** Well, I have a rather considerable staff and many responsibilities with regard to marketing plans and day-to-day decisions regarding our sales force and advertising. So I really don't have the time. But we have a very highly trained sales force, and they are talking to customers all the time.

> **Sales Force:** Sure, we are in continuous contact with our customers and we bring back new ideas all the time. But nobody in management has the time to listen.

Obviously, this business lacks marketing leadership at the top. To build a strong market orientation, all levels of management, and senior management in particular, need to have a strong customer focus. Market orientation and marketing leadership start at the top.

For example, IBM's top 470 executives are personally responsible for more than 1,300 customer accounts.[23] In addition, IBM gives frontline employees the authority, without prior management approval, to spend up to $5,000 per complaint to solve problems for a customer on the spot. Nordstrom has created a market-based culture in which every customer interaction is an opportunity to build customer satisfaction.[24] This initiative is led from the top and permeates all levels of the Nordstrom management hierarchy. Starbucks senior management believes that the first four hours of new employee training are the most important in shaping an employee's market orientation. To the degree that management fails to communicate its customer orientation during this training, it will have failed to shape Starbucks' market orientation.

Every marketing decision implicitly or explicitly sends a message to employees relative to management's commitment to a market orientation. The actions and words of senior and middle management set the tone of a business's market orientation. Their market orientation and leadership are essential in building a market-based business culture. A top management decision to unjustifiably raise customer prices in order to meet short-term profit objectives sends a clear signal of the business's lack of commitment to a market orientation. Thus, consistent market-based leadership is a requirement for building a market-oriented business culture.

Market Orientation and Employee Satisfaction

Think about calling a business with a complaint and interacting with a person who hates his or her job and the company he or she works for. What kind of reception do you think you will get? Employee satisfaction is a key factor in delivering customer satisfaction.[25] As shown in Figure 1.12, employee satisfaction affects customer service, which in turn influences customer satisfaction and retention. And, as we have already shown, higher levels of customer satisfaction contribute to higher levels of customer retention and profitability.

Sears found that in all of its many stores, there was a high correlation between customer satisfaction, employee satisfaction, and store profitability.[26] NCR found that,

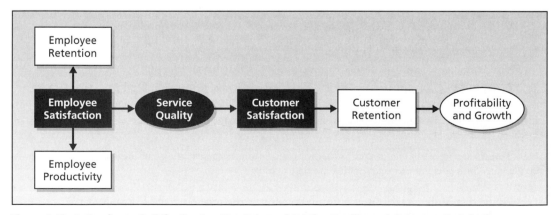

Figure 1.12 ◆ Employee Satisfaction Is a Key Driver of Service Quality and Customer Satisfaction

among 12 manufacturing operations, higher levels of employee job satisfaction corresponded with higher levels of customer satisfaction.[27] Thus, building a strong market orientation requires a healthy business environment in which employees enjoy their jobs and working for the organization.

SUMMARY

The strength of a business's market orientation is directly related to its ability to develop market-based strategies that deliver high levels of customer satisfaction. For years, many observers would have considered that statement to be a nice academic philosophy that had little to do with a company that was in business to make a profit. Today, however, there is considerable evidence that businesses that operate with higher levels of customer satisfaction are more profitable. They are more profitable because they are able to retain a high percentage of customers, have less rework as a result of poor product or service quality, and need to spend less time and money attracting new customers to replace lost customers. Thus, businesses with a strong market orientation are able to deliver higher levels of both customer satisfaction and profitability.

As is true of most concepts, the words come much more easily than the results. There are three critical components to achieving a strong market orientation:

- A business must have strong individual market orientation among all its managers and employees. A business's market orientation is only as strong as the collective sum of all the individual market orientations of its managers and employees.
- A business must have a senior management team dedicated to a strong market orientation that leads by example and reinforces its market orientation through company communications and employee reward systems.
- The ultimate goal of a strong market orientation is to develop and implement marketing strategies that attract, satisfy, and retain target market customers. Formal measures of customer satisfaction, dissatisfaction, and retention play an important role in achieving a strong market orientation.

A business with a strong market focus is in a position to develop marketing strategies that are responsive to customer needs and competitive forces. By delivering higher levels of customer satisfaction and value, these businesses are able to retain a higher proportion of their customers. Having higher customer satisfaction and retention lowers the cost of serving customers and acquiring new ones. Perhaps more important, it creates the opportunity to keep customers throughout their customer life cycle. Keeping customers contributes to both current and future profits, enabling a business to invest in other market opportunities. In the end, a strong market orientation rewards customers, employees, and shareholders.

MARKET-BASED LOGIC AND STRATEGIC THINKING

1. What is a market orientation? How would a business with a strong market orientation differ from one with a weak market orientation?
2. How are a strong market orientation and commitment to understanding customer needs related to shareholder value?

APPLICATION PROBLEM: AIRCOMM

AirComm is a wireless communication service with 5 million customers and annual sales of $1.9 billion. Though profitable, AirComm has never measured its customer satisfaction. To better understand customer satisfaction, usage, and what customers do when they are dissatisfied, AirComm conducted a comprehensive study of 1,000 customers, the key results of which are outlined below.

Customer Satisfaction

- Sixty-seven percent of AirComm's customers are satisfied and 33 percent are dissatisfied.
- Satisfied customers produce an average revenue of $400 per year and an average margin of $250.
- Dissatisfied customers who are retained produce an average revenue of $300 per year and an average margin of $150.
- Dissatisfied customers who discontinue their service produce an average $200 in revenue per year and an average margin of $100.

Customer Complaint Behavior

- Only 5 percent of AirComm's dissatisfied customers complain to AirComm about dissatisfaction. Of these, 90 percent are retained and 10 percent discontinue their service.
- Ninety-five percent of AirComm's dissatisfied customers do *not* complain. Of these, 20 percent are retained as customers and 80 percent discontinue their service.

New Customers

- New customers generate an average revenue of $150 and an average margin of $50 the first year.
- AirComm actively seeks new customers to maintain its customer base of 5 million in an increasingly competitive market.

Marketing Costs

- The average marketing cost for retaining a satisfied customer is $50.
- The average marketing cost of managing a dissatisfied customer is $100.
- The average marketing cost to attract a new customer is $250.

Questions

For Internet discussion, go to www.prenhall.com/phbusiness.

1. Build a Customer Retention Tree (as illustrated in Figure 1.6), and determine AirComm's current rate of customer retention.

2. What is AirComm's average customer life expectancy at their current rate of customer retention? At this level of customer life expectancy, what is the net present value of a customer who is satisfied until the year he/she leaves? (Use a 12 percent discount rate.)

3. How would customer retention change if customer satisfaction were improved (from 67 percent to 77 percent)?

3. Why are customer satisfaction and customer retention important drivers of profitability?
4. Why are average measures of customer satisfaction misleading indicators of market-based performance?
5. How does the mix of customers who are satisfied, neutral, and dissatisfied affect a business's net profits?
6. Using the Customer Retention Tree in Figure 1.6, determine how customer retention would change if the business increased its percentage of satisfied customers from 70 to 80 percent.
7. Why do high levels of customer dissatisfaction make attracting new customers more difficult?
8. How do high levels of customer dissatisfaction increase the cost of marketing and hence lower net profits?
9. Why are satisfied customers crucial to a business's net profits?
10. If the average customer life of a credit card (see Figure 1.10) were extended one year, what would be the level of customer retention required? Also, if the profit obtained in the sixth year is the same as that in the fifth year, what is the net gain in customer value (net present value)?
11. How does customer selection affect customer retention?
12. Why is marketing education an important element in building a strong market orientation?
13. What role does employee training play in building market orientation? Why is a market orientation important at all levels of an organization?
14. What role does marketing leadership play in building the market orientation of a business?
15. How can the senior management of an organization destroy a business's market orientation?
16. Why should employee satisfaction impact customer satisfaction? Why would it be difficult to build customer satisfaction when employee satisfaction is low?

NOTES

1. Bradley Gale, *Managing Customer Value* (New York: Free Press, 1994): chapter 2.
2. Ajay K. Kohli and Bernard J. Jaworski, "Market Orientation: The Construct, Research Propositions, and Managerial Implications," *Journal of Marketing,* 54 (April 1995):1–18; Bernard J. Jaworski and Ajay K. Kohli, "Market Orientation: Antecedents and Consequences," *Journal of Marketing,* 57 (July 1993):53–70; Ajay K. Kohli, Bernard J. Jaworski, and Ajith Kumar, "Markor: A Measure of Market Orientation," *Journal of Marketing,* 30 (November 1993):467–77; John C. Narver and Stanley F. Slater, "The Effect of a Market Orientation on Business Profitability," *Journal of Marketing,* 54 (October 1990):20–35; and Stanley F. Slater and John C. Narver, "Does Competitive Environment Moderate the Market Orientation-Performance Relationship," *Journal of Marketing,* 58 (January 1994):46–55.
3. Frederick F. Reichheld and W. Earl Sasser Jr., "Zero Defections: Quality Comes to Services," *Harvard Business Review* (September–October 1990):106–11; and Frederick F. Reichheld, "Loyalty-Based Management," *Harvard Business Review* (March–April 1993):64–73.
4. M. Menezes and J. Serbin, "Xerox Corporation: The Customer Satisfaction Program," Harvard Business School Publishing.

5. Patrick Byrne, "Only 10% of Companies Satisfy Customers," *Transportation and Distribution* (December 1993); and Tom Eck, "Are Customers Happy? Don't Assume," *Positive Impact* (July l992):3.

6. Valarie Zeithaml, A. Parasuraman, and Leonard Berry, *Delivering Quality Service* (New York: Free Press, 1990): chapter 1; and John Goodman, Ted Mama, and Liz Brigham, "Customer Service: Costly Nuisance or Lower Cost Profit Strategy?" *Journal of Bank Retailing* (Fall 1986):12.

7. TARP, "Consumer Complaint Handling in America: An Update Study," White House Office of Consumer Affairs, Washington, DC, 1986; TARP, "Consumer Complaint Handling in America, Final Report," U.S. Office of Consumer Affairs, Washington, DC, 1979; and Kathy Rhoades, "The Importance of Customer Complaints," *Protect Yourself* (January 1988):15–18.

8. J. Singh, "Consumer Complaint Intentions and Behavior," *Journal of Marketing* (January 1988):93–107; Jack Dart and Kim Freeman, "Dissatisfaction Response Styles Among Clients of Professional Accounting," *Journal of Business Research,* 29 (January 1994):75–81.

9. A.M. McGahan and Panlcaj Ghemawat, "Competition to Retain Customers," *Marketing Science,* 13 (Spring 1994):165–176; Mark H. McCormack, "One Disappointed Customer Is One Too Many," *Positive Impact,* 4 (September 1993):7–8, Jeffery Gitomer, "Customer Complaints Can Breed Sales If Handled Correctly," *Positive Impact,* 5 (February 1994):10–11; Financial Services Report, "Most Popular Trends in Retention—Appealing to Your 'Best' Customers," *Positive Impact,* 5 (May 1994):24; and Sreekanth Sampathkumaran, "Migration Analysis Helps Stop Customer Attrition," *Marketing News,* 28 (August 1994):18–19.

10. T. Lucia, "Domino's Theory—Only Service Succeeds," *Positive Impact* (February 1992):6–7.

11. Bernice Johnston, *Real World Customer Service—What to Really Say When the Customer Complains* (Small Business Source Books, 1996).

12. See the following articles in *Positive Impact:* Debbie Mitchell Price, "More Than Ever, It Pays to Keep the Customer Satisfied," 3 (February 1992):7–8; Rosalie Robles Crowe, "Customer Satisfaction Paramount," 5 (April 1994):7–8; Rod Riggs, "More-Than-Satisfied Customer Now the Goal," 5 (January 1994):4–5; Peter Larson, "Customer Loyalty Is a Commodity Worth Fighting For," 4 (November 1993):4; and Julie Bonnin, "L.L. Bean Keeps Its Customers Returning," 5 (January 1993):7–8.

13. Steven Schnaars, *Marketing Strategy* (New York: Free Press, 1998):186–205.

14. Reichheld and Sasser, "Zero Defections: Quality Comes to Services," 106–111; and Reichheld, "Loyalty-Based Management," 64–73.

15. Thomas Jones and W. Earl Sasser Jr., "Why Satisfied Customers Defect," *Harvard Business Review* (November–December 1995):88–89.

16. Roger Best and Terrance Reilly, "Customer Life Expectancy and Customer Retention," unpublished working paper.

17. Roberta Clarke, "Addressing Voluntary Disenrollment," *CDR Healthcare Resources* (1997):10–12.

18. Steve Schriver, "Customer Loyalty—Going, Going . . . ," *American Demographics* (September 1997):20–23.

19. Peter Peacock, "Data Mining in Marketing: Part I," *Marketing Management* (Winter 1998):12.

20. Michael Anthony, "More Customers or Right Customers: Your Choice," *Marketing News,* 31 (August 1998):13.

21. Roger Best, "Determining the Marketing IQ of Your Management Team," *Drive Marketing Excellence* (November 1994), New York: Institute for International Research.

22. Mary Connelly, "Chrysler Adopts Disney Mindset for Customers," *Automotive News* (February 1992).

23. Robert Hiebeler, Thomas Kelly, and Charles Ketteman, *Best Practices: Building Your Business with Customer-Focused Solutions* (New York: Simon and Schuster, 1998):167–200.

24. Rosalind Bentley, "The Name Nordstrom—Aim to Keep Customer Happy Is Legendary," *Positive Impact* (July 1992):5.

25. Anthony Rucci, Steven Kirin, and Richard Quinn, "The Employee—Customer Profit Chain at Sears," *Harvard Business Review* (January–February 1998):82–97.

26. Jack W. Wiley, "Customer Satisfaction and Employee Opinions: A Supportive Work Environment and Its Financial Costs," *Human Resource Planning*, 14 (1991):117–23; Anita Bruzzese, "Happy Employees Make Happy Customers," *Positive Impact*, 4 (November 1993):8–9; Jim Cathcart, "Fill the Needs of Employees to Better Serve Customers," *Positive Impact*, 5 (November 1994):7–8; and Peter Lawson, "Studies Link Customer–Employee Satisfaction," *Positive Impact*, 3 (March 1992):11–12.

27. Leonard A. Schlesinger and Jeffery Zomitsky, "Job Satisfaction, Service Capability, and Customer Satisfaction: An Examination of Linkages and Management Implications," *Human Resource Planning*, 14 (1991):141–49.

APPENDIX 1.1—PRESENT VALUE TABLE

Period (N)	DR=8%	DR=9%	DR=10%	DR=11%	DR=12%	DR=13%	DR=14%	DR=15%
0	1.000	1.000	1.000	1.000	1.000	1.000	1.000	1.000
1	0.926	0.917	0.909	0.901	0.893	0.885	0.887	0.870
2	0.857	0.842	0.826	0.812	0.797	0.783	0.769	0.756
3	0.794	0.772	0.751	0.731	0.712	0.693	0.675	0.658
4	0.735	0.708	0.683	0.659	0.636	0.613	0.592	0.572
5	0.681	0.650	0.621	0.593	0.567	0.543	0.519	0.497
6	0.630	0.596	0.564	0.535	0.507	0.480	0.456	0.432
7	0.583	0.547	0.513	0.482	0.452	0.425	0.400	0.376
8	0.540	0.502	0.467	0.434	0.404	0.376	0.351	0.327
9	0.500	0.460	0.424	0.391	0.361	0.333	0.308	0.284
10	0.463	0.422	0.386	0.352	0.322	0.295	0.270	0.247
11	0.429	0.388	0.350	0.317	0.287	0.261	0.237	0.215
12	0.397	0.356	0.319	0.286	0.257	0.231	0.208	0.187
13	0.368	0.326	0.290	0.258	0.229	0.204	0.182	0.163
14	0.340	0.299	0.263	0.232	0.205	0.181	0.160	0.141
15	0.315	0.275	0.239	0.209	0.183	0.160	0.140	0.123
16	0.292	0.252	0.218	0.188	0.163	0.141	0.123	0.107
17	0.270	0.231	0.198	0.170	0.146	0.125	0.108	0.093
18	0.250	0.212	0.180	0.153	0.130	0.111	0.095	0.081
19	0.232	0.194	0.164	0.138	0.116	0.098	0.083	0.070
20	0.215	0.178	0.149	0.124	0.104	0.087	0.073	0.061

Present Value Formula

$$PV = \frac{1}{(1 + DR)^N}$$

PV = Present Value of $1.00
N = Number of periods before the $1.00 will be received
DR = Discount Rate (cost of borrowing or desired rate of return)

Example I: N = 5 periods and Discount Rate (DR) = 10%

$$PV = \frac{1}{(1 + 0.10)^5} = \frac{1}{1.611} = 0.621 \text{ (\$1.00 received in 5 years is worth \$0.621 today)}$$

Example II: N = 2.33 periods and Discount Rate (DR) = 10%

$$PV = \frac{1}{(1 + 0.10)^{2.33}} = \frac{1}{1.249} = 0.801 \text{ (\$1.00 received in 2.33 years is worth \$0.801 today)}$$

chapter 2

Market-Based Performance

CommTech is a $454 million business that manufactures a wide range of imaging and data transmission products for medical, industrial, and business-to-business markets. Five years ago, a new management team was put in place after several years of disappointing performance. The new management team reorganized the business and designed programs to lower unit costs, control overhead expenses, and facilitate better management of assets. In addition, the new management team put in place an extensive sales training program that enabled the sales force to improve its sales productivity from $1.4 million to $2.2 million per salesperson.

The results were sensational! In five years, the new management team almost doubled sales and more than tripled net profits. As shown in Figure 2.1, CommTech's return on sales grew from 6.3 percent to 12.1 percent, and its return on assets increased from 11.3 percent to 26.7 percent. On the basis of this information

- How would you rate CommTech's performance over the last five years?
- What aspects of CommTech's performance were most impressive?
- Should CommTech follow the same strategy for the next five years?

MARKET VS. FINANCIAL PERFORMANCE

Most of us would be quick to conclude that CommTech's performance over the last five years was outstanding. Who would not like to have run a business in which the sales almost doubled and the profits more than tripled over a five-year period? Despite those

Performance (millions)	Base Year	1	2	3	4	5
Sales Revenue	$254	$293	$318	$387	$431	$454
−Cost of Goods Sold	183	210	230	283	314	331
Total Contribution	$ 71	$ 83	$ 88	$104	$117	$123
−Marketing and Sales	18	23	24	26	27	28
−Operating Expenses	37	38	38	41	40	40
Net Profit (before taxes)	$ 16	$ 22	$ 26	$ 37	$ 50	$ 55
Return on Sales (%)	6.3	7.5	8.2	9.6	11.6	12.1
Assets (millions)	$141	$162	$167	$194	$205	$206
Return on Assets (%)	11.3	13.6	15.6	19.1	24.4	26.7

Figure 2.1 ◆ CommTech's Five-Year Performance

impressive increases, it is probably a mistake to evaluate CommTech's performance in such rosy terms when all the criteria used to arrive at this judgment are *financial* measures of performance. Sales revenues, net profits, return on sales, assets as a percentage of sales, and return on assets are all excellent measures of internal financial performance. These measures, however, do not provide an *external or market-based view* of performance. As a result, we do not know how CommTech has performed relative to external benchmarks such as market growth, competitive prices, relative product and service quality, and satisfying and retaining customers. Therefore, following the same strategy for the next five years may or may not be the best strategy for achieving profitable growth.

While using traditional methods of tracking performance, most would judge CommTech to be a real success story. But it can be demonstrated that, in reality, its efforts represent a cumulative loss to the corporation and its shareholders of $122 million in net income and cash flow over the five-year period. This difference in performance is due largely to a lack of market-based performance metrics and an overreliance on traditional financial measures as a guide to strategic thinking and performance evaluation.

To complement a business's internal financial performance, a business needs a parallel set of external metrics to track market-based performance.[1] Although these measures may not have the additive elegance of financial accounting, individually and collectively they provide a different and more strategic view of business performance. In Figure 2.2 is a set of market-based performance metrics that paints a different picture of CommTech's performance over the past five years.

One can readily see several strategic flaws in CommTech's market-based performance. First, CommTech sales, while showing impressive growth, were increasing at a rate less than the market growth rate. This analysis shows that CommTech was actually losing market share over the past five years. New product sales, product quality, and service quality each eroded *relative to competition*. Declines in relative product and service quality do not necessarily mean that CommTech's actual product or service quality declined.

Market-Based Performance	Base Year	1	2	3	4	5
Market Growth (dollars)	18.3%	23.8%	16.3%	31.4%	24.9%	16.9%
CommTech Sales Growth	12.8%	17.8%	13.3%	24.9%	18.2%	7.7%
Market Share	20.3%	18.8%	17.5%	16.2%	14.4%	13.0%
Customer Retention	88.2%	87.1%	85.0%	82.2%	80.9%	80.0%
New Customers	11.7%	12.9%	14.9%	24.1%	22.5%	29.2%
Dissatisfied Customers	13.6%	14.3%	16.1%	17.3%	18.9%	19.6%
Relative Product Quality	+19	+20	+17	+12	+9	+7
Relative Service Quality	+0	+0	−2	−3	−5	−8
Relative New Product Sales	+8	+8	+7	+5	+1	−4

Figure 2.2 ◆ CommTech's Five-Year Market-Based Performance

In many instances, the competition simply moved ahead in delivering a higher level of product and service quality. On a relative basis, the competition's more rapid progress caused CommTech to lose ground to competitors in these areas.

Declines in quality, along with declines in relative new product sales, made it more difficult to hold customers as customer satisfaction declined and the percentage of dissatisfied customers grew. The net results were an eroding market-based performance, high levels of customer turnover, and a steady decline in market share.

A Market-Based Strategy

What would have been the impact of a strategy to hold market share? To hold a 20 percent share in a growing market, the marketing budget and product R&D would have needed to keep pace with market demand and the competition. At this level of investment and a 20 percent market share, the results presented in Figure 2.3 would have been plausible.

Although the market-based strategy to hold share would have delivered approximately the same return on assets as the internally driven strategy, it would have produced an additional $122 million in net profit (before taxes). Thus, over the five-year period, the business gave up $122 million in cash to the bottom line. Furthermore, CommTech's lost income will be even greater over the next five years even if share erosion is halted and market growth completely subsides. If the market continues to grow, and market share continues to erode, CommTech's lost profit opportunity could easily approach $500 million over the next five years.

Market-Based Performance

The foundation of market-based management is a strong commitment to market-based performance metrics, market-level profitability, and the management of marketing expenses to achieve a high level of marketing productivity. Businesses that are market-based

Performance (millions)	Base Year	1	2	3	4	5
Sales Revenue	$254	$312	$363	$477	$596	$697
−Cost of Goods Sold	183	216	251	330	415	484
Total Contribution	$ 71	$ 96	$112	$147	$181	$213
−Marketing and Sales	18	24	27	32	41	50
−Operating Expenses	37	41	45	52	59	66
Net Profit (before taxes)	**$ 16**	**$ 31**	**$ 40**	**$ 63**	**$ 81**	**$ 97**
Return on Sales (%)	6.3	9.9	11.0	13.2	13.6	13.9
Assets (millions)	$141	$172	$196	$253	$310	$355
Assets (% of sales)	55.5	55.1	54.0	53.0	52.0	50.9
Return on Assets (%)	11.3	18.0	20.4	24.9	26.1	27.3
Lost Income (cash flow)*	**$ 0**	**$ 9**	**$ 14**	**$ 26**	**$ 31**	**$ 42**
* Difference between net profits in Figures 2.1 and 2.3.						

Figure 2.3 ◆ **Market-Based Strategy to Hold a 20 Percent Market Share**

are able to create a business culture in which managers possess strong individual market orientations and work across functions to achieve marketing excellence. However, to fully leverage market-based management and market orientation and attain superior performance, a business needs to manage itself with respect to:

- **Market Performance Metrics:** External measures of market performance.
- **Marketing Profitability:** Measures of profitability at the market level.
- **Market-Based Organization:** Business structure built around markets.

Each of these elements of market-based performance is critical in taking a business to a higher level of marketing effectiveness and overall success.

MARKET-BASED PERFORMANCE METRICS

The CommTech situation underlines the importance of market-based performance metrics. Most business systems are set up to track revenues, costs, factory overhead, accounts receivable, operating expenses, and profits. Yet a business's customers are its most important asset and the only significant source of positive cash flow. Giving up customers in a period of growth simply means that the business has to work harder and spend more in order to replace each lost customer.

Internal vs. External Performance Metrics

To be successful, a business needs both internal and external performance metrics.[2] As presented in Figure 2.4, internal measures are critical for tracking unit costs, expenses, asset utilization, employee and capital productivity, and overall measures of profitability. Market-based performance metrics are equally important in providing an external view of the business's market-based performance. While CPA firms have done an excellent job in developing procedures for internal measures of a business's performance, the next frontier for either CPA firms or market research firms will be the development of stan-

Internal Performance Metrics	External Performance Metrics
Unit Cost	Market Share
Manufacturing Overhead	Relative Share
Marketing Expenses	Customer Satisfaction
R&D Expense	Market Coverage
Sales/Employee	Product Awareness
Inventory Turn	Relative Quality
Days Accounts Receivable	Relative Price
Return on Sales	Customer Preferences
Asset Turnover	Relative New Product Sales
ROI and ROE	Response Time to Problems

Figure 2.4 ◆ Internal and External Measures of Performance

dardized procedures for external measures of a business's market-based performance. With both sets of performance metrics, managers as well as financial analysts and shareholders will be in a much better position to evaluate a business's marketing effectiveness and business performance.

In-Process vs. End-Result Performance Metrics

The primary purpose of market metrics is to maintain an ongoing measure of market performance. And, because many market metrics precede financial performance, they are critical to strategy implementation and financial performance. However, not all market metrics are leading indicators of business performance. There are *in-process market metrics* and *end-result market metrics.*[3] Both are important, but in-process market metrics are particularly important because they are also leading indicators of financial performance. End-result metrics correspond more closely to financial performance.

Product awareness, intention to purchase, product trial, and customer satisfaction and dissatisfaction, along with customer perceptions of relative product quality, service quality, and customer value, all serve as in-process market metrics. Changes in each, positive or negative, generally precede actual changes in customer purchase behavior. As a result, these in-process measures of customer thinking and attitude are important leading indicators of future purchase behavior and, hence, of revenue and profit performance.

For example, perhaps customers are satisfied, but their perceptions of the value they derive from your product, relative to competing alternatives, is steadily diminishing. You may well have done nothing wrong to dissatisfy customers; the competition may have simply improved in delivering customer value based upon a combination of total benefits in comparison to total cost. However, the net effect is that customer perceptions of the value derived from your product have diminished. This change in customer perceptions, in turn, opens the door to competitors' products that your customer may be inclined to try or purchase. With an early warning signal, a market-based business can take corrective action before customers switch their purchase to a competitor. Without in-process market metrics, problems may go undetected and unresolved until after declines in financial performance.

End-result market metrics include market share, customer retention, revenue per customer, and others, as outlined in Figure 2.5. End-result market metrics are likely to occur at the end of a financial performance period. However, each provides a different set of performance diagnostics and insights.

For example, let's assume that sales revenues are increasing and are ahead of forecast, and financial performance is also better than expected. Most businesses would feel pretty good about their performance. However, if end-result performance metrics show that the business is losing market share in a growing market, and poor customer retention is masked by new customer growth, there should be cause for concern. Without end-result market metrics, the business has only an internal perspective of end-result performance.

MARKETING PROFITABILITY

Although market-based performance metrics are essential to understanding external performance, it is also important that a business be managed to grow and to protect profits and shareholder value. Consider, for example, the Santa Fe Sportswear Company. The

Measurement Perspective	Time of Measurement	
	In-Process Metrics	**End-Result Metrics**
Internal (in-company)	Product Defects Late Deliveries Billing Errors Accounts Receivable Inventory Turnover	Net Profit/Earnings Return on Sales Margin per Unit Return on Assets Asset Turnover
External (in-market)	Customer Satisfaction Relative Product Quality Relative Service Quality Intentions to Purchase Product Awareness	Market Share Customer Retention Relative New Product Sales Revenue per Customer Market Growth Rate

Figure 2.5 ◆ **Internal vs. External and In-Process vs. End-Result Performance Metrics**

company's sales of $125 million were built around five product lines. The company was profitable overall, but two of the product lines had not performed well. In response, the senior management team of Santa Fe Sportswear met to review its product line performance. In preparation for the senior management review, the finance manager prepared the product line profitability summary presented in Figure 2.6.

Using this information, the finance manager argued the following:

> We are wasting resources on Product Lines P4 and P5. One makes no money and the other loses money. I recommend we drop both product lines and refocus our efforts on Product Lines P1, P2, and P3.

Would this be a good decision? How should the marketing manager present her interpretation of the performance of Product Lines P4 and P5? Before we address those two questions, let's examine the role marketing plays in building net profits.

MARKET-BASED MEASURE OF PROFITABILITY

To create a measure of marketing profitability, we need to examine more closely the elements of profitability and determine which come under the influence of the marketing function. To do this, we need to systematically break down the elements of profitability

Area of Performance	Product Line					Company Total
	P1	**P2**	**P3**	**P4**	**P5**	
Sales Revenues	$60.0	$25.0	$15.0	$10.0	$15.0	$125
Variable Expenses	37.5	15.5	7.5	8.5	11.0	80
Total Contribution	$22.5	$ 9.5	$ 7.5	$ 1.5	$ 4.0	$ 45
Fixed Expenses	17.0	7.0	4.0	3.0	4.0	35
Net Profit	**$ 5.5**	**$ 2.5**	**$ 3.5**	**$–1.5**	**$ 0.0**	**$ 10**

Figure 2.6 ◆ **Santa Fe Sportsware: Product Line Profitability**

and marketing strategy to better understand how they interact.[4] The best method is to start with a very broad definition of net profit and then break down the profit equation into a definition that encompasses a market-level measure of profitability. Thus, in its most basic terms, a business's net profit is simply revenues minus expenses:

$$\text{Net Profits (before taxes)} = \text{Revenues} - \text{Expenses}$$

However, from a marketing point of view, we would want to break down sales revenues and expenses into more meaningful market-based strategic variables. Revenues can be decomposed into unit volume sold times the price per unit, and unit volume can be further broken down into market demand and a business's share of that demand, as shown:

$$\text{Sales Revenues} = \text{Unit Volume} \times \text{Price per Unit}$$
$$= \text{Market Demand} \times \text{Market Share} \times \text{Price per Unit}$$

For marketing purposes, this is a more meaningful expression of revenue because it is based on a particular combination of market demand (units), market share (percentage of market demand), and price per unit. In this manner, we can readily understand three ways in which revenue can change. Market demand can change because of market growth, expanded market definition, or new market entry. Likewise, share of market and price can vary depending on a combination of marketing strategies and changes in competitive conditions.

With regard to expenses, we can break them down into *variable* expenses and *fixed* expenses. Variable expenses are *volume-sensitive* and can be broken down in the same manner as sales revenue:

$$\text{Variable Expenses} = \text{Unit Volume} \times \text{Variable Cost per Unit}$$
$$= \text{Market Demand} \times \text{Market Share} \times \text{Variable Cost per Unit}$$

Changes in unit manufacturing cost, purchased materials, sales commissions, and transportation costs generally determine the variable cost of each unit sold, as described in Figure 2.7. As volume changes, the overall variable expenses will also change.

Fixed expenses (also described in Figure 2.7) are made up of those expenses that are not volume-sensitive and are, therefore, less likely to change in the short run for a given level of production capacity. However, from a market-based management perspective, it is very important that these expenses also be decomposed into two important sources of fixed expense, as shown:

$$\text{Fixed Expenses} = \text{Marketing Expenses} + \text{Operating Expenses}$$

To manage profits at the market level we need to separate fixed marketing expenses from other fixed *operating* expenses.[5] Operating expenses, as described in Figure 2.7, include R&D and administrative expenses needed to run the business.

NET MARKETING CONTRIBUTION

If we combine revenues, variable expenses, and marketing expenses, we can create a measure of marketing profitability. However, to manage profit at the market level, we need to rewrite the net profit equation based on how we break down revenues and variable and fixed expenses as they are related to the profit impact of marketing strategies. Because the

Variable Cost per Unit	Costs that vary with unit volume sold
Cost of Materials	Per unit cost of products sold to customers that is made up of raw materials, semifinished goods, and component products
Direct Labor	Per unit cost of personnel needed to manufacture and/or assemble products sold
Transportation Costs	Per unit cost of shipping to and holding finished goods for customers
Sales Commissions	Per unit cost of commissions paid to the sales force or sales agents
Sales Promotions	Per unit cost of price discounts or co-op advertising used to promote products
Marketing Expenses	**Direct fixed expenses that vary with market strategy**
Sales Force Expense	Salaries paid to the sales force and personnel who support the sales force
Advertising Expense	Advertising dollars spent to communicate the business's message to the served market
Customer Service	Fixed expense of providing customer service to the served market
Marketing Support	Market research and administration that supports the efforts directed at the served market
Sales Promotions	Special promotions and public relations intended to stimulate potential or served market demand
Marketing Administration	Fixed cost of the marketing management team and associated administrative expenses
Operating Expenses	**Indirect fixed expenses that will not vary in the short run and are independent of volume**
Research and Development	Expense of improving products and developing new products
Administrative Overhead	Expenses allocated to business units to cover corporate expenses associated with legal counsel, professional services, corporate communications, and the salaries of senior management and staff

Figure 2.7 ◆ Variable Costs, Marketing Expenses, and Operating Expenses

volume portion of revenues and that of variable expenses are the same, we can express net profit in *marketing terms* in the following way:

$$\text{Net Profit (before taxes)} = \underbrace{\left[\text{Market Demand} \times \text{Market Share} \times \left(\text{Price per Unit} - \text{Variable Cost per Unit} \right) \right] - \text{Marketing Expenses}}_{\text{Net Marketing Contribution (NMC)}} - \text{Operating Expenses}$$

The portion bracketed as *net marketing contribution* is our measure of marketing profitability. These are the components of profitability that are largely under the control of the marketing function. Operating expenses are generally not under the control of the marketing function. Thus, we can rewrite the net profit of a business as shown, where marketing controls the net marketing contribution (NMC) component of net profit:

Net Profit (before taxes) = Net Marketing Contribution – Operating Expenses

From this perspective, a marketing strategy produces a net marketing contribution.[6] This net marketing contribution has to cover the business's operating expenses and more in order for the business to make a profit.

Using net marketing contribution as a measure of profitability, the marketing manager can more readily evaluate the profit impact of a marketing strategy. Each product or market should be managed to produce a *positive* net marketing contribution. In this way, marketing decisions can be evaluated with respect not only to revenue and share gains but also to how they will affect profits by the level of net marketing contribution they produce.

Recognizing net marketing contribution as the measure of marketing profitability, we need to reexamine Santa Fe Sportswear's product line profitability. For example, Santa Fe Sportswear's marketing strategy for Product Line P1 currently produces a net marketing contribution of $15.5 million, as shown in Figure 2.8. This level of marketing profitability is the result of a 12.5 percent share of a 12 million unit market demand, a price of $40 per unit, a variable cost of $25 per unit, and marketing expenses of $7 million.

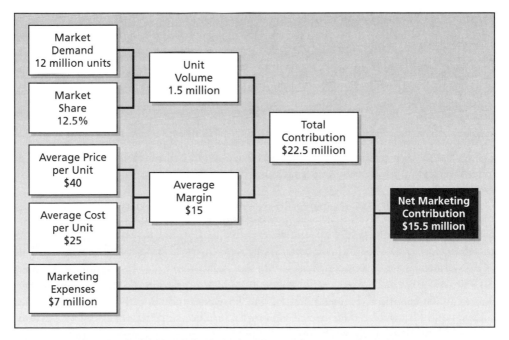

Figure 2.8 ◆ Net Marketing Contribution: Santa Fe Sportswear Product Line P1

$$\begin{array}{l}\text{NMC} \\ \text{(P1)}\end{array} = \left[\begin{array}{c}\text{Market} \\ \text{Demand}\end{array} \times \begin{array}{c}\text{Market} \\ \text{Share}\end{array} \times \left(\begin{array}{c}\text{Price} \\ \text{per Unit}\end{array} - \begin{array}{c}\text{Variable Cost} \\ \text{per Unit}\end{array} \right) \right] - \begin{array}{c}\text{Marketing} \\ \text{Expenses}\end{array}$$

$$= [12 \text{ million} \times 0.125 \times (\$40 - \$25)] - \$7 \text{ million}$$

$$= [1.5 \text{ million} \times \$15 \text{ per unit}] - \$7 \text{ million}$$

$$= \$22.5 \text{ million} - \$7 \text{ million}$$

$$= \$15.5 \text{ million}$$

To demonstrate how the profit impact of a marketing strategy can be assessed, assume that the marketing manager of Santa Fe Sportswear's Product Line P1 proposed to cut price by 10 percent in order to grow share from 12.5 to 15 percent. As shown below, this marketing strategy would produce 300,000 more units in sales volume, but at a lower margin ($15 vs. $11). The net result of this marketing strategy would be a decrease in net marketing contribution from $15.5 million to $12.8 million and, therefore, a decrease in net profits of the same amount.

$$\text{NMC (P1)} = [12 \text{ million} \times 0.15 \times (\$36 - \$25)] - \$7 \text{ million}$$

$$= [1.8 \text{ million} \times \$11 \text{ per unit}] - \$7 \text{ million}$$

$$= \$19.8 \text{ million} - \$7 \text{ million}$$

$$= \$12.8 \text{ million}$$

Net Marketing Contribution and Business Unit Profitability

When a business has several product lines, it produces several sources of net marketing contribution. The sum of the net marketing contributions of all these product lines is the only source of cash flow produced by the business; everything else is expense, as shown:

$$\begin{array}{l}\text{Net Profit} \\ \text{(before taxes)}\end{array} = \underbrace{\begin{array}{c}\text{NMC} \\ \text{Product (1)}\end{array} + \begin{array}{c}\text{NMC} \\ \text{Product (2)}\end{array} + \cdots + \begin{array}{c}\text{NMC} \\ \text{Product (n)}\end{array}}_{\text{NMCs from all served markets}} - \begin{array}{c}\text{Operating} \\ \text{Expenses}\end{array}$$

Now, let's return to the questions raised earlier: Would eliminating Product Lines P4 and P5 be a good idea? And would such a decision improve the net profits of Santa Fe Sportswear?

First, Figure 2.9 presents a market-based view of Santa Fe Sportswear's product line profitability and overall company net profits (before taxes). As shown, each product line produces a positive net marketing contribution. Thus, each product line is making a positive contribution to operating expenses and net profit (before taxes). If we assume that the operating expenses of the business would not change with the elimination of Product Lines P4 and P5, the business would actually reduce net profits by the amount of net marketing contribution Product Lines P4 and P5 were producing. Eliminating Product Lines P4 and P5 would reduce overall sales by $25 million and net profits by $2.5 (from $10 to $7.5 million), as shown below:

Sante Fe Sportswear Area of Performance	Product Line					Company Total
	P1	P2	P3	P4	P5	
Market Demand (000)	12,000	6,250	5,000	3,750	3,000	30,000
Market Share	12.5%	8.0%	10.0%	8.0%	6.7%	10.0%
Unit Volume (000)	1,500	500	500	300	200	3,000
Sales Revenues (millions)	$ 60	$ 25	$ 15	$ 10	$ 15	$125.0
Average Price (per unit)	$ 40	$ 50	$ 30	$33.3	$ 75	$ 41.7
–Average Variable Cost	25	31	15	28.3	55	26.7
Average Margin	$ 15	$ 19	$ 15	$ 5	$ 20	$ 15.0
Total Contribution (millions)	$ 22.5	$ 9.5	$ 7.5	$ 1.5	$ 4.0	$ 45.0
–Marketing Expenses	7.0	3.0	2.0	1.0	2.0	15.0
Net Mktg. Cont. (millions)	**$ 15.5**	**$ 6.5**	**$ 5.5**	**$ 0.5**	**$ 2.0**	**$ 30.0**
–Operating Expenses	10.0	4.0	2.0	2.0	2.0	20.0
Net Profit (before taxes)	**$ 5.5**	**$ 2.5**	**$ 3.5**	**$ –1.5**	**$ 0.0**	**$ 10.0**

Figure 2.9 ◆ Santa Fe Sportswear: Product Line Marketing Profitability

$$\text{Net Profit (before taxes)} = \text{NMC(P1)} + \text{NMC(P2)} + \text{NMC(P3)} - \text{Operating Expenses}$$
$$= \$15.5 \text{ mil} + \$6.5 \text{ mil} + \$5.5 \text{ mil} - \$20 \text{ mil}$$
$$= \$7.5$$

Another way for the marketing manager to demonstrate how each product line contributes to overall net profits is presented in Figure 2.10. As shown, each product line is producing a positive net marketing contribution. As a result, each makes a contribution toward covering operating expenses and producing net profit. Eliminating any of these products without a commensurate reduction in operating expenses would result in a reduction in net profits.

MARKET-BASED MARKETING PROFITABILITY

Accounting systems are generally built around producing something. Revenues and costs are directly associated with the production of something whether it be a product or a service. Costs that are not directly related to production are allocated to products or services using some agreed-upon accounting rules that have nothing to do with satisfying customers or making money. To develop marketing strategies that satisfy customers and

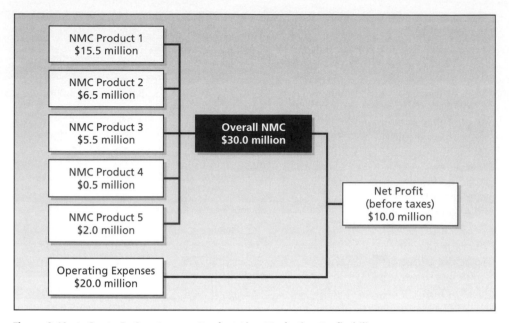

Figure 2.10 ◆ Santa Fe Sportswear: Product Line Marketing Profitability

grow profits, we need to extend the accounting unit of analysis to better assist the marketing function in managing marketing profitability. To accomplish this, we need an alternative way to track a business's revenues, variable costs, fixed expenses, and net profits.

It is convenient to report performance by product, but there are several reasons we should also track performance by markets and customers. Regardless of the technical or psychological appeal of a business's products or services, cash flow is produced only when a customer buys a business's product or service. There are many products and services a business may produce; but there are only a finite number of actual and potential customers in any given market. The objective of a marketing strategy should be to attract, satisfy, and retain target customers in a way that grows the profits of the business.

Using customers and the market segments they belong to as the accounting units, we can create a more insightful understanding of market-based profitability and ways to grow it. But, let's first see what a market-based profitability statement would look like.

In Figure 2.11, we have rebuilt the performance of Santa Fe Sportswear around the three markets served. One can quickly observe that product-based and market-based approaches produce the same total revenue, total contribution, net marketing contribution, and net profits. However, each presents a different insight into market-based management. Both are important and meaningful. The product-based accounting statement (Figure 2.9) helps us understand product unit volume, product price, and unit margin for products. Market-based accounting (Figure 2.11) helps us understand customer demand, customer share, customer volume, revenue per customer, and variable cost per customer. In both cases, we have units of analysis producing net losses (or no net gain). In Figure 2.9, it is Product Lines P4 and P5, and in Figure 2.11 it is Segment S3. However, each produced a positive net marketing contribution and, thus, contributed to covering operating expenses and producing net profit.

Santa Fe Sportwear Area of Performance	Market Segment			Company Total
	S1	S2	S3	
Market Demand (000 customers)	6,800	3,600	1,600	12,000
Market Share	9.0%	6.3%	10.1%	8.3%
Customer Volume (000)	612	227	161	1,000
Sales Revenue (millions)	$ 55	$ 31	$ 39	$125
Revenue per Customer	$ 90	$137	$242	$125
–Variable Cost per Customer	55	80	175	80
Margin per Customer	$ 35	$ 57	$ 67	$ 45
Total Contribution (millions)	$ 21	$ 13	$ 11	$ 45
–Marketing Expenses (millions)	6	4	5	15
Net Marketing Contribution	**$15.4**	**$ 8.9**	**$ 5.8**	**$30.1**
–Operating Expenses (millions)	8	5	7	20
Net Profit (millions)	**$ 7.4**	**$ 3.9**	**$–1.2**	**$10.1**

Figure 2.11 ◆ Santa Fe Sportswear: Customer-Based Marketing Profitability

MARKET-BASED STRATEGIES AND PROFITABLE GROWTH

Recognizing the product or customer as the unit of analysis, we can evaluate different aspects of net marketing contribution in order to gain a better insight into the development of marketing strategies designed to grow profitability.[7] As shown in Figure 2.12, each element of the net marketing contribution equation offers the potential to create a marketing strategy that will affect profits. In each case, the net marketing contribution of a proposed strategy must exceed the current net marketing contribution in order to grow the net profits of the business. In light of this fact, there are a limited number of fundamental marketing strategies that a business can consider in order to grow net marketing contribution.

Figure 2.12 ◆ Fundamental Market-Based Strategies and Profitable Growth

Consider, for example, Santa Fe Sportswear's performance in Segment S1, as presented in Figure 2.11. As shown below, Segment S1 currently produces a net marketing contribution of $15.4 million. This is derived from a 9 percent share of a market demand of 6.8 million customers, revenues of $90 per customer, variable costs of $55 per customer, and marketing expenses of $6 million.

$$\begin{aligned} \text{NMC} \atop \text{(Segment S1)} &= \left[{\text{Market} \atop \text{Demand}} \times {\text{Market} \atop \text{Share}} \times \left({\text{Revenue per} \atop \text{Customer}} - {\text{Variable Cost} \atop \text{per Customer}} \right) \right] - {\text{Marketing} \atop \text{Expenses}} \\ &= [6.8 \text{ million customers} \times 0.09 \times (\$90 - \$55)] - \$6 \text{ million} \\ &= [612,000 \text{ customers} \times \$35] - \$6 \text{ million} \\ &= \$21.4 \text{ million} - \$6 \text{ million} \\ &= \$15.4 \text{ million} \end{aligned}$$

Marketing strategies to grow marketing profitability are many. In the remainder of this section, we will discuss the market-based strategies suggested in Figure 2.12 and assess how selected strategies in each area might affect the profits of Santa Fe Sportswear.

Strategies to Grow Market Demand

In many markets, a large part of the marketing challenge is to bring more customers into the market. If you think about the Sony Walkman, cellular telephones, and personal computers, you realize that a good portion of the profitable growth comes from new customers. Thus, marketing strategies to attract more customers and grow market demand offer one way to grow the net profits of a business. If a business is able to hold or grow share while attracting new customers to the market, there is a potential to grow profits. Profits will grow, however, only when the net marketing contribution produced by the proposed marketing strategy exceeds the current net marketing contribution.

For example, the Santa Fe Sportswear's Segment S1 marketing manager believes that segment demand could be grown from 6.8 million customers to 8.0 million customers with a 50 percent increase in marketing effort. If this increase could be achieved, and Santa Fe Sportswear were able to maintain a 9 percent share, volume would increase by 108,000 customers. But would this proposed strategy improve Segment S1's marketing profitability and increase the business's overall profitability?

We can see from the calculations below that this would be a worthwhile marketing strategy. Net marketing contribution would increase by $0.8 million (from $15.4 to $16.2 million). The gain of 108,000 new customers would produce enough additional total contribution to cover the additional $3 million in marketing expenses required.

$$\begin{aligned} \text{NMC (Segment S1)} &= [8.0 \text{ million customers} \times 0.09 \times (\$90 - \$55)] - \$9 \text{ million} \\ &= [720,000 \text{ customers} \times \$35 \text{ per unit}] - \$9 \text{ million} \\ &= \$25.2 \text{ million} - \$9 \text{ million} \\ &= \$16.2 \text{ million} \end{aligned}$$

In some instances a business may actually take lower net marketing contributions in the short run in order to build demand and future net marketing contributions.

However, the discounted cash flow from the long-term strategy has to exceed that of the current strategy in order for this approach to be viable.

Strategies to Increase Market Share

Perhaps the most common marketing strategy to grow revenue and profits is market share penetration. For any served market, a strategy is developed to grow the business's share of its served market. The same rules apply; a market penetration strategy is likely to cost money, margin, or both, and the net marketing contribution of the penetration strategy needs to exceed the current net marketing contribution for the business to improve profitability. For example, in Segment S1, Santa Fe Sportswear could consider a strategy to increase its market share from 9 to 11 percent by lowering its prices 10 percent. As shown below, the overall 136,000 customer gain would not be sufficient to offset the lower margin that would result from a 10 percent price decrease. The net result is a projected decrease in net marketing contribution from $15.4 million to $13.45 million.

$$\begin{aligned} \text{NMC (Segment S1)} &= [6.8 \text{ million customers} \times 0.11 \times (\$81 - \$55)] - \$6 \text{ million} \\ &= [748,000 \text{ customers} \times \$26 \text{ per customer}] - \$6 \text{ million} \\ &= \$19.45 \text{ million} - \$6 \text{ million} \\ &= \$13.45 \text{ million} \end{aligned}$$

Strategies to Increase Revenue per Customer

In a mature market with a strong share position, a business may not find it feasible or profitable to grow market demand or market share. However, the business's customers still remain its best strategic asset, and an examination of customer needs might reveal new products and services to better serve those needs and grow revenues. To evaluate the overall profit impact of such a marketing strategy, a business would have to project what higher prices could be attained and what increases in the average cost per unit would be required.

Also, to be considered are potential additional marketing expenses, such as the additional advertising dollars that would be necessary to make existing customers aware of product or service improvements. Thus, it is important to examine all aspects of the strategy to ensure that a strategy to increase price per unit leads to an increase in net marketing contribution.

To illustrate the profit impact of a strategy to build revenue per customer, let us consider that, in Segment S1, a major product line improvement would be able to raise average revenue per customer from $90 to $100. However, this improvement would also raise the average variable cost per customer by $5 because of increased materials costs. In addition, another $2 million in marketing expense will be needed to introduce the improved product line and to communicate its benefits. As shown below, this marketing strategy would produce an incremental gain of $1.1 million in net marketing contribution when compared with the current net marketing contribution of $15.4 million.

$$\begin{aligned} \text{NMC (Segment S1)} &= [6.8 \text{ million customers} \times 0.09 \times (\$100 - \$60)] - \$8 \text{ million} \\ &= [612,000 \text{ customers} \times \$40 \text{ per customer}] - \$8 \text{ million} \\ &= \$24.5 \text{ million} - \$8 \text{ million} \\ &= \$16.5 \text{ million} \end{aligned}$$

Strategies to Lower Variable Cost

Another way to grow net profits is by lowering the variable cost per unit. For example, perhaps the transportation costs and sales commissions could be lowered with a new distribution strategy for a given market or market segment. This strategy would lower variable expenses per unit and increase margin per unit, but the business has to be concerned about the level of customer satisfaction that will be delivered by this alternative distribution system. If customer satisfaction lessens, so will customer retention. And, in the long run, net profits will erode even though the business has achieved a lower variable cost and higher margin per unit. Thus, a successful marketing strategy must hold or increase customer satisfaction while growing net profits through increases in net marketing contribution.

Continuing with the Santa Fe Sportswear example, Segment S1's management is evaluating a new customer order entry and billing system that would improve customer satisfaction and lower the variable cost of serving a customer by $5 per customer. However, this new system will add $1 million per year in fixed marketing expense. This system would improve customer satisfaction and lower variable costs, but would it improve profitability? As shown below, the proposed order entry and billing system would improve the net marketing contribution by $2.1 million, improving both customer satisfaction and profitability.

$$\text{NMC (Segment S1)} = [6.8 \text{ million customers} \times 0.09 \times (\$90 - \$50)] - \$7 \text{ million}$$
$$= [612,000 \text{ customers} \times \$40 \text{ per customer}] - \$7 \text{ million}$$
$$= \$24.5 \text{ million} - \$7 \text{ million}$$
$$= \$17.5 \text{ million}$$

Strategies to Increase Market Efficiency

Another way to improve the profitability of a marketing strategy is to lower fixed marketing expenses: that is, to be more efficient in the use of marketing expenses to achieve a particular performance objective. The more focused a business is with respect to target customers, the fewer marketing dollars it has to expend in order to achieve a desired marketing objective. Likewise, alternative forms of distribution affect the fixed marketing expenses needed. For example, a business short on financial resources may elect to use a distributor rather than incur the fixed cost of direct selling and distribution.

Santa Fe Sportswear currently uses a direct sales force in Segment S1 and, as we have seen, spends $6 million in marketing expenses to obtain a market share of 9 percent. The business is considering shifting to manufacturers' representatives as a way to lower marketing expenses. The reps would be paid a 10 percent sales commission, and the business could reduce its marketing expenses by $2 million. As shown below, the 10 percent sales commission would be too costly in terms of reduced margin. As a result, the business is better off with its current marketing strategy because the current net marketing contribution ($15.4 million) is greater than the net marketing contribution of the projected marketing strategy.

$$\text{NMC (Segment S1)} = [6.8 \text{ million customers} \times 0.09 \times (\$90 - \$9 - \$55)] - \$4 \text{ million}$$
$$= [612,000 \text{ customers} \times \$26 \text{ per unit}] - \$4 \text{ million}$$
$$= \$15.9 \text{ million} - \$4 \text{ million}$$
$$= \$11.9 \text{ million}$$

MARKETING PRODUCTIVITY

Recognizing net marketing contribution as the measure of marketing profitability, a manager can readily evaluate the profit impact of marketing strategies, as has been illustrated. In addition, we can evaluate the efficiency of the marketing budget used to produce a given level of marketing profitability (net marketing contribution) by creating the following measure of marketing productivity.

$$\text{Market Productivity} = \frac{\text{Net Marketing Contribution}}{\text{Marketing Budget}}$$

The ratio of net marketing contribution to marketing budget (marketing and sales expenses) provides a measure of how efficient a given marketing budget is in producing marketing profits. For example, Santa Fe Sportswear produces an overall net marketing contribution of $30.1 million with a marketing budget of $15 million. This is a market productivity ratio of 2.0, which means that each dollar of marketing budget produces $2 of net marketing contribution:

$$\text{Market Productivity} = \frac{\text{Net Marketing Contribution}}{\text{Marketing Budget}}$$

$$= \frac{\$30.1 \text{ million}}{\$15 \text{ million}}$$

$$= 2.0$$

We can also assess the marketing productivity of each segment served by Santa Fe Sportswear. Using the net marketing contribution and marketing expenses reported in Figure 2.11, we can see that each segment strategy is producing a good level of net marketing contribution for each dollar of marketing budget. Segment S1 produces the largest sales revenue, and the marketing strategy used in this segment is the most efficient in producing marketing profits. And, while segment S3 is reported to produce an overall loss of $1 million, the marketing strategy developed for segment S3 is profitable and produces $1.20 of marketing profits for each dollar of marketing budget.

Market Performance Metric	Seg. S1	Seg. S2	Seg. S3	Overall
Net Marketing Contribution (mil)	$15.4	$8.9	$5.8	$30.1
Marketing and Sales Expenses (mil)	$ 6	$ 4	$ 5	$ 15
Marketing Productivity	**2.5**	**2.25**	**1.2**	**2.0**

This market-based performance metric helps managers evaluate the relative efficiency with which they are growing net marketing contribution. It may be that two marketing strategies yield an equivalent net marketing contribution, but one is more efficient because it has a higher marketing productivity. Put simply, one strategy can produce the same level of marketing profitability (net marketing contribution) but for fewer dollars of marketing budget. This, of course, is an advantage to any business, since those extra dollars can be used for other purposes.

Another benefit to this market metric is that it can be used in comparisons with competitors or benchmark businesses. Figure 2.13 presents the marketing productivity of three

Area of Performance (billions)	Personal Computer Conpany			Consumer Goods Company		
	Compaq	**Dell**	**Gateway**	**Ralston Purina**	**General Mills**	**PepsiCo**
Sales Revenues	$24.6	$7.7	$6.3	$4.5	$6.0	$20.9
–Cost of Goods Sold	17.9	6.1	5.2	2.3	2.4	8.4
Total Contribution	$ 6.7	$1.6	$1.1	$2.2	$3.6	$12.5
Marketing Expenses	2.1	.8	.8	1.6	2.5	9.2
Net Mktg. Cont.	$ 4.6	$ .8	$ .3	$ .6	$1.1	$ 3.3
Mktg. Productivity*	**2.2**	**1.0**	**0.38**	**0.38**	**0.44**	**0.36**

* A ratio of Net Marketing Contribution to Marketing Expenses (marketing, sales, and administrative expenses).

Figure 2.13 ◆ Net Marketing Contribution and Marketing Productivity

competing computer companies. In this case, Compaq is more efficient in generating marketing profits than either Dell or Gateway. Also presented in Figure 2.13 is the marketing productivity of three well-known consumer goods companies. Each of these companies produced a marketing productivity ratio of less than 1. However, in this case, the three consumer goods companies shown have very similar levels of marketing productivity.

MARKET-BASED ORGANIZATIONS

Over time, businesses develop extended product lines. Unfortunately, as these businesses evolve from single- to multiple-product organizations, they rarely alter their organizational structure. What normally emerges over time is a product-driven organization, as illustrated in Figure 2.14. In this example, five separate motor manufacturing operations each serve multiple markets. This arrangement is both expensive for the business and

Figure 2.14 ◆ Product-Focused Organizational Structure

confusing for customers. It is expensive for the business because there are obvious marketing redundancies in sales, support, and distribution. For customers, it is frustrating to deal with two or more separate businesses with respect to invoices, service levels, sales coverage, etc. Even worse, each product-focused business is looking to sell only its own products and becomes myopic in its view of the market.[8] As a result, a product-oriented organizational structure is less likely to see a broader range of customer needs and, hence, market opportunities.

Thus, an important characteristic of a market-managed business is that it will reengineer its marketing organization as more markets are served or as these markets change.[9] An important element of this characteristic of market-based management is that businesses are built around markets, not around products or manufacturing operations. If customers are the primary focus of a market-based business, then why not start with the customer and work backward with respect to how we design our business and marketing organization to serve target customers?[10] In this way, the organizational focus is on the market where customers buy, and not on the factory where products are made.

To become market-focused, a business needs to formulate a market-based organizational structure. In this structure, the *market unit* is a market-focused entity. It is assigned the task of understanding customer needs and competitor positioning in a given market and developing and implementing marketing strategies to achieve target objectives for that market.[11] Hence, the market unit is responsible for all aspects of the marketing and business directed at target customers in its market. For example, consider the motor manufacturer. While the company may have a number of different manufacturing operations to produce a range of motors, it serves several markets through market units. As illustrated in Figure 2.15, this market-based structure provides a much better systems linkage between customer markets and the organization. This structure facilitates more responsive market strategy development, implementation, and market-based performance tracking.[12]

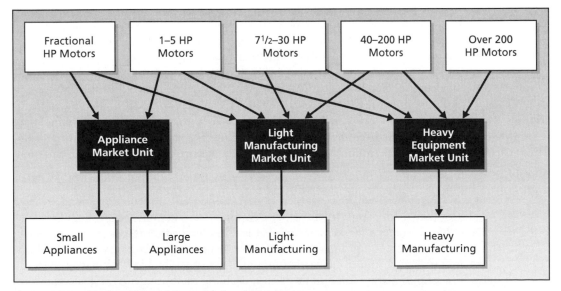

Figure 2.15 ◆ **Market-Focused Organizational Structure**

Figure 2.16 ◆ Sales-Based vs. Market-Based Organizational Structure

Figure 2.16 illustrates how a specialty steel manufacturer shifted from a sales-oriented to a market-oriented organizational structure. The business sold products in both the mining and construction markets. It had done well in mining but poorly in construction markets because they were much more difficult to reach. However, the construction market, while very fragmented, was several times larger. The only way to perform better in the construction market was to have a market unit (marketing team) in charge of that market whose sole responsibility was that market. When a construction market unit team was put in place, within a short time they found they had ineffective dealers, an incomplete product line, and the wrong marketing systems to serve the more price-sensitive and delivery-conscious construction market. In other words, a great deal was different from the mining market, and it required a completely different marketing approach to satisfy customers. The results were phenomenal. Within 18 months, the sales in the construction market grew by over 40 percent. Further, this increase was accomplished with no change in personnel, just a reorganization of existing marketing, sales, and product management personnel.

Market units are organized around customer markets such that maximum market focus can be achieved without conflict in developing and implementing market-based strategies that deliver high levels of both customer satisfaction and profitability. Each market unit becomes a marketing team that is solely focused on the needs of a particular group of customers.[13] This organizational structure makes market-based measures of performance such as customer satisfaction meaningful and actionable. The market units can also be set up as market-level profit centers, enabling the business to evaluate and track profitability at the market level.

SUMMARY

A market-based business engages in three important distinguishing practices:

- It tracks market-based measures of performance.
- It measures marketing profits by product, market, or both.
- It organizes around markets rather than products.

Without an external set of market-based performance metrics, a business will never know its market performance. For CommTech, an overreliance on traditional measures of internal performance cost the business and its shareholders $122 million in net profits. Thus, an important step in becoming a market-based business is the development of a key set of external market-based measures of performance. These external market metrics can include in-process metrics, which typically precede financial performance measurement, and end-result market metrics, which are more likely to coincide with financial performance measurement.

To develop and implement marketing strategies that are going to increase customer satisfaction and grow profits, a business needs to be able to measure the profitability of a marketing decision. This means understanding the revenues that result from serving a target market of customers and all the costs associated with serving that market. A common problem often arises here in most accounting systems: the need to allocate overhead costs. This has the potential to distort profitability and can lead to decisions that actually reduce profitability. To grow profits, a business needs to grow net marketing contribution. Allocating overhead costs will distort net marketing contribution. If the accountants persist in allocating cost, simply ask that costs be allocated after the net marketing contribution has been computed so that market-level profitability can be clearly observed.

With market-based management, the focus is on the customer. How much revenue does a customer produce? What are the costs of acquiring a customer? What are the costs of serving those customers after they have been acquired? What is the net marketing contribution per customer in different segments of the market? Measures of marketing profitability and marketing productivity help us evaluate the profit impact and spending efficiency of a marketing strategy.

Marketing is manipulation, but what should be manipulated is the business, not the customer. Businesses that are able to reengineer their organizational structures around markets and new market opportunities are in the best position to respond to customer needs and changing market conditions. Thus, a market-based organizational structure is evolutionary. It will change as markets change in order to maximize its ability to attract, satisfy, and retain target market customers.

MARKET-BASED LOGIC AND STRATEGIC THINKING

1. Why are market-based measures of performance critical to achieving profitable growth?
2. How do market-based measures of performance differ from internal measures of performance? Why are both necessary?

APPLICATION PROBLEM: DELL COMPUTER

Dell Computer is a direct marketer of personal computers with sales in 1997 of over $7.76 billion and net profit before tax of $705 million. At that time, Dell's product line included desktop computers, portable computers, and servers/workstations. Eighty-five percent of sales were gained through direct marketing and 15 percent via the Internet. Dell planned to derive 50 percent of their sales from the Internet in two years.

The average margin for Dell computer products was 21.4 percent. Marketing expenses ran about 10.7 percent of sales. However, marketing on the Internet was reported to be roughly half as expensive. Dell's operating overhead was among the lowest in the industry at 1.6 percent of sales. The average selling price for PCs had been eroding at roughly eight percent per year. Outlined below are specific details for each of Dell's major product–markets in 1997.

Desktop PC Market

- Market demand was estimated to be 33 million units per year and growing at 16 percent per year.
- Dell's market share is 6 percent, average selling price $2,250 per unit, and margin 18 percent.
- Marketing expenses in this segment averaged 12.4 percent of sales.

Portable PC Market

- The market was estimated to be 13.5 million units per year and growing at 25 percent per year.
- Dell's share was five percent. Average selling price was $2,750 per unit, which provided margins of 25 percent.
- Marketing expenses in the portable PC segment averaged 10.2 percent of sales.

Server/Workstation Market

- This (low-end server) market was 5.5 million units per year and growing at 27 percent per year.
- Dell's market share was 6 percent. Dell's average price was $4,500 with a margin of 27 percent of sales.
- Marketing expenses for the low-end server market segment were 6 percent of sales.

Questions

For Internet discussion, go to www.prenhall.com/phbusiness.

1. What was Dell's net marketing contribution in each major product–market? What were Dell's overall net marketing contribution and net profit?

2. How would Dell's net marketing contribution in portable computers change the next year if the company able to hold market share and margins while average prices continued to erode at eight percent per year?

3. Which of Dell's product–markets had the highest marketing productivity?

3. Why does a business need both internal (financial) measures of performance and external (market-based) measures of performance?

4. What roles do market-based measures of performance play in achieving profitable growth?

5. Why are performance metrics important?

6. What is the fundamental difference between a market performance metric and a financial performance metric?

7. Why are in-process metrics an important part of a successful marketing strategy? What is the relationship between in-process metrics and end-result metrics?

8. What are some of the fundamental differences between product-based accounting and customer-based customer accounting?

9. How does net marketing contribution enable a business to better understand the profit impact of a marketing strategy?

10. What is the difference between a variable cost and a fixed expense?

11. Why are marketing expenses considered semi-variable expenses and cost of goods a variable expense?

12. How can treatment of operating expenses distort interpretations of profitability?

13. How can one assess the profit impact of a specific marketing strategy?

14. Under what conditions would you expect operating expenses to change with changes in marketing strategies?

15. What fundamental marketing strategies can a business pursue to grow marketing profits?

16. Explain how any given marketing strategy might affect different components of net marketing contribution.

17. Why would a business want to measure its profitability by market segment?

18. What does a marketing productivity of 0.5 mean? What does it mean when a competitor with approximately the same market share has a marketing productivity of 1.0?

NOTES

1. Bradley Gale, "Tracking Competitive Position Drives Shareholder Value," *Global Management* (1992):367–71.

2. Robert Kaplan and David Norton, "The Balanced Scorecard—Measures That Drive Performance," *Harvard Business Review* (January–February 1992):71–79; and Robert Eccles, "The Performance Measurement Manifesto," *Harvard Business Review* (January–February 1991):131–37.

3. George Cressman, "Choosing the Right Metric," *Drive Marketing Excellence* (November 1994), New York: Institute for International Research.

4. John Shank and Vijay Govindarajan, *Strategic Cost Analysis* (New York: Irwin, 1989):99–112.

5. John Shank and Vijay Govindarajan, "The Perils of Cost Allocation Based on Production Volumes," *Accounting Horizons,* 4 (1988):71–79; and John Shank and Vijay Govindarajan, "Making Strategy Explicit in Cost Analysis: A Case Study," *Sloan Marketing Review* (Spring 1988):15–30.

6. Michael Morris and Gene Morris, *Market-Oriented Pricing* (New York: NTC Business Books, 1990):99–100; and Don Schultz, "Spreadsheet Approach to Measuring ROI for MCI," Marketing News, 28 (February 1994):12.

7. William Christopher, "Marketing Achievement Reporting: A Profitability Approach," *Industrial Marketing Management* (New York: Elsevier North Holland, Inc. 1977):149–62; Patrick Dunne and Harry Wolk, "Marketing Cost Analysis: A Modularized Contribution," *Journal of Marketing*

(July 1977):83–94; Stanley Shapiro and V. H. Kirpalard, *Marketing Effectiveness: Insights from Accounting and Finance* (Needham Heights, MA: Allyn and Bacon, 1984):377–424; and Jean-Claude Larreche and Hubert Gatignon, *MARKSTRAT* (New York: Scientific Press, 1990):22–23.

8. Theodore Levitt, "Marketing Myopia," *Harvard Business Review* (July–August 1968):45–56.

9. Frederick Webster, *Market-Driven Management* (New York: Free Press 1994): chapter 8.

10. B. Joseph Pine II, *Mass Customization: The New Frontier in Business Competition* (Boston: Harvard Business School Press, 1993).

11. George Day, "Aligning the Organization to the Market," in *Reflections on the Future of Marketing,* ed. D. Lehmann and Katherine Tocz, (Cambridge, MA: Marketing Science Institute, 1994):67–96; George Day, "The Capability of Market-Driven Organizations," *Journal of Marketing* (January 1994):37–52; and John Workman Jr., Christian Hornburg, and Kjell Graner, "Marketing Organization: An Interactive Framework of Dimensions and Determinants," *Journal of Marketing* (July 1988):21–41.

12. Vijay Govindarajan and A. Gupta, "Linking Control Systems to Business Unit Strategy: Impact on Performance," *Accounting, Organizations and Society,* 10 (1985):51–66.

13. George Day, "Building a Market-Driven Organization," *Market Driven Strategy* (New York: Free Press, 1990): chapter 14.

part II

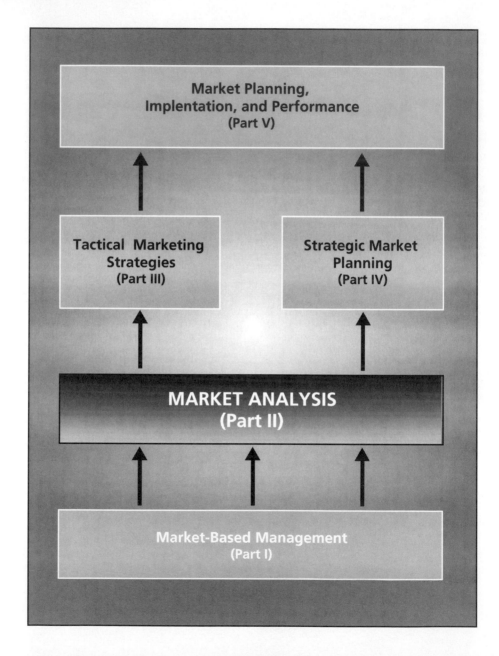

Market Planning,
Implentation, and Performance
(Part V)

Tactical Marketing
Strategies
(Part III)

Strategic Market
Planning
(Part IV)

MARKET ANALYSIS
(Part II)

Market-Based Management
(Part I)

Market Analysis

If you're in a meeting, any meeting, for 15 minutes, and we're not talking about customers or competitors, raise your hand and ask, "why"? If it goes on for half an hour, leave! Leave the meeting!

—Jerry Stead, AT&T

Market analysis is an essential input to the development of market-based management strategies that deliver superior levels of customer satisfaction and profitability. The continuous pursuit of customer needs, ongoing monitoring of competitors' moves and capabilities, and tracking of market-based performance are the core competencies of market-focused business.

Part II includes four chapters that are built around the fundamental inputs of market analysis: market demand, customer analysis, market segmentation, and competitor analysis. Chapter 3 focuses on market definition, market potential, market demand, and market growth opportunities. However, markets do not buy products; customers buy products. Chapter 4 covers customer analysis and the discovery of benefits that deliver a superior value.

Because customers in any market differ in many ways, rarely can one marketing strategy adequately serve their needs. Chapter 5 addresses needs-based market segmentation and the development of segment strategies. Finally, chapter 6 focuses on competitor analysis, competitive position, and sources of competitive advantage.

chapter 3

Market Definition, Potential, and Demand

At any point in time, the overall demand for a product or service is finite. That is, there is a fixed number of customers who buy at a certain rate of purchase; thus, there is a certain level of market demand, whether for fast food, personal computers, or automobiles. At any point in time, there are *existing* customers who make up current market demand and *potential* customers who provide the opportunity for growing market demand.

Potential customers help us define the level of future market demand. In mature markets, the market potential (maximum number of customers) is close to the market demand (existing number of customers). In emerging or growing markets, market demand will grow as more customers enter the market. However, for a business to achieve a desired level of performance in a market, it needs to obtain a desired share of that market. To manage performance over time, a business needs to understand

- The market's existing level of demand and potential demand.
- The rate of replacement purchase and new customer purchase.
- The business's market share and potential market share.

With a good understanding of these dimensions of performance, a business can assess the market's current and future volume. The purpose of this chapter is to understand the factors that shape market demand, the forces that influence market growth, and the parameters of marketing strategy that yield a certain level of market share and unit volume.

MARKET DEFINITION

The cola wars of the 1980s lured soft drink manufacturers into a limited vision and, hence, a limited definition of their markets. Strategies to hold share and grow market demand in an intensely competitive market blurred their market vision. Though there is nothing inherently wrong with a narrow product–market focus, a pure product–market focus limits a business's view of other market opportunities and competitive threats. Many observers would agree that this limited focus was the only choice these manufacturers had because the loss of one market share point in the soft drink market is worth almost $600 million in retail sales. Losing one share point in this market has to hurt profits because marketing and overhead expenses are not likely to go down in the midst of a battle to hold market share. Thus, their aggressive moves to hold share could be legitimately defended.

The battle to hold share in the soft drink market, however, represents only one portion of the battlefield. Adjacent to this battlefield is a whole new set of competitive threats that have emerged over the last 25 years. As illustrated in Figure 3.1, these new product markets include mineral waters, sports drinks, fruit juices, fruit drinks, and specialty tea and coffee products.

Because of their focus on the soft drink market, soft drink manufacturers were late to react to these new forms of competition. Yet where did the consumers of Perrier, Gatorade, Snapple, Ocean Spray, and New York Express Iced Coffee come from? Many came from the soft drink market into these new product–markets while others were drawn away from alcoholic beverages and hot-served coffees and teas. Collectively, these substitute products produce $30 billion in annual retail sales, approximately half that of the soft drink market. In response to these new market opportunities, Coca-Cola and Pepsi have aggressively entered these markets. They are working to better position themselves to gain share as these markets continue to grow at twice the rate of the soft drink market.

Market Vision

Perhaps the biggest threat to business survival and a major cause of missed market opportunities is the lack of a broad market vision: that is, being unable to see the broader picture of customers, market demand, and the forces that shape unserved market de-

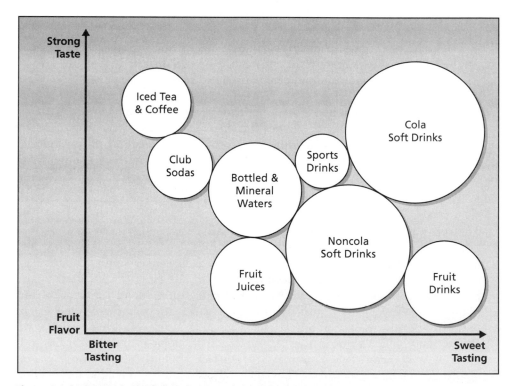

Figure 3.1 ◆ Strategic Market Definition of the Beverage Market

mand.[1] Theodore Levitt's timeless perspective on marketing myopia, applies today as well as it did when he first wrote on the subject more than 40 years ago: "A myopic vision of the potential markets a business might serve translates into a narrow product-focused market definition."[2]

Individuals with a broad market vision usually see the world differently. Their view of market demand goes beyond a view of existing products and customers and enables them to see more clearly untapped or emerging market opportunities that most cannot see or others conclude are too small or foolish. With unrestricted market vision, these businesses moved quickly to control their own destinies.[3]

Strategic Market Definition

The first step in understanding market demand is to develop a broad vision of what the market is. A market definition that is limited to a particular product focus maintains the status quo. A business with a narrow market focus sees only the *articulated needs of served* customers.[4] A broad market vision encourages discovery of *unarticulated needs* and uncovers new *unserved* opportunities. For Fred Smith, founder of Federal Express, a broad market focus meant a vision of overnight mail, new choices for customers, and a profitable business opportunity that bankers, professors, and industry experts could not envision and said would not work. For Phil Knight, founder of Nike, it meant a market vision for running and sports footwear as well as sports clothing. And, for Bill Gates, co-founder of Microsoft, it meant a market vision of people using computers in a variety of ways.

To avoid a narrow market definition and, hence, its potential to restrict discovery of new market opportunities, a business needs a broad *strategic market definition*. This includes a broader definition of all product–markets that are potential substitutes for the product–markets currently served by the business. For example, the market definition for soft drinks could be limited to the soft drink product domain and not include important substitute product–markets. A broader strategic market definition would include all relevant substitute products. The degree of substitutability in a broad strategic market definition is represented by the distance between markets.[5] The closer one market is to another, the greater the likelihood that customers will substitute one product for another.

A broad strategic market definition enables managers to see a broader set of customer needs and potential new market opportunities. This ability, of course, provides a wider range of market-based strategies as management assesses which markets it would like to participate in, recognizing its own core competencies and capabilities. Thus, a broad strategic market definition provides three key benefits to a market-based business:

- It opens the window of opportunity to a broader set of customer needs.
- It provides better understanding of potential substitutes and competitive threats.
- It helps a business better understand fundamental customer needs.

Vertical vs. Horizontal Market Opportunities

With a broader market vision, a business is able to see more opportunities for growth. These broader market opportunities often exist in adjacent *vertical* and *horizontal* markets. Vertical markets represent market opportunities along the vertical market's "value chain." A business can either *forward* or *backward integrate* to expand its market domain and opportunity for growth.[6] A manufacturer who takes over the retail sale of its products is expanding its vertical market domain and opportunity to grow. Horizontal market opportunities exist in substitute product markets. For soft drink manufacturers, the various markets shown in Figure 3.1 represent horizontal market opportunities. However, companies without a broad market vision rarely take such opportunities seriously.

Nevertheless, adjacent vertical and horizontal markets offer potential growth opportunities that require consideration for any business seeking growth. For example, as illustrated in Figure 3.2, Ocean Spray has expanded its vertical market domain from bulk-processing capabilities to vertically integrate into processed goods that initially included cranberries and fruit juice. Changing customer needs also created a horizontal market opportunity, and, in response, Ocean Spray developed a line of fruit drinks. The combination of both vertical and horizontal market expansion has contributed significantly to the overall growth of Ocean Spray.

Served Market Definition

With a broad market definition, a business is now in a position to better define the market domains in which it will elect to compete. Recall that the primary determinant of market vision is the *fundamental customer need* we are serving. This fundamental customer need has a tremendous impact on how the business defines its market and the size of market it

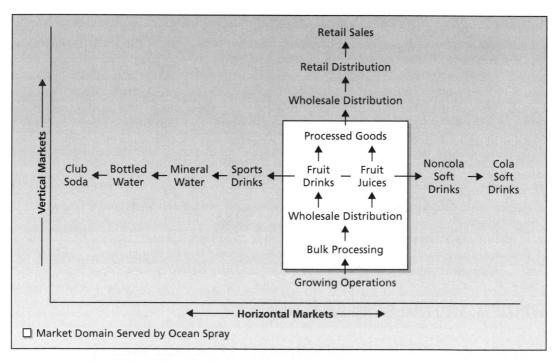

Figure 3.2 ◆ Vertical and Horizontal Markets and Growth Opportunities

will develop and serve. A *served market* is defined as the market in which a business competes for target customers.[7] It includes both the business's and its competitors' customers.

For example, the served market for Lexus is much different from that for Tercel, though both are Toyota products. Each has a separate and distinct set of customers and competitors that make up unique served markets. The automotive market, while broadly defined as a transportation market, is made up of many smaller served markets based on the unique needs of customers for price and car benefits. Likewise, a broad market definition of the beer market has enabled Anheuser-Busch to create several served market definitions. As the beer market matured, it fragmented into many new market opportunities along with new types of customers and competitors. It required a broad market vision and more than one served market definition to effectively manage penetration of these new market opportunities.

MARKET POTENTIAL

Once a served market definition has been established, a business is in a better position to understand several important aspects of market demand. The first, and most crucial, is how many customers make up the maximum potential for this market definition.[8] This perspective creates a sharp contrast between a product-focused and a market-based business.

> A product-focused business is interested in product volume, whereas a market-based business is interested in how many customers make up a market.

Product volume and sales revenues can vary with customer behavior and competitive strategies. However, the potential number of customers within a market domain is a finite number of great strategic significance because it places the true upper limit on the number of consumption units.

For example, what is the market potential for disposable diapers? The number of babies between newborn and 2 years of age might be a reasonable estimate of the maximum number of consuming units. But, do all households with children in this age bracket purchase disposable diapers? No! Some cannot afford them; others oppose them because of their negative environmental impact; still others may simply prefer the advantages they see in cloth diapers. Thus, the number of consuming units is almost always less than the maximum market potential (maximum number of customers).

Untapped Market Opportunities

Many new markets and most global markets are well below their full market potential. That is, there are large numbers of possible customers who have not yet entered the market. For example, the market potential (maximum number) for personal computers is estimated to be one billion. In 1999, the level of market penetration was approximately 425 million, as illustrated in Figure 3.3. Thus, still less than half of the market potential had been developed by 1999. But, one could ask, why was this market not at its full market potential. There are five major market forces that can restrict a market from reaching its full potential, as illustrated in Figure 3.4.

Awareness   This does not mean just *product awareness* but *complete comprehension of benefits*. If potential customers are unaware of a product, or do not fully or accurately un-

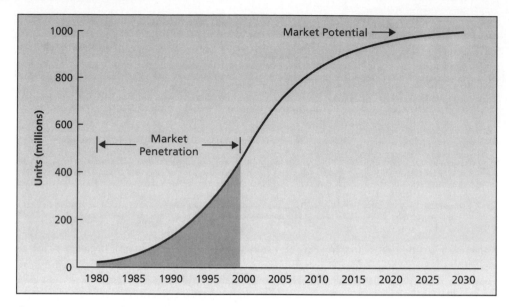

Figure 3.3 ◆ Personal Computer Market Development

derstand its benefits, then they will not be fully informed and they will be unable to discern the product's potential value to them. For the personal computer, most potential customers in a worldwide market would be aware of the product, but many may not fully comprehend the benefits. Because the product is complex and experiential, many of the benefits are understood only after a period of use.

Availability   A second force that restricts market demand is lack of *availability*. Personal computers can be readily purchased by many people, but services to support them might not be available in many geographic markets. For most mature markets, product availability is not a significant force that restricts market demand. However, lack of availability of products that may be in short supply, or difficult to make available, or lack services to support their use, can be an important source of reduced market demand.

Ability to Use   The inability to use a product can also restrict expansion of a market to its full potential. People in many parts of the world would benefit from the use of a personal computer, but if you do not have electricity, you cannot use one even when the product is available. Perhaps more important, the ability to use a personal computer requires a certain level of specialized education. In response to this need, businesses such as Apple Computer and Microsoft have funded educational programs that should contribute to the market development of the personal computer market.

Benefit Deficiency   For some consumers, the benefits of a given type of product are not attractive or compelling enough for them to enter the market. For others, such as those consumers who oppose disposable diapers for environmental reasons, the benefit proposition is simply deficient and not strong enough to stimulate purchase even if the product is available and affordable and a proper use situation exists. Because consumers have a wide range of product and lifestyle needs, it may be difficult to accommodate all the

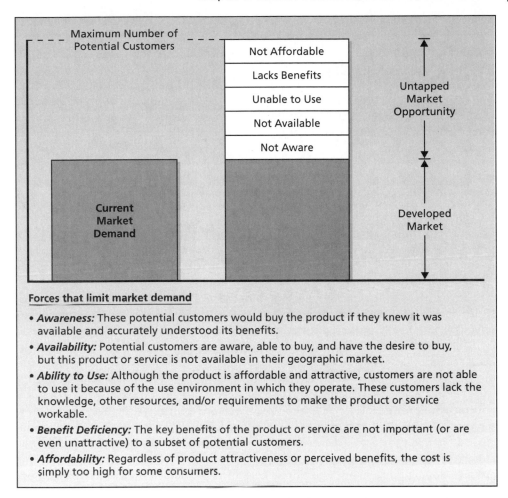

Figure 3.4 ◆ **Maximum Market Potential and Current Market Demand**

needs and desired benefits in any given market. So there is a practical limit that may restrict any market from reaching its maximum market potential. For example, many older people may not see a benefit in owning a personal computer. However, with the expansion of e-mail and Internet home shopping, this growing segment of the population could become an important source of new customer growth that would contribute to further development of the PC market.

Affordability   Finally, many of the products some people take for granted are simply not affordable for others. While the benefits are known and attractive, the product is too expensive given the income available to many potential customers. Once again, businesses with narrowly focused product orientation will never see beyond their current customer market. As a result, they will never challenge their engineers and production managers with the task of building a lower-cost version of their products. The largest portion of new customer purchases in the PC market is in the under-$1,000 segment. This price point triggered the entry of a new group of buyers based on affordability. As low-end PC prices approach the price of low-end televisions and VCRs, the PC will continue to attract price-sensitive buyers into the market.

Market Development Index

The real benefit of a broader market definition is in knowing both the overall potential of a market and the forces that currently restrict market demand. If we create a ratio of maximum market potential to current market demand, we can index the opportunity for market development.

$$\text{Market Development Index} = \frac{\text{Current Market Demand}}{\text{Maximum Market Demand}} \times 100$$

A market development index (MDI) of less than 33 would suggest that there is considerable growth potential. As shown in Figure 3.3, the personal computer market is in its first half of market development. Although price declines for personal computers have contributed to market development, this market's maximum market potential probably will not be reached for many years.

The first third of the market potential can generally be served with higher prices and basic benefits. To bring more customers into the market, businesses have to lower prices, offer a wider range of product alternatives, and expand distribution to increase availability. When the market development index is between 33 and 67, development of the market is based on addressing benefit deficiencies and price reductions that bring more customers into the market at a more affordable price.

When the market development index goes above 67, there still exists considerable opportunity for growth. However, the task will be more difficult as the business faces the more difficult causes that restrict full market development. These forces are likely to include affordability, benefit deficiency, and inability to use. Overcoming these hurdles will require real market-based, customer-focused solutions. Though a tougher marketing task, developing this untapped portion of customers provides a more differentiated position and one that competitors may find hard to copy. Thus, while the challenge may be greater, the rewards of market ownership could also be greater.

Market Potential and Market Growth

Recognizing that every market has some upper limit (its market potential), marketing people are intrigued by the question of how fast the market will grow as it expands to its full potential. Shown in Figure 3.5 are the market growth curves for several products. The upper limit in each case represents the market potential for each product–market. The rate at which customers enter a market is a market-specific phenomenon based on product attractiveness, customer characteristics, and marketing efforts.[9] However, the early pattern established by the rate of customer entry into a market provides sufficient information to accurately project the market growth rate in most instances.[10]

There are three fundamental forces that capture the shape of the market growth curve and hence the rate of market growth:

- **Market Potential:** The maximum number of customers who can enter the market given a specific served market definition.

Figure 3.5 ◆ Market Penetration and Market Development Index

- **Market Penetration:** The total number of customers who have entered that market at a specific point in time.
- **Rate of Entry:** The rate at which new customers enter the market.

The combination of these three forces defines the shape and individual parameters of a market's customer attraction and growth. However, some markets grow faster and reach their full potential much faster than others. But why? Why do some product markets grow at a fast rate and others at a comparatively slow rate? The next section addresses these questions and marketing strategies that can be developed to accelerate market growth.

Rate of Market Development

New markets depend on finding new customers. Most potential customers are not going to be the first to buy a new product. New products are often higher priced, more complex, and less accepted by mainstream society than are established products. As a result, there are a variety of risks associated with being among the first buyers of a new product or technology.

Emerging markets are initially relatively small and made up of *innovators* and *early adopters,* as shown in Figure 3.6. In general, the customers who make up the *early market* possess more knowledge, are less price-sensitive and more benefit-driven, and are less dependent upon what others do or think than are most people. These *lead customers* are critical. If they cannot be attracted, satisfied, and retained, the market is likely to die because the mainstream market will not buy if the lead customers do not. The first job in successfully developing a new product market is to identify lead customers and penetrate the early market.

However, for a new market to move from the *early market* to the *mainstream market* requires the development of *complete solutions.*[11] Although customers in the early market

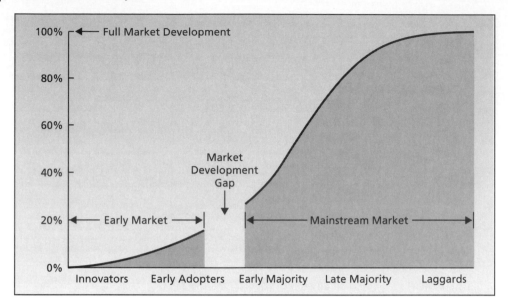

Figure 3.6 ◆ Customer Adoption and Market Development

are willing to struggle to make new products workable, those in the mainstream market are less willing to put up with less-than-complete solutions; they want a 100 percent solution. Thus, to successfully reach the mainstream market, a business needs to create a complete solution, one that has all the necessary features, functions, and supporting products and services.[12]

Unfortunately, there is one more problem. The mainstream market is made up of many segments, each with a different view of what it considers a complete solution.[13] To successfully reach the mainstream market, a business must carefully identify its target customers and focus on the delivery of what those target customers consider a complete solution. And, just as there are lead customers in the early market, there are *lead segments* in the mainstream market. As a result, further success in the mainstream market is partially dependent on the influence of one segment over another. The more quickly businesses address the complete solution needed to close the *market development gap* shown in Figure 3.6, the faster the market growth.

Accelerating Market Growth

Developing and delivering a complete solution requires more than further product development. The rate at which the mainstream market adopts a new product is also dependent upon customer characteristics, product positioning, and market influences. Given adequate product awareness and availability, there are 11 forces that act to accelerate or slow customer attraction and the rate of market growth.[14]

Customer Influences   As shown in Figure 3.7, there are four customer characteristics that affect the rate at which customers enter a market. When the *felt need* for the product is low, customer attraction will be slow. For years, many customers simply did not feel a

	Slows Market Development								Accelerates Market Development
Customer Influences									
Felt Need	Low	—	—	—	—	—	—	—	High
Perceived Risk	High	—	—	—	—	—	—	—	Low
Innovativeness	Low	—	—	—	—	—	—	—	High
Decision-Making Unit	Group	—	—	—	—	—	—	—	Individual
Product Influences									
Relative Advantage	Minimal	—	—	—	—	—	—	—	Substantial
Relative Cost	High	—	—	—	—	—	—	—	Low
Complexity	Extensive	—	—	—	—	—	—	—	Minimal
Ease of Use	Difficult	—	—	—	—	—	—	—	Easy
Market Influences									
Observability	Do Not See	—	—	—	—	—	—	—	Easily Seen
Trialability	Cannot Try	—	—	—	—	—	—	—	Easy to Try
Marketing Effort	Minimal	—	—	—	—	—	—	—	Extensive

Figure 3.7 ◆ Forces That Affect the Rate of Mainstream Market Growth

strong need to have a microwave oven, and the lack of a felt need slowed the rate at which customers entered this product–market. Also, many customers perceived a safety risk with microwave ovens, and this perception also slowed market growth. Customer perceptions of risk can include a variety of *perceived risk* factors such as perceived safety, social, and economic risk.

A third customer factor is the degree to which the market is made up of *innovative* customers. Younger people tend to be innovative and likely to try new things, whereas many older people are conservative and slow to try new products. The demographics and lifestyles of target customers can play a key role in the rate of new customer attraction. Finally, the nature of the *decision-making unit* influences the rate of new customer market entry. Group decisions, whether in a business or in a family, slow the rate of customer entry. Individual decision-making units are less likely to be inhibited by others and are freer to make decisions quickly. Collectively, when all the customer characteristics line up on the positive side, they provide an accelerating effect on the rate customers enter a given product–market.

Product Influences   The strength of a product's positioning (relative benefits) also plays a key role in the rate of market growth. The stronger the *relative advantage* and the lower the *relative cost,* the greater the customer value created by the product and the faster the rate of customer market entry. However, this is the point at which many businesses stop. They do not follow through and examine more closely the *perceived complexity* and *ease of use* perceived by potential customers. If the product is not compatible with the way things are normally done, or it is difficult to use, customers may be reluctant to try or purchase the product.

When first introduced, the microwave oven, while expensive, had some attractive benefits. However, many people did not buy a microwave oven because they thought they were too complex and hard to use because they required a different way of cooking.

Likewise for many high-tech products: The relative advantages are enormous, but the perceived complexity and the difficulty in using them can be deterrents in attracting customers and growing market demand.

Market Influences   If a product does not offer a complete solution, potential customers are reluctant to enter a market. To accelerate customer market entry, a business needs to ensure that all related products and services are available to create a complete solution. Mainstream customers want "plug-in" solutions that are easy to use. In addition, the market demand for products that are *easily observed* such as a Walkman, color TV, or fashionable sunglasses grows faster than for products that are less observable such as household cleaners, insurance programs, or bed sheets. Also, the easier it is to try a product without buying, the faster its rate of market penetration. The Walkman is both *observable* and *easy to try.* Insurance programs are difficult to observe and cannot be tried without purchasing the product. Finally, the more extensive the *marketing effort* supporting the product, the faster the rate of market development.

MARKET DEMAND

Based on the rate of market development, at any point in time, the market demand for a product is made up of the number of customers in the market and the amount they purchase. Because some customers are new to the market while others have been in the market for some time, their purchase amounts may differ. Thus, we can decompose market demand in any given period into existing and new customers and their respective purchase behaviors.

$$\binom{\text{Market}}{\text{Demand}} = \left(\binom{\text{Existing}}{\text{Customers}} \times \binom{\text{Purchase}}{\text{Amount}}\right) + \left(\binom{\text{New}}{\text{Customers}} \times \binom{\text{Purchase}}{\text{Amount}}\right)$$

The cellular phone market attracts approximately 5 million new customers each year. The customer base is expected to be approximately 65 million by the year 2000. However, new customers typically consume at a lower rate than existing customers. In fact, each year the average customer purchase amount goes down as more low-use customers enter the market. As shown below, this combination of new and existing customers produces an estimated usage of 25 billion minutes per year.

$$\binom{\text{Market}}{\text{Demand}} = \left(\binom{\text{60 Million}}{\text{Customers}} \times \binom{\text{400 Minutes}}{\text{per Year}}\right) + \left(\binom{\text{5 Million}}{\text{Customers}} \times \binom{\text{200 Minutes}}{\text{per Year}}\right)$$

$$= 25 \text{ Billion Minutes per Year}$$

The market demand for personal computers in any given year is a little more complex. First, existing customers repurchase at an average rate of every four to five years. This means the market demand in the current year will be, at least in part, a result of the number of buyers four to five years earlier. Thus, a portion of the year 2000 market demand derived from existing customers is based on the average number of units sold in 1995 and 1996. As shown in Figure 3.8, approximately 60 million units were sold in 1995 and 70 million in 1996. Thus, we would expect the average of 65 million replacement purchases in the year 2000. Also, referring to Figure 3.3, we could estimate that by

Figure 3.8 ◆ Market Demand for Personal Computers

the turn of the century 65 million new customers should enter the market. Together, these estimates yield an estimated market demand for personal computers of:

$$\begin{array}{c}\text{Market Demand} \\ \text{(year 2000)}\end{array} = \begin{array}{c}\text{Replacement Purchases} \\ \text{from 1995 and 1996}\end{array} + \begin{array}{c}\text{Number of New Customers} \\ \text{Entering the Market in 2000}\end{array}$$

$$= \quad 65 \text{ million} \quad + \quad 65 \text{ million}$$

$$= 130 \text{ Million Units Sold}$$

Using the combination of the number of existing customers, their rate of repurchase, and new unit sales, one can create the market demand forecast shown in Figure 3.8.

PRODUCT LIFE CYCLE

As markets evolve, they are supported by an evolution of products that also go through a life cycle. Shown in Figure 3.9 is the PC market demand over the product life for five generations of Intel products. In each case there was an emerging market period followed by a period of rapid growth. Growth in this case was driven by both *new customers* entering the market and *expanding purchase amounts by existing customers.* In this example, the growth phase was followed by a very short mature market period and then a stage of rapid decline in market demand.

All of these product life cycles had very similar durations (less than 10 years), and each subsequent product achieved a higher level of life cycle demand. Furthermore, there was an overlap between product life cycles. This type of market growth and product life cycle behavior is typical of many high-tech product markets. However, many more mature markets such as the automotive, commercial aircraft, and housing markets have much longer product life cycles. Growth in these markets is largely dependent on increases in the population and favorable economic factors that affect customer purchase behavior.

Figure 3.9 ◆ Intel Product Life Cycles

MARKET SHARE AND SHARE POTENTIAL

The potential of a market, its growth rate, and the shape of the product life cycle provide key insights into current and future market demand. A business needs to translate this information into a sales forecast of unit volume. Somebody has to decide how much to produce and how big a manufacturing operation to build. A business's estimate of sales volume can have a dramatic impact on profitability. If the unit volume forecast is correct, and a plant with the right level of capacity is built, total production volume will be near plant capacity, and the best production economies will be achieved. On the other hand, if a business overbuilds capacity, manufacturing overheads will be higher, and lower overall profits will result. And, if the business underbuilds capacity because of poor sales planning, it will forgo a great deal of potential profit due to lost customer sales.

A first step in developing a good estimate of sales is to develop a good estimate of market demand. The market demand sets an upper limit on sales. If a business had a 100 percent market share, then its sales would equal the total market demand. Following this logic, a business's sales are equal to the product of its market share and market demand, as shown here:

$$\text{Volume (units)} = \text{Market Demand (units)} \times \text{Market Share}$$

As an example, Kodak film sales are approximately 400 million rolls of film per year, a 67 percent share of a 600 million roll American film market. Next year's sales depend on two factors: What will the total market demand be? and What will Kodak's share of that demand be? If this is a mature market, the demand will not change drastically. And, depending on competitive conditions, share change could also be minimum. However, for growth markets with considerable competitor entry, both market demand and market share can change dramatically from one year to another.

Share Development Tree

Although market share estimation can involve a complex set of mathematical propositions, there is a simple marketing logic that provides a reasonable estimate of what a business's market share should be. Market share can be estimated from the combination of a set of hierarchical market share effects, as shown in Figure 3.10. Each step along the *Share Development Path* indicates how customer response influences market share.[15] Because there are many other factors that can affect actual market share, the market share index is simply an indicator of what market share *should* be, given certain expected levels of market performance. Each step along the Share Development Path and its impact on share is explained in the remainder of this section.

As shown in Figure 3.10, an index of market share can be created from a combination of market share effects. The Share Development Path traces a hierarchy of market share effects that leads to a particular level of indexed market penetration. Perhaps more important is that the overall share index is the interaction between effects. Should one perform poorly, the overall index will perform poorly. Further, each share effect is derived from a particular component of what we call the "marketing mix." The marketing mix for a given group of target customers includes:

$$\text{Market Share} = \text{Promotion} \times \text{Product} \times \text{Price} \times \text{Place}$$

- **Promotion** strategies intend to create awareness of a product and its benefits.
- **Product** positioning strategies build around benefits designed to create product attractiveness and preferences.
- **Price** strategies are designed to enhance intentions to buy based on a price that creates an attractive customer value.
- **Place** strategies ensure that there is adequate availability and service to facilitate purchase.

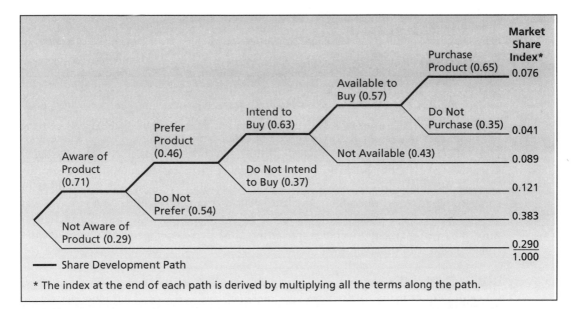

Figure 3.10 ◆ Share Development Tree

As shown in Figure 3.10, each of these marketing mix factors creates a different impact on target customer response and share development. In managing market share, a business must develop a successful strategy for each element of the marketing mix.

Product Awareness The first share effect in the Share Development Tree is product *awareness:* the percentage of the market that is aware of the product. For very mature products such as Coca-Cola, Kodak film, or Ford cars, product awareness would not be an issue because virtually all target market customers would know about the company's product. However, if a business has low awareness, then its market share is limited by a marketing communications problem.

In the early 1980s, Hewlett-Packard began to think about products such as computers and printers for the consumer market. HP had already established its name to some degree with HP calculators, so it thought awareness would not be an issue. However, a survey of U.S. households in the early 1980s showed that less than 10 percent had any awareness of Hewlett-Packard.

Awareness is a particular problem for many industrial and commercial businesses. They rely mostly on specialized advertising, trade shows, sales promotions, and sales calls to communicate their product awareness and positioning. Consumer goods manufacturers are able to better utilize a variety of mass media and in-store merchandising techniques to build awareness of their products. Nevertheless, the first marketing challenge in building market share, whether as a consumer goods business or as a manufacturer of capital equipment, is to build a broad base of product awareness among target market customers.

Product Preference Even if target customers are aware of a product, the product needs to be *attractive* to target customers. That is, target customers have to have favorable attitudes and interest in the product and the benefits it offers at a particular price. If customers are indifferent or negative, the purchase path is short-circuited and market share is dramatically reduced, as illustrated in Figure 3.10. When this is the case, there is very little chance of gaining market share from these customers. In the example presented in Figure 3.10, 71 percent of the target market customers are aware of the product, but only 46 percent of these customers prefer it (find it attractive). As a result, a significant portion of the business's share potential is lost.

This marketing problem is most likely a product positioning problem. Well-positioned products with attractive benefits and price are likely to be in the customer's choice set; products that are not well positioned are simply not considered in a purchase decision. Of course, if there are very few close substitutes, then it is easier to capture a higher percentage of favorable predispositions. For IBM in the personal computer market, the product differentiation between IBM and competitors decreased and the number of competitors increased throughout the late 1980s and into the 1990s. As a result, it was difficult to hold a dominant position as the most favored personal computer manufacturer. The percentage of customers preferring IBM over other personal computers declined, as did IBM's market share.

Intention to Buy If a large percentage of customers is favorably attracted to a product, we would expect many to also have high *intentions to buy* the product. However, owing to economic constraints, customers are not always able to switch or to buy immediately.

Understanding why these customers have low intentions to buy when interested in a product could uncover a creative marketing solution that would help grow share. In the example shown in Figure 3.10, 63 percent of the customers who are aware of the product and are attracted to it also intend to purchase. Those customers who do not intend to purchase cost the business another 12 percent of its potential market share. To stimulate intentions to purchase, a business may have to give the customers extra incentives to purchase its product. This is where sales promotion programs can be a valuable marketing tool to offset high price barriers and to stimulate trial usage. Once customers have tried the product, we would hope that they would be able to more fully comprehend the product's benefits. In addition, buy-back programs and customer financing could provide customer solutions when attractiveness is high but intentions to buy are low.

Product Availability   A fourth share management factor in building market share is product *availability.* If potentially interested customers seek a product and cannot find it at their preferred point of purchase, there is a loss of potential market share. As shown in Figure 3.10, the lack of product availability results in an 8.9 percent reduction in potential market share. If a business could succeed in building its availability to customers intending to buy from 57 percent to 70 percent, it could increase its overall market share index from 7.6 percent to 9.3 percent.

Product Purchase   Finally, while the Share Development Path shown in Figure 3.10 takes a customer to the point of purchase, we cannot assume that a *purchase* will actually occur. The fact that customers may actually prefer one product over others does not ensure that they will always purchase it. In-store influences such as inadequate display or poor location, as well as temporary price promotions or persuasive sales presentations, may switch customers to competing products at the time of purchase. As shown in Figure 3.10, the business's product is selected 65 percent of the time when there is an intention to buy and the product is available.

Market Share Index

If we follow the Share Development Path from awareness to product preference, intention to purchase, product availability, and actual purchase, we can create a *Market Share Index.* The Market Share Index is the product of these five share performance factors along the Share Development Path shown in Figure 3.10. In the example, a Market Share Index of 0.076 is derived as follows:

$$\begin{array}{c}\text{Market}\\\text{Share}\\\text{Index}\end{array} = \begin{array}{c}\text{Product}\\\text{Awareness}\end{array} \times \begin{array}{c}\text{Product}\\\text{Preference}\end{array} \times \begin{array}{c}\text{Intention}\\\text{to Buy}\end{array} \times \begin{array}{c}\text{Product}\\\text{Availability}\end{array} \times \begin{array}{c}\text{Product}\\\text{Purchase}\end{array}$$

$$= \quad 0.71 \quad \times \quad 0.46 \quad \times \quad 0.63 \quad \times \quad 0.57 \quad \times \quad 0.65$$

$$= 0.076 \ (7.6\%)$$

[handwritten margin note: How are these numbers derived?]

Although a business's actual market share may be slightly higher or lower, this market share index is a reasonable approximation. It provides us three important benefits:

- It helps identify important sources of lost market share opportunity.
- It provides a mechanism to assess the market share change when a certain level of improvement is directed in a key area of poor performance.
- It enables us to estimate what might be a reasonable market share potential, given reasonable levels of performance in each area along the purchase path.

Share Potential and Market Share Management

Summarized in Figure 3.11 are the marketing performance gaps between actual customer response and *desired* customer response along the Share Development Path. For each area of performance, the performance gap highlights the degree to which market share is lost along the purchase path. On the basis of the performance gaps shown in Figure 3.11, a business could estimate the share and revenue loss due to below-expected levels of share performance. For example, assume that a business serves a $500 million market and has a 7.6 percent market share index based on the actual response in each area of performance shown in Figure 3.10. If the business could improve product awareness from 71 percent to 80 percent, it should increase its market share and revenue. We cannot determine the exact extent of the impact on share, but a reasonable estimate can be made based on the planned improvement, as shown:

$$\text{Market Share Index} \atop \text{(current awareness)} = \mathbf{0.71} \times 0.46 \times 0.63 \times 0.57 \times 0.65 = 0.076 \ (7.6\%)$$

$$\text{Market Share Index} \atop \text{(improved awareness)} = \mathbf{0.80} \times 0.46 \times 0.63 \times 0.57 \times 0.65 = 0.085 \ (8.5\%)$$

This is an estimated increase of 0.9 percent market share. And 0.9 percent of a $500 million market is $4.5 million in incremental gain in sales revenue. If the business focused instead on the performance gap created by product availability, increasing actual availability from 57 to 70 percent, it could improve its market share index by 1.7 percent, as shown:

Market Share Index (improved availability) $= 0.71 \times 0.46 \times 0.63 \times \mathbf{0.70} \times 0.65 = 0.093 \ (9.3\%)$

Share Performance Factor	Current Response	Desired Response	Performance Gap*
Product Awareness	0.71	0.80	−0.09
Product Preference	0.46	0.60	−0.14
Intentions to Buy	0.63	0.80	−0.17
Product Availability	0.57	0.70	−0.13
Product Purchase	0.65	0.75	−0.10
Market Share Index	**0.076**	**0.202**	**−0.126**

*Performance Gap = Current Response – Desired Response

Figure 3.11 ◆ **Current vs. Potential Market Share Index**

This level of share impact would increase sales revenue by $8.5 million. Of course, in each case, management must assess the cost of marketing efforts needed to affect the level of these changes in order to assess the profit impact (change in net marketing contribution).

Market Share Potential

Establishing a *desired level of response* at each step along the share development path provides a basis for estimating a business's market share potential. For example, in Figure 3.11, if we compute the market share index on the basis of desired response, we can estimate our share potential as shown below.

Market Share Index (potential) $= 0.80 \times 0.60 \times 0.80 \times 0.70 \times 0.75 = 0.202$ (20.2%)

This means that if the business achieves the desired level of performance at each step along the customer purchase path, it should achieve a share index considerably greater than the current share index. In this way, a business can assess its actual share relative to its share potential and can assess the degree to which further growth can be achieved with market share gains.

Share Development Index

Having determined its market share potential, a business is now in the position to assess its opportunity for market share development. In our example, the business's current market share index should have been 7.6 percent. However, owing to a variety of other factors, the actual market share was only 6.3 percent. Furthermore, we estimated that the business's market share index potential would be 20.2 percent if the business achieved the desired level of customer response along the share development path. A ratio of actual market share to potential market share provides a Share Development Index (SDI), as shown:

$$SDI = \frac{\text{Actual Market Share}}{\text{Potential Market Share}} \times 100$$

$$= \frac{6.3\%}{20.2\%} \times 100 = 31$$

In this case, the Share Development Index is 31. That is, the business has achieved only 31 percent of its potential market share performance given full effectiveness of its delivered marketing strategy at each step along the Share Development Path.

If we combine the Market Development Index presented earlier with the Share Development Index, we are able to create an important planning matrix that can help uncover opportunities for growth, as illustrated in Figure 3.12. On the vertical axis is the Market Development Index, the degree to which the market has been developed, and on the horizontal axis is the Share Development Index, the business's level of market share development. Depending on the situation, the business may find one of several strategies to aid it in its development of marketing strategies that will contribute to profitable growth. As illustrated in Figure 3.12, further growth could be achieved with either market or share development. Thus, the combination of these two indexes provides a good way to access growth opportunities and the type of growth strategy that should be pursued.

Figure 3.12 ◆ Market Development–Share Development Matrix

UNIT VOLUME VECTOR

Coca-Cola releases its estimates of unit case-volume growth toward the end of each quarter. Analysts watch the unit volume estimates very closely to gauge the earnings outlook. These volume estimates provide an early indication of earnings for the quarter.

At any point in time, a business's unit volume is simply the business's market share times the current market demand. To estimate future unit volume we can create a *unit volume vector* based on current market demand, market growth rate, and the business's target share at some future point in time, as shown below:

Unit Volume (Period N) = Market Demand × Market Growth^N × Market Share

By understanding these three elements of unit volume, a business can estimate the unit volume of different marketing strategies. For example, assume that the PC market has a current market demand of 130 million units and is growing at 15 percent per year. A PC manufacturer with a 5 percent market share would currently sell 6.5 million units. A strategy (S1) to *hold share* over the next three years would produce a volume vector estimate of 9.88 million units, as illustrated below:

Unit Volume (Year 3) = (130 million units) × $(1 + 0.15)^3$ × (0.05)

= 130 million × 1.52 × 0.05 = 9.88 million units

An alternative strategy (S2) would be to grow market share in this growing market. A strategy to grow share from 5 percent to 7.5 percent in three years would yield a unit volume of 14.83 million units, as illustrated below:

Unit Volume (Year 3) = (130 million units) × $(1 + 0.15)^3$ × (0.075)

= 130 million × 1.52 × 0.075 = 14.83 million units

A third strategy (S3) could be to grow market share to the business's full share potential of 10 percent in this growing market. As shown below, this share growth strategy would yield a volume estimated to be 19.77 million units in three years:

Figure 3.13 ◆ Three-Year Unit Volume Vector for Alternative Share Strategies

$$\text{Unit Volume (Year 3)} = (130 \text{ million units}) \times (1 + 0.15)^3 \times (0.10)$$
$$= 130 \text{ million} \times 1.52 \times 0.10 = 19.77 \text{ million units}$$

When each of the three strategies is represented in the volume vector in Figure 3.13, one can readily see the impact of each strategy. A simple *hold share* strategy (S1) yields a 52 percent gain in unit volume in three years. More aggressive *share growth* strategies (S2 and S3) yield significantly greater unit volume gains. However, one has to determine the cost of achieving these target shares to determine if either is more profitable than a hold share strategy. The unit volume will be a key component in determining the profitability of each strategy.

SUMMARY

A critical first step in any marketing strategy is to determine the size of the market. A business with a narrow product focus will see only the products it sells. Therefore, it is important to start this process with a broad, strategic view of the market that encompasses a wide range of substitute products. From a broad market vision, a business can begin to see more of its markets, as well as adjacent markets that might serve as new opportunities for growth.

With a broader market definition, a business can begin to understand the maximum potential of the market it intends to serve. In some instances the market may be underdeveloped and well below its maximum potential demand. When this is the case, it is important to determine the sources of lost market demand. That is, what is preventing customers from entering the market? Factors such as a lack of awareness, preferences, intention to buy, and availability, contribute to lost market opportunity. A Market Development Index helps quantify when efforts should be made with respect to market development. In many instances, good opportunities for growth exist when a business can look beyond its current customers and the current needs it is serving.

Market demand over time is an important aspect of market planning and strategy development. For many markets, today's market demand is made up of both new customers and existing customers making replacement purchases. Based on the rate at which new customers come into the market, the time it takes for all potential customers to enter the market, and the rate of product replacement, a unique market demand occurs over time. The rate at which a market approaches its full potential is a function of target customer characteristics, product positioning, and marketing effort. Each of these factors can be influenced by the marketing strategies developed by a firm and its competitors. As a result, marketing strategies can influence the rate of market development and growth.

The demand for a business's products is also based on the share of market it can extract from a given level of market demand. Market share is simply the proportion of sales a business can obtain from the total market demand at any given point in time, but a business needs to know if its share performance is at, above, or below what it should expect. Four marketing mix factors (promotion, product, price, and place) are used to create an index of market share response. The Market Share Index helps a business understand its share potential.

Combining the Market Development Index with a Share Development Index allows us to better discover sales volume and opportunities to grow sales volume. For a given segment or geographic market we can determine what our best opportunities for sales growth are. In instances where the market is fully developed and we have achieved the full potential of our market share performance, defensive strategies can be developed. Although this approach may sound simplistic, many businesses may be hurting profits by trying to grow share in markets where further share or market development is not warranted.

APPLICATION PROBLEM: OREGON CHAI

Oregon Chai, launched in 1994, produces a "tea latte." The majority of Oregon Chai customers are tea drinkers seeking variety. However, Oregon Chai, with sales of $5.4 million in 1997, can hardly be found in the specialty coffee market ($3 billion) or specialty tea market ($2.7 billion).

Oregon Chai is sold through specialty retailers as well as grocery stores. By the end of 1997, Oregon Chai was in all 50 states, in over 6,000 retail locations. This was a big jump from 400 retail locations three years earlier. Oregon Chai is sold to retail customers at $3 per quart and to retailers at a 25 percent discount off the retail price. The management of Oregon Chai aspires to build the business to $50 million in sales over the next five years.

Questions

For Internet discussion, go to www.prenhall.com/phbusiness.

1. What should Oregon Chai use as a served market definition? On the basis of this market definition, what is its market share?

2. What level of market share would Oregon Chai have to obtain to meet its long-run goal of $50 million sales?

3. Using the concept of a Shared Development Tree (see Figure 3.10), discuss what Oregon Chai would have to accomplish along the Share Development Path in order to reach its long-run market share objective.

MARKET-BASED LOGIC AND STRATEGIC THINKING

1. How would a product-focused market definition differ from a broad, strategic market definition?
2. What are some of the benefits of a broad, strategic market definition?
3. Why is market vision an important element of market demand?
4. What is the difference between vertical and horizontal market opportunities?
5. Why is it important to establish the maximum potential for market demand?
6. What would be the maximum market potential for disposable diapers?
7. What forces would restrict today's market demand for disposable diapers from reaching the maximum market demand?
8. What factors help accelerate market growth? How can a business affect these factors to accelerate market growth?
9. How does a Market Development Index help a business in its market planning?
10. What are the ways a business could affect the rate of market development?
11. Why is it important to decompose market demand into replacement and new purchases?
12. What performance factors underlie market share performance?
13. How would a business use an index of its current and potential market share?
14. What are the advantages of computing a Market Share Index?
15. Why might a business's actual market share be different from its Market Share Index for a given target market?
16. How could the Market Development–Share Development matrix be used to develop international marketing strategies?

NOTES

1. Noel Tichy and Stratford Sherman, *Control Your Destiny or Someone Else Will* (New York: Harper Business, 1993); and Richard Ott, "The Prerequisite of Demand Creation," in *Creating Demand* (Burr Ridge, IL: Business One Irwin, 1992): 3–10.
2. Theodore Levitt, "Marketing Myopia," *Harvard Business Review* (July–August 1960):45–56.
3. Jerry Porras and James Collins, "Successful Habits of Visionary Companies," *Built to Last* (New York: Harper Collins, 1994); and Burt Nanus, *Visionary Leadership* (San Francisco: Jossey-Bass, 1992).
4. Gary Hamel and C. K. Prahalad, *Competing for the Future* (Cambridge, MA: Harvard Business School Press, 1994): 103.
5. R. E. Bucklin and V. Srinivasan, "Determining Interbrand Substitutability through Survey Measurement of Consumer Preference Structures," *Journal of Marketing Research* (February 1991):58–71; "Car Makers Use Image Map As Tool to Position Products," *Wall Street Journal* (March 22, 1984):33; and "Mapping the Dessert Category," *Marketing News* (May 14, 1982):3.
6. Michael Porter, *Competitive Advantage* (New York: Free Press, 1985): 37; and Jeffrey Rayport and John Sviokla, "Exploiting the Virtual Value Chain," *Harvard Business Review* (November–December 1995):75–85.
7. Derek Abell and John Hanunond, *Strategic Market Planning* (Upper Saddle River, NJ: Prentice Hall, 1979), 185–86.
8. Philip Kotler, *Marketing Management,* 7th ed. (Upper Saddle River, NJ: Prentice Hall, 1991): 240–60.

9. Roger Calantorte, Anthony di Benedetto, and Sriraman Bhoovaraghavan, "Examining the Relationship between the Degree of Innovation and New Product Success," *Journal of Business Research,* 30 (June 1994):143–48; and Fareena Sultan, John Farley, and Donald Lehmann, "A Meta-Analysis of Applications of Diffusion Models," *Journal of Marketing Research* (February 1990):70–77.

10. Frank Bass, Trichy Krishonan, and Dipak Jain, "Why the Bass Model Fits without Decision Variables," *Marketing Science* 13 (Summer 1994):203–23.

11. Geoffrey Moore, *Inside the Tornado* (New York: Harper Collins, 1985): 11–26.

12. William Davidson, *Marketing High Technology* (New York: Free Press, 1986).

13. John Naisbitt, *Global Paradox: The Bigger the World Economy, the More Powerful Its Smallest Players* (New York: Morrow, 1994).

14. Delbert Hawkins, Roger Best, and Kenneth Coney, *Consumer Behavior—Implications for Marketing Strategy,* 6th ed. (New York: Irwin, 1995): 174–81.

15. Doug Schaffer, "Competing Based on the Customer's Hierarchy of Needs," *National Productivity Review* (Summer 1995).

chapter 4

Customer Analysis and Value Creation

In developing a customer strategy for the Lexus, the Lexus marketing team starts with current customers. They conduct in-depth interviews with current customers, many in the homes of the customers, to determine their likes and dislikes as well as their lifestyles. From this customer input and comparisons with competing luxury cars, the Lexus team identifies product improvements that range from more leg room to better fuel economy to a longer coat hook (customers complained that the conventional coat hook was not long enough to carry dry cleaning). They believe that product improvements that enhance product benefits are critical to delivering a superior customer value. To further build customer value, the Lexus marketing team seeks to also find a price that enhances customer value, as illustrated in Figure 4.1.

DISCOVERING CUSTOMER BENEFITS

The Lexus marketing team does more than just survey target customers. They try to understand all aspects of the customers' product usage, lifestyles, and demographics. Gathering this information requires more than a survey of customer perceptions and pref-

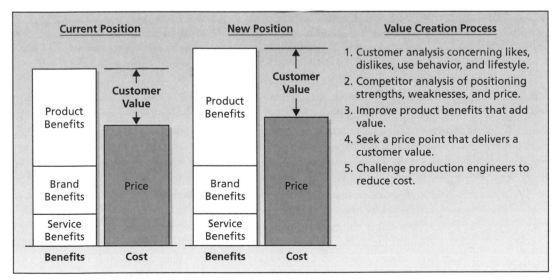

Figure 4.1 ◆ Lexus's Customer Value Creation Process

erences. To discover customer benefits, one needs to understand the total customer environment, not simply the product features customers like or do not like. What we really need to find out is *what the customers want but cannot get from the products they purchase.*

A Day in the Life of a Customer

One way to better understand customer needs is to become the customer.[1] Although customers' descriptions of their needs are important, customers do not always reveal (or think of) the frustrations they encounter in the purchase, use, and disposal of a product when asked. For example, to better understand how customers used their car trunks, Honda employees videotaped people loading groceries. Different cars, different consumers, and different grocery bags all affected how much car owners had to struggle to get the bags into their car trunk. Some arranged their plastic bags to keep them from tipping over; others paused to rest a bag on the edge of the trunk wall and then had to lift the lid again after it partly closed. Watching the videos, Honda engineers put themselves in the customers' shoes. They could see and feel users' experiences and envision better trunk designs.

Empathic Design Process

Videotaping customer product use is one form of the *Empathic Design Process.*[2] This is an observational approach to understanding customer needs and discovering customer benefits. Intuit, the maker of the personal-finance software Quicken, has a *Follow Me Home* program. Product developers gain permission from first-time buyers to observe their initial experience with the software in their own homes. In this way, they learn what other software applications are running on the customer's system and how that software can interfere with or complement Quicken. Product developers can also see what other data files the customer refers to and accesses and whether they are on paper or in electronic form. From in-home observations, Intuit designers discovered that many small-business owners were using Quicken to keep their books; that discovery led to a whole new product line.

Although actual observation might be preferred, it may not be possible to observe customers in many consumer, business, or industrial markets. As an alternative, one could develop two *hypothetical videos.*[3] Video I requires a customer to describe the product he or she wants to buy and, in a sequence of scenes, the *process* he or she goes through in the acquisition, installation, use, maintenance, and disposal of this product. It is particularly important to note the parts of each scene that create customer problems or frustrations. Remember that Video I is not product-specific; it is a *narrative of the process* the customer goes through in acquiring and using the product of interest. Video I describes a typical day in the life of a business's customer.

Video II requires the customer to *re-describe* the scenes of Video I with improvements they would *desire* in each scene. This video provides the opportunity to discover new customer benefits. For example, a marketing team from the Weyerhacuser Corporation visited a large furniture maker to better determine what they wanted when they purchased particle board. The furniture maker made it clear that what they wanted was a *low price with reliable quality.* Weyerhaeuser presented a compelling case for higher quality, but the customer was not swayed. Weyerhaeuser was left with no basis for creating customer value because they could not compete on price against a competitor that had a considerable cost advantage.

This is where most businesses would stop in their analysis of customer needs. However, Weyerhaeuser put together a multifunctional team to revisit the furniture manufacturer to gain a more complete picture of how the manufacturer purchased, inventoried, used, and processed particle board in making furniture (Video I). This time they wanted to understand the customer process in using the product, not just product-specific purchase criteria. By focusing on the process, and not just on the product, they discovered that the customer had to laminate purchased particle board to make thicker pieces because manufacturers could not reliably produce thicker board. They also observed that saw blades wore out at a relatively fast rate because of the grit in particle board. In Video II (desired situation), the customer would eliminate the lamination process and not have to replace saw blades so often.

With these customer insights, Weyerhaeuser responded with thicker, cleaner (less grit) particle board. Although more expensive per unit, the new product saved the customer money; thicker pieces of particle board eliminated the laminating process, and less grit reduced tool wear, each providing significant savings. These product features translated into meaningful customer benefits, as presented in Figure 4.2.

Staple Yourself to an Order

A product-focused business rarely looks beyond the product features and price the business offers. A market-based business will seek to understand customer needs and the benefits they are seeking in solving a particular problem. However, the process of under-

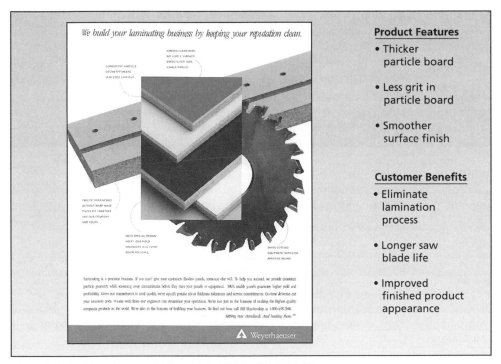

Figure 4.2 ◆ Weyerhaeuser Value-Added Customer Benefits

standing customer needs must go beyond the product and the process of using it. A market-based business will look at the entire *customer order process* as well as the benefits a product provides a customer at a given price. Another way to discover customer problems and understand customer frustrations in the customer buying process is to "staple yourself to an order."[4]

This customer analysis process, outlined in Figure 4.3, involves tracking the customer order process from the early stages of order planning to the resolution of claims when after-purchase problems arise. Each step of the customer order cycle presents potential customer problems and frustrations we have all experienced. The earlier these problems occur in the cycle, the less likely a customer is to buy from a business. Problems or frustrations that occur later in the process hurt the chances of repurchase and, hence, lower customer retention.

One way to operationalize this process is to ask, What are the worst things we could do to a customer at each stage of the customer order cycle? On the basis of the level of customer frustration these problems create and the frequency with which they occur, a market-based business would identify the opportunities to build customer value by improving the customer buying process. While product-oriented competitors are focused on product features and price, a market-based business focusing on product benefits and the customer order cycle can develop important sources of customer value competitors will never see.

Customer Benefits and Customer Value

Weyerhaeuser's, Intuit's, and Honda's efforts to create increased customer benefits went beyond product-specific thinking. They each engaged in an analysis of the customer situation and the various problems customers encountered. With a deeper understanding of the use situation, they were able to engineer customer solutions that went beyond those provided by currently available products.[5] Had Weyerhaeuser focused only on the prod-

Stage in the Customer Order Cycle	Potential Problems, Customer Frustrations, and Opportunities to Build Value
Order Planning	Customers do not recognize your solution in solving a problem
Order Development	Insufficient or incorrect information on your solution
Order Evaluation	Misperceptions or incomplete information limit fair evaluation
Order Placement	Difficulties in placing order with your business
Order Entry	Order recorded or priced incorrectly
Order Processing	Order in process but customer not aware of order status and delivery
Order Delivery	Product delivered late or damaged; wrong product delivered
Customer Invoice	Bill has errors, no one to contact, and calls lead to voice mail hell
After-Sale Services	Problems after purchase with no one to call; calls not returned
Product Usage	Inadequate instructions; no hot line offered
Product Problems	Product does not work and must be returned at customer's expense
Returns and Claims	Customer has to fight to get warranty claim resolved

Figure 4.3 ◆ **Stages in the Customer Order Cycle and Opportunities to Build Value**

uct features and not on the customer needs, they would not have discovered their customer solution. Or, if Intuit had only sold the product but had not sought to understand how it was used, they would not have discovered new products.

A more comprehensive understanding of customer needs and use situations provides a business with a better opportunity to create customer benefits that add value for customers. However, the overall value derived from customer benefits needs to exceed the costs of acquiring those benefits:

$$\text{Customer Value} = \text{Customer Benefits} - \text{Cost of Purchase}$$

Creating attractive benefits at a very high cost could result in negative customer value. Thus, a business needs to be sensitive to both the benefits it creates in response to customer needs and the total cost of acquiring those benefits. In the following sections, we will examine several ways in which a business can create customer benefits and deliver a greater value to target customers.

ECONOMIC BENEFITS AND VALUE CREATION

To deliver a customer value that creates a superior *economic value* requires that the customer achieve a *net economic gain*. For example, Weyerhaeuser created an economic value for furniture manufacturers even though the cost of the purchased product was higher than the cost of competing products. The savings created by eliminating the need for lamination to make thicker furniture legs and the reduced cost of saw blade wear more than offset the higher price of the new, improved product. Thus, the customer value created was greater than that of competitors' products, and it was measurable in actual savings (economic value).

There are six primary sources of economic value creation, as outlined in Figure 4.4.

Figure 4.4 ◆ Economic Benefits and Value Creation

The price paid for a product or service stands out as the most obvious cost of purchase to most customers. As a result, a business with a lower price and the same quality can easily communicate its economic value to target customers. Because customers may not look beyond a product's price, other sources of economic value may go unnoticed. However, other sources of value creation can include costs associated with acquisition, usage, maintenance, ownership, and disposal of a product. Discovering these value creation opportunities is marketing's job and one of the key benefits of spending a day in the life of a customer.

Low Price

Quite often, price or terms of payment can destroy customer value. Regardless of benefits and potential economic value, the product may simply be unaffordable, or the price may be too high relative to the benefits provided. For example, DuPont found that for more expensive blood analyzers, large hospitals could justify a high price based on overall benefits. Smaller hospitals simply did not have the volume of blood chemistry work to justify purchasing a higher-priced, more sophisticated blood analyzer. As DuPont rolled out subsequent new product improvements, they met resistance from large hospitals that wanted to buy the newer products but could not economically justify the purchase because the existing product worked well and was still relatively new. This situation led to a strategy in which DuPont bought back the old blood analyzers from the large hospitals, refurbished them, and then resold them to smaller hospitals. In this way, DuPont created an affordable combination of benefits and price for both large and small hospitals.

Acquisition Costs

With respect to acquisition costs, American Hospital Supply found that one-half of every dollar spent by hospitals on pharmaceuticals, chemicals, and hospital equipment went to the acquisition and inventory of such products. As identified in Figure 4.4, acquisition costs are a part of the total cost of purchase. By putting computers in hospitals to streamline order entry, logistics, and inventory procedures, American Hospital Supply created an economic value for hospital customers, saving them a significant portion of their acquisition and inventory costs. American Hospital Supply won a large share of this market by creating an economic value that was real and measurable by hospital customers.

Usage Costs

The cost associated with using a product is an obvious area of potential value creation and the one that enabled Weyerhaeuser to deliver a greater economic value even with a higher price. The same is true for a manufacturer's telecommunications switch, as shown in Figure 4.5. The customer's current telecommunications switch had a total (life cycle) cost of purchase of $1,000. The purchase price was only $300, but an additional $200 was spent for installation and start-up, as well as $500 in usage and other postpurchase costs. The business's new product offered a customer a solution that could cut the start-up costs in half and reduce the usage cost by $100. As shown in Figure 4.5, this solution created an economic value of $500. However, the product had to be priced in a way that created

Figure 4.5 ◆ Economic Value of a Telecommunications Switch

economic value for both customers and the business. In response, the business set its price at $375, $75 more than the existing customer solution of $300. However, at this price, it created a solution that added $125 per switch to the customer's bottom line.[6]

A second example is presented in Figure 4.6. Sealed Air's AirCap provided an economic value of $0.65 even though its price was $0.25 higher than the price of the competition's product. The $0.65 economic value was made possible by reduced costs of labor and freight relative to those for the competing product.

Maintenance Costs

The cost of repair and maintenance can be expensive for both customers and businesses. The cost of repair for products under warranty is generally the responsibility of the business that sold the product. After warranty, repair and normal maintenance are costs to the customer. As presented in Figure 4.4, General Motors designed the Saturn to be easily repaired in the event of an accident. This design saves both customers and insurers potentially millions of dollars. The savings are so significant over the life of the car that the customer's cost of insurance for a Saturn can be hundreds of dollars lower than for a comparable car.

A second example is Loctite's Quick Metal. Quick Metal can be applied to worn or cracked machine parts during routine maintenance to prevent an extended shutdown. Quick Metal's value proposition, "Keep the machinery running until the new part arrives," tells customers how Quick Metal can create an important savings (economic value) for them.

Ownership Costs

Some products are simply more expensive to own than others. These products often have purchase prices that require financing or higher insurance costs or both. General Electric,

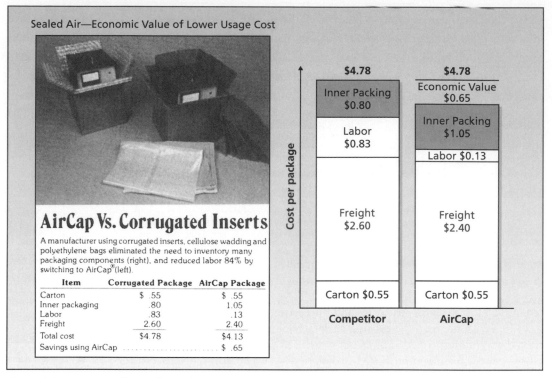

Figure 4.6 ◆ Lower Labor and Freight Costs Drive AirCap's Economic Value

many years ago, developed GE Capital to create affordable ownership with GE financing. GE Capital has been very successful and is today a large business, serving both GE and non-GE customers.

Ownership also has the risk of dissatisfaction: What happens after a product warranty expires? Copiers, for example, have potentially high ownership cost if the product goes bad. As a response to this risk, Xerox created a customer satisfaction program that guarantees product performance for an extended period of time.

Disposal Costs

The way products are disposed of offers another important source of economic value creation. FP International (FPI) manufacturers styrene packaging materials from waste styrene packaging that it picks up from its customers. FPI then sells its recycled styrene packaging back to the customer at a premium price. Because FPI lowers the total cost of the product by solving the customer's disposal problem, it is able to charge a higher price for its product.

A second example is described in Figure 4.7. Kathon MWX is a product that creates a significant economic value for machine shop owners by extending the life of metalworking fluids. The net result is a significant reduction in the cost of disposing of these fluids.

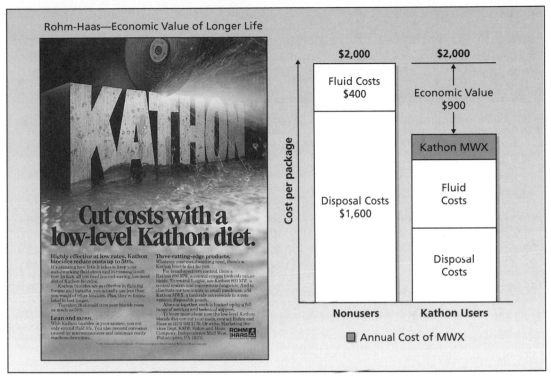

Figure 4.7 ◆ Lower Cost of Disposal Is the Value Driver

PRICE-PERFORMANCE AND VALUE CREATION

While economic value provides a powerful basis for creating a cost-based customer value, there are aspects of product performance that are more difficult to quantify in the total cost of purchase. Performance can also include product features and functions that do not save money but enhance usage and, in that way, create customer value. For example, a car has cost-based value drivers in its fuel economy, maintenance requirements, insurance, and resale value. A car also offers safety, reliability, design, and other features such as front-wheel drive, luggage racks, and comfort. Although these latter components of customer value are difficult to quantify with respect to the total cost of owning a car, they can be evaluated with respect to performance. *Consumer Reports* provides one way to rate the performance of consumer products.

Relative Performance

The overall performance rating for 15 toasters based on the *Consumer Reports'* evaluations of eight product features[7] is shown in Figure 4.8. On a scale that ranged from zero to 100, the overall performance of the toasters listed ranged from a low of 55 to a high of 88, with an average performance of 69. We can create a relative measure of performance by dividing the overall rating of each toaster by the overall average. This measure of

No. Name of Toaster	Overall Performance	Relative Performance	Toaster Price	Relative Price	Relative Value
1 Cuisinart CPT-60	88	128	$70	215	–85
2 Sunbeam	82	119	28	85	34
3 KitchenAid	81	117	77	237	–119
4 Black & Decker	77	112	25	77	35
5 Cuisinart CPT-30	75	109	40	123	–14
6 Breadman	74	107	35	108	–1
7 Proctor-Silex 22425	72	104	15	46	58
8 Krups	70	101	32	98	3
9 Oster	65	94	45	138	–44
10 Toastmaster B1021	63	91	16	49	42
11 Proctor-Silex 22415	60	87	35	108	–21
12 Toastmaster B1035	58	84	21	65	19
13 Betty Crocker	58	84	25	77	7
14 Proctor-Silex 22205	57	83	11	34	49
15 Rival	55	80	13	40	40
Average	**69**	**100**	**$33**	**100**	**0**

Figure 4.8 ◆ Toaster Relative Price-Performance and Relative Value

product performance will help us more readily assess performance around a benchmark average of 100, as shown below.

$$\text{Relative Performance} = \frac{\text{Product Performance}}{\text{Average Performance}} \times 100$$

When each toaster's *Consumer Reports* rating is divided by the average of all ratings (69) and multiplied by 100, we have a measure of relative performance in which the average performance is equal to 100. Now we can readily assess performance as it varies from a low of 80 to a high of 128, where 100 is average. Sunbeam, for example has a relative performance of 119. This means that Sunbeam's overall performance is 19 percent better than the average of the 15 toasters evaluated, as illustrated below.

$$\frac{\text{Relative}}{\text{Performance}} = \frac{82}{69} \times 100 = 119$$

Relative Price

To acquire Sunbeam's above-average relative performance requires paying a certain amount of money. Their price is reported as $28, but it is difficult to readily infer the attractiveness of this price in absolute dollars. Thus, a measure of relative price is also important in understanding value creation. For the 15 toasters evaluated, the overall average price was $33. When the average price is used as a performance benchmark, Sunbeam's relative price is 85, as shown below.

$$\text{Relative Price} = \frac{\text{Product Price}}{\text{Average Price}} \times 100$$

$$\begin{array}{l} \text{Relative Price} \\ \text{(Sunbeam)} \end{array} = \frac{\$28}{\$33} \times 100 = 85$$

This means that the price of Sunbeam's toaster is 15 percent lower than the average price of the 15 toasters evaluated. As shown in Figure 4.8, the relative price of the 15 toasters ranged from a low of 34 to a high of 237. At the lowest price, a customer could buy a toaster 67 percent below the average price, and at the high end a customer would pay 137 percent more than the average price. Thus, the Sunbeam relative price, although attractive, is not the lowest relative price of the 15 toasters considered.

Customer Value

With measures of relative performance and relative price, we can readily identify products that are above or below average in performance or price. However, to infer customer value we need to compute the difference in these two relative measures, as shown below for Sunbeam.

$$\text{Customer Value} = \text{Relative Performance} - \text{Relative Price}$$
$$\text{Customer Value (Sunbeam)} = 119 - 85 = 34$$

In this example, Sunbeam has a positive customer value of 34. A customer value of zero would mean that the relative performance was offset by the relative price. This offset could occur for a product with above- or below-average performance. For example, the Breadman toaster has an above-average relative performance (107) that is almost entirely offset by an above-average relative price (108). The net difference is a customer value of –1.

Using this measure of customer value, we can assess the value of different combinations of performance and price. As shown in Figure 4.8, the customer value for these 15 toasters ranges from a low of –119 to a high of +58. To better understand this range of customer value we need to examine these results a little further.

Value Map

A graph of relative performance versus relative price allows us to create a *value map,* as illustrated in Figure 4.9. As shown, all the toasters to the right of the diagonal line have positive customer values. However, four of the nine toasters that stand out as having above-average performance have below-average price. For these four brands, customer value is created with very attractive prices. Thus, price-sensitive customers might find alternative 7 the most attractive value, because it has both a low relative price and slightly above-average relative performance. A performance-oriented customer would probably find Sunbeam (alternative 2) particularly attractive, because it offers above-average performance with a lower-than-average price.

Alternatives 1 and 3 may seem to be overpriced relative to performance. This method of inferring customer value, however, does not take into account the perceived status or

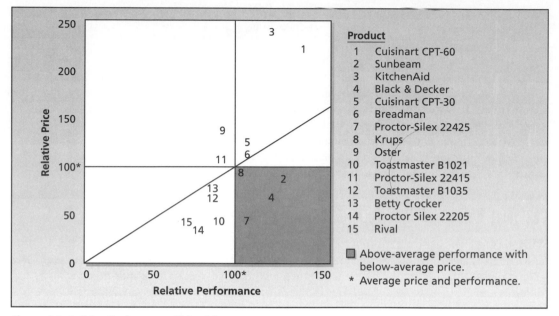

Figure 4.9 ◆ Price-Performance Value Map

reputation of a brand, which can also be an important source of value creation and one that we can include in a measure of customer value.

PERCEIVED BENEFITS AND VALUE CREATION

Economic value and price-performance relative value provide an excellent measure of customer value. However, our evaluation of products often needs to go beyond economic and price-performance measures of customer values. Customer *perceptions* of service quality, brand reputation, and costs other than price also affect customer value. This next section examines how we can utilize customer perceptions of a broader range of benefits and costs to infer the level of customer value for a business's products or services.

Product Benefits

Value creation is logically affected by perceptions of product benefits. These perceived benefits are not easily translated from economic benefits or objectively rated measures of product performance. Yet, it is customer perceptions of product benefits that drive purchase behavior.[8] We need a method for measuring customer perceptions of product benefits and the relative value derived from them when compared with a competitive benchmark.[9]

Shown in Figure 4.10 are four product benefits sought in the purchase and use of a commercial copier. Each product benefit is weighted with respect to relative importance. For instance, in this example, *Machine Up Time* is weighted twice as important as *Image Quality*, four times as important as *Ease of Use,* and so on. To determine the degree to which a relative advantage in delivering these product benefits is created by a business, the business needs to evaluate each customer benefit relative to competing products. In

Customer-Determined Product Benefits	Relative Importance	Business Rating	Competitor			Relative Advantage
			A	B	C	
Machine Up Time	40	8	7	5	6	27
Print Speed	30	9	8	5	5	20
Image Quality	20	7	7	7	6	0
Ease of Use	10	4	6	7	6	−10
	100					37

Relative Product Benefits = 100 + 37 = 137

Figure 4.10 ◆ Measuring Perceived Product Benefits

this case, three competitors were used to benchmark the business's perceived performance and overall relative advantage.

The ratings shown for the business and each competitor are ratings of perceived machine up time that range from zero (disastrous) to 10 (outstanding). If the business outperforms a competitor by more than one point, it receives a portion of the importance allocated to that customer benefit. For example, in Figure 4.10, competitor A is rated only one point lower than the business, whereas competitors B and C are rated more than one point lower. As shown below, the business derives no perceived advantage over competitor A and, hence, gets zero points. However, because the business is perceived to be better than competitors B and C (by more than one point), it receives the 40 points attached to perceived machine up time from each competitor. When these three perceived performance impacts are averaged, an overall relative advantage of 27 is obtained, as computed below:

$$\text{Machine Up Time} \quad \frac{0 + 40 + 40}{3} = \frac{80}{3} = 27$$

For *print speed*, the business also outperformed two of the competitors by more than one point and, therefore, received two-thirds of the relative importance allocated to print speed. However, the business achieved no relative advantage in *image quality* and was hurt by being rated more than one point below each of the three competitors with respect to *ease of use*.

When the relative advantage is added up for all four product benefits, this business produces an overall relative advantage of 37. This means that, on the basis of perceived ratings of product benefits relative to the competition, the business produces 37 percent greater benefits. When this overall relative advantage is added to a base index of 100, a relative product benefit index of 137 is produced.

Service Benefits

For many markets (or segments), product differentiation may be minimal, because competitors are able to emulate the best features of each other's products. When this is the case, service quality can be a crucial source of differentiation and competitive advantage.[10] To measure a business's perceived service benefits, we can use the same approach we used for perceived product benefits.

Shown in Figure 4.11 is a measure of perceived service benefits for the same business

Customer-Determined Product Benefits	Relative Importance	Business Rating	Competitor			Relative Advantage
			A	B	C	
Repair Time	60	5	7	6	5	−20
Response to Problems	30	5	5	6	2	10
Quality of Service	10	7	7	6	8	0
	100					−10
Relative Service Benefits = 100 − 10 = 90						

Figure 4.11 ◆ Measuring Perceived Service Benefits

as that evaluated in Figure 4.10. In this case, the business is roughly equal to two and behind one of its benchmark competitors with respect to *repair time*. This position detracts from its overall perceived service benefits because 60 percent of the importance is attached to this aspect of service benefits. With respect to *response to problems,* the business roughly matches competitor A and competitor B, and outperforms competitor C. The net result is a slight relative advantage. However, there is an excellent opportunity to move ahead of fairly average competitor performance, as illustrated:

$$\frac{\text{Response to}}{\text{Problems}} = \frac{0 + 0 + 30}{3} = \frac{30}{3} = 10$$

With respect to *quality of service,* the business failed to capture any relative advantage. Overall, the business produced a service benefit index of 90. This implies that the business is 10 percent less attractive than its competitors in delivering service benefits to target customers.

Company or Brand Benefits

A third source of customer benefit is a business's brand or company reputation. Whether a brand such as Lexus or Perrier, or a company such as Nordstrom or Hewlett-Packard, the company or brand name itself provides potential benefit to some customers. For Lexus and Perrier, the name adds social status to the product. This is an intangible benefit that could be of great importance to many customers. For Nordstrom, the reputation for customer service creates an added company benefit that goes beyond actual customer service. For HP, its reputation for innovation is valued by many customers and creates a customer benefit that is neither product- nor service-specific.

To measure a business's perceived brand or company benefits, we can use the same method we used for measuring perceived product or service benefits. As shown in Figure 4.12, the company benefits for this copier company were driven by two factors: *customer commitment* and *reputation for quality.* In this case, the business leads two benchmark competitors in customer commitment and has no relative advantage in reputation for quality. The net result of these customer perceptions is an overall index of 140 with respect to company benefits.

Customer-Determined Product Benefits	Relative Importance	Business Rating	Competitor			Relative Advantage
			A	B	C	
Customer Commitment	60	8	7	6	4	40
Reputation for Quality	40	9	8	9	8	0
	100					40
Relative Company Benefits = 100 + 40 = 140						

Figure 4.12 ◆ Measuring a Business's Brand or Company Benefits

Overall Customer Benefits

To arrive at an overall measure of perceived customer benefits, we need a way to combine these three key sources of customer benefits. Combining them requires weighing the relative importance of each of these major sources of customer benefit. In this example, the majority of the weight was given to product benefits (0.60), and smaller amounts to service (0.30) and company (0.10) benefits, as illustrated in Figure 4.13.

When the relative index for each area of benefit is weighed by the proportions shown, an overall index of perceived benefits can be obtained. In this case, the overall perceived benefit score of 123 can be interpreted to mean that the business is 23 percent ahead of the competition in delivering perceived customer benefits. But has the business created a superior customer value? We don't know. The level of perceived customer value cannot be determined until we also determine the perceived cost of acquiring these benefits.

Perceived Cost of Purchase

Before we can determine the overall level of value created for customers, we need to determine the perceived cost of purchase. The first step is very similar to computing overall perceived benefits. We have to first determine the cost components considered by the customer in a purchase decision and the relative importance of each component. In Figure 4.14, there are four sources of cost to be considered in the customer's total cost of purchase. The purchase price carries the majority of the relative importance. Other factors, such as service and repairs, toner, and paper are also significant cost components of the customer's total perceived cost of purchase.

Customer-Determined Benefits	Relative Importance	Competitive Position	Overall Customer Perceived Benefits
Product Benefits	0.60	137	82
Service Benefits	0.30	90	27
Company Benefits	0.10	140	14
	1.00		123
Overall Relative Benefits = 123			

Figure 4.13 ◆ Measuring Overall Perceived Customer Benefits

Customer-Determined Cost of Purchase	Relative Importance	Competitive Position	Cost Multiplier	Overall Cost of Purchase
Purchase Price	40	+15%	1.15	46
Service and Repair	30	+10%	1.10	33
Toner	20	0%	1.00	20
Paper	10	−20%	0.80	8
	100			107
Overall Relative Cost of Purchase = 107				

Figure 4.14 ◆ Measuring the Total Costs of Purchase

In this case, the business is perceived to be 15 percent higher in purchase price, and, as a result, the competitive position multiplier is 1.15 (a constant of 1 plus the relative position). By simply multiplying the relative importance for price (40) by the competitive position multiplier (1.15), we can index the overall perceived position of the business on purchase price as 46. Note that a positive competitive position multiplier increases the total cost of purchase, whereas a negative position reduces the total cost of purchase.

The business's competitive position with respect to service and repair is perceived to be higher than the competitors', which increases the perceived total cost of purchase. However, the business is perceived to be less expensive with regard to the cost of paper, which decreases the perceived total cost of purchase. Because there is no perceived difference in the cost of toner between this business and its competitors, the cost multiplier is 1.00 and the relative weight of 20 translates to a value of 20 for the overall perceived position on this factor.

The sum of these four areas of perceived cost produces an index of overall perceived cost of purchase, which in this case is 107. This can be interpreted to mean that the business is perceived to be 7 percent more expensive to do business with than its competitors; the difference can be traced back to its higher prices and higher service and repair costs, despite a lower cost of paper.

Perceived Customer Value

Once customers' perceptions of overall benefits and total cost of purchase have been obtained, a business can evaluate the degree of value it creates for its customers. Shown in Figure 4.15 is the customer value created by the copier company. Each area of perceived benefit and perceived cost is graphed using the results presented in Figures 4.13 and 4.14. The difference between the overall customer benefits (123) and the total cost of purchase (107) creates an index of perceived customer value score of 16. This means that the business has been able to create a superior customer value while commanding a 15 percent price premium. If a business wanted to further improve its perceived customer value without lowering price, it could strive to improve key weaknesses in areas of importance to customers. Ease of use, repair time, and service and repair are all areas that detract from customer value. To the degree that these areas could be improved, the business could improve the value it creates for customers while maintaining a price premium.

Figure 4.15 ◆ Perceived Benefits, Costs of Purchase, and Customer Value

EMOTIONAL BENEFITS AND VALUE CREATION

So far, we have looked at customer benefits that could be described largely as *rational* bene-fits. The rational appeal of an automobile includes gas economy, maintenance cost, insur-ance, resale value, size, and price. Less tangible rational benefits might include quality of re-pair service, friendliness of service personnel, and manufacturer reputation. For many customers there are also *emotional* benefits that are tied to psychological needs that are more personal in nature.[11] The same can be true in many business-to-business purchases, in which emotional benefits could be tied to security, reputation, or friendship. Thus, to be complete in our understanding of customer benefits and value creation, we need to also understand sources of emotional customer benefits and how they contribute to customer value.

Emotional Benefits and Psychological Value

Each of us has both physical and psychological needs. Physical needs such as hunger, thirst, sleep, and safety generally come first. But as those needs are met, our psychological needs such as the need for warm relationships, affiliation, status, recognition, respect, fun, enjoy-ment, excitement, and self-fulfillment become more important to us. Because many prod-ucts have personalities with psychological meanings, our psychological needs can be served with the purchase of products that offer a set of emotional benefits that are consistent with those needs. As shown below, our psychological needs will draw us to products with a brand personality that satisfies our psychological needs. To the degree that a product's brand per-sonality delivers desired emotional benefits, our psychological needs can be fulfilled.

Psychological Needs → Brand Personality → Emotional Benefits

As an example, a consumer with a need to be seen as rugged, tough, and self-sufficient might be attracted to a Chevy truck and the advertising that positions the Chevy truck as strong, independent, and rugged. On the other hand, consumers with a need for status, recognition, sophistication, and respect might be attracted to a Mercedes. Thus, for products that project a "brand personality" there is the opportunity to create customer value through the delivery of emotional benefits.

Brand Personality and Value Creation

In a comprehensive study of human personality and brand personality, five dominant brand personalities were identified,[12] as presented in Figure 4.16. As you look over the five dominant brand personalities and their related personality traits, ask yourself which of the five would best describe the following brands or companies: Nike, Gateway Computer, Lexus, Timberland, and Hewlett-Packard.

Most people would align Nike with excitement. Nike's brand personality has been carefully honed to exemplify daring, spirit, imagination, and being ahead of the crowd (up-to-date). Gateway Computer, on the other hand, projects an image of being down-to-earth, honest, and wholesome, which translates into sincerity. Timberland footwear has a brand personality that projects ruggedness. Lexus seeks to project sophistication. Hewlett-Packard products project an image of competence built around intelligence, success, and reliability.

In each case, consumers with psychological needs that match well with the brand personality of a product will be drawn to that product. This conclusion assumes that other product benefits, service benefits, and price needs are adequately met. To the degree that the brand delivers these emotional benefits, it will contribute to the overall value a customer can derive from the purchase of one product over another.

For example, what if Nike had used John Wooden (a famous college basketball coach) instead of Michael Jordan to endorse Nike Air basketball shoes (later named Air Jordan)? The personality of the Nike brand would be very different, and the emotional benefits created by the product would be considerably less for the target customers. Products

Brand Personality	Personality Trait	Not at All Descriptive				Extremely Descriptive
Sincerity	Down-to-earth	—	—	—	—	—
	Honest	—	—	—	—	—
	Wholesome	—	—	—	—	—
	Cheerful	—	—	—	—	—
Excitement	Daring	—	—	—	—	—
	Spirited	—	—	—	—	—
	Imaginative	—	—	—	—	—
	Up-to-date	—	—	—	—	—
Competence	Reliable	—	—	—	—	—
	Intelligent	—	—	—	—	—
	Successful	—	—	—	—	—
Sophistication	Upper-class	—	—	—	—	—
	Charming	—	—	—	—	—
Ruggedness	Outdoorsy	—	—	—	—	—
	Tough	—	—	—	—	—

Figure 4.16 ◆ **Brand Personality and Personality Traits**

have personalities. The spokesperson and ad copy used to promote a product help create the product's brand personality and emotional benefits.

CUSTOMER TRADE-OFFS AND VALUE CREATION

With an understanding of customer benefits and how they contribute to value creation, a business needs to create a positioning strategy based on some combination of those benefits and the costs of acquiring them. To evaluate the overall attractiveness of this positioning strategy and the value it creates relative to competing alternatives, a customer must make some trade-offs. To better understand how customers make these trade-offs between benefits, different levels of the same benefits, and costs, we can utilize the method called *conjoint analysis*.[13] This involves a systematic arrangement of key customer benefits and price in such a way that a fair representation of all combinations of price and benefits is created. Customers are asked to evaluate alternatives that are arranged systematically and indicate their preference for each.

In Figure 4.17, four customer buying factors (speed, software, manufacturer, and price) are systematically arranged to create nine alternative personal computers. None of those shown may actually represent any of the products on the market. What is created is a systematic representation of the three customer benefits and price in a way that all combinations of price and benefits are fairly represented as alternative computer systems. These alternatives are often presented on 5×7 cards. Customers are instructed to carefully examine the alternatives and then rank them from most preferred to least preferred. Also shown in Figure 4.17 is one customer's ranking of these nine alternative personal computers.

Customer Trade-Offs: Benefits vs. Price

In the process of ranking alternatives, customers have to decide how important different customer benefits are at different performance levels. They are forced to make trade-offs between different combinations of benefits and price. A customer sensitive to price would most likely use price as a dominant factor in evaluating and ranking the nine alternatives. On the other hand, a customer who needed greater speed and extensive software would most likely prioritize those customer benefits over price. The rank order of alternatives is unique and related to a unique set of underlying benefit and price preferences that can be estimated using a conjoint analysis program. A cursory look at the customer preferences presented in Figure 4.17 reveals that the customer was most sensitive to personal computers that had faster speeds and lower prices (as evidenced by the customer's first three choices: D, H, and G). Using the conjoint analysis program, we can fully discover the underlying customer sensitivity to each customer benefit, as illustrated in Figure 4.18.

The preference curves shown in Figure 4.18 are unique to the preferences provided by customers.[14] If we change the order of even one alternative, a new set of curves will result. Thus, the preference curves shown are unique representations of the overall preferences provided by a customer and, when applied to the alternatives presented in Figure 4.17, they would produce the same rank order preference as provided by the customer. In this case, the customer puts a lot of value on speed. But more important from a product-positioning point of view is the fact that greater value is created by 3× speed. Thus, in

Figure 4.17 ◆ Alternative Computer Systems in a Customer Choice Set

positioning a product to create the most value for this customer, it is important to offer a 3× speed. A 2× speed, while creating some value for the customer, is only incrementally better than the current speed.

Price is the most important positioning factor because it covers the whole range (zero to 1.0). Using the range of each factor, we can estimate its relative importance, as shown

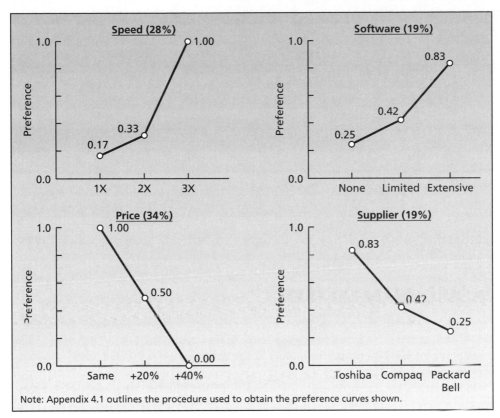

Figure 4.18 ◆ **Customer Preference for Different Customer Benefits**

in Figure 4.19. The range for speed is 0.83, whereas the range for price is 1.00. When the range of all buying factors shown is added up, a total of 2.99 is obtained. If we divide 2.99 into each range, a normalized score is obtained. When added up, the four customer benefits total 1.00. Expressing the normalized scores in percentage terms enables us to communicate to management the meaning of these results. In this case, price was not the only factor affecting customer product preference, but it was the most important. It accounted for 34 percent of the importance attached to this customer's preference for the four benefits shown. Thus, for a business to offset a higher price and still create a supe-

Customer Benefit	Low	High	Range	Normalized	Importance
Speed	0.17	1.00	0.83	0.28	28%
Software	0.25	0.83	0.58	0.19	19%
Price	0.00	1.00	1.00	0.34	34%
Manufacturer	0.25	0.83	0.58	0.19	19%
Total			**2.99**	**1.00**	**100%**

Figure 4.19 ◆ **Importance of Customer Benefits and Price**

Customer Benefit	Toshiba		Compaq		Packard Bell	
	Product Position	Customer Value	Product Benefit	Customer Value	Product Benefit	Customer Value
Speed	3×	1.00	2×	0.33	1×	0.17
Software	Extensive	0.83	Extensive	0.83	None	0.25
Price	+40%	0.00	+20%	0.50	Current	1.00
Manufacturer	Toshiba	0.83	Compaq	0.42	Packard Bell	0.25
Overall Attractiveness		2.66		2.08		1.67

Figure 4.20 ◆ Product Positioning, Customer Benefits, and Customer Value

rior customer value, it will have to position its product with attractive levels of performance on the nonprice customer benefits.

Positioning and Customer Value

Using the customer preference curves shown in Figure 4.18, we can now evaluate the overall attractiveness of a business's product position based on the value it creates.[15] The positioning of three personal computers is shown in Figure 4.20. For each computer, product position produces an overall customer value score based on the results presented in Figure 4.18. For example, Toshiba is positioned in this example with a 3× speed, which produces a customer benefit of 1.00 based on the customer preference for speed. Toshiba also derives a certain level of customer benefit from its name (0.83) and extensive software (0.83), but there is no benefit derived from a 40 percent higher price. The total score of 2.66 is an index of overall customer attractiveness that has meaning only within the context of competing alternatives. In this example Toshiba has a higher index than Compaq (2.08), and Compaq has a higher index than Packard Bell (1.67). Compaq could improve its product positioning, however, by improving its speed from 2× to 3× and could surpass Toshiba in overall customer attractiveness if everything else remained unchanged.

SUMMARY

At the core of any market-based strategy are a strong customer focus and an ongoing commitment to understanding customers' needs and the problems customers encounter. Too often, businesses oversimplify the analysis of customer needs by narrowly focusing on specific product features and price. Although this assessment is important, it is also important for a business to look beyond current product features and price to more broadly see and understand the complete process or cycle the customer goes through in acquiring and using a product. Spending a day in the life of a customer provides a practical way for managers to more fully understand customers' needs and discover new opportunities to improve customer value and satisfaction.

We examined three areas of customer analysis that influence customer benefits (economic benefits, perceived benefits, and emotional benefits) and the way customers derived value from these customer benefits. Economic benefits are a measurable difference in savings that enables a business to create an economic value that is greater than that of competing products. Although a lower price is an obvious source of economic value, there are nonprice areas from which economic benefit can be created. Savings derived from lower acquisition, usage, ownership, maintenance and repair, and disposal costs offer ways to lower the total cost of purchase for a target customer. However, not all benefits can be quantified into an economic value expressed in dollar savings.

Customer benefits derived from a product's appearance, exceptional service, or reputation are more difficult to put a dollar value on. Likewise, customer perceptions of performance have a strong influence on product preference and purchase behavior. By measur-

---

APPLICATION PROBLEM: ADVANTECH SOFTWARE

AdvanTech Software is a start-up company that designs and markets software engineering products. Industry surveys report that the average software engineer costs $100,000 per year (including all benefits). Industry data also show that software engineers are productive (i.e., actually producing code) only 40 percent of the time. AdvanTech Software can improve software engineering productivity 60 percent.

A competing product from a well-known company is already on the market, but it provides only a 50 percent level of productivity. This competitor licenses its software for $1,000 per software user per year. The average customer has 30 software engineers.

Before it launched its new product, AdvanTech Software performed a customer analysis in which it measured customer perceptions with respect to product, service, and company (reputation) benefits as well as the overall cost of purchase. The results are summarized below.

Product Benefits (60%)	Relative Imp.	AS	C1	C2	C3	Service Benefits (30%)	Relative Imp.	AS	C1	C2	C3
Compatibility	60	8	8	5	6	Tech Support	70	5	8	6	7
Ease of Use	40	9	7	5	5	Support Availability	30	5	7	6	7

Product Benefits (10%)	Relative Imp.	AS	C1	C2	C3	Overall Cost of Purchase	Relative Imp.	Competitive Position
Known/Reliable	60	5	9	7	6	Impact on Labor	80	−20%
Leading Edge	40	8	8	6	5	Price of Software	20	100%

Questions

For Internet discussion, go to www.prenhall.com/phbusiness.

1. How much economic value does AdvanTech's competitor create? And, how much economic value does AdvanTech create with a price that is twice that of its lead competitor?

2. How much perceived customer value does AdvanTech create relative to its lead competitor?

3. What is your overall assessment of AdvanTech's customer value at a price that is twice that of its lead competitor?

ing customer perceptions of product benefits, service benefits, and brand benefits relative to competition, we are able to develop an overall index of total benefits derived from a particular business's product. By also measuring perception of price and nonprice costs of purchase relative to competition, we can develop an overall index of the total cost of purchase. The difference between total perceived benefits and cost provide a measure of perceived customer value. The larger the customer value, the greater the potential to attract, satisfy, and retain customers.

A third area of customer benefit and value creation is emotional benefits. Products that serve an underlying psychological need, type of personality, or personal values are creating emotional benefits that add value for the customer. Understanding these aspects of a target market are important in positioning a product and enhancing its perceived value. Products, like people, have personalities, and the closer we are able to position the product with respect to the target customer's emotional needs, the greater potential value we will be able to create with a given product.

Finally, trade-off analysis was introduced to help us better quantify the value created by different combinations of price and product positioning. The customer trade-off process enables us to uncover the degree to which different aspects of a product are driving customer preference. This analysis in turn enables a business to index the value it creates relative to key competitors and to evaluate the impact alternative positioning strategies would have on customer preference and relative value. Overall, customer analysis and value creation are important inputs in developing marketing strategies designed to yield high levels of customer satisfaction.

MARKET-BASED LOGIC AND STRATEGIC THINKING

1. What is the danger in asking customers what is important to them in a particular product purchase?
2. How do product features differ from customer benefits?
3. What is meant by "Staple Yourself to an Order"? How would this process increase opportunities to improve customer value?
4. How does Empathic Design help a business to discover customer problems and new opportunities for value creation?
5. What is the purpose of spending a day in the life of a customer?
6. Why should the scenes in each videotape of a day in the life of a customer go beyond the use of our product or service?
7. What is economic value to the customer?
8. What are the ways in which a business can create a more attractive economic value?
9. Why is it important to measure perceived benefits and perceived costs?
10. What are the ways in which a business can improve the perceived value of its product?
11. How should customer preference and purchase behavior change as a function of different levels of perceived customer value?
12. Why are emotional benefits important?
13. How do psychological motives help shape emotional benefits and customer perceptions of value?

14. How does the personality of a spokesperson help shape the emotional benefits of the product being endorsed?
15. Using Figure 4.16, discuss the brand personalities of Kodak film, Mountain Dew, and Prudential Insurance, and how these brand personalities were created?
16. What is trade-off analysis? How does it help us understand customer preferences?
17. How could a business determine if customers would prefer a new service?

NOTES

1. Readings in *Positive Impact*: William Henry Jr., "Walking in the Customer's Shoes" (November 1994):6–7; Paul Tulenko, "It's Important to Know What Customers Want" (August 1994):9–10; American Marketplace, "Author Says Success Lies in Customer Value Management" (August 1994):11–12.
2. Dorothy Leonard and Jeffrey Rayport, "Spark Innovation through Empathic Design," *Harvard Business Review* (November–December 1997).
3. Michael Lanning, *Delivering Profitable Value* (Reading, MA: Perseus Books, 1998):228–253.
4. Benson Shapiro, V. Kasturi Rangan, and John Sviokla, "Staple Yourself to an Order," *Harvard Business Review* (July–August 1992):113–22.
5. Robert Yeager, "Customers Don't Buy Technologies; They Buy Solutions: Here's How Five Advanced Technology Marketers Saw the Light and Avoided Becoming High-Tech Commodities," *Business Marketing* (November 1985):61–76.
6. John Forbis and Nitin Mehta, "Value-Based Strategies for Industrial Products," *Business Horizons* (May 1981):32–42.
7. "Ratings and Recommendation: Toasters and Toaster-Oven/Broilers," *Consumer Reports* (August 1998):42–43.
8. Kenneth Teas, "Expectations, Performance Evaluation and Consumers' Perceptions of Quality," *Journal of Marketing* (October 1993):18–34.
9. Bradley Gale, *Managing Customer Value* (New York: Free Press, 1994).
10. Morris Holbrook, "The Nature of Customer Value: An Axiology of Services in the Consumption Experience," in *Service Quality: New Directions in Theory and Practice*, ed. Roland Rust and Richard Oliver (London: Sage Publications, 1991):21–71.
11. Delbert Hawkins, Roger Best, and Kenneth Coney, "The Changing American Society: Values and Demographics," in *Consumer Behavior: Implications for Marketing Strategy*, 6th ed. (New York: Irwin, 1995):66–88.
12. Jennifer Aaker, "Dimensions of Brand Personality," *Journal of Marketing Research* (August 1997):347–56.
13. Donald Tull and Delbert Hawkins, *Marketing Research: Measurement and Method*, 6th ed. (New York: Macmillan, 1993):406–18; and M. Agarwal and P. Green, "Adaptive Conjoint Analysis versus Self-Explicated Models," *International Journal of Research* (June 1991):141–46.
14. John Morton and Hugh Devine, "How to Diagnose What Buyers Really Want," *Business Marketing* (October 1985):70–83.
15. J. Axelrod and N. Frendberg, "Conjoint Analysis," *Marketing Research* (June 1990):28–35; P. Green and V. Srinivasan, "Conjoint Analysis in Marketing Research," *Journal of Marketing* (October 1990):3–19; D. Wittink and P. Cattin, "Commercial Use of Conjoint Analysis," *Journal of Marketing* (July 1989):19–96; and A. Page and H. Rosenbaum, "Redesigning Product Lines with Conjoint Analysis," *Journal of Product Management* (1987):120–37.

APPENDIX 4.1—TRADE-OFF ANALYSIS COMPUTATIONS

STEP 1. Determine individual scores for each attribute (factor/level) by summing the scores for that attribute.

Speed	Price		
	Current	20%	40%
1X	Compaq Limited (A) ⟨5⟩	Packard Bell Extensive (B) ⟨6⟩	Toshiba None (C) ⟨8⟩ = 19
2X	Toshiba Extensive (D) ⟨1⟩	Compaq None (E) ⟨7⟩	Packard Bell Limited (F) ⟨9⟩ = 17
3X	Packard Bell None (G) ⟨3⟩	Toshiba Limited (H) ⟨2⟩	Compaq Extensive (I) ⟨4⟩ = 9
	= 9	= 15	= 21

Software

None	= 8 + 7 + 3	= 18
Limited	= 5 + 9 + 2	= 16
Extensive	= 6 + 1 + 4	= 11

Manufacturer

Compaq	= 5 + 7 + 4	= 16
Toshiba	= 8 + 1 + 2	= 11
Packard Bell	= 6 + 9 + 3	= 18

STEP 2. Rank attributes and summed attribute scores from lowest to highest. (X's below)

	$\underline{X}$	$\underline{Y}$
3X Speed	9	1.00
Current Price	9	1.00
Extensive Software	11	0.83
Toshiba	11	0.83
Price + 20%	15	0.50
Limited Software	16	0.42
Compaq	16	0.42
2X Speed	17	0.33
No Software	18	0.25
Packard Bell	18	0.25
1X Speed	19	0.17
Price + 40%	21	0.00

STEP 3. Determine the maximum score, minimum score, and difference between the maximum and minimum scores.

STEP 4. Rescale the raw scores (X's) using the following Normalization Formula:

Normalization Formula:

$$Y = \frac{X_{max} - X}{X_{max} - X_{min}}$$

$$Y = \frac{21 - X}{21 - 9}$$

$$Y = \frac{21 - X}{12}$$

Now, all scores will vary between zero and one, depending on their overall attractiveness to this customer segment.

chapter 5

Market Segmentation and Segmentation Strategies

Market segmentation is the cornerstone of a market-based strategy. A market segment is a specific group of customers with unique customer needs, purchase behaviors, and identifying characteristics. Market segmentation opens the door to multiple market-based strategies and greater marketing efficiency. It creates the opportunity for sales and profit growth.

For example, many retail gasoline companies operated for more than 20 years on the fundamental belief that gas purchases were made primarily on the basis of price. This marketing belief guided their marketing strategy. However, a study of gas station customer needs uncovered five distinct segments, only one of which would be described as price shoppers.[1] The top three segments illustrated in Figure 5.1 are more concerned with quality, service, and the availability of other products such as coffee, soft drinks, sandwiches, and snack foods. In addition, each of the top three segments in the figure (Road Warriors, Generation F3, and True Blues) produced more revenue per customer than Home Bodies (convenience buyers) and Price Shoppers.

These three target segments, which make up 59 percent of the gas customers, produce higher revenue per customer because they buy more gas, premium products, and food products. In addition, the average margin per customer in each of these segments is also higher than in the other two groups because the products they buy often have higher margins. By focusing on these three segments, a gas retailer could implement a series of marketing strategies to better serve the needs of these target segments and, if successful, grow its revenues and profits.

CUSTOMER NEEDS AND MARKET SEGMENTATION

Most businesses have unique capabilities and limited resources. The idea of market segmentation is to focus a business's resources on opportunities that match its capabilities. Without a marketing focus, the business could end up not achieving its objectives.

A business with a strong market orientation will seek to understand customer needs and to develop strategies to attract, satisfy, and retain target customers. Understanding customer needs goes beyond the more obvious product and price needs to include the more subtle *personal* needs that are unique to target customers. Because potential customers will rarely all have the same needs, a business with a strong market orientation

Segment	Size	Core Customer Needs	Use Behavior	Key Demographics
Road Warriors	16%	Premium Products and Quality Service	Drive 25,000 to 50,000 miles a year; buy premium gas, drinks, and sandwiches.	Higher income, middle-aged men.
Generation F3	27%	Fast Fuel, Fast Service, and Fast Food	Constantly on the go; drive a lot, snack heavily, and want fuel and food fast.	Upwardly mobile men and women, half under 25.
True Blues	16%	Branded Products and Reliable Service	Brand- and station-loyal; buy premium gas, pay cash.	Men and women with moderate to high income.
Home Bodies	21%	Convenience	Use whatever gasoline is conveniently located.	Usually housewives who shuttle children around during day.
Price Shoppers	20%	Low Price	Neither brand- nor station-loyal	Usually on tight budget.

Figure 5.1 ◆ Mobil Corporation's Segment Selection and Multisegment Strategy

will divide customers into segments based upon the similarity of their needs. In this way, each segment should be distinct[2] in its needs and the benefits it seeks to obtain from a product or service. It is useful to first understand why customers have different needs.

Forces That Shape Consumer Market Needs

There are so many ways in which we are each different. It should not be surprising that we would differ in our needs and preferences for automobiles, toothpaste, and entertainment. Although there are many factors that contribute to these differences,[3] there are three primary forces that shape the needs of consumers, as summarized in Figure 5.2.

Demographic Influences   Consider how customer needs and preferences for an automobile change as one moves *demographically* from college student to management trainee. Changes in income, occupation, and educational status each contribute to a changing set of customer needs for a variety of products such as an automobile. A few years later, the same person may get married and start a family; changes in marital status and household will once again shift needs and automobile preferences. Because there are a large number of demographic differences between both individuals and households, we should expect a large array of differences in what these consumers need, can afford, and buy.

Lifestyle Influences   Demographics are not alone in shaping customer needs and market demand. *Lifestyle forces* created by differences in values, attitudes, and interests also contribute to differences in customer needs. Two consumers who are demographically the same may differ significantly in their attitudes and value orientations. A consumer with

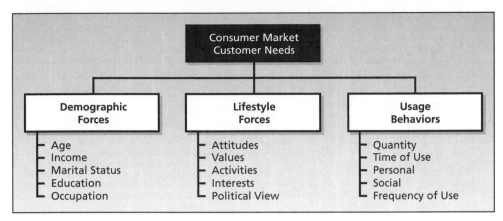

Figure 5.2 ◆ Fundamental Forces That Shape Differences in Consumer Needs

strong environmental values is likely to prefer a different type of car than a demographically identical person whose values are more focused on fun, enjoyment, and personal gratification. These differences, as well as differences in preferred activities and interests, contribute to lifestyle forces that shape customer needs and product preferences.

Usage Behaviors A third major force in shaping customer needs is *usage behavior.* How the product is used, when it is used, and how much it is used are likely to shape customer needs for certain products. A family with two or three children under 10 will have a different set of usage behaviors for an automobile than a family with two children over the age of 16. In addition, if parents are buying a first car for their child as a graduation gift, their needs are likely to be different from those of people who are buying a car for the family or for business.

Forces That Shape Business Market Needs

Quite often, discussions of market segmentation are limited to consumer markets and, as a result, managers in business-to-business industrial, high-tech, and commercial markets are left to extrapolate how segmentation might apply to their markets. Actually, there is very little difference in how fundamental forces shape customer needs, but there are fairly large differences in the types of factors that contribute to these fundamental forces, as shown in Figure 5.3.

Firmographics In consumer markets, one of the key forces is *demographics.* A more appropriate term in business-to-business markets would be *firmographics.* Differences in the size of a commercial or industrial business in both employees and sales are likely to contribute to differences in customer needs. Industries can also be identified by the Standard Industrial Classification (SIC) code.

These industry differences often correspond to different product applications and different needs for products. Likewise, the newness of a business, number of locations, and financial stability are also important firmographics that may play a role in shaping customer needs in nonconsumer, business-to-business markets.

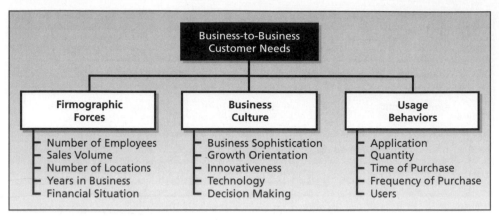

Figure 5.3 ◆ Fundamental Forces That Drive Differences in Business-to-Business Customer Needs

Business Culture   Just as consumer markets have lifestyles, businesses have *cultures* (styles) that can have a profound impact on their needs. Two firms that are very similar in firmographics may have very different needs due to major differences in their corporate style, or culture. A firm with a strong technological base and growth orientation is going to have a different set of needs from a commodity business with no aspirations for growth. Other differences in attitudes with respect to innovation and risk and centralized versus decentralized decision making are also likely to shape the customer needs and requirements in a purchase decision.

Usage Behaviors   Finally, as in consumer markets, usage behavior can play a role in shaping business customer needs. How much a business buys, how often it purchases, who uses the product, and how it is used all influence the specific needs a business-to-business customer will have in selecting one vendor or product over another. Quite often, it is not simply the product a customer is buying but the support, service, and integrity of the company from which it is buying.

For example, though there are several million small businesses in the United States, they can be divided into two core segments: *growth-oriented entrepreneurs* and *cost-focused sustainers*. As shown in Figure 5.4, each segment is different in business need, firmographics, and purchase behavior. Growth-oriented entrepreneurs are better educated, more sophisticated, and better organized, and they have a passion to grow their business. By contrast, cost-focused sustainers are more centered on maintaining the status quo at the lowest cost. These small businesses also tend to be less sophisticated in their operations, have a lower level of formal education, and are less likely to have a working financial plan. To sell successfully in either segment requires a strategy that recognizes the unique needs and behaviors of each segment.

NEEDS-BASED MARKET SEGMENTATION

Understanding customer needs is a tenet of market orientation and the first step in successful market segmentation. Although demographics, lifestyle, and usage behaviors help shape customer needs, we should not start the segmentation process with those variables.

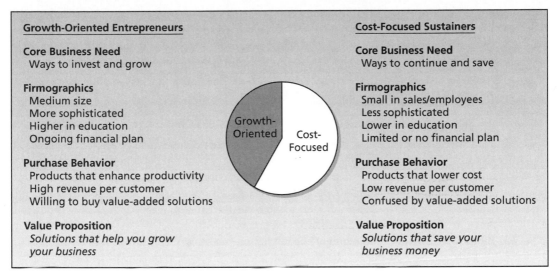

Growth-Oriented Entrepreneurs

Core Business Need
Ways to invest and grow

Firmographics
Medium size
More sophisticated
Higher in education
Ongoing financial plan

Purchase Behavior
Products that enhance productivity
High revenue per customer
Willing to buy value-added solutions

Value Proposition
Solutions that help you grow
your business

Cost-Focused Sustainers

Core Business Need
Ways to continue and save

Firmographics
Small in sales/employees
Less sophisticated
Lower in education
Limited or no financial plan

Purchase Behavior
Products that lower cost
Low revenue per customer
Confused by value-added solutions

Value Proposition
Solutions that save your
business money

Figure 5.4 ◆ Market Segmentation of the Small Business Market

There are simply too many variables and too many meaningless combinations. Instead, the market segmentation process should start with customers:

> *First*, group customers with like needs and then discover which demographics, lifestyle forces, and usage behaviors make them distinct from customers with different needs.

In this way, we are able to let customer needs drive the market segmentation process and let the unique combination of external forces that shaped them follow. This approach reduces the chance of an artificial segmentation of the market based on a combination of demographics and usage behaviors that are *not* the key forces that shape customer needs. However, before we proceed with the process of needs-based segmentation, let's first examine the *demographic trap*.

The Demographic Trap

Quite often, marketers new to market segmentation will fall into the *demographic trap*. Given the strong role demographics, lifestyle, and usage play in shaping customer needs, it would seem logical to segment a market on the basis of these differences. For example, in the consumer financial services market we could segment the market on the basis of differences in income, education, and age, as well as differences in amount invested, frequency of transactions, and type of investments purchased. If we created three meaningful categories for each of these six variables, we would have over 700 possible market segments!

$$\text{Number of Segments} = (3 \text{ categories per variable})^6 = 729$$

This is too many segments to consider if we are to develop a meaningful marketing strategy for each customer group. Perhaps even more important, it is possible that none of the over 700 segments have anything to do with customer needs. It may be convenient to group customers into demographic, lifestyle, or usage categories, but the demographics selected may or may not be relevant in shaping customer needs. Although markets are heterogeneous, and people differ from one another by demographics, personal attitudes, and life circumstances, *demographic segmentation seldom provides much guidance for product development or message strategies.*[4] Thus, it makes more sense to start the market segmentation process with customer needs and group customers on the basis of similar needs.

Needs-Based Market Segments

To illustrate the importance of needs-based segmentation, consider how we might segment the market for investment services. Relevant demographics that might be considered to cause differences in needs could include income, assets, age, occupation, marital status, education, and, perhaps, others. Relevant use behaviors might include experience with investments, size of investment portfolio, portfolio diversification, and amount of average transaction. Each of these influences could be legitimately argued to be an important force in shaping customer needs. However, consider the hopeless task that would emerge if one were to attempt to segment the market on the basis of all of these differences.

Instead, the first step in the market segmentation process outlined in Figure 5.5 is to determine customers' investment needs and the benefits they hope to derive from their investment decisions. A study of female investors' needs produced three *needs-based segments:*[5]

- **Segment A:** Investors who sought investments that outperform inflation with minimum tax consequences.

Steps in Segmentation Process	Description
1. **Needs-Based Segmentation**	Group customers into segments based on similar needs and benefits sought by customer in solving a particular consumption problem.
2. **Segment Identification**	For each needs-based segment, determine which demographics, lifestyles, and usage behaviors make the segment distinct and identifiable (actionable).
3. **Segment Attractiveness**	Using predetermined segment attractiveness criteria, determine the overall attractiveness of each segment.
4. **Segment Profitability**	Determine segment profitability (net marketing contribution).
5. **Segment Positioning**	For each segment, create a "value proposition" and product-price positioning strategy based on that segment's unique customer needs and characteristics.
6. **Segment "Acid Test"**	Create "segment storyboards" to test the attractiveness of each segment's positioning strategy.
7. **Marketing Mix Strategy**	Expand segment positioning strategy to include all aspects of the marketing mix: product, price, promotion, and place.

Figure 5.5 ◆ Key Steps in a Needs-Based Market Segmentation Process

- **Segment B:** Investors who sought investments that provide appreciation with limited risk.
- **Segment C:** Investors who sought investments that produced high levels of current income with minimal risk.

It would not take much of a financial adviser to figure out which type of investments would best suit each segment of investors. However, on the basis of needs alone, we do not know who these customers are. The primary *benefit* of needs-based market segmentation is that segments are created around specific customer needs. The primary *disadvantage* is that we do not know who these customers are. We need to determine what observable demographics and behaviors differentiate one segment from another in order to make a needs-based segmentation actionable.

Segment Identification

After grouping customers into needs-based segments, step 2 in the segmentation process is segment identification.

> For a segmentation scheme to be actionable, it must characterize segments by demographic variables for purposes of targeting and positioning.[6]

For each needs-based segment, we need to determine the demographics, lifestyles, and usage behaviors that make one segment meaningfully different from another. The key descriptive factors that make segment A distinct from the other segments are career orientation, occupation, college education, and above-average income, as shown in Figure 5.6. Women in this segment are also more likely to be self-confident and competitive and to have interests outside the home. On the basis of these characteristics, this segment is labeled the *career woman*. With accurate delineation of segment needs and identification, one can begin to visualize a self-confident career woman who has discretionary income to invest but wants her investments to grow at a rate greater than inflation without the burden of additional taxes.

Although segment B is in the same general age category as segment A, customers in segment B have lower incomes, are more likely to have young children, and are less likely to be married. They have less experience with investments and are more likely to be fearful of investment decisions. This segment is labeled the *single parent,* given both the unique family situation and lifestyle orientation.

Segment C is called the *mature woman,* because of age, conservative outlook, and wealth position. These investors want investments that deliver high levels of current income with limited risk. Thus, all three segments have unique needs and identities that enable us to successfully accomplish the first two steps in the needs-based segmentation process outlined in Figure 5.5.

Segment Attractiveness

What makes one segment attractive and another not attractive? Although every business might answer this question somewhat differently according to its industry perspective, when we step back and look more broadly at the factors that make a market attractive, we find few differences. Common to most assessments of segment attractiveness would be measurements of *market growth, competitive intensity,* and *market access.*

Segment Profile	Segment: Segment Need		
	A: Growth without Taxes	**B: Appreciation with Minimal Risk**	**C: Income with Minimal Risk**
Demographics			
Age	35–45	35–55	55–75
Income > $50,000	86%	3%	63%
Working	100%	43%	17%
Professional	83%	9%	13%
Married	56%	13%	35%
Youngest Child < 5	24%	83%	5%
College Educated	78%	23%	17%
Lifestyle			
Investments Attitude	Confident	Concerned	Conservative
Interests	Sports/Reading	Family	Leisure
Entertainment	Concerts	Movies	Television
Key Value	Individualistic	Cooperative	Traditional
Usage Behaviors			
Experience	Some/Extensive	None/Limited	Limited/Moderate
Risk Preference	Moderate/High	Low	Low/Moderate
Net Worth	Growing	Fixed	Fixed

Figure 5.6 ◆ Segment Identification: Female Investor Market Segments

Market Growth   As shown in Figure 5.7, forces that shape market growth include the size of the segment, rate of growth, and market potential. Large, growing segments with potential for future growth are more attractive than combinations of small segments without potential for growth. Each of these forces directly affects the opportunity for profitable growth. A first step in assessing segment attractiveness is to identify the key market forces that contribute to an attractive market opportunity for growth.

Figure 5.7 ◆ Forces That Shape Segment Attractiveness

Competitive Intensity   The number of competitors, the number of substitutes, and the competitive rivalry among competitors affect the attractiveness of a segment. Even if the market growth for a segment is attractive, the competitive intensity could more than offset its attractiveness and opportunity for profitable growth. If there are many competitors and market entry is relatively easy, market attractiveness diminishes because it becomes more difficult to achieve market share and margin objectives. In addition, if there are many substitute products and very limited product differentiation, margins will be further compressed. An attractive segment is one with relatively few competitors, little price competition, very few subsitutes, and high barriers to competitor entry.

Market Access   To be attractive, a segment has to be accessible. The first requirement is access to channels that reach target segment customers. Without customer familiarity and channel access, there is little opportunity for success. Market access also requires a good fit between a business's core capabilities and target segment needs. The better the match between customer needs and a business's sources of advantage, the easier it is to access markets. Without sufficient marketing resources, market access is greatly impeded. Segment attractiveness is greatly enhanced when a business has good customer access, sufficient marketing resources to access customers, and a good fit between business capabilities and customer needs.

Segment Profitability

Although the market attractiveness of a segment may be acceptable, a business may elect not to pursue that segment if it does not offer a desired level of profit potential. To estimate segment profitability, we can use the net marketing contribution expected with a certain level of segment market penetration.

For any segment there is a certain level of market demand. For example, the segment demand among *growth-oriented entrepreneurs* in the small-business market may be 100,000 in a particular geographic region. Assume that a business believes it can achieve a 10 percent penetration of this market segment with an average revenue per customer of $1,000 per year and variable cost per customer of $600. Marketing expenses are estimated to be $1 million. Based upon these estimates, the net marketing contribution, or segment profitability, would be $3 million, as shown below.

$$\begin{aligned}
\text{Net Marketing} \atop \text{Contribution} &= \left[{\text{Segment} \atop \text{Demand}} \times {\text{Segment} \atop \text{Share}} \times \left({\text{Revenue per} \atop \text{Customer}} - {\text{Variable Cost} \atop \text{per Customer}} \right) \right] - {\text{Marketing} \atop \text{Expense}} \\[4pt]
&= [100{,}000 \times 0.10 \times (\$1{,}000 - \$600)] - \$1 \text{ million} \\
&= 10{,}000 \times \$400 - \$1 \text{ million} \\
&= \$4 \text{ million} - \$1 \text{ million} \\
&= \$3 \text{ million}
\end{aligned}$$

The importance of market segmentation and segment profitability is highlighted in Figure 5.8. Without a segmentation of customers, this health insurance business attempted to sell to all willing buyers. However, customer segmentation based on insurance needs revealed that their greatest market penetration was in the smallest and least profitable segment, segment I. Given the relative attractiveness of the other two segments because of their revenue per customer and claims problems, the health insurance provider revised its marketing efforts around segments II and III.

Health Insurance Market Segment	Have and Will Not Drop	Do Not Have, But Intend to Add	Plan to Drop to Cut Cost	Do Not Have and Would Not Add
Segment I: Insurance Minimizers				
Life Insurance				
Accidental Death				
Prescription Drugs				
Long-Term Disability				
Second Opinion of Surgery				
Separate Coverage for Accidents				
Segment II: Basic Buyers				
Life Insurance				
Accidental Death				
Prescription Drugs				
Long-Term Disability				
Second Opinion of Surgery				
Separate Coverage for Accidents				
Segment III: Premium Buyers				
Life Insurance				
Accidental Death				
Prescription Drugs				
Long-Term Disability				
Second Opinion of Surgery				
Separate Coverage for Accidents				

■ Denotes segment average

Segment	Size	Revenue per Customer*	Claims Problems*	Company Share
Insurance Minimizers	30%	100	100	40%
Basic Buyers	34%	163	71	27%
Premium Buyers	36%	181	66	19%

*Indexes set equal to 100 for Insurance Minimizers.

Figure 5.8 ◆ Market Segmentation of the Business Insurance Market

A key benefit of market segmentation is identifying segments that should *not* be pursued. As Chuck Lillis, the CEO of MediaOne Group, put it, "I will know when our businesses are doing a good job of market segmentation when they can articulate who we should *not* sell to." Businesses that do not segment their markets generally sell to everyone, and in doing so may hurt profits without even knowing it.

Segment Positioning

For each target segment, a new set of marketing challenges needs to be addressed. A business needs to develop a customized *value proposition* and *positioning strategy* that deliver value to target customers in each segment.[7] A value proposition includes all the key elements of the situation and the benefits the target customer is looking for in this purchase. For the female investor market described in Figure 5.6, segment A included middle-aged professional women who were seeking investments that would have above-average growth with minimal tax consequences. The value proposition developed for this segment was: "How to beat inflation and taxes with thoughtful investment planning"

Ideally, the value proposition for a segment should be built around the key benefits sought by the target customer. As a result, the value proposition for segments B and C would be radically different because the needs, benefits, and purchase behaviors of these segments are radically different.

To develop a *segment positioning strategy* for each of the three segments, we need to return to Figure 5.6 as a guide. Because the three segments differ in primary needs, demographics, lifestyle, and purchase behaviors, it is important to use all this information in developing a customized positioning strategy for each segment.

Although there could be many possible strategies for each segment, Figure 5.9 outlines a *value proposition* and *positioning strategy* designed to meet the unique needs of each of these three segments. Product differences based on segment needs are relatively easy to determine. This is the first sign of a good segmentation program. If a business can readily link customer needs to specific product features and benefits, then it is on the right track in developing a successful segment strategy. If this linkage is difficult or arbitrary, target customers will be less likely to recognize a segment strategy as being unique.

Because pricing is less important in the investment market than in, for example, the retail market, it is not a key part of the segment positioning strategy for any of the three segments. Had a segment emerged as price-sensitive, then pricing may have become a critical issue in both the value proposition and the segment positioning strategy.

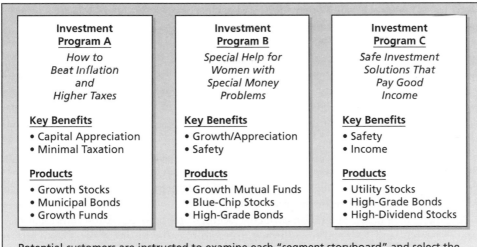

Investment Program A	Investment Program B	Investment Program C
How to Beat Inflation and Higher Taxes	*Special Help for Women with Special Money Problems*	*Safe Investment Solutions That Pay Good Income*
Key Benefits	**Key Benefits**	**Key Benefits**
• Capital Appreciation • Minimal Taxation	• Growth/Appreciation • Safety	• Safety • Income
Products	**Products**	**Products**
• Growth Stocks • Municipal Bonds • Growth Funds	• Growth Mutual Funds • Blue-Chip Stocks • High-Grade Bonds	• Utility Stocks • High-Grade Bonds • High-Dividend Stocks

Potential customers are instructed to examine each "segment storyboard" and select the one that best fits their investment needs. The degree to which target segment customers select the storyboard designed for them determines the degree to which the segment positioning strategy would be judged to be working.

Figure 5.9 ◆ Segment Storyboards for Acid Test of Segment Strategies

Promotion is critical in delivering the value proposition and communicating the identity of the customer it is intended for. Thus, both the ad copy and the media selected for advertising communications are crucial. For segment A, the ad copy would portray a career woman in a business setting; potential media could include *Business Week.* Segment B requires a different approach because the family plays a larger role, as does limited experience in financial planning. Likewise, the promotion strategy for segment C has to be carefully customized to the needs, lifestyles, and usage behaviors of mature female investors.

To reach customers in each of these segments, a business has to again be sensitive to the needs and lifestyle of the target customer. For the career woman, lunchtime seminars at or near her place of work are used to more effectively deliver the value proposition and product portfolio that would best serve her needs and desired benefits. Morning or evening seminars at local schools are more likely to meet the place needs of the single parent segment. A convenient location would be a key consideration in drawing mature women to a seminar customized to their needs. Interestingly, seminars targeted at the mature segment are given on cruise ships, where participants are able to write off a portion of their trip by attending a short seminar each day.

Segment Strategy Acid Test

To test our understanding of segment needs and our ability to translate that understanding into a value proposition, the next step in the segmentation process is an *acid test* of our strategy.[8] To conduct an acid test, we need to create at least three distinct *segment storyboards,* each of which delineates a different value proposition and segment positioning strategy. We would then ask potential customers to examine the segment storyboards and to select the one that best meets their needs. Figure 5.9 illustrates a sample storyboard for each of the female investor segments. A sample of female investors would be asked to evaluate each value proposition and each segment storyboard and to select the one that most appealed to them and their situation.

If the strategy is successful, the majority of the potential customers from any given target segment will select the segment storyboard created for them. The higher the percentage of correct classification, the better the chance the business has of delivering a meaningful segment strategy. Of course, if target segment customers indicate that none of the segment storyboards fits their needs, then the business has failed to translate segment needs into a meaningful value proposition and segment positioning strategy.

A telecommunications business found in an acid test that five segments found the storyboard created for them attractive, though they had suggestions on how to improve them, while one segment failed to find any of the segment storyboards attractive. The business had to do more research, probing deeper into the overall needs of customers in the segment that failed to find an attractive segment storyboard. After additional customer research, and a second time through the acid test, the business was able to attract enough target segment customers to a revised storyboard to warrant moving forward in the segmentation process.

In another acid test, a segment of bank customers rejected a segment storyboard designed for them because it did not include the cost of a new service. A revised value proposition included both the benefits and the cost of this new service. In all cases, an important part of the acid test is to ask customers for ways the value proposition can be modified to better fit their needs, usage behavior, and lifestyle.

Segment Marketing Mix Strategy

Although this last step may seem a bit trivial given the preceding steps, a major cause of failure is ineffectively *executing* the segment strategy. To be successful, the segment strategy next needs to be expanded to include all elements of the marketing mix. The segment positioning strategy may include both product and price, but a complete marketing mix strategy needs also to include promotion (communications) and place (sales and distribution) strategies.[9] If target segment customers are not adequately aware of the segment value proposition or cannot acquire the product at preferred points of purchase, the segment strategy will fail.

For example, in Figure 5.10 we can see how DuPont developed different advertisements to execute a multisegment strategy for Kevlar. Note the attention to distinct segment value propositions and product positioning differences that are unique to each target segment.[10] A generic ad highlighting product features would not have the impact that each segment-specific ad was designed to have.

Commercial Fishing

"This boat hull of Kevlar saves fuel, gets there faster and can carry home more fish."

Value Proposition: *This boat hull of Kevlar saves fuel, gets there faster, and can carry more fish.*

Aircraft Design

"Our L-1011 is 807 lbs. lighter because of Kevlar 49."

Value Proposition: *Our L-1011 is 807 pounds lighter because of Kevlar 49.*

Figure 5.10 ◆ DuPont Segment Value Propositions and Positioning Strategies

SEGMENTATION STRATEGIES

On the basis of segment attractiveness, profit potential, and available resources, there are several segment strategies a business could pursue. As shown in Figure 5.11, segment strategies can range from a *mass market* strategy with no segment focus to a *mass customization* strategy with numerous niche segments within segments. This section discusses these various segment strategies and the circumstances under which they are used.

Mass Market Strategy

When differences in customer needs are small or demographics are not distinctive, a business may elect to use a mass market strategy. This strategy presents a generic value proposition built around the core customer need and the business's generic positioning strategy. Wal-Mart, for example, pursues a mass market strategy built around a low-cost value proposition that has worked very effectively for 30 years. Coca-Cola, Caterpillar, Sony, Marlboro, Phillips, Toyota, Volvo, and Kodak are some of many well-recognized global brands that use a global marketing strategy while sometimes modifying their products and market communications to meet specific customer needs in specific international markets.

Large Segment Strategy

When a market is segmented and marketing resources are limited, a business could elect to pursue a *large segment* strategy. As illustrated in Figure 5.11, a mass market strategy could be segmented into three core segments. A large segment strategy would focus on

Figure 5.11 ◆ Segmentation Hierarchy: Mass Market to Mass Customization Strategies

segment A, because it is the largest, representing 50 percent of the market. Unlike a mass market strategy, a large segment strategy addresses one set of core customer needs. Thus, a large segment strategy engages the benefits of market segmentation while also providing a relatively large market demand. Chevy's truck strategy is a large segment strategy. Because market demand is somewhat limited and a large segment exists, this large segment strategy provides a cost-effective way to reach a large number of target customers.

Adjacent Segment Strategies

Quite often, businesses find themselves in a situation in which they have pursued a single segment focus but have reached the point of full market penetration. When this is the case, an *adjacent segment* strategy offers an attractive opportunity for market growth. Because resources are limited, a closely related attractive segment is tackled next. With profits derived from the primary target segment, the next most attractive adjacent segment is addressed.

In Figure 5.11, segment B is profiled to be the next most similar to segment A. A business that reaches full penetration of segment A with a large segment strategy may pursue new growth by entering segment B, an adjacent segment with respect to product and price needs.

An example of this segmentation strategy is Toyota's adjacent segment strategy in the U.S. car market. Toyota entered the U.S. market with the Corona at the low-price end of the market (today the Tercel serves this segment). As Toyota penetrated this segment, it moved to an adjacent segment in terms of price and quality by adding the Corolla, as shown in Figure 5.12. By the late 1980s, additional products were developed for higher price–quality segments. Next came entry into the luxury car segment with Lexus and an adjacent segment for the Supra and Avalon. Over a 30-year period, Toyota effectively used an adjacent segment strategy, and today it has a strong market position in each segment.

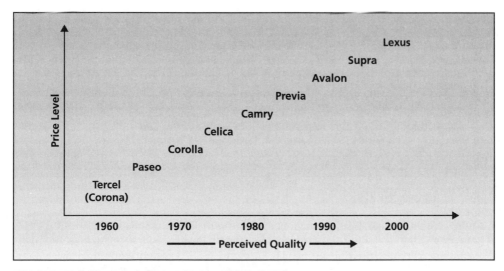

Figure 5.12 ◆ Toyota's Adjacent Segmentation Strategy

Multisegment Strategies

Quite often, the segmentation process will uncover several segment opportunities, and resources will be available to pursue more than one. On the basis of the results of the female investor segmentation study presented earlier, Merrill Lynch developed three distinct segment strategies, one for each of the three segments described. In these situations, a business has the added challenge of developing and implementing more than one segment positioning strategy, as illustrated in Figure 5.9.

Perhaps an even more challenging multisegment marketing strategy was one developed by an electric equipment manufacturer. The power generation and distribution market in the United States includes 7,000 entities. A segmentation study of this market produced 12 distinct needs-based segments that differed in customer needs, firmographics, and usage behavior,[11] as shown in Figure 5.13. At one extreme was a segment that included large, publicly owned utilities that had large engineering and maintenance staffs, and at the other extreme were small rural co-ops that produced electricity for small farm communities. Another segment actually included businesses that produce electricity for their own consumption and sell excess power to the local utilities. The Los Angeles Performing Arts Center is a customer in this segment.

The electric equipment manufacturer found each of the segments attractive and already had sales to customers in each of the segments. The only difference was that before the segmentation study the business used a mass market strategy and treated all customers roughly the same. On the basis of the unique needs of each segment, 12 separate marketing programs were designed. Designing them required 12 different segment product-positioning and marketing approaches in order to build a strong value proposition for each segment.

The year the multisegment strategy was implemented, the entire market experienced a decline of 15 percent in sales. The previous year market sales had also declined by 8 percent. In addition, one regional vice president had elected to not participate in the implementation of the multisegment marketing strategy. Thus, without trying, the business had created a perfect experiment from which to evaluate the results of the multisegment marketing strategy: They had a control group and, with a 15 percent decrease in market demand, a known direction from which to evaluate sales change. For the multisegment strategy to be effective, it would have to create a net sales change that outperformed a 15 percent market decline. The year the multisegment strategy was implemented, there were significant increases in sales in regions A and B and a smaller increase in region C, the control group, as shown in Figure 5.13. Overall, the business achieved a sales growth of more than 10 percent in a year that the market declined by 15 percent in sales volume. It is also important to note that this increase was achieved with essentially no change in marketing budget—simply better market focus and reallocation of marketing resources.

Small Segment Strategy

Although a market may provide three segment opportunities, a business with limited resources and certain capabilities may elect to compete in the smallest segment. The smallest segment, as represented by segment C in Figure 5.11, is often ignored by large com-

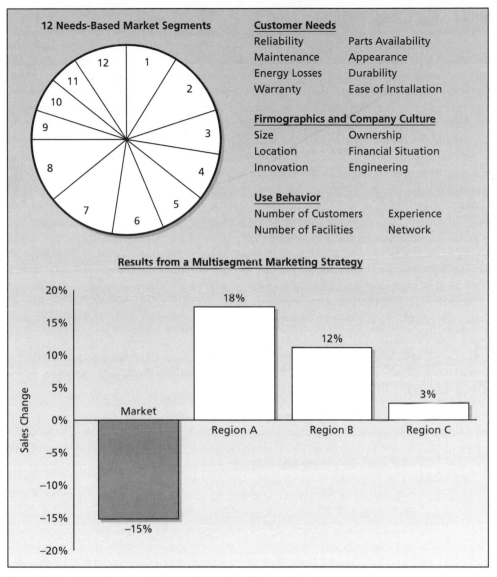

Figure 5.13 ◆ Multisegment Power Generation Market Strategy

petitors, who may use mass market or large segment strategies. Even businesses with a multisegment strategy may not be able to compete effectively with a business that has a singular-focus small segment strategy.

For example, Mercedes for many years used a small segment strategy to stay focused on the luxury car market. Having built a certain prestige in this market, Mercedes was reluctant to move down into lower price–quality adjacent segments. However, because of the increased attractiveness of adjacent segments, Mercedes is now pursuing a dual-segment strategy.

Niche Segment Strategies

Market segmentation is a process of grouping customers with like needs into homogeneous segments, but the process is never perfect. That is, even when customers in a given segment share common needs, there are still differences in demographics or usage behaviors that cannot be fully addressed with a single segment strategy. As a result, there is the opportunity for a business to carve out a niche within a segment and further customize its marketing effort to that group of target customers.

Consider the case of Sub-Zero refrigerators.[12] This business, with less than a 2 percent market share of the U.S. refrigerator market, competes with industry giants who have large economies of scale and marketing resources. However, Sub-Zero holds 70 percent of the "Super Premium" segment, a niche market segment in the refrigerator market. Sub-Zero specializes in very expensive built-in refrigerators that start at $3,500. Target customers claim, "to own a Sub-Zero refrigerator is to have something special."

It is hard to outperform niche competitors such as Sub-Zero because they have all their marketing resources focused on the specific needs of a certain type of customer. Within that segment, Sub-Zero can focus on a *niche market* that includes only high-end customers who are seeking a super premium refrigerator. For Sub-Zero, a needs-based market strategy is customized to the specific needs, lifestyle, and usage behavior of their niche customer.

Mass Customization

The complete opposite of a mass market strategy is a *mass customization* strategy. A mass customization strategy treats every unique group of customer needs as a niche market. As shown in Figure 5.11, a mass customization strategy recognizes all 10 unique groups of customer needs. The objective is to customize a segment strategy for each customer segment. *Mass customization* is a term used in conjunction with database marketing. With the use of customer databases,[13] a segment can be further divided into customized subsegments, as shown in Figure 5.11. A business serving segment A could build a customized database for each of the subsegments, or niches, within segment A. With this added degree of customer focus, a business can customize its value proposition and positioning strategy for customers in these subsegments. For example, the value proposition and segment positioning strategy developed for customers in the career women segment in Figure 5.6 could be further broken down and customized for different subsegments such as physicians, architects, CPAs, executives, and business owners.

Mass customization combines the advantages of a niche segment strategy while retaining the breadth of opportunity available with multisegment marketing strategies. The whole process of segmentation should be viewed as a *nested hierarchy*. At one extreme is a mass market strategy in which all customers are treated the same. And at the other extreme is mass customization, in which subsegments are created in order to more closely match the particular needs of a niche segment strategy. In between are varying degrees of market segmentation and target segment focus.

SUMMARY

At the heart of market-based management is a skillful execution of market segmentation. It is the core of a market-based strategy because it is built around customer needs, unique lifestyles, and usage behaviors. To the degree to which a business understands differences in customer needs, it can translate them into actionable segment strategies.

A specific segmentation process was presented with special emphasis on creating needs-based segments. Although it may be easy to create segments on the basis of differences in demographics or behavior, doing so may lead to a marketing strategy that does not deliver a needs-based customer solution. However, needs-based segments need to be demographically identified so that actionable strategies can be created for each segment. These first two steps are crucial.

The next steps in the segmentation process require that we index overall segment attractiveness and estimate segment profit potential to select target segments. A value proposition and marketing mix strategy must be developed for each target segment selected. To ensure that we have accurately translated target customer needs and identity characteristics into our positioning strategy (value proposition and marketing mix), a segment acid test is carried out. This enables a business to determine if customers are adequately attracted to the combination of a target segment value proposition and segment strategy designed for them. On the basis of customer feedback, a revised strategy can be finalized and implemented.

In some instances, resources may be limited and only a single segment or niche (subsegment) within a segment may be pursued. In other instances, a multisegment strategy may fit the resources and capabilities of a business. Of course, the more segment strategies a business has, the more difficulty it encounters in maintaining a distinct marketing strategy for each segment. With the use of database marketing, a business can actually take either a segment strategy or a multisegment strategy one step further with mass customization. With mass customization, a business is able to further customize its value proposition and segment positioning through customized product positioning and communications. Mass customization enables a large business to obtain the advantages of a niche marketer while also serving many segments and niches within segments.

MARKET-BASED LOGIC AND STRATEGIC THINKING

1. How did market segmentation help Mobil Corporation in its marketing strategy?
2. Why should customer needs be the driving force in segmenting a market?
3. What kind of problems can occur if a business segments a market on the basis of demographics or usage?
4. How are customer needs shaped, and what role do these forces play in the segmentation process?
5. What happens when a business is able to segment a market on the basis of needs but unable to demographically or behaviorally identify the segments?
6. How does firmographics help shape business-to-business customer needs?
7. What forces shape market attractiveness, and how should they be measured in order to develop an overall index of market attractiveness?

APPLICATION PROBLEM: THE WEB DEPOT

The Web Depot is a Web-based business that helps small businesses develop Web-based business offerings to better reach and serve current customers and attract new customers. The business is relatively new, with $10 million in sales revenue, and it is growing at 30 percent per year. But it is not making a profit. In fact, The Web Depot is losing $1.25 million per year.

Currently, The Web Depot has 5,000 customers who spend an average of $2,000 per year. Variable cost per customer ($1,450) is quite high because it is a labor-intensive business. The work is custom-designed Web site home pages, product catalog, and customer order processing. Fixed expenses are $4 million, of which $1.75 million is spent on marketing and the rest on facilities, equipment, and management salaries and overhead.

Market Segmentation Study

A team of students from a local university was assigned to The Web Depot for the school year. The team was given the assignment of finding out more about The Web Depot's customers and recommending a way that The Web Depot could grow and be profitable. The customer analysis and market segmentation study revealed three market segments, each with different needs, usage levels, and business characteristics:

Segment Characteristic	Segment A	Segment B	Segment C	Overall
Business Objectives	Maintain	Grow	Grow	Hold–Grow
Number of Customers	2,500	1,500	1,000	5,000
Computer/Web Experience	Limited	Some	Wide	Limited–Wide
The Web Depot Product Interest	Narrow	Moderate	Wide	Narrow–Wide
Revenue per Customer	$1,000	$2,000	$4,500	$2,000
Margin per Customer	$ 200	$ 600	$1,350	$ 550
Marketing Expenses per Customer	$ 300	$ 400	$ 400	$ 350

Questions

For Internet discussion, go to www.prenhall.com/phbusiness.

1. What is the segment profitability of each segment (i.e., the net marketing contribution of each segment)?

2. What type of segmentation strategy would you recommend in order for The Web Depot to be more profitable?

3. Assuming that overhead (fixed) expenses are proportional to sales, what would be the profit impact of your segmentation strategy next year and in five years at an annual growth rate of 30 percent?

8. What criteria should be used in determining which segments a business should pursue?
9. What is a segment value proposition? Why is it a crucial part of the segmentation process?
10. How would you develop a value proposition for a retail gasoline business's target customers?
11. What is a segment marketing mix strategy? How did the marketing mix strategy differ for each of the three segments of the female investor services market?
12. What is an "acid test"? What are the advantages of performing an acid test?
13. How did DuPont create an effective multisegment strategy for Kevlar?
14. What is an adjacent segment strategy? Why would a business pursue an adjacent segment strategy when more than one segment of the market is attractive and offers good profit potential?
15. When would a business pursue a single segment market strategy?
16. Why is a niche strategy often difficult for competitors to outperform?
17. What is mass customization? How could a business using a mass customization strategy match the effectiveness of smaller niche competitors?

NOTES

1. Allanna Sullivan, "Mobil Bets Drivers Pick Cappuccino Over Parties," *Wall Street Journal* (January 30, 1995).
2. Wendell Smith, "Product Differentiation and Market Segmentation As Alternative Marketing Strategies," *Marketing Management* (Winter 1995):63–65.
3. Delbert Hawkins, Roger Best, and Kenneth Coney, *Consumer Behavior: Implications for Marketing Strategy*, 6th ed. (New York: Irwin, 1995):4–25.
4. Marshall Greenberg and Susan McDonald Schwartz, "Successful Needs/Benefits Segmentation: A User's Guide," *Journal of Consumer Marketing* (Summer 1989):29–36.
5. "Merrill Lynch Campaign Targeted at Women Stresses Investment Options," *Marketing News* (November 30, 1979):11.
6. Sachin Gupta and Pradeep Chintagunta, "On Using Demographic Variables to Determine Segment Membership in Logit Mixture Models," *Journal of Marketing Research* (February 1994):128.
7. Michael Lanning, *Delivering Profitable Value* (Reading, MA: Perseus Books, 1998):39–88.
8. William Band, "Customer-Accelerated Change," *Marketing Management* (Winter 1995):19–33.
9. P. Dickson and J. Ginter, "Market Segmentation, Product Differentiation, and Marketing Strategy," *Journal of Marketing* (April 1987):1–10.
10. G. Coles and J. Culley, "Not All Prospects Are Created Equal," *Business Marketing* (May 1986):52–59.
11. Dennis Gensch, "Targeting the Switchable Industrial Customer," *Marketing Science* (Winter 1984):41–54.
12. J. Levine, "Cool!" *Forbes* (April 1996):98.
13. Stan Rapp and Tom Collins, *MaxiMarketing* (New York: McGraw-Hill, 1987); Jonathan Berry, "Database Marketing—A Potent New Tool for Selling," *Business Week* (September 5, 1995):56; Robert Buzzell and Rajendra Sisoda, "Information Technology and Marketing," in *Companion Encyclopedia of Marketing*, ed. Michael Baker (Los Angeles: Rutledge, 1995).

chapter 6

Competitor Analysis and Competitive Position

When one thinks about General Motors, NBC, or IBM, one does not have to go back too far in time to see how the competitive position of each of these market leaders has changed. For General Motors, it was foreign competition that eroded its competitive position, first with lower prices, and then with higher levels of product quality. For NBC, CBS, and ABC, it was first ESPN, CNN, and Fox and then a multitude of cable networks and the Internet. And for IBM, DEC, and others, it was Compaq, Dell, Toshiba, and a flood of new competitors. These competitors could buy the basic hardware and software for a computer and assemble and market it at lower prices.

In each case, the market leader once held a strong, almost impenetrable competitive position. And, in each case, new competitive forces emerged and the competitive position of the market leader was seriously eroded. It is important to recognize that in each example, the market leader had not lowered quality, raised prices, or cut back on marketing efforts. On the contrary, each had made serious efforts to improve products, reduce prices, and expand marketing efforts to retain customers. However, in each case, the competitive forces brought to bear on its market first challenged, and then eroded, the market leader's competitive position.

COMPETITION AND COMPETITIVE POSITION

There are three important aspects of competition that affect a business's competitive position and profitability, as outlined in Figure 6.1. The first, *industry forces,* has to do with the competitive forces within an industry. These competitive forces shape a market's attractiveness and profit potential. An important step in market analysis is an industry analysis of markets in order to select those markets that offer the best profit potential.

Second, within an industry or market, it is important for a business to benchmark its *competitive position.* External market measures of *relative* product quality, service quality, customer satisfaction, brand awareness, and market share are crucial market metrics that benchmark the strength of a business's competitive position. Internal metrics such as unit cost, order cycle time, delivery costs, accounts receivable, and sales per employee are equally important in benchmarking and managing competitiveness. However, to improve on an important competitive weakness, a business needs to benchmark world-class performance outside its industry in order to gain a competitive advantage.

Finally, to achieve a superior level of profitability, a business needs to attain a source of sustainable *competitive advantage.* This could be a cost advantage that yields more at-

Figure 6.1 ◆ Competitive Forces That Shape Competitive Position and Profitability

tractive prices, a quality advantage that enhances product preference or price premiums, or a marketing advantage that achieves greater customer awareness and availability. The purpose of this chapter is to examine each of these areas of competition and how each is used in the development of market-based strategies.

INDUSTRY ANALYSIS

A first step in industry analysis is to determine the attractiveness of the competitive environment. Developing a strong competitive position in an unattractive market has the potential to lessen profitability even when a business's competitive position in that industry is relatively strong.[1] Picking the right markets (industries) in which to compete is a crucial step in market analysis and strategy development.

Shown in Figure 6.2 are industry forces that shape the attractiveness of a competitive environment. Each of these industry forces can be evaluated along a continuum from unfavorable to favorable. As the sum of these forces favor a more attractive competitive environment, there is greater profit potential. A business in a market with low entry barriers, high exit barriers, high levels of customer and supplier power, many substitutes, and intense rivalry among competitors will have a lower profit potential than a business with a more favorable set of competitive forces.

Barriers to Entry

Market entry can be blocked in many ways. Many international markets are blocked by political barriers. These barriers reduce competition and enhance profit potential for protected competitors. Technology or low-cost manufacturing can also create entry barriers. Businesses with a superior cost or technological advantage create a market entry barrier that discourages competitors from entering a market. In addition, the resources needed to compete in a given market could be so great that entry is limited. High advertising expenditures, R&D spending, and sales force expenditures can each require resource levels that can block market entry for businesses with limited resources. For example, barriers to entry in the pharmaceutical industry are relatively high. Patents on prescription drugs, high R&D investments, and large sales forces needed to contact physicians each deter competitor entry and contribute to the attractiveness of this competitive environment.

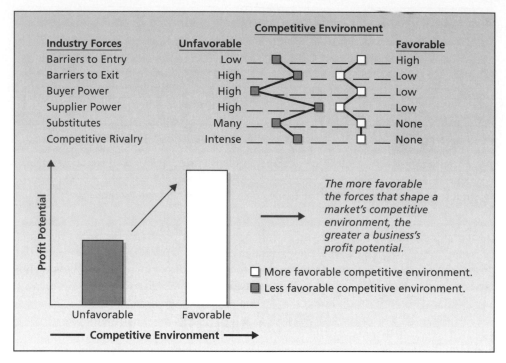

Figure 6.2 ◆ Industry Analysis: Industry Forces and Profit Potential

Barriers to Exit

The competitive environment is also enhanced when weak competitors can easily exit a market. Legal barriers, specialized assets, or the strategic importance of a business often prevent businesses from exiting markets when they should. A pharmaceutical company that is losing money on a particular prescription drug may want to exit, but legal, political, or social forces could create an environment in which market exit would be very difficult. The struggle to survive can lead to competitive practices that adversely affect industry profits.

Likewise, a business that has invested in specialized assets (capital or people or both) may find it difficult to exit a market because these assets are not easily sold or transferred to another business application. Businesses that have specialized in nuclear fuel reprocessing may find market exit difficult because of their specialized assets. Finally, a business that is dependent on products that are strategically important to its image or ability to market other products may not exit a market even though it is producing less-than-desired levels of profitability.

Customer Buying Power

When relatively few customers buy in large quantities, and can easily switch suppliers, there is considerable customer buying power, which lowers market attractiveness. Large, concentrated groups of customers possess a buying power that enables them to negotiate lower prices or better terms and conditions of sale. Likewise, when customers can easily switch from one supplier to another, they force increased competition, which can lower prices as well as raise the cost of serving customers. In addition, when the purchased product or service is of limited importance to the customer, supplier dependence is much lower.

For the pharmaceutical industry, customer buying power is relatively low. Many well-known prescription drugs, such as Prozac, have many individual customers to whom the product is extremely important and who have limited opportunities to switch. As a result, the pharmaceutical industry has relatively low customer buying power, which enhances the competitive environment and profit potential.[2]

Supplier Selling Power

The flip side of customer buying power is supplier selling power. If a business is a large purchaser of a commodity product (less important to the buyer) and is in an industry in which switching costs are low, supplier power is generally low. For a business, this is an attractive market situation that contributes to industry attractiveness and profit potential. For many pharmaceutical businesses, supplier power is relatively low for these reasons, which contributes to the overall attractiveness of the industry.

Product Substitutes

The more substitute products available to customers, the easier it is for them to switch. Ease of switching intensifies competition and lowers profit potential and industry attractiveness. For example, in the soft drink industry, there are many product substitutes, so premium pricing is impossible. However, if the market definition is broadened to include non-soft drink substitutes, such as mineral water, fruit drinks, fruit juices, and sports drinks, one can begin to understand the enormous pressure this level of choice brings to bear on competitors serving these markets. It is important to have a broad market definition as presented in chapter 3 in order to understand the full impact of substitutes in evaluating industry attractiveness. For example, in the pharmaceutical industry, there are fewer substitutes than in the beverage or automobile industry.

Competitive Rivalry

The more competitors in an industry, the lower the differentiation between competitors, and the larger the excess industry capacity, the more likely the industry will engage in intense competitive rivalry. More intense competitor rivalry tends to lower prices and margins and raise marketing expenses in the battle to attract and retain customers. The net effect is a less attractive competitive environment in which the profit potential is lower.

The personal computer industry is an industry that is becoming increasingly more competitive due to price rivalry. The market has attracted many competitors with considerable capacity. In addition, product differentiation among personal computer products has become minimal. These factors, along with slower market growth, have intensified competition. By contrast, the pharmaceutical industry has fewer competitors for specific drugs, and product differentiation is much greater. As a result, the pharmaceutical industry is less likely to engage in intense competitive rivalry.

Prisoner's Dilemma

Intense competitive rivalry can evolve into what is known as a *prisoner's dilemma*.[3] In such situations, downward price moves by one competitor force "follower moves" by other competitors in order to minimize lost profits. Actually, all competitors would be better off if none cut prices to begin with.

Consider the example presented in Figure 6.3. The current scenario with both the business and its competitor holding price yields a total contribution (margin per unit multiplied by unit volume) of $40 million. If the competitor cuts price by 5 percent and the business holds price, the business will lose two share points and $8 million in total contribution. Of course, if the business were to lead with a price cut against a competitor who did not follow, the business could gain two share points and $2.0 million in total contribution. The worst effect of the prisoner's dilemma occurs when one competitor cuts price and the other matches that price in order to minimize losses. As shown in Figure 6.3, this combination results in no share gain or loss and a total contribution $5 million lower than when the two competitors both held at the higher price.

COMPETITOR BENCHMARKING

Although selecting competitive environments that favor profit potential is an important aspect of competitive analysis, it has been shown that it is equally important for businesses to develop a strong competitive position in the markets in which they compete.[4] To understand the degree to which a business has a position of competitive advantage, we need to engage in a detailed analysis of competitors. An important question is "Which competitors should a business analyze?" We want to maintain a very broad market definition to include all meaningful competing substitutes, but, at the same time, a business cannot engage in a detailed analysis of every competitor.[5] Thus, we need a mechanism to help us identify a relevant competitor set that will help us prioritize which competitors to analyze and benchmark.

Business's Marketing Strategy	Competitor's Marketing Strategy	
	Hold Price	Cut Price 5%
Hold Price	Market Share = 10% Volume = 1 million units Price = $100 per unit Margin = $40 per unit Total Cont. = $40 million	Market Share = 8% Volume = 800,000 units Price = $100 per unit Margin = $40 per unit Total Cont. = $32 million
Cut Price 5%	Market Share = 12% Volume = 1.2 million units Price = $95 per unit Margin = $35 per unit Total Cont. = $42 million	Market Share = 10% Volume = 1 million units Price = $95 per unit Margin = $35 per unit Total Cont. = $35 million

Figure 6.3 ◆ **Performance Impact of Price Rivalry and Prisoner's Dilemma**

Benchmark Competitors

There are a variety of ways to identify a business's competitors. Perhaps the best is to have customers evaluate the degree to which they consider competitors as interchangeable substitutes. The closer customers perceive two competitors to be, the more likely they are to switch from one to the other. Likewise, the more dissimilar customers perceive any pair of competitors to be, the less likely they are to switch from one to the other. In addition, customers can rate each competitor on the basis of how far that competitor is from their ideal product or supplier. From these customer perceptions we can create a *perceptual map,* which is very useful in gaining a better understanding of both competitive position and key competitors to benchmark.

Perceptual mapping is a technique used to capture customer perceptions of competing products or services.[6] Without specifying criteria for evaluating differences between competing products, customers are simply asked to rate the degree to which they perceive each pair of competitors to be *different* from one another. For example, in the luxury car market, the Volvo 700, Mercedes 420, BMW 525, Lincoln Towncar, Buick Regal, and Honda Prelude are competing substitutes. As shown in Figure 6.4, the Volvo 700 and BMW 525 were rated very close in *perceived similarity,* whereas the Lincoln Towncar and Honda Prelude were rated as very dissimilar.

By asking customers to also rate each car shown with respect to how close it is to their *ideal* car, we can gain a better understanding of competitive position and key competitors. In the example presented in Figure 6.4, the customer ratings of the cars shown relative to the ideal car produced two different segments. There were two different sets of customer needs and product preferences operating in this sample market. The ideal car for segment A is almost equidistant from the Honda Prelude, Buick Regal, BMW 525, and Volvo 700. Thus, these four competitors would be the most likely choices for customers in segment A. If you were on the marketing team for Buick Regal, you should view Honda, Volvo, and BMW as your key competitors in serving segment A, even though Mercedes and the Lincoln Towncar are equally close to the Buick Regal. However, if Buick Regal were more interested in serving segment B, then Lincoln Towncar and Mercedes would be their competitors to benchmark.

A variety of multidimensional scaling programs can be used to create a perceptual map,[7] such as the one shown in Figure 6.4. In this example, a graphical representation of interbrand differentiation was created in two dimensions.[8] In most applications, over 90 percent of competitor differentiation can be captured in two dimensions. With a perceptual map of competition, a business can easily discern two things: (1) which competitors it will compete against in a particular market segment and (2) its competitive position relative to these competitors in attracting and satisfying customers in this segment. However, to improve or maintain a position relative to competitors and the customer's ideal car, a business must also know on what basis target customers are differentiating competing products.

Competitor Analysis

Once a business has identified which competitors it should benchmark, the business now has to engage in a more detailed analysis of these competitors. A competitor analysis such as this is difficult to conduct and something a business may do only periodically.

Competing Alternatives	◄——————— Degree of Perceived Differentiation ———————►										
	Very Similar									Very Different	
Mercedes–Volvo	0	1	2	3	4	5	(6)	7	8	9	10
Mercedes–Towncar	0	1	(2)	3	4	5	6	7	8	9	10
Mercedes–Prelude	0	1	2	3	4	5	6	7	8	(9)	10
Mercedes–Buick	0	1	2	3	4	5	(6)	7	8	9	10
Mercedes–BMW	0	1	2	(3)	4	5	6	7	8	9	10
Mercedes–Ideal A	0	1	2	3	4	5	(6)	7	8	9	10
Mercedes–Ideal B	0	1	(2)	3	4	5	6	7	8	9	10
Volvo–Towncar	0	1	2	3	4	5	6	(7)	8	9	10
Volvo–BMW	0	1	2	(3)	4	5	6	7	8	9	10
Volvo–Buick	0	1	2	3	(4)	5	6	7	8	9	10
Volvo–Prelude	0	1	2	3	4	(5)	6	7	8	9	10
Volvo–Ideal A	0	1	(2)	3	4	5	6	7	8	9	10
Volvo–Ideal B	0	1	2	3	4	(5)	6	7	8	9	10
Towncar–Prelude	0	1	2	3	4	5	6	7	8	9	(10)
Towncar–BMW	0	1	2	3	(4)	5	6	7	8	9	10
Towncar–Buick	0	1	2	3	4	5	(6)	7	8	9	10
Towncar–Ideal A	0	1	2	3	4	5	6	7	(8)	9	10
Towncar–Ideal B	0	1	(2)	3	4	5	6	7	8	9	10
BMW–Prelude	0	1	2	3	4	5	6	7	(8)	9	10
BMW–Buick	0	1	2	3	4	(5)	6	7	8	9	10
BMW–Ideal A	0	1	2	3	4	(5)	6	7	8	9	10
BMW–Ideal B	0	1	2	(3)	4	5	6	7	8	9	10
Buick–Prelude	0	1	2	3	4	(5)	6	7	8	9	10
Buick–Ideal A	0	1	(2)	3	4	5	6	7	8	9	10
Buick–Ideal B	0	1	2	3	(4)	5	6	7	8	9	10
Prelude–Ideal A	0	1	2	3	(4)	5	6	7	8	9	10
Prelude–Ideal B	0	1	2	3	4	5	6	7	8	(9)	10

Perceptual Map

Figure 6.4 ◆ Customer Perceptions of Interbrand Differentiation

However, a market-based business with a strong market orientation is *gathering competitor intelligence all the time* and, as a result, has continuously evolving competitor profiles from which to evaluate its own competitiveness and competitive advantages.[9]

Competitor Intelligence

A great deal of competitive intelligence is public and readily available from dealers, trade press, business press, industry consultants, trade shows, financial reports, industry reports, general press, government documents, and customers.[10] However, unless a business has created a market-based culture in which everyone in the organization is an *information gatherer,* the more valuable and difficult to find sources of competitive intelligence will slip by unnoticed.

In today's growing information age, information on markets and competitors is becoming rapidly more available. For example, the reference librarian at Multnomah County Library in Portland, Oregon, was challenged to see how much competitor intelligence he could gather in one hour. Five questions were posed with respect to the Merix Corporation, a small circuit board manufacturer. Outlined in Figure 6.5 is a summary of the competitive information and sources used to answer the questions posed. As shown, all five questions were adequately answered in one hour by a skilled person.[11]

A Sample Competitor Analysis

Compaq Computer is the market share leader in the personal computer market. Although there are more than 150 competitors in the personal computer market, it is important for Compaq to understand its strengths and weaknesses relative to its two largest competitors, Dell Computer and Gateway Computer. Using publicly available information, Compaq can create a competitor analysis of these two benchmark competitors.

As shown in Figure 6.6, Compaq dominated both Dell and Gateway in five market-based performance measures in 1997. Particularly important was the fact that Compaq had over twice the marketing productivity (dollars of net marketing contribution per $1 of marketing budget). However, with regard to operating performance, Compaq followed Dell Computer in asset turnover, accounts receivable, and inventory turnover. This difference was largely due to a difference in marketing strategies; Dell and Gateway were direct marketers, whereas Compaq relied more on PC resellers to reach target customers.

The level of detail included in a competitor analysis can vary considerably from what is shown in Figure 6.6. In the example shown in Figure 6.7, the competitor analysis is broken down into two categories: *market-based performance* and *operating performance.* And, as shown, each area is further broken down into more specific performance metrics and then measured for the business and a benchmark competitor. In this example, the business has almost one-third of the market share of the benchmark competitor. This competitive gap corresponds closely with similar competitive gaps in number of distributors, number of distributor locations, and sales force coverage. To close its share gap, the business undoubtedly needs to address adverse competitive gaps in distribution and sales coverage.

Overall, the business is behind its benchmark competitor in most aspects of market-based performance. The competitive gaps shown help create performance targets and

> **Outlined below are the questions posed and the sources of information from which competitive intelligence was gathered in one hour by a research expert.**
>
> **1. How big is the circuit board market served by Merix, and what is its current market share?**
>
> The *Market Share Reporter* gives market size and share of hundreds of sectors in the economy, but Merix did not appear. *Predicast* provides market sizes and reference to *SMT Trends* (a trade journal) that reports the market share statistics of the top 10 circuit board producers, but not Merix. However, the *CorpTech Dictionary of Technology Companies* turned out to be the mother lode. It gives Merix's SIC (standard industrial classification) and lists other companies in that sector. From this information, an estimate of market size and share was computed.
>
> **2. Merix has been dependent on a few large customers. Is it adding to its customer base?**
>
> A search of a local newspaper uncovers an article "Merix Wants More Customers." It quotes the company as saying 70 percent of revenues come from its top five customers. Merix's most recent annual report also states that 69.3 percent of revenues come from four customers. In addition, the *SEC Edgar* Web site reports Merix's 10K and states that not much progress has been made in adding new customers to its customer base.
>
> **3. Develop a biographical profile of Merix's CEO and her approach to business.**
>
> Standard and Poor's *Register of Directors and Executives* provides a short bio on the CEO, Debi Coleman, and her e-mail address. The *Biography and Genealogy Master Index, Dun & Bradstreet Reference Book of Corporate Management, Who's Who,* and *Who's Who of American Women* provide no details. However, *Who's Who in Finance and Industry* provides a detailed resume.
>
> **4. Will Merix have a booth at any upcoming trade shows? If so, where and when?**
>
> *Trade Shows Worldwide* and the current editions of *Trade Show and Exhibits Schedule* and *Trade Show Week Data Book* provide the answers needed.
>
> **5. Merix hired a new chief operating officer. What biographical information is available?**
>
> *Predicast* reported that a chief operating officer was hired, and *Business Wire* press releases provided a bio on the new COO.
>
> Other sources considered but not used included *Business News Bank* (a CD-ROM database), *Business Index* (another CD-ROM database), *Value Line,* and *Red Chip Review.* Had time permitted, the *Manufacturers Register* (every state has one) and trade magazines would have been used.

Figure 6.5 ◆ A Competitor Information Search

management incentives to close these gaps. This, of course, is a key input into the development of a successful market-based strategy. From an internal perspective, this business is also poorly positioned in almost all areas of operating performance. Higher overhead costs and accounts receivable and lower return on sales per employee each lower profitability and productivity. Each of these gaps may be difficult to close, and competitors are not likely to help. Thus, to successfully close important competitive gaps, a business may have to go outside its industry to find better competitive practices.

Market-Based Performance	Compaq	Dell	Gateway	Advantage
Market Share: Desktops	15%	6%	5%	Compaq
Market Share: Portables	11%	< 5%	3%	Compaq
Marketing Budget (% sales)	8.6%	10.7%	12.8%	Compaq
New Marketing Contribution (millions)	$4,580	$830	$290	Compaq
Marketing Productivity	2.18	1.00	0.38	Compaq
Operating Performance				
Return on Sales	7.5%	6.6%	1.7%	Compaq
Return on Assets	12.6%	6.6%	1.7%	Compaq
Asset Turnover	1.7	2.6	3.1	Gateway
Days of Inventory	26	13	14	Dell
Days Accounts Receivable	43	37	69	Dell

Figure 6.6 ◆ **Competitor Analysis (1997): Compaq vs. Benchmark Competitors**

Competitive Benchmarking

Competitive benchmarking is a process developed initially at Xerox to improve its competitive position relative to key competitors. The idea is for a business to identify a key area of competitive weakness, such as billing errors in Figure 6.8, and then benchmark a com-

Dimension of Competitiveness	Business Performance	Competitor Performance	Performance Gap*
Market-Based Performance			
Market Share	6%	17%	11 behind
Relative Price	115	100	15 higher
Relative Product Quality	115	105	10 better
Relative Service Quality	93	113	20 worse
Number of Distributors	87	261	174 fewer
Sales Force (number)	36	60	24 fewer
Advertising & Promotion (% of sales)	0.5%	0.5%	0 equal
Marketing Budget (% of sales)	16.0%	17.0%	1.0 lower
Operating Performance			
Unit Manufacturing (% of sales)	48.0%	50.8%	2.8 lower
Direct Materials (% of sales)	26.0%	17.6%	8.4 higher
Overhead (% of sales)	38.0%	31.0%	7.0 higher
Return on Assets (%)	17.1%	19.5%	2.4 lower
Return on Sales (%)	7.4%	11.1%	3.7 lower
Asset Turnover	2.3	1.6	0.7 higher
Accounts Receivable (days)	46	38	8 higher
Sales per Employee	$1.5 mil	$2.1 mil	0.6 lower
* Performance Gap = Business Performance − Competitor Performance			

Figure 6.7 ◆ **Competitor Analysis for an Industrial Business**

Competitive Benchmarking	Xerox: Billing Errors
1. Identify a key area of competitive weakness.	1. Xerox found billing errors were more frequent than competitors.
2. Identify a benchmark company.	2. Xerox looked at Citicorp, AT&T, and American Express.
3. Track the benchmark company's process advantage.	3. With the cooperation of American Express, Xerox developed new systems to reduce billing errors.

Figure 6.8 ◆ Competitive Benchmarking: Xerox Billing Errors

pany, *outside* its industry, that is recognized as a *world-class performer* in this area.[12] In this way, a business can hope to gain access to the underlying processes that produce this *best practice* and develop a system that, when successfully implemented, has the potential of being better than that of its key competitors.

The first step in competitive benchmarking is to identify a key area of competitive weakness that affects customer satisfaction or profitability or both. For Xerox, a large number of billing errors was an annoying competitive weakness, as outlined in Figure 6.8. This was a source of considerable customer frustration and hurt overall perceptions of performance and customer satisfaction. The second step was to identify several companies that would be recognized as among the very best in the world in this area of performance. Xerox identified Citicorp, American Express, and AT&T. After talking with these companies, Xerox selected American Express and gained the cooperation of American Express in order to study its billing systems, which had a significantly lower error rate and many more transactions.

Once inside American Express, Xerox could observe the systems and processes that led to a more error-free billing system. This knowledge was transferred into several programs to begin the process of becoming more competitive in this key area of competitive weakness. Performance benchmarks were set in an effort to work toward decreasing billing errors. These efforts took time, but Xerox reached its goal and turned a competitive weakness into a competitive strength. Xerox had a similar success story in competitive benchmarking of order cycle time (the time it takes to deliver the product after the customer places the order), using L.L. Bean as a benchmark company.

COMPETITIVE ADVANTAGE

As a business begins to more fully grasp its position relative to key competitors, it can gain a better insight into potential sources of competitive advantage. For a source of relative advantage to be a competitive advantage requires (1) that the area of relative advantage be meaningful to target customers and (2) that the relative advantage be sustainable (not easily copied by competitors).

Wal-Mart, for example, has developed a low-cost advantage that has enabled it to attract and satisfy target customers by offering lower prices. Hewlett-Packard, by contrast, has built a differentiation advantage with product innovation and quality, and Nordstrom has built a differential advantage with service quality. Each attracts and satisfies customers with differentially superior products or services. Nike, on the other hand, has developed a marketing advantage with creative and aggressive marketing efforts and with retailing that attracts and satisfies target customers.

In each case, the business developed a source of competitive advantage that is meaningful to target customers. It becomes an area they work on each day in order to sustain their level of competitive advantage. While there are potentially many areas of competitive advantage, the three primary areas are described next and in Figure 6.9.

- **Cost Advantage:** A significantly lower cost position from which to create lower prices while still achieving desirable profit margins.
- **Differentiation Advantage:** A meaningful differentiation that creates desired customer benefits at a level superior to competition.
- **Marketing Advantage:** A marketing effort that dominates the competition in sales coverage, distribution, or brand recognition, or some combination of the three.

COST ADVANTAGE

A business can achieve three different types of cost advantage, as outlined in Figure 6.9. It can achieve a lower variable cost per unit sold, a lower level of marketing expenses, or a lower level of operating and overhead expense. Each of these cost advantages is achieved in different ways.

Variable Cost Advantage

Businesses with a lower unit cost are able to achieve the same (or better) unit margin at lower prices than competing businesses. Unit or variable costs include manufacturing costs and variable costs associated with distribution, such as discounts, sales commissions, transportation, and other variable transaction costs. As demonstrated in Figure 6.10, a unit cost advantage relative to competition contributes to higher levels of profitability.

But how does a business achieve a low variable cost advantage? Volume is a key factor. Businesses with a substantial market share (volume) advantage can generally achieve a lower unit cost.[13] As volume increases, the cost per unit generally decreases. For example,

Figure 6.9 ◆ Major Sources of Competitive Advantage

Figure 6.10 ◆ Profit Impact of a Variable Cost Advantage

as demonstrated in Figure 6.11, the cost of cellular phone service decreases at the rate of 18 percent every time the volume of customers in a geographic market doubles. Thus, when a cellular business in a given market doubles its customer base from 400,000 to 800,000, the unit cost decreases by 18 percent. In this case, the business that attains the largest customer penetration (volume) achieves a lower unit cost.

A larger production volume allows for production and purchasing economies that lower the unit cost of a product, thereby creating a *scale effect*. With volume purchases,

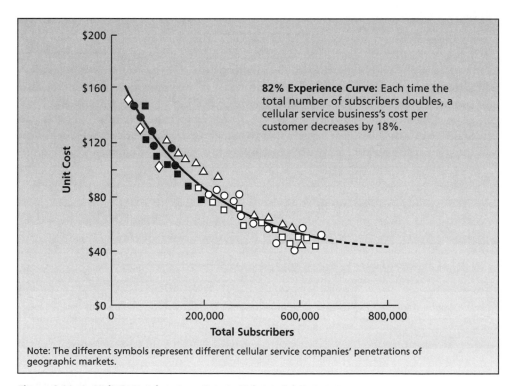

Note: The different symbols represent different cellular service companies' penetrations of geographic markets.

Figure 6.11 ◆ Unit Cost Advantage Due to Volume Advantage

Wal-Mart has been able to negotiate a lower cost of goods. The same scale effect would occur for a manufacturer who had twice the production capacity. For example, as Honda has moved from one level of production capacity to an increased capacity, there has been some reduction in unit cost due to a scale effect for certain component products, as illustrated in Figure 6.12.

Likewise, as a business adds products to its product line that have similar purchased materials and manufacturing processes, it is able to lower the average unit cost of all products. This is a *scope effect*. For Honda, the cost of ignition switches is lower because the same ignition switch components are used in cars, motorcycles, lawnmowers, all-terrain vehicles, snow blowers, snowmobiles, jet skis, and generators, as illustrated in Figure 6.12. In each case, the addition of another product line provides a volume-cost advantage across product lines for common component parts such as ignition switches, spark plugs, carburetors, and so on.

Finally, as a business builds more of the same product, there is a greater opportunity for *learning effects*. These are nonscale, nonscope effects that contribute to lower cost through process improvements that are the result of learning. Each unit produced provides additional learning and the opportunity to build the next unit more efficiently. Naturally, the business with more production experience has the best opportunity to learn from experience. This learning normally leads to improvements in processes that result in a lower cost per unit.

Marketing Cost Advantage

Quite often, businesses may not look beyond variable costs for sources of cost advantage. However, marketing cost efficiencies can be derived from product line extensions. For example, it takes a certain number of salespeople to adequately cover a target market. As the sales force is given more products to sell to the same customers, a *marketing cost scope*

Figure 6.12 ◆ Ignition Switch Cost Advantage Due to Scale and Scope Effects

effect is created. As illustrated in Figure 6.13, Procter & Gamble sales force expense per pound of soap detergent sold should decrease as more brands of soap detergent are added to its product line. A competitor with far fewer brands would have to have the same sales call frequency to adequately serve retailers and, therefore, would experience a higher cost per pound sold because it had fewer brands to sell.

Another area of marketing cost advantage is derived from the advertising cost efficiency of a brand extension strategy. For example, Campbell's Soup is the banner brand from which a whole line of soup brands has been created. Each time an individual soup is advertised, it is reinforcing top-of-the-mind awareness of Campbell's Soup and each soup in the product line. In this way, the scope effect created by additional soups should lower the advertising dollars spent per ounce of soup sold.

Operating Cost Advantage

Although an operating cost advantage is generally outside the control or influence of the marketing function, lower operating expenses relative to competitors contribute to a low-cost advantage. For example, Wal-Mart achieves an operating expense to sales ratio under 20 percent of sales; many of its competitors' operating expenses are well over 20 percent. This difference gives Wal-Mart another source of cost advantage from which to create greater customer value with lower prices and greater shareholder value with lower operating expenses.

Likewise, McDonald's has been able to cut the cost of construction of new McDonald's restaurants by 50 percent since 1990 by sticking to standardized building designs. Because the building is an asset that needs to be depreciated, this source of operating expense is drastically lower than it would be if each building had a unique design. Using a standardized design, along with rapid store expansion, has contributed to McDonald's earnings and shareholder value.

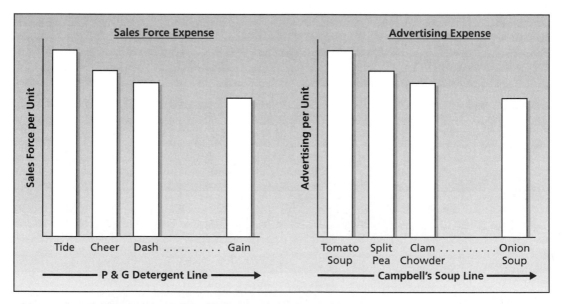

Figure 6.13 ◆ Product Scope and Marketing Cost Advantage

DIFFERENTIATION ADVANTAGE

Every business must manage its costs, but not every business can have a cost advantage. To achieve above-average profits, a business needs some source of competitive advantage. A differentiation advantage with respect to product, service, or brand reputation is a potential source of competitive advantage as outlined earlier. However, as do all sources of competitive advantage, a differentiation advantage has to be meaningful to target customers and sustainable (not easily duplicated by competitors).

Product Advantage

There are many aspects of a product around which a business can build a differentiation advantage. A product's durability, reliability, performance, features, appearance, and conformance to a specific application each has the potential of being a differential advantage.[14] For example, the ESCO Corporation is a manufacturer of earth-moving equipment parts that are used in very demanding mining and construction applications. The company has developed a differential advantage in the wearlife of its products due to proprietary steel chemistry and product design. The end result is that its products last longer and are less likely to break than are the products of its competitors. Both of these customer benefits save the customer money even when its products are sold at a higher price. Overall, businesses with a relative advantage in product quality produce higher levels of profitability, as illustrated in Figure 6.14.

Service Advantage

A business can achieve a differentiation service advantage in the same way it can achieve a differential product advantage.[15] The same baseline conditions are required: First, the service advantage has to be meaningful and important to target customers, and second, it has to be sustainable. FedEx tracks its performance each day on 10 service quality indicators (each weighed by the customer pain a failure creates). This service quality index is carefully monitored each day to help FedEx maintain a service quality advantage. As its

Figure 6.14 ◆ Profit Impact of a Differentiation Product and Service Advantage

service quality index improves, customer satisfaction improves and the overall cost per package decreases. Thus, on the days that its service quality is at its highest level, FedEx is able to create greater overall customer satisfaction with fewer errors, lower costs, and greater profits for shareholders. As shown in Figure 6.14, businesses with a service quality advantage produce higher levels of profitability.

Reputation Advantage

Another source of differential competitive advantage is brand reputation. Although competing watchmakers may match the quality of a Rolex watch, they cannot easily match Rolex's brand reputation advantage. Products such as Chanel, Nikon, and Perrier have built successful brand reputations that provide a source of competitive advantage in their ability to attract target customers. Their reputation or status adds a dimension of appeal that is an important customer benefit to many less price-sensitive, more image-conscious consumers.

A brand reputation advantage can be measured in the same way as a product or service differential advantage. We find that businesses with an advantage in brand reputation are able to both attract customers and obtain a price premium. As shown in Figure 6.15, the reputation of a consumer product or service can have a bigger impact on price premiums than a product advantage. Even in business-to-business markets, an advantage in brand or company reputation helps to support price and, hence, margins.

MARKETING ADVANTAGE

A business that dominates markets with a relative advantage in distribution, sales coverage, or marketing communications can control (and often block) market access. This is also a source of competitive advantage. Whether through sales and distribution or marketing

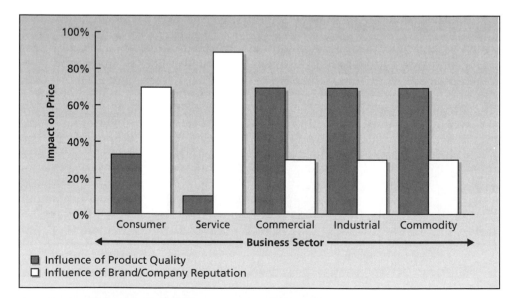

Figure 6.15 ◆ Price Impact of Relative Quality and Reputation

communications, Eastman Kodak, Procter & Gamble, Campbell Soup, and many others have developed a source of competitive advantage around their marketing expertise.

Channel Advantage

In all markets in which distribution is required for market access, there are a finite number of distributors, whether retailers in consumer markets or dealers in business-to-business markets. Furthermore, there are even fewer top-notch distributors. Therefore, a business that is able to dominate these distributors can control channels in a given market and, to some degree, control market access. This is a source of competitive advantage independent of cost or differential advantage.

Shown in Figure 6.16 is the relationship between distributor share and market share, along with the impact of market share advantage on profitability. What this suggests is that as a business is able to dominate the channels to market, it is able to achieve a higher relative market share. As shown, larger relative shares tend to correspond with greater levels of profitability.[16]

Sales Force Advantage

In both consumer and business-to-business markets, certain levels of sales call frequency and after-sale service are required. Because there is a limit to how many sales calls a salesperson can make in a given time period, a business with more salespeople will simply be able to reach and serve more customers. For example, on the basis of a certain call frequency and purchase behavior in a given industry, assume that the sales per salesperson is $2 million per year. If one business has 100 salespeople, it is able to achieve sales of $200 million. A business with 20 salespeople would achieve an estimated sales level of $40 million, assuming equal sales force capabilities and competitive products in terms of price and quality. Thus, the business with a sales force that is five times larger has a marketing advantage. For the competing business to neutralize this advantage, it would have to increase its sales coverage, assuming no change in price or differentiation advantage.

Figure 6.16 ◆ Indirect Distribution Outlet Share vs. Market Share

Brand Awareness

Nike has very good products with attractive prices. But what makes Nike a tough competitor is the level of market awareness and identity it has been able to develop with creative ad copy, pervasive promotion of the Nike swoosh, careful selection of product spokespersons, and heavy advertising. This level of competitive advantage makes it difficult for competitors who may in fact have a better product or lower price with comparable quality. Nike's name, logo recognition, and top-of-the-mind awareness make it easier for Nike to attract customers for existing products and to launch line extensions or entirely new product lines under the Nike name and logo.

This type of competitive advantage, like all others, is relevant only when the communications created are meaningful and important to target customers. To obtain and sustain a marketing communications advantage takes more than advertising dollars. It goes right to the core of market-based management. Who are our customers? What do they want? And how do we communicate our product in a way that best serves their needs?

SUMMARY

Competitive analysis is an important aspect of marketing strategy and market orientation. There are three primary dimensions to competitor analysis: industry forces, competitor benchmarking, and competitive advantage. The first aspect of competitive analysis is an analysis of industry forces. Industry forces such as competitor entry and exit, number of substitutes, buyer and supplier power, and competitive rivalry each affect profit potential. When the collective sum of these forces is favorable, the profit potential is greater. Thus, to obtain the best profit potential, a business needs to assess its industry forces.

Competitor analysis is a way of bringing all these sources of competitiveness together to help understand a business's competitive position in a given market. A complete competitor profile enables a business to better understand its key strengths and weaknesses. Quite often, a business may be overlooking several fundamental weaknesses in its competitive makeup. A competitor gap analysis is intended to expose these major weaknesses.

Often, a competitor analysis will lead to an area of weakness that needs to be further examined and better understood. Competitive benchmarking is a process in which a business identifies a business outside its industry that is known for excellence in a given area. By studying a world-class business, a business can hope to not only improve in its area of weakness but to also improve to the extent it could gain a competitive advantage over its competitors.

There are three primary sources of competitive advantage: cost advantage, differentiation advantage, and marketing advantage. A cost advantage in either variable costs, marketing expenses, or overhead expenses enables a business to price more aggressively in building customer value. Share leaders often have a cost advantage due to economies of scale, economies of scope, and experience curve effects. Niche businesses can also achieve a cost advantage with lower overhead and lower marketing expenses.

Differentiation is a second major source of advantage. An advantage in product quality, service quality, or reputation (image) provides a unique source of differential advantage. In

APPLICATION PROBLEM: NEWVECTOR CONSULTING

NewVector Consulting is a marketing consulting firm that helps client businesses develop a sustainable competitive advantage. NewVector Consulting specializes in industrial markets that serve business customers. An important part of NewVector's marketing consulting is its industrial business database. The database includes over 500 industrial businesses that report several measures of financial and market-based performance. As important, each business also reports its position relative to competition on cost, differentiation, and marketing. From this database, NewVector built the industry performance model shown above.

The numbers along each path reflect the relative impact of that variable. The profit impact of a business's competitive position is based on its sources of advantage that have a direct effect on financial performance and indirect effects that are derived from market-based performance. To estimate the profit impact of a business's competitive position, NewVector determines the business's relative competitive position with respect to cost, differentiation, and marketing and then estimates an index of financial performance using the model above.

$$\frac{Financial}{Performance} = 100 + \left[0.60 \times \frac{Cost}{Position}\right] + \left[0.20 \times \frac{Differentiation}{Position}\right] + \left[1.5 \times \frac{Market}{Performance}\right]$$

where:

$$\frac{Market}{Performance} = \left[0.40 \times \frac{Cost}{Position}\right] + \left[0.75 \times \frac{Differentiation}{Position}\right] + \left[0.90 \times \frac{Marketing}{Position}\right]$$

For example, assume that a business has a 30 percent cost advantage, no advantage with respect to differentiation, and is 10 percent behind competitors with respect to marketing. Using the model above and this information, NewVector can estimate an index of financial performance for the business.

$$Financial\ Performance = 100 + [0.60 \times 30] + [0.20 \times 0] + 1.50[(0.40 \times 30) + (0.75 \times 0) + (0.90 \times -10)]$$
$$= 100 + \quad 18 \quad + \quad 0 \quad + \qquad [1.50(12 + 0 - 9)]$$
$$= 122.5$$

A financial performance index of 122.5 means that the business should do 22.5 percent better than average with respect to financial performance. While this is important information to clients, NewVector adds value by pointing out to this business that it is giving up even higher levels of financial performance because of below-average marketing.

Questions

For Internet discussion, go to www.prenhall.com/phbusiness.

1. What would be the profit impact if the business matched competitors with respect to marketing position while maintaining its 30 percent cost advantage? What would be the impact of a 20 percent advantage in marketing position?

2. For each index of profit impact estimated in question 1, explain to senior management what portion of the financial performance was due directly to the business's cost advantage and what portion was due directly to market-based performance.

3. On the basis of NewVector's industry performance model, what level of differentiation advantage would a competitor with no marketing advantage need to equal NewVector's client financial performance of 122.5? Assume that the competitor would have no advantage or disadvantage with respect to cost position.

each case, a business with a differential advantage that is meaningful to target customers is in a position to charge more for its products and enhance profitability through higher margins. For markets in which service quality is more important than product quality, profitability is even greater. In some industries, particularly service industries, a business's reputation for quality has a very large impact on its price positioning.

A third major source of advantage is a marketing advantage. A business with a strong distribution system can control market access and limit competitors' ability to reach target customers. Likewise, a business with a large, well-trained, and well-supported sales force is able to better serve customers and respond more quickly to their problems or changing needs. This again is a considerable source of market-driven advantage. Finally, businesses that have a core competency in marketing communications are able to build and sustain market awareness and customer preference effectively and cost efficiently. Again, this is a tremendous source of advantage because these businesses will be able to more easily attract new customers and maintain a presence with existing customers.

MARKET-BASED LOGIC AND STRATEGIC THINKING

1. Why is competitor orientation an important element of a business's market orientation?

2. How could the industry forces for a regional phone company be different from the industry forces for a regional bank?

3. How will the industry change as competitors enter the regional phone market? How will profit potential be affected?

4. What impact would Procter & Gamble's everyday low price strategy have on competitive rivalry and the prisoner's dilemma?

5. How will the Internet affect competitor intelligence gathering? What traditional sources of competitor intelligence will most likely be available on the Internet?

6. What is the benefit of a competitor gap analysis? How would the results be used in strategy development?

7. When should a business do a competitive benchmarking study?

8. What are the benefits of competitive benchmarking?

9. Cost and differentiation are well-known sources of competitive advantage, but why is a marketing advantage also a potential source of competitive advantage?
10. What are the various ways a business can achieve a cost advantage?
11. Why do share leaders often have a cost advantage?
12. What areas of relative advantage does Wal-Mart use to drive its competitive position? How should Kmart and Sears drive their competitive positions?
13. Why are businesses with a relative advantage in either market share, unit cost, or product quality more profitable than businesses that have no advantage in any of those areas?
14. Identify for each area of differential advantage a business that uses this as a source of competitive advantage. Explain how each source of differential advantage helps the business attract and satisfy target customers.
15. Identify businesses that have developed different types of marketing advantage, and explain for each how this advantage affects profitability.
16. How could a business with a niche market strategy develop a marketing advantage as a source of competitive advantage?

NOTES

1. Michael Porter, *Competitive Strategy* (New York: Free Press, 1980): chapter 1.
2. Anita McGahan, "Industry Structure and Competitive Advantage," *Harvard Business Review* (November–December 1994):115–24.
3. Sharon Oster, "Understanding Rivalry: Game Theory," in *Modern Competitive Analysis,* 2nd ed. (Kinderhook, NY: Oxford 1994), 237–51.
4. George Day and Prakash Nedungadi, "Managerial Representations of Competitive Advantage," *Journal of Marketing* (April 1994):31–44; Richard Rumelt, "How Much Does Industry Matter?" *Strategic Management Journal* (March 1991):67–86; and Ralf Boscheck, "Competitive Advantage: Superior Offer or Unfair Dominance," *California Management Review* (Fall 1994):132–51.
5. Joseph Porac and Howard Thomas, "Taxonomic Mental Models of Competitor Definition," *Academy of Management Review* 15 (1990):224–40.
6. Hugh Devine Jr. and John Morton, "How Does the Market Really See Your Product?" *Business Marketing* (July 1984):70–79.
7. Donald Tull and Delbert Hawkins, *Marketing Research: Measurement and Method,* 6th ed. (New York: Macmillan, 1993):431.
8. Glen Urban and Steven Star, *Advanced Marketing Strategy* (Upper Saddle River, NJ: Prentice Hall, 1991):144.
9. Stanley Slater and John Narver, "Does Competitive Environment Moderate the Market Orientation–Performance Relationship?" *Journal of Marketing* (January 1994):46–55; and John Narver and Stanley Slater, "The Effect of Market Orientation on Business Profitability," *Journal of Marketing* (October 1990):20–35.
10. Leonard Fuld, *The New Competitive Intelligence—The Complete Resource for Finding, Analyzing, and Using Information about Your Competitors* (New York: John Wiley & Sons, 1995).
11. "Intelligence," *Oregon Business* (May 1988):28–32.
12. Robert Camp, *Benchmarking—The Search for Industry Best Practices That Lead to Superior Performance* (Milwaukee, WI: Quality Press, 1989); Kathleen Leibfried and C. McNair, *Benchmarking: A Tool for Continuous Improvement* (New York: Free Press, 1992); Jeremy Main, "How to Steal the Best Ideas Around," *Fortune* (October 9, 1992):102–6; Gregory Watson, *Strategic Benchmarking* (New York: Wiley, 1993); and Gregory Watson, *Benchmarking for Competitive Advantage* (Portland, OR: Productivity Press, 1993).

13. William Boulding and Richard Staelin, "A Look on the Cost Side: Market Share and the Competitive Environment," *Marketing Science* (Spring 1993):144–66.

14. David Garvin, "Competing on the Eight Dimensions of Quality," *Harvard Business Review* (November–December 1987):101–9.

15. Bradley Gale, *Managing Customer Value* (New York: Free Press, 1994):309.

16. Robert Buzzell and Bradley Gale, *The PIMS Principles: Linking Strategy to Performance* (New York: Free Press, 1987).

part III

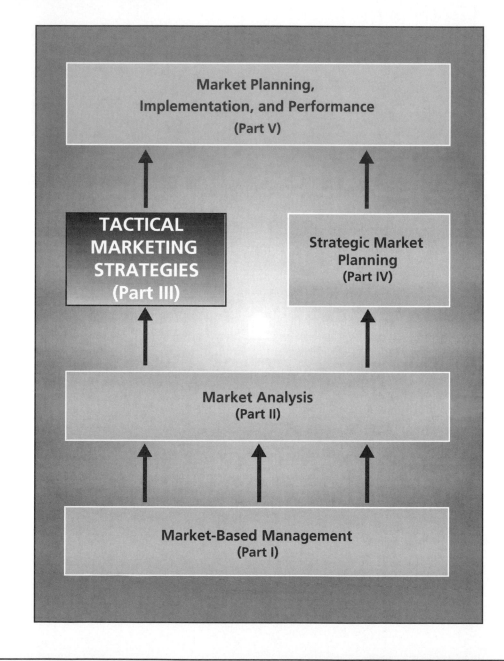

Market Planning,
Implementation, and Performance
(Part V)

TACTICAL
MARKETING
STRATEGIES
(Part III)

Strategic Market
Planning
(Part IV)

Market Analysis
(Part II)

Market-Based Management
(Part I)

Tactical Marketing Strategies

When it comes to pricing, most businesses simply check what the competition is charging or mark up their products or services by a standard industry margin or just use their intuition. They sacrifice a lot of profit that a shrewder pricing approach would provide.

—H. Simon

Businesses that lack a market orientation are more likely to price their products by simply checking the competition or marking up their costs to achieve a desired profit margin. There are good odds that these businesses will hurt their customer value, market share, and profit margins. A market-based business will set prices based on customer needs and the strength of its product position relative to competitors.

Part III focuses on short-run tactical marketing strategies designed around the marketing mix for a particular target market. The market analysis presented in Part II is a prerequisite for the development of a tactical marketing strategy because these strategies are built around market demand, the needs of a target segment, and within the context of a competitive environment.

Chapter 7 is devoted to product positioning, differentiation, and new product development, and chapter 8 presents alternative market-based pricing strategies. The combination of product and price creates a certain level of customer attractiveness for a business's product position. Without a strong marketing effort in terms of sales effort, distribution, advertising, and promotion, however, the share potential of a business cannot be fully realized. Chapter 9 examines the various marketing systems (channels and sales) that can be used to effectively reach target customers, and chapter 10 focuses on the role marketing communications play in delivering a successful tactical marketing strategy.

chapter 7

Product Positioning and Product Strategies

When the Loctite Corporation launched a product branded RC-601, management was confident that it had the potential to be a great success. RC-601 could be applied, shaped, and cured to repair worn or broken metal machine parts. In one customer test, one tube of RC-601 saved 800 hours of machine downtime.

Because production engineers were suspicious of using a gel-like substance to repair critical machine parts, Loctite's marketing strategy was to confront the production engineers' skepticism head on. Sales literature and advertising copy were created with great technical detail in order to convincingly document the strength and engineering characteristics of RC-601.

The pricing was also designed to be attractive and to not present a barrier to trial usage. Pricing RC-601 under $10.00 per tube, the new product team felt there should be little opposition to trying the new Loctite product. What more could the target customer want than an *inexpensive solution to machine downtime when a part breaks or needs repair?*[1]

Unfortunately, the RC-601 marketing strategy failed. After an extensive marketing effort, Loctite distributors were requesting refunds on RC-601 inventory that was not selling. Though the product was proven to work reliably, the market failed to accept it, even at an inconsequential price. RC-601 was removed from the market less than one year after its market launch.

After several months of internal speculation, a customer research project was designed to determine why customers rejected RC-601. This research uncovered the fact that production engineers were risk-averse and wanted proven solutions. The low price may have created even greater suspicions with regard to reliability and quality. Moreover, the customer research also revealed that the real target customer was the maintenance worker, not the production engineer or supervisor. Maintenance workers were more open to new ideas, preferred pictures of how things worked, and could purchase supplies such as RC-601 when they cost under $25.00. With this customer intelligence, a revised target market strategy was formulated around maintenance workers' *product* needs as well as their *personal* needs. Recognizing these needs, the company included the following changes in its revised product positioning strategy:

- RC-601 was renamed Quick Metal to better communicate the primary benefits of the product (speed and strength). Also, the advertising copy focused on "how to use" the product rather than on technical data.
- A new logo and new packaging were created that featured a metallic-colored tube and a box with bold lettering, as shown in Figure 7.1.

Figure 7.1 ◆ **Loctite's Product Positioning for Quick Metal**

- The price was modified to capture more of the economic value created by the product while keeping the purchase decision within the discretion of the maintenance worker.

The revised product positioning strategy was a huge market success. This success was based upon finding the right target customer and then building a product positioning strategy around the needs of that target customer. Thus, the first step in successful product positioning is to determine the appropriate target customers and to understand their needs, both product and personal.

PRODUCT POSITIONING

The cordless drill market is partitioned into five needs-based product segments, as illustrated in Figure 7.2.[2] At the low end are light-duty cordless drills, which are relatively low in power, torque, and endurance (time to a battery change). At the other extreme are heavy-duty power cordless drills, which are high in power, torque, and endurance. Sears has elected to position products in each of the price-performance segments. Black & Decker, on the other hand, has positioned itself in four of the five segments at much lower prices. DeWalt (a Black & Decker brand) is positioned higher than Sears in four of the five segments.

Although the Sears product positioning strategy covers all five price-performance segments, its relative position is not the same in all five segments. At the low-price end of the market (light duty), Sears is higher-priced than Black & Decker for roughly the same

Figure 7.2 ◆ Cordless Drill Product Line Positioning

performance. At the high-price end of the market (heavy duty power), Sears is priced just below DeWalt. In the midprice segments (medium duty, all-purpose, and heavy duty), Sears faces both brands. In these segments, Sears is rated and priced slightly lower than DeWalt. Black & Decker is rated and priced significantly lower in the all-purpose and heavy-duty segments.

PRODUCT POSITIONING AND MARKET SHARE

The goal of a positioning strategy is to create a product-price position that is attractive to target customers and creates a good source of cash flow for the business. Achieving a certain level of market share is a key factor in the success of a marketing strategy and directly dependent on the strength of a business's *product positioning* and *marketing effort.*

As shown in Figure 7.3, market share is represented as the business's product position multiplied by its marketing effort. Thus, a weak product position with a strong marketing effort will fail to deliver a desired level of market share. Likewise, an attractive product position that is supported with a weak marketing effort will also fail to achieve a desired level of market share. To be successful, a business needs both.

Also shown in Figure 7.3 are the various factors that contribute to a business's product position and marketing effort. Product differentiation, price, product breadth, new products, service quality, and brand image each contribute to the strength of a business's overall product position. As these inputs to product positioning outperform those of competitors, the strength of a business's product position increases and becomes more attractive to target customers. In this chapter, we will cover each of the inputs to product positioning shown in Figure 7.3. In chapter 8, we will focus on pricing strategies used to enhance a business's product position. Inputs to marketing effort include the sales force,

Figure 7.3 ◆ Product-Price Position, Marketing Effort, and Market Share

customer support, distribution, retailing, advertising, and sales promotions. The importance of each input to marketing effort varies from business to business, but the combination in any specific marketing situation is critical. Marketing effort and the inputs shown in Figure 7.3 will be addressed in chapters 9 and 10.

PRODUCT MANAGEMENT STRATEGIES

To create an attractive product position and achieve a desired level of market share and profitability requires several ongoing product management efforts. The first is very basic. Who is our target customer? What is our positioning strategy? Will the positioning strategy create a superior value for target customers? For a particular target price, a business needs to develop a position based on either a low price or some source of product positioning and differentiation that is meaningful to target customers. As shown in Figure 7.4, a differential advantage could be built around some combination of price, product, service, and brand.

A second important area of product management is product line strategies. How broad should the product line be? How should products be positioned in the product line in order to maximize customer attractiveness and profitability? To what degree

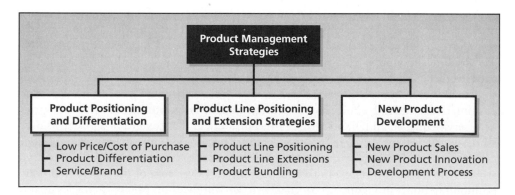

Figure 7.4 ◆ Core Elements of Product Management Strategy

should product line additions be extensions of the core brand? And when should we bundle or unbundle products in order to attract and satisfy target customers? From a core product positioning strategy, these types of product line strategies need to be developed in order to fully leverage a business's capabilities and profit potential.

And finally, no business can survive without continuous improvement of its existing products and the development of new products. How do new product sales contribute to sales growth? To what degree does a competitive advantage in new product sales contribute to sales growth? How does a market-based business discover new product ideas? And what process is used in developing new products that create both a superior value for target customers and a desired level of profit for the business? The impact of new product sales on product positioning and market share is important in retaining current customers and attracting new customers. The remainder of this chapter is devoted to the three areas and specific topics identified in Figure 7.4.

PRODUCT POSITIONING AND DIFFERENTIATION

On the basis of target customer needs, a business must develop a product position that is in some way differentially superior to competitors' product positions. In a price-sensitive market, product positioning generally requires a lower price, because other sources of differentiation are not valued by target customers. For markets in which differentiation is possible and valued by target customers, a variety of strategies are possible. Product, service, and brand image differences that are meaningful to target customers and differentially superior to those of competitors each offer the potential to create a more attractive product position. Regardless of the product positioning strategy pursued, our goal is to create a customer value superior to that offered by competitors, as illustrated in Figure 7.5. The remainder of this section will be devoted to these product positioning and differentiation strategies.

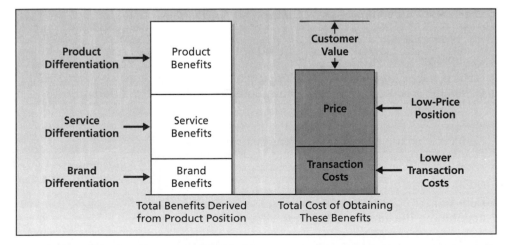

Figure 7.5 ◆ Differentiation and Customer Value

Product Differentiation

Many customers are not seeking the lowest price, and many are willing to pay a higher price for products that deliver important customer benefits. Differences in product quality, reliability, and performance can attract customers who are seeking products that perform better than average products. There are eight dimensions of product quality that can serve as bases for product differentiation.[3] These dimensions can be arranged into four hierarchical categories of product quality, as shown in Figure 7.6. If a business fails to deliver acceptable or expected levels of reliability and conformance, an advantage in other dimensions of product quality will not matter. At the other extreme, quality aesthetics as a source of differentiation is of value only when all other aspects of quality are met with respect to customer quality expectations.

Quality Killers Customers expect reliability and conformance to specifications. Whether they are buying a computer, an automobile, or a Boeing jet, customers expect the product to conform to the specifications that are basic elements of the product. For example, Nescafé creates different blends of coffee to match customers' taste preferences in different international markets. This is conformance to expectations (i.e., specifications).

Customers also expect products to operate reliably. Companies such as General Electric, Motorola, and Allied Signal have engaged in *six sigma* programs. At two sigma, a business with one million products would experience 40,000 failures. At six sigma, the failure rate drops to as close to failure-free as one could expect to get. GE has spent $1 billion to convert all its divisions to six sigma principles. Higher conformance to specifications and fewer failures enhance customer retention and are also raising GE profit margins.

Quality Drivers Performance and durability are the workhorses of product quality. Improvements in steering, braking, and fuel economy have been key aspects of im-

---

Quality Killers
Reliability: Time to failure or malfunction for a given product
Conformance: Incidence of defects that should not have occurred

Quality Drivers
Performance: Operational characteristics that distinguish product performance
Durability: Product life and ability to endure demanding use conditions

Quality Enhancers
Features: Number and type of options that can be added
Serviceability: Ease, speed, and cost of maintenance and repair

Quality Aesthetics
Appearance: The fit, finish, and appearance of a product
Reputation: The image created by the brand name or company

Figure 7.6 ◆ Dimensions of Product Quality

proved automobile performance. For example, BMW adds an extra coat of paint to its vehicles sold in Japan in order to meet the quality expectations of the Japanese luxury car buyer.

Manufacturers who cannot keep pace with performance improvements will simply lose market share over time. Those who can lead with improved product performance will have created a position on a basis of product differentiation and competitive advantage. Intel, for example, seeks to stay ahead of competitors by continuously improving its products. For over three decades, Intel has followed *Moore's Law: Every 18 months the operating performance per unit of space should double.* This pursuit of performance has enabled Intel to dominate the market it serves, with an 85 percent market share.

Durability is also a key component of product quality. Customers have expectations with respect to how long the product should last and how well it should stand up in normal usage. A business that fails to meet customer expectations with respect to durability will face difficulty in both attracting new customers and retaining existing customers. Durability is a common source of advantage in demanding industrial product use situations. For example, ESCO corporation is a specialty steel manufacturer that makes wear parts for front-end loaders and buckets for mining and construction applications. With proprietary steel chemistry and product designs, ESCO is able to offer customers greater product durability that extends the life of its products and reduces the incidence of breakage in extreme earthmoving applications.

Quality Enhancers   A product that meets customer expectations with respect to conformance, reliability, performance, and durability can be differentiated with enhanced quality features. Additional options that can improve the use, safety, or enjoyment of a product can be important sources of product differentiation. Air bags, automotive entertainment systems, cruise control, and navigation maps are examples of features that have been added to automobiles to enhance their quality. Features, as a source of differentiation, become more important as a business serves more affluent segments of the market. These customers often want more than the basic elements of product quality. They are seeking enhanced quality in the products they purchase.

Serviceability is another quality enhancer. Products that are easier to maintain and repair save time and money. The Saturn was engineered to make automotive repair easier and less time-consuming. The net result is lower repair costs. This design has also produced lower insurance costs due to lower-than-normal cost of repair in the event of an accident. Both lower the total cost of ownership for Saturn owners.

Quality Aesthetics   The appearance of a product and its reputation can also serve as sources of product differentiation. In Japan, the appearance of a product, or even of the package around the product, can have an enormous impact on the success of that product. For example, a British stereo manufacturer introduced its very high quality system into the Japanese market but failed because the box it was packaged in did not match the quality of the product it contained.

Likewise, the image a brand projects or reputation a company has established can be important in some markets. The quality of products such as Porsche, Rolex, and Chanel is judged not only on their functional characteristics but also on their aesthetic characteristics, which are derived from the image they project. A watch comparable on all seven other aspects of quality listed in Figure 7.6, but not made by Rolex, will fail to attract customers who value the Rolex name and the image it projects.

Service Differentiation

Nordstrom, FedEx, and Caterpillar are well-recognized businesses that have sought to attain a superior position in the area of service differentiation. Many competitors carry the same brand name products and can match the atmospheres found in Nordstrom stores. However, Nordstrom's positioning strategy has always been an unparalleled service advantage. This position of superior service differentiates it from competitors by creating a customer benefit that target customers find attractive. In this way, Nordstrom delivers a greater customer value to target customers.

For FedEx, the promise of "when it absolutely, positively has to get there" communicates its service position around reliability. And, as shown in Figure 7.7, reliability is one of the key dimensions of service quality.[4] The other service dimensions shown in Figure 7.7 are also important and may provide a good opportunity to build a service advantage in other business situations. For example, Caterpillar has sought to strengthen its competitive position and customer benefits with a differential advantage in responsive service. A 24-hour parts and repair service anywhere in the world has helped Caterpillar differentiate itself from competitors and create a valued service benefit for Caterpillar customers.

Brand Differentiation

In many consumer and business-to-business purchases, customers are influenced by the status of a brand name or by the assurance of a well-known company. Brands such as Lexus and Mercedes have strong associations with prestige or status. The importance of these brand benefits to many target customers enhances their positioning and differential advantage.[5]

Brand differentiation provides another way to position a business's products relative to competitors and to create incremental customer benefits and value, as illustrated in Figure 7.8. For example, Marriott estimated that adding its name to Fairfield Inn increased Fairfield Inn's occupancy by 15 percent. Kellogg found that in matched product tests, customer choice of corn flakes cereal increased from 47 percent, when the brand was not known, to 59 percent, when the Kellogg name was identified. And when Hitachi and a competitor jointly manufactured TVs in England, Hitachi sold its TVs at

Reliability:	Ability to perform the promised service dependably and accurately
Responsiveness:	Willingness to help customers and provide prompt service, and readiness to provide prompt service
Assurance:	Employee knowledge, courtesy, and ability to convey trust and confidence
Empathy:	Caring, individualized attention the business offers its customers
Tangibles:	Facilities that enhance service quality

Figure 7.7 ◆ Key Dimensions of Service Quality

Figure 7.8 ◆ Differentiation and Customer Value

a $75 price premium and achieved a higher market share.[6] Each of these examples illustrates the importance of brand benefits to target customers and the brand equity these brand reputations create for the business.[7]

A strong brand enhances positive evaluations of a product's quality, maintains a high level of product awareness, and provides a consistent image or brand personality. A strong brand, such as Coca-Cola, extends each of these positive customer evaluations to brand extensions that include Coke Classic, Diet Coke, Caffeine Free Coke, and Cherry Coke. Brand differentiation can be an important source of differentiation and extend the positioning benefits of a core brand to many closely related flanker brands. However, there are limits to brand extensions.[8] At some point, it may be necessary to create new brand names and build another area of brand equity as Coca-Cola did when entering the sports drink market with Powerade and the fruit juice market with Fruitopia.

Low-Price Position

Thus far, we have focused on the benefit side of differentiation. A business can also create a source of advantage with low price, and, hence, lower the cost of purchase. Businesses with a low-cost advantage in markets in which price is an important determinant of customer value can utilize a low price as a basis for product positioning. However, in these market situations, a business cannot ignore product, service, or brand issues. A business must still meet customer expectations in these areas, even though the strength of its product position is built around a more attractive price.

For example, Wal-Mart utilizes low prices to create an attractive position relative to competing retail stores. With a low-price positioning strategy, Wal-Mart must achieve a lower cost of buying, inventorying, and retailing the products it sells. This positioning strategy requires Wal-Mart to continuously find ways to contain or lower costs in order to maintain low prices as a source of competitive advantage while still meeting target customer needs for product, service, and brand. With this positioning strategy, Wal-Mart creates customer value and a competitive advantage by offering lower prices.

Gateway Computer and Dell Computer have positioned themselves with a lower cost of purchase by eliminating the retailer markup. Target customers who are price-sensitive can achieve greater customer value with lower prices by purchasing directly from these businesses but must give up the convenience and confidence of buying from a local retailer. Of course, using low price as a positioning strategy requires these businesses to pay attention to all aspects of achieving a low-cost position because they are not the only ones pursuing a low-price advantage. Gateway, for example, is able to achieve its low-price positioning strategy with a lower cost of operations by locating in South Dakota, where wage rates and taxes are low.

Lower Transaction Costs

The total cost of purchase also includes transaction costs, as shown in Figure 7.5. These are costs associated with the acquisition of a product. A business can build a low-cost advantage and customer value by lowering these nonprice costs of purchase. For example, American Hospital Supply found that $0.50 of every $1 a hospital spent to buy hospital equipment was spent on acquiring and inventorying the equipment. In response, American Hospital Supply devised a computerized ordering and inventory management system that would lower a hospital's cost of acquiring and inventorying equipment by 50 percent. In lowering these transaction costs, American Hospital Supply created a greater customer value and developed a source of advantage that enabled American Hospital Supply to grow to become the market share leader in this market.

PLUS-ONE PRODUCT POSITIONING

In most competitive markets, businesses are able to emulate the best features of competitors' products. As a result, it is difficult to stand out as unique. To succeed in these markets, a business needs some source of differentiation in order to build a unique product position. It needs to establish a plus-one product position.[9]

A plus-one product position is one in which a business can equal competitors on all areas of product and service quality and find one area of performance in which it is clearly superior. For example, Volvo, in the luxury car market, must meet customer expectations in all aspects of performance but uses safety as its plus-one product differentiation strategy. This is what makes Volvo uniquely different, and it is a central part of its product positioning and value proposition. On the other hand, Lexus uses performance as its plus-one strategy, and Mercedes uses its reputation.

PRODUCT LINE POSITIONING

The more products a business has to sell, the more ways it has to attract and satisfy potential customers. A broad line of products creates more selling opportunities for the sales force and channel partners. A business with a narrow line of products has to be more focused in order to be cost-effective in its marketing efforts.

Because a broad product line provides a business with more potential customers and the potential to sell more to each customer, this type of marketing efficiency translates into more sales and higher levels of profitability. For example, in Figure 7.9, we can see that businesses with broad product lines are more profitable during the emerging and growing stages of a product life cycle than are businesses with a narrow product line. Thus, it is particularly important to expand a business's product line during these stages of the product life cycle. This is exactly what Microsoft did in the 1980s and 1990s in growing the computer market.

Product Line Development

Quite often, a company will want to expand from one market segment into an adjacent segment in order to grow sales and profits. Product line expansion requires considerable product differentiation and careful positioning because the same company is now going to ask for a different price for a different combination of product, service, and brand benefits. Toyota sequentially expanded its product line from a very low product-price segment in the 1960s to the point where, today, Toyota offers a full line of automobiles, each with a different product-price position and unique brand name identity, as illustrated in Figure 7.10.

In the beer market, Anheuser-Busch's product line strategy utilizes separate brand names for each of the five beer marketing positioning strategy it has pursued, as outlined in Figure 7.10. Each brand has a distinct product-price position that is attractive to different types of customers or different use situations. In recent years, Anheuser-Busch

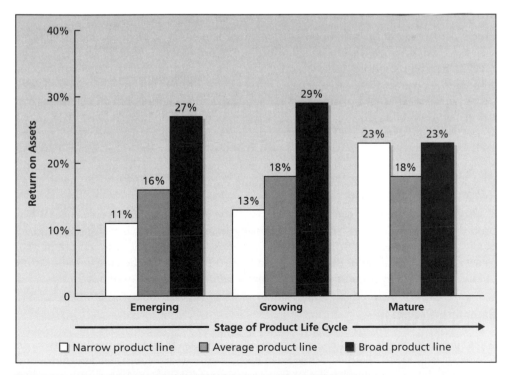

Figure 7.9 ◆ Breadth of Product Line and Return on Invested Assets

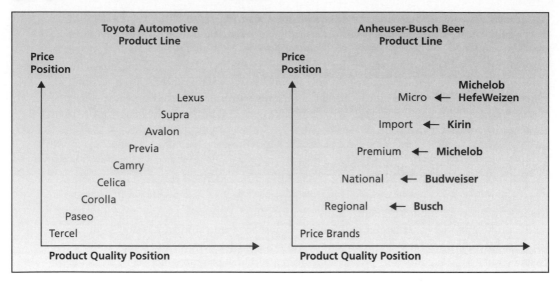

Figure 7.10 ◆ Product Line, Branding, and Differentiation Strategy

expanded its product line to the micro beer segment with the introduction of Michelob HefeWeizen, and it added Kirin to create an import brand position.

Product Line Extensions

Product line extensions offer important potential benefits to a business. First, the same sales force can often be used to sell additions to the product line. Second, manufacturing capacity can be more fully utilized and lower the allocated manufacturing overhead for all brands. These benefits can be derived with a product line extension that could include new brands or extensions of an existing brand. Procter & Gamble has an extensive soap and detergent product line, with over 20 separate brands (Tide, Cheer, Dash, Gain, etc.) as well as brand extensions (Tide, within the line). Although each brand may have size variations, each of the brands pretty much stands alone. On the other hand, Eastman Kodak has several consumer film products under the Kodak brand name (Kodak Gold, Kodak Royal Gold, Kodak Ektar, Kodachrome, etc.), each of which leverages Kodak's brand name, manufacturing capability, and sales force.

Product line extension strategies can also achieve greater advertising efficiency. When product line extensions are built off an existing brand name that is well known for its quality, the line extension or flanker brand achieves a faster rate of customer awareness. Likewise, the advertising of the flanker brand keeps the name of the core brand in front of customers, thereby lowering the cost of maintaining core brand awareness.

Umbrella Branding

An *umbrella brand* is the core product of a business such as Ivory (soap), American Express (credit cards), Betty Crocker (cake mix), Gerber (baby food), Kodak (film), and Johnson & Johnson (baby shampoo). From a consumer's point of view, the core product is the most visible embodiment of the brand name. Accumulated exposure and experience with the core product solidifies a certain image and quality expectation. Umbrella branding involves the transfer of quality perceptions derived from a core product or brand to product line extensions that use the same brand name. The intent of umbrella branding is to enhance the effectiveness of marketing programs and to increase demand for product extensions by transferring brand awareness and perceptions of quality from the umbrella brand.[10]

The purpose of brand and line extensions is to leverage the awareness and image of the flagship brand while, at the same time, not diluting its image or perceived quality. However, line extensions may not grow market demand and can cannibalize the core brand or other extensions while raising the total cost of marketing. Thus, careful product line accounting is needed to ensure that product line extensions are profitable and, overall, that they incrementally improve the profitability of the entire product line.[11]

Product Bundling

Bundling products serves to create a complete customer solution that has the potential to create a superior customer value and attract customers. Products such as living room sets, entertainment packages, and software offered with the purchase of computers are product bundles that have the potential to create a superior value (economic and perceived) for target customers. There are two approaches to product bundling.

A *pure product bundling* strategy involves the sale of two or more products at an overall price lower than the total price that would be paid if the products were purchased separately. Even when the products are offered individually at a discounted price that makes the total cost equal to the bundled purchase price, customers rate the bundled offering higher in perceived value.

A *mixed bundling* strategy offers the customer the opportunity to purchase each of the items separately at a sale price or bundled with an additional level of savings. There is evidence that when both options are available, customer perceptions of value exceed those produced with a pure bundling strategy.[12] In addition, a mixed bundling strategy has been shown to be more profitable than pure bundling strategies.[13]

Product Unbundling

Unbundling a set of products that is normally sold as an integrated bundle or system can also be desirable in attracting and satisfying customers. For many complex industrial and commercial purchases, customers may want to purchase individual products or components and integrate them into a certain configuration that best serves their needs.[14] In some instances, value-added resellers (VARs) fulfill this role. For specialized applications in architecture, agriculture, or chemical processing, VARs will purchase unbundled products and integrate them in a customized bundle that best suits the target customers' application. Hewlett-Packard may have a very attractive product bundle, but it cannot meet the specific needs of all customers. By unbundling and selling individual products or component products to VARs and systems integrators, HP has been able to create value for its customers and sales growth opportunities for the business.

In the early evolution of a market, customer needs are generally less fragmented than in the later stages, and bundled product solutions are often very attractive. However, as markets grow and new customers enter, segments of the market emerge, and more customized product solutions are needed to satisfy different customers.[15] As a market matures, unbundling often becomes more important in attracting and satisfying customers.[16]

NEW PRODUCT DEVELOPMENT

Why do some businesses seem to thrive on new product innovation and others struggle? If we look at those that thrive, such as 3M, Hewlett-Packard, and Procter & Gamble, we will find that these businesses have a strong market orientation. These businesses will start the new product development process with target customers and include their technical people in hearing customer needs and desires.[17] From the *"voice of the customer"* and the benefits they articulate, along with how well competitors serve their needs, a business must examine its capabilities and technologies. In this manner, technology and product development are market-driven.

New Product Sales

Over the past several years Hewlett-Packard has grown at the rate of almost $2 billion per year. During this period, HP has created additional revenues each year greater than the size of many Fortune 500 businesses. Underlying this phenomenal growth is a commitment to new product development and reduced time to market in the development process. Well over two-thirds of HP's revenues in any given year is the result of new products and upgrades of existing products introduced over the previous four years.

Whether product line extensions or entirely new products, their development and marketing are critical to the survival and growth of a business. Figure 7.11 demonstrates the importance of new product sales to sales growth. The higher the level of new product sales, the greater the real sales growth (growth with inflation removed). Furthermore, businesses that outperform their competition in new product sales achieve an even higher rate of real sales growth.

Commitment to Innovation

To achieve a high rate of new product development requires more than highly trained engineers. It requires a business culture that encourages and empowers all employees to engage in the process of new product development, and then rewards them for it. In a business culture where innovation is highly valued, the process does not start and stop as new products are developed; it is an ongoing process that cuts across functions of an organization. For example, 3M, well known for its product innovation, has established the following organizational guidelines.[18]

- **Vision:** Learn how work done today can be turned into a product tomorrow.
- **Foresight:** Make sure the market is ready for this new product innovation.
- **Ambitious Objective:** Strive for bold but attainable sales goals in four years.
- **Empowerment:** Allow all employees time to develop their own ideas.
- **Networking:** Encourage different job functions to combine their expertise.
- **Recognition:** Have an active program of recognizing quality and performance.

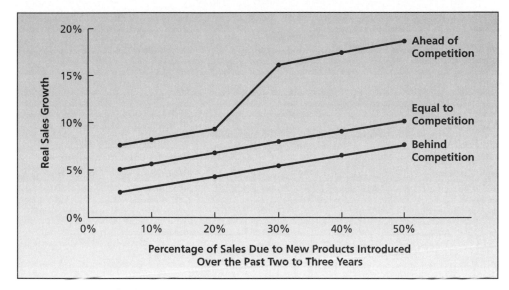

Figure 7.11 ◆ New Product Sales and Real Sales Growth

With these guidelines, 3M has developed many successful product innovations that range from Scotch Tape to Post-it Notes.

Development Process

The new product development process requires a combination of process inputs, design, and testing, and process outputs as outlined in Figure 7.12. Businesses that are able to manage this process efficiently are able to achieve a fast time to market and high levels of profitability, as noted in the following comment.

> There are significant economic rewards that stem from faster NPD (new product development). Earlier product introduction improves profitability by extending a product's sales life, creating an opportunity to charge a premium price, and allowing development and manufacturing cost advantages.[19]

Process Inputs   New product development has three important inputs: customers, competitors, and technologies, as illustrated in Figure 7.12.[20] From these inputs, a business needs to develop a new product that addresses the key benefits sought by consumers and is differentially superior to competing products.

For example, in the development of an improved microwave, Whirlpool began with customers and a series of customer interviews. The purpose was to gain insights into *what was important to microwave oven customers* and *what customers would like that they couldn't currently get in a microwave oven.* What Whirlpool found to be important to consumers was consistent cooking performance and ease of use. What customers also wanted, but could not get, was the *crispiness* that one gets in baking or broiling. To achieve crispiness, Whirlpool had to evaluate alternative technologies and select a combination that would yield customer benefits not available in competing products.

Figure 7.12 ◆ **New Product Development of a Microwave Oven**

New Product Concept Testing   Testing is an important step in the new product development process. Customer evaluation is critical. If customers do not value the new product offerings, a decision to go further could be an expensive mistake.

A customer trade-off analysis (described in chapter 4) is commonly used to determine how much customers value product benefits such as crispiness or ease of use in a new product concept. In this case, by varying these product features across three performance levels, along with three price levels ($150, $250, and $350), and three manufacturers (Kenmore, GE, and Whirlpool), Whirlpool could create a set of new product alternatives, as shown in Figure 7.13. One customer's ranking of these nine alternatives, shown at the bottom of Figure 7.13, would produce the preference curves shown in Figure 7.14. This result would suggest that this customer values crispiness and ease of use and would be willing to pay extra for a microwave that had those features.

Cross-Functional Teams   Designing a new product requires several critical cross-functional interrelationships to ensure that a product is developed that not only meets customer needs but also creates a value that is superior relative to competing products.[21] For this reason, businesses form cross-functional new product development teams. Teams facilitate understanding, leverage required skills, and coordinate efforts across the functions needed to bring a new product to market.[22] One of the advantages of using cross-functional teams is that it speeds up the time to market in the product development cycle.[23]

Komatsu, for example, requires that a cross-functional team consisting of at least one person each from engineering, manufacturing, and marketing make 50 customer site visits before a new product design is finalized. Each member of this team is a necessary link

Figure 7.13 ◆ Alternative Combinations of Product Features, Brand, and Price

in the successful development of a new product. As each hears from the customer first-hand, three important benefits result. First, because the information is real, and in the customer's own words, both the accuracy and credibility of the information are enhanced. Second, interviewers are able to ask questions to further clarify what the customer means and so can reduce the potential for misinterpretations and tell the customer of the benefits of alternatives of which, perhaps, the customer is unaware. And third, after the customer site visit, the team can discuss what they heard and better understand their role in the new product development process.

Process Outputs Throughout the new product development process, it is important to estimate the cost of each new product component and, ultimately, the unit cost of the whole new product. People in marketing need to set price levels and estimate marketing expenses needed to achieve a particular sales volume. At this point, a product is designed and priced to deliver a superior customer value. But will it achieve the desired sales vol-

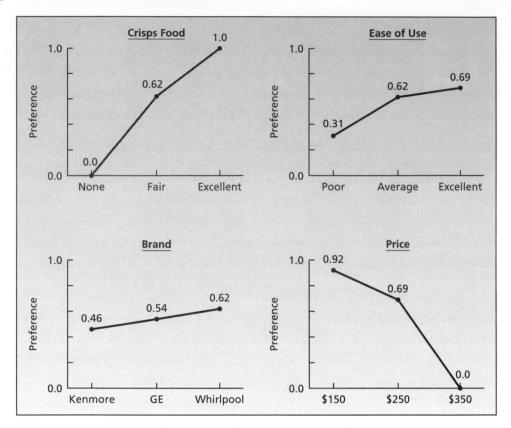

Figure 7.14 ◆ **Customer Preference for Different Customer Benefits**

ume and meet the profit expectations of the company? To answer that question, the team needs to combine all the price, cost, expense, and investment estimates to make a projection of profitability and assessment of risk.

If the new product design does not yield an acceptable level of profitability, there are only two options to consider. First, is there another way to lower the cost of the present product design without diminishing any of the customer benefits? And second, is there an alternative new product design (alternative combination of technologies) that will yield the same level of benefits and value but at a lower cost? If neither is possible, then the new product development project should be dropped. Raising the price to produce a desirable profit works for the profitability analysis but destroys the value created for customers. And with little or no customer value, it will be difficult to attract customers to this product and achieve a desired level of sales volume.

The process of developing a new product involves a complex combination of process, testing, and people. Process inputs and outputs, both internal and external, drive the new product development process. Throughout this process, we need to stay in touch with the customer. Staying in touch involves continual customer testing. And the process works only when people work well together. Each of these elements of the new product development process is critical to a new product's success.

SUMMARY

For any specific target segment, a business needs to develop a tactical marketing strategy that involves positioning its product with respect to products and price and marketing its product with respect to promotion and place. This chapter focused on product position and product strategies, but a successful marketing strategy requires a highly integrated mix of product, price, promotion, and place.

Product positioning and differentiation are key parts of a successful marketing strategy. How should a business position its products relative to customer needs and competitors? And what source of differentiation is needed to make this product position differentially superior to competitors' products? Low-price differentiation is an important position to develop for businesses serving price-sensitive markets. However, lowering the customer's transactions costs can also be a valuable way to achieve a low-cost advantage. For markets in which differentiation is possible, a business could build its differentiation around a product or package advantage, service advantage, or an advantage in brand reputation. To be successful, the differentiation underlying the positioning strategy must be meaningful to target customers and sustainable (not easily duplicated by competitors).

To grow, a business needs to leverage its product knowledge, production capabilities, marketing systems, and brand equity. Product line strategies provide an excellent oppor-

---

APPLICATION PROBLEM: APOLLO PRINTER

In 1999, Hewlett-Packard (HP) introduced the Apollo Printer, the first HP product ever not to carry the Hewlett-Packard name. The Apollo Printer was positioned for the under $100 ink jet printer market. Prior to this new product position, HP's lowest priced ink jet printer was $127. The under $100 ink jet market segment was 1.4 million units in 1998, 5 percent of the entire ink jet market. By the year 2000, this market was projected to have a market demand of 5.1 million units, 11 percent of the total ink jet market. HP's share of the total ink jet market in 1998 was approximately 50 percent.

HP's Apollo Printer strategy was in response to a market need and effort to protect the HP name and image. HP looked to companies, such as the Gap, that have successfully introduced new product positions such as Old Navy (see chapter 8, Figure 8.1). HP's strategy was to enter the under $100 price segment with innovative product designs that would differ considerably from traditional HP product designs.

Questions

For Internet discussion, go to www.prenhall.com/phbusiness.

1. If HP could hold a 50 percent market share in markets priced greater than $100, what would its overall market share be in the year 2000 if it did not enter the under $100 printer segment?

2. If HP is able to obtain a 50 percent share of the under $100 ink jet printer market by 2000, how much sales revenue will the Apollo Printer produce (assume an average selling price of $85)?

3. How will the Apollo branding strategy protect the HP brand name and minimize HP product line cannibalization?

tunity to grow and leverage current assets and expenses. Related product line extensions that are built off an existing brand or a new brand are important ways to achieve profitable growth. Brands that are well known for above-average quality create a basis from which to create flanker brands. One has to be mindful of sales cannibalization, damaging the image of the core brand, and the diminishing returns of adding a number of brands. Product bundling and unbundling are also product strategies that can enhance customer attractiveness in certain customer markets.

Finally, new product development is an essential part of market-based product management. Without new product success, a business's long-run survival is in question, as is its short-run ability to grow the business. The higher a business's percentage of new product sales, the higher its level of real sales growth will be. And when new product sales are also a source of relative competitive advantage, even higher rates of sales growth are achievable. A market-based business should manage the new product development process on the basis of three important areas of input: customer, competitor, and technology. The goal is to develop a new product that is responsive to an unfulfilled customer need in a manner that is superior to what the competition is offering. This market-driven goal requires technological input to develop such a new product. To be successful requires that the new product create a superior customer value and a desirable level of profitability.

MARKET-BASED LOGIC AND STRATEGIC THINKING

1. Why did Loctite's initial Quick Metal marketing effort fail?
2. How would you evaluate the product line positioning of Black & Decker relative to Sears in terms of customer choice and customer value? See Figure 7.2.
3. How does Compaq's product positioning strategy differ from IBM's?
4. How could a business with a very attractive product position achieve a lower market share?
5. What is Dell's source of customer attractiveness and differentiation? How does Compaq approach the same market?
6. How would a business use the eight dimensions of quality differentiation in developing a product and package differentiation strategy?
7. What is a plus-one product positioning strategy? Give an example of such a strategy and the value proposition used to communicate the business's plus-one advantage.
8. How does a business such as McDonald's develop a positioning strategy around some aspect of service differentiation?
9. Why would a brand name such as Kodak, Disney, or Coca-Cola create customer value and provide a basis for product positioning and differentiation?
10. Why would the occupancy of a Fairfield Inn increase by 15 percent when the Marriott name is added to the building?
11. What would a mere extension of a line of related products contribute to higher levels of profitability?
12. What is the marketing logic that underlies Anheuser-Busch's product line and bundling strategy for the beer market?
13. What are the advantages of a product strategy involving a strong core brand with flanker brands? Under what conditions would this product line strategy fail?
14. How would bundling help the sale of computers, software, and printers from three different manufacturers? When would it be better to offer these products unbundled?

15. To what degree do new product sales affect real sales growth? How does this relationship change when a business has a competitive advantage in the area of new product development and sales?

16. How did Whirlpool approach the development of a new microwave oven that offers a crisping feature? What had to happen to make this new product a success?

17. How are cross-functional teams likely to contribute to the successful development of a new product? Why is a cross-functional team likely to shorten the new product-to-market cycle time?

NOTES

1. Bill Abrams, "Consumer-Product Techniques Help Loctite Sell to Industry," *Wall Street Journal* (April 2, 1981).

2. "Drills for All Reasons," *Consumer Reports* (November, 1997):24–28.

3. David Garvin, "Competing on Eight Dimensions of Quality," *Harvard Business Review* (November–December 1987):101–5.

4. Valarie Zeithaml, A. Parasuramon, and Leonard Berry, *Delivering Quality Service* (New York: Free Press, 1990): chapter 1.

5. Bradley Gale, "Creating Power Brands," in *Managing Customer Value* (New York: Free Press, 1994), 153–74.

6. Peter Farquhar, "Managing Brand Equity," *Marketing Research* (September 1989):24–33.

7. David Aaker, *Managing Brand Equity: Capitalizing on the Value of a Brand Name* (New York: Free Press, 1991).

8. Daniel Sheinin and Bernd Schmitt, "Extending Brands with New Product Concepts: The Role of Category Attribute Congruity, Brand Affect, and Brand Breadth," *Journal of Business Research* 31 (1994):1–10.

9. G. Moore, *Inside the Tornado* (New York: HarperCollins, 1995).

10. T. Erdem, "An Empirical Analysis of Umbrella Branding," *Journal of Marketing Research* (August 1998); 339–51; David Aaker, *Building Strong Brands* (New York: Free Press, 1995); P. Dacin and D. Smith. "The Effect of Brand Portfolio Characteristics on Consumer Evaluations of Brand Extensions," *Journal of Marketing Research* (May 1994): 229–42; A. Rangaswamy, R. Burke, and T. Oliver, "Brand Equity and Extendibility of Brand Names," *International Journal of Research in Marketing* (March 1993):61–75.

11. Bruce Hardle, "The Logic of Product-Line Extensions," *Harvard Business Review* (November–December 1994):53–62.

12. Manjit Yadav and Kent Monroe, "How Buyers Perceive Savings in a Bundle Price: An Examination of a Bundle's Transaction Value," *Journal of Marketing Research* (August 1993): 350–58.

13. William Adams and Janet Yellen, "Commodity Bundling and the Burden of Monopoly," *Quarterly Journal of Economics* (August 1976):475–98; and Richard Schmalensee, "Gaussian Demand and Commodity Bundling," *Journal of Business* 57(1984):211–30.

14. Lynn Wilson, Allen Weiss, and George John, "Unbundling of Industrial Systems," *Journal of Marketing Research* (May 1990):123–38.

15. Roger Best and Reinhard Angelmar, "Strategies for Leveraging Technology Advantage," in *Handbook on Business Strategy* (Boston: Warren, Gorham, and Lamont, 1989):2-1–2-10.

16. Barbara Jackson, *Winning and Keeping Industrial Customers* (Lexington, MA: Lexington Books, 1985); and Michael Porter, *Competitive Advantage* (New York: Free Press, 1985).

17. Peter Bloch, "Seeking the Ideal Form: Product Design and Consumer Response," *Journal of Marketing* (July 1995):16–29.

18. W. Coyne, *Training* (3M Corporation).

19. N. Karagozoglu and W. Brown, "Time-Based Management of the New Product Development Process," *Journal of Product Innovation Management* 10, no. 3 (1993):204.

20. John Hauser and Don Clausing, "The House of Quality," *Harvard Business Review* (May–June 1988):63–73.

21. Roger Calantone, C. Anthony di Benedetto, and Sriraman Bhoovaraghavan, "Examining the Relationship between Degree of Innovation and New Product Success," *Journal of Business Research* 30(1994):143–48.

22. John Narver and Stanley Slater, "The Effect of Market Orientation on Business Profitability," *Journal of Marketing* (October 1990):20–35.

23. C. Ittner and D. Lacker, "Product Development Cycle Time and Organizational Performance," *Journal of Marketing Research* (February 1997):13–23.

chapter 8

Market-Based Pricing and Pricing Strategies

The Gap is well known for its product positioning as expressed by its merchandise, pricing, locations, and advertising. However, the customers and needs served by the Gap are limited. As the Gap grew sales and profits through expansion of a successful market focus, it also reached a point of diminishing returns. In response, the Gap developed new product positions at both higher and lower prices.

As shown in Figure 8.1, the Banana Republic enables the Gap to reach a higher-priced, more fashion-oriented segment with an array of higher-quality products at higher prices. Old Navy, on the other hand, steps down in price to better serve another price point with more basic products. The combination of these three market-based positioning and pricing strategies has enabled the Gap to grow both sales and profits.

MARKET-BASED VS. COST-BASED PRICING

The Gap uses market-based pricing: a price developed around target market needs and price sensitivity. However, many businesses use cost-based pricing: a price based on variable costs and a desired level of profit margin. For example, in the early nineties,

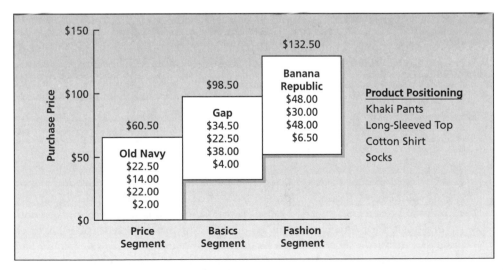

Figure 8.1 ◆ The Gap's Market-Based Pricing

Cost-Based Pricing	Market-Based Pricing
Compute cost of all parts and labor to build a personal computer.	Each cost center develops plan to meet target cost.
↓	↑
Add on to the total cost a 40 percent margin to determine Compaq's price to retailers.	Deduct from the Compaq price to retailers a 30 percent margin to determine total product cost.
↓	↑
Retailers buy at Compaq's price and add (markup) 15 percent for their retail price.	Deduct from the street price an amount equal to a 15 percent retailer markup.
↓	↑
Market Price for a Compaq Computer	**Market Price** set by market forces

Figure 8.2 ◆ **Compaq Computer's Cost-Based vs. Market-Based Pricing**

Compaq Computer used cost-based pricing, as described below and illustrated in Figure 8.2.

> In the past, product designers totaled up the cost of the features they wanted on the machine, figured out which sole supplier provided each part at what price, and added on a margin of 40 percent. This was the price to dealers, who typically added another 15 percent markup.[1]

A shift to market-based pricing drastically reshaped Compaq's pricing process, as described below:

> Now the process is reversed. Managers must decide what they want the street price to be, based on competitive factors. Then they must assume a dealer markup, subtract a gross profit margin—about 30 percent today—instruct departments of materials, engineering, manufacturing, and marketing to resolve among themselves how to allocate the remaining costs to make the product.[2]

It may appear that market-based pricing is the preferred approach to pricing in a market-focused business, but there are situations in which cost-based pricing may be the better approach. What is the same in both cases is the inputs to a pricing strategy. As outlined in Figure 8.3, the process starts with customers, competitors, and positioning. On the basis of different combinations of these three fundamental inputs, a business might pursue either a market-based or a cost-based pricing strategy.

MARKET-BASED PRICING

Market-based pricing starts with customer needs and the benefits a product creates relative to competitors' products.[3] On the basis of customer benefits, price is set relative to competition to create a superior value. In this way, price is set in the market, not at the factory or in the financial department. The goal of market-based pricing is to create a price that delivers a superior value. As discussed in chapter 4, this value could be real in terms of *economic value* or a *perceived value* based on differences between perceived benefits and perceived costs.

Figure 8.3 ◆ Pricing Strategy Process Template

Economic Value Pricing

By considering the total cost of ownership incurred by target customers, a business can price its product to produce an attractive savings (economic value). For example, in Figure 8.4, the price of a business's product is higher than the price of the competitor's product, but the customer's total cost of ownership is lower. The business saves the customer money on the basis of lower acquisition, use, and maintenance costs over the life of the product.

The level of economic value and price are set relative to what is an attractive savings to customers, not on the cost of manufacturing and marketing the product. The cost and margins are the business's problem, not the customer's. Customers are interested in savings or economic value, and the higher the savings, the more attractive the business's product. Chapter 4 discusses in detail the various ways a business can lower the cost of ownership and, hence, achieve higher price levels while still creating a superior value for target customers.

Perceived Value Pricing

Some customer benefits are more difficult to quantify in terms of economic value, yet they have an important perceived value. Another approach to market-based pricing is *perceived-value pricing*. As illustrated in Figure 8.4, the perceived benefits derived from the product, service, and brand (image or reputation) yield a certain level of total perceived benefits. The overall perceived cost of purchase is made up of the price paid, the terms of purchase, and any transaction costs that contribute to the total perceived cost of purchase. The net difference between perceived overall benefits and cost is perceived customer value. In this example, the strength of the business's overall benefits enables it to

Figure 8.4 ◆ Market-Based Value Pricing

charge a price higher than the competition's (price premium) and still create a larger overall perceived value for customers. Chapter 4 provides a detailed discussion of how to measure perceived customer value and the various ways a business can improve its perceived benefits in order to obtain higher prices and still create a superior value when compared with competitors.

Segment Pricing

Market-based pricing starts with target customers, and the goal is to create a superior customer value, so it seems reasonable that segment price strategies would be developed in response to different segment product-price needs. Customers in different segments generally have different product needs and different price needs. A price-sensitive segment would be attracted to low price regardless of additional product or service benefits. A quality-sensitive segment may pay more for the extra benefits (product, service, or brand) they desire. Thus, the market-based price could be different for different segments within a market.

Let's consider the cellular phone market. There are many potential segments, but the three outlined in Figure 8.5 are typical of many cellular phone markets. Customers in the *field office* segment are heavy users who work away from the office. The *package plan,* which provides a fixed monthly cost for a wide range of usage, provides considerable economic value and cost certainty to businesses in the field office segment. Customers in the *time management* segment work at and away from their offices but use the cellular phone to manage their time, both business and personal. Their usage varies from month to month. A *flex plan* best fits their needs because it provides for usage discounts during periods of heavy use. Finally, the *personal* user is a nonbusiness customer with low usage. This

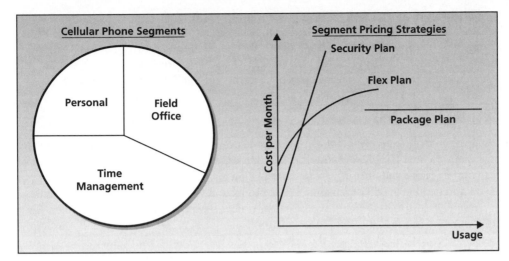

Figure 8.5 ◆ **Cellular Phone Market-Based Segment Pricing**

user is sensitive to the cost of cellular phone service but likes the security and convenience a cellular phone offers. For this segment, a *security plan* offers a very low minimum monthly access fee but a higher usage fee. Because all three price programs are available to any customer, we would expect customers in the various segments to prefer the market-based pricing alternative that best fits their usage patterns and price sensitivity.

COST-BASED PRICING STRATEGIES

Market-based pricing starts with the customer, competition, and a business's competitive position, as illustrated in Figure 8.2. In this manner price is set in the market to create a desired level of customer attractiveness and delivered customer value. In contrast, cost-based pricing starts with the cost of the product and a desired margin. On the basis of these requirements, a price is set and the product is sold to channel intermediaries who mark up the price to a level that allows them to achieve a desired margin. This, of course, is the price the customer sees in the marketplace, as illustrated in Figure 8.2. In markets where product differentiation is minimal, cost-based pricing is often a reasonable alternative to market-based pricing.

Commodity Pricing

In commodity markets, cost-based pricing strategies are often necessary. In these markets, competitors face the same cost of supply. Products are priced with normal industry markups and are adjusted on the basis of competitor price strategies. Because the products are designed, built, and delivered to a required specification, the purchase decision is made primarily on the basis of price. Cost and margin need to be managed closely in light of competing prices in order to obtain market share and be profitable. Even in these markets, it is important to know how competitors price. A pure cost-based pricing strategy could result in over- or underpricing a product.

Oil companies, for example, buy crude oil, process it, and sell it to gas station retailers. As the cost of oil goes up, they adjust their prices upward. As the cost of oil goes down, some competitors will lower prices to build volume, and others will follow to maintain market share. Thus, in this situation, cost is a primary driver of prices, and pricing decisions are made on the basis of cost, margins, and competitors' prices.

Cost Leader Pricing

A business with a cost advantage can price more aggressively in an attempt to build market share and volume. Higher volume further contributes to a lower cost position because of economies of scale and learning effects. Formosa is a low-cost producer of resins and can price below competitors in order to maintain large production volumes and a lower cost per unit.

Although cost leader pricing is cost-based, it does have market-based implications. Cost leader pricing can lead to prices so low that not many businesses can survive. For example, in the integrated circuit market, the price of DRAMs (Dynamic Random Access Memory) follows a steady decline as a function of cumulative output,[4] as shown in Figure 8.6. To remain price competitive, businesses in this market have to remain cost competitive.

Competitive Bid Pricing

Cost-based pricing is also used in competitive bid markets. In such markets, bidders are prequalified and bids must meet product specifications and delivery dates in order to be considered. Of those meeting the required specifications, suppliers are selected on the basis of the lowest price. For example, in the corporate purchase of personal computers, product features are specified, bidders qualified, and price bids submitted. In 1998, Dell Computer was successful in winning 50 percent of its bids. "Competitive bid" pricing is a cost-based pricing strategy designed for this type of pricing.

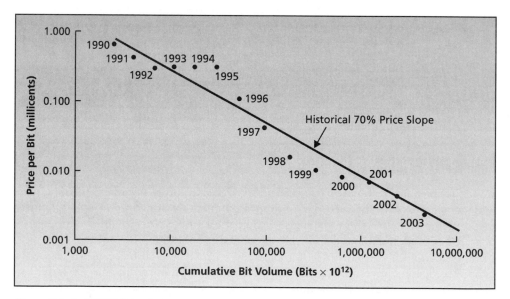

Figure 8.6 ◆ DRAM Price Curve

Shown in Figure 8.7 is a ratio of price to cost called the *bid ratio.*[5] Alongside the bid ratio is a history of winning bids that the company obtained at different bid ratios. For example, a bid ratio of 1.2 (price is 20 percent over cost) resulted in winning bids 63 percent of the time. The probability of actually winning is also a function of the number of bidders. In this example, there are two bidders, and the probability of winning a bid with a 1.2 bid ratio is 0.40. The profit at this price level is $1 million, and the expected value, based on the probability of a winning bid, is $400,000. In this case, a bid ratio of 1.2 (with two bidders) is also the best cost-based price because it provides the highest expected value. Thus, in a given year, if the business bid 100 contracts in competition against one other bidder, and used a 1.2 bid ratio, it would achieve the best level of overall profitability for the year. Of course, as the number of bidders increases, the probability of winning decreases, and a lower bid ratio would be needed in order to maximize profits.

On the basis of this logic, we might expect a business to always use a certain cost-based price bid ratio, but this is not the case. For example, consider an aerospace contractor that is using a 1.2 bid ratio but has won more bids than expected and is now approaching full manufacturing production capacity. For the next bid, this contractor might purposely bid higher, knowing the chances of winning are lower. However, if the bid was won, it would be at a higher profit level and it would be worth the extra cost needed to complete another job while at full capacity. The opposite might also be true. If that contractor's capacity utilization is very low, it may bid below the optimal bid price to improve its odds of winning. In these instances, volume is needed, and the business may forgo higher profits in exchange for a better chance of obtaining a certain volume of work.

REFERENCE PRICE AND PRICE STRATEGY

A market-based price is set relative to the price of competing products. When a business's price is lower than the competitor's, the business can use a competitor's price as a reference point to enhance the likelihood of customer purchase.

Bid Ratio	Percentage of Winning Bids	Probability* of Winning	Profit of Winning Bid (millions)	Expected Value	Cost-Based Pricing Logic
0.90	100	1.00	−$.05	−$500,000	A price
1.00	92	0.85	0	0	20 percent
1.10	80	0.64	+$.50	+$320,000	higher than cost
1.20	63	0.40	+$1.0	+$400,000 ←	offers the best
1.30	21	0.04	+$1.5	+$60,000	long-run
1.40	3	0.00	+$2.0	+$0	profitability.

$$* \text{ Probability of Winning} = \left(\frac{\% \text{ Winning Bids}}{100\%}\right)^{\text{No. of Bidders}} = \left(\frac{63\%}{100\%}\right)^2 = 0.40$$

Expected value = 0.40 × $1 million = $400,000

Figure 8.7 ◆ **Cost-Based Competitive Bid Price Strategy**

On the other hand, if the business's price is higher than the competitor's price, the probability of customers' purchasing the business's product decreases.[6] What does a business do if its product is priced higher than competitors'? Although there are many potential strategies, one could set the reference price with respect to products priced at the next higher level along a product-price continuum. In this way, the reference price is higher for both the business and its competitors.

For example, consider two reference prices, one the lowest in a line of competing products and the other the highest. When the products are presented from the lowest-priced product to highest-priced, we create a situation with a low reference price. On the other hand, if we present the same products from the most expensive to the least expensive, we create a high reference price. Shown in Figure 8.8 is the average price paid, based on either a bottom-up (low reference price) or top-down (high reference price) product-price presentation. When the top-down approach is used and a higher reference price set, the average price paid is much higher.

Flagship Products

When a business has products at each point along the product-price continuum, it is difficult to set a reference price for products at the high end of the product line. In this situation, some businesses have developed *flagship products*. These are higher-priced, full-feature products that few customers are expected to buy. However, the presence of a flagship product creates an even higher reference price. In a study of VCR purchase preferences, a top-down presentation led to a preference for higher-priced VCRs. With the addition of a flagship product (an even higher reference price) the average price of the preferred VCR moved to an even higher price level.[7]

Thus, it is important to establish a high reference price in order to enhance customer purchase. In addition, businesses with a broad product line and many levels of price should present their product line from the top down. This approach creates a high reference price for the entire product line and enhances the probability that customers will purchase higher-priced products. Finally, it may be advantageous for price leaders to develop a flagship product in order to create a higher reference price.

Product Area	Bottom-Up Presentation (Low Reference Price)	Top-Down Presentation (High Reference Price)	Price Gain	Percent Gain
Electric Shaver	$20.58	$24.00	$3.42	16.6
After-Shave	2.28	3.56	1.28	56.1
Shirt	4.85	6.69	1.84	37.9
Sports Coat	39.85	44.64	4.79	12.0
Shoes	15.85	17.83	1.98	12.5
Blouse	7.37	49.27	1.90	25.8

Figure 8.8 ◆ Purchase Price and High vs. Low Reference Price Presentation

PRICE ELASTICITY AND PERFORMANCE

Market demand and market growth are often dependent on price level. At high prices, many customers simply cannot enter the market, as described in chapter 3. As the price of cellular phone services, CD players, and computers decreased, more customers entered these markets. In one sense, price regulates both the size of a market and how fast it will grow.

For example, Figure 8.9 shows how market demand for voice messaging (a telecommunications service) varies as a function of price. A business that wants to limit initial demand because of a lack of capacity to add the service may price the service at $5 per minute. This price produces an estimated demand of 9,000 customers in a particular geographic market. In addition, at this price, the price elasticity is –2.20, which means that for each 1 percent reduction in price, demand would grow by approximately 2.2 percent. Therefore, a 10 percent price reduction from $5 to $4.50 should yield a 22 percent increase in customer demand (from 9,000 to 10,980).

A business might continue to lower price to grow demand, but when the price elasticity reaches –1.0, the sales revenue will have reached its maximum. At this point, up or down price moves will result in lower overall sales revenue. This is the price point at which a nonprofit organization doing fund-raising events would be able to maximize the revenues received, if that is their objective. However, a business wanting to grow profits may price above or below this price point, at which *revenues,* not necessarily *profits,* are maximized.[8]

Inelastic Price Performance

As shown in Figure 8.10, when a price is inelastic, all aspects of performance are improved when prices are increased. Lowering price when it is inelastic will hurt sales, margins, and total contribution and increase unit volume, as presented in Figure 8.10. For

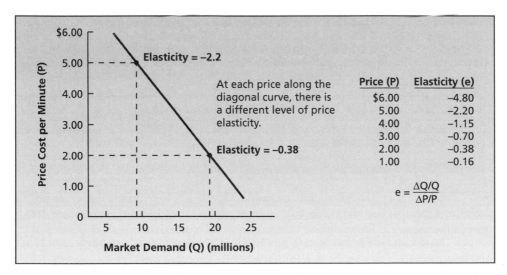

Figure 8.9 ◆ Voice Messaging Price Elasticity of Demand

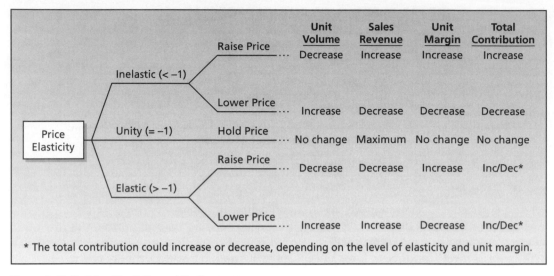

		Unit Volume	Sales Revenue	Unit Margin	Total Contribution
Inelastic (< −1)	Raise Price	Decrease	Increase	Increase	Increase
	Lower Price	Increase	Decrease	Decrease	Decrease
Unity (= −1)	Hold Price	No change	Maximum	No change	No change
Elastic (> −1)	Raise Price	Decrease	Decrease	Increase	Inc/Dec*
	Lower Price	Increase	Increase	Decrease	Inc/Dec*

Price Elasticity

* The total contribution could increase or decrease, depending on the level of elasticity and unit margin.

Figure 8.10 ◆ **Price Elasticity and Performance**

example, Yellow Page advertising is known to be price inelastic, with an elasticity of approximately −0.7. What would be the consequence of a Yellow Pages business lowering prices on its $100 ads by 10 percent? Assume that the business normally sells 1 million of these ads and that its variable cost is $50 per ad. The results are a unit margin of $50, sales revenues of $100 million, and a total contribution of $50 million, as shown below.

Current Price Situation

Price per Ad = $100	Variable Cost per Ad = $50
Ad Volume = 1 million ads	Margin per Ad = $50
Sales Revenue = $100 million	Total Contribution = $50 million

A decision to lower prices by 10 percent when the price elasticity is equal to −0.70 would produce the following performance:

Lower Price Strategy

Price per Ad = $90	Variable Cost per Ad = $50
Ad Volume = 1.07 million ads	Margin per Ad = $40
Sales Revenue = $96.3 million	Total Contribution = $42.8 million

As shown above, a decision to lower price by 10 percent when prices were inelastic lowered margins by $10 per ad, lowered sales by $3.7 million, and lowered total contribution by $7.2 million, even though volume increased. This would have been a disastrous pricing decision. A business that did not know that its price was inelastic could easily follow a strategy of lowering prices in response to competitors or customer concerns about price.

The correct strategy in this case would be to raise price, because the price is inelastic. A strategy to raise price by 10 percent when the price elasticity is −0.70 would produce the following estimate of performance:

Raise Price Strategy

Price per Ad = $110	Variable Cost per Ad = $50
Ad Volume = 0.93 million ads	Margin per Ad = $60
Sales Revenue = $102.3 million	Total Contribution = $55.8 million

As shown, this strategy would increase margins by $10 per ad, sales by $2.3 million, and total contribution by $5.8 million. Knowing the correct direction to move price improved this business's total contribution by 10 percent, while giving up 70,000 ads. Although there was a loss of unit market share (ads sold), dollar market share improved significantly.

Elastic Price Performance

Figure 8.10 also shows that price strategy is more difficult when prices are elastic. Although sales revenues will increase with a price cut and decrease with a price increase, the change in total contribution will depend on the level of price elasticity. Though a price may be elastic, it may not be sufficiently large to produce a volume increase large enough to more than offset the margin decrease created by a price cut.

For example, let's assume that the price elasticity for the same Yellow Page ad is -1.5. This is clearly an elastic price, and one that may lead many businesses to lower price to grow both unit volume and sales revenue. However, as shown below, a strategy to lower price by 10 percent would lower total contribution by $4 million.

Lower Price Strategy

Price per Ad = $90	Variable Cost per Ad = $50
Ad Volume = 1.15 million ads	Margin per Ad = $40
Sales Revenue = $103.5 million	Total Contribution = $46 million

A strategy to raise prices by 10 percent when the price elasticity is equal to -1.5 would yield less ad volume and less sales revenue but would produce higher margins and a larger total contribution.

Raise Price Strategy

Price per Ad = $110	Variable Cost per Ad = $50
Ad Volume = 0.85 million ads	Margin per Ad = $60
Sales Revenues = $93.5 million	Total Contribution = $51 million

Competitor Price Response

The question that keeps many managers awake at night is, "What will my competitors do in response to my price change?" If a business lowers price to gain share, and competitors follow, there is likely to be very little real share gain. And at reduced margins, with a limited increase in volume, total contribution is likely to go down. On the other hand, if a business raises prices to improve margins and competitors do not follow, the business could lose share and lower total contribution, even with higher margins.

In any given market, competitor response to price change is going to depend on a variety of supply and demand forces,[9] as outlined in Figure 8.11. As the supply and demand forces in Figure 8.11 align to the left, competitors are less likely to respond to a price cut.

	Competitor Response Elasticity		
	None	**Partial**	**Full**
Supply Forces			
Variable Cost Structure	High	_____	Low
Capacity Utilization	Full	_____	Low
Product Perishability	None	_____	High
Product Differentiation	High	_____	None
Competitor Financial Position	Poor	_____	Strong
Strategic Importance	Low	_____	High
Demand Forces			
Price Elasticity	Inelastic	_____	Elastic
Efficiency in Price Shopping	Low	_____	High
Customer Loyalty	High	_____	Low
Market Growth Rate	High	_____	Low
Complementary Products	None	_____	Important
Substitute Products	None	_____	Many

Figure 8.11 ◆ Forces That Help Shape Competitor Price Response

As these forces shift to the right, they will contribute to the likelihood of a full and fast competitor response to a price cut. Overall, there is generally a high degree of price interdependence among competing firms. One study showed that the average competitor price response elasticity was 0.71.[10] This means that if a business lowered its prices by 10 percent, it could expect competitors to follow with a 7.1 percent price decrease.

PRODUCT LINE PRICING

As a business adds more products to its product line, it enhances sales growth but also increases the chances of cannibalization of existing product sales. It is necessary to know both a product's price elasticity and the degree to which there is a cross-elasticity with other products. Products that have a *positive* cross-elasticity are *substitutes;* lowering the price of one product will decrease the demand for the other product. Products that have a *negative* cross-elasticity are *complementary* products; lowering the price for one product will increase the demand for both products. Because the margins may be different for alternative products in a product line, one has to give careful consideration to any price change to ensure that the total profits are increased for the entire product line.

Pricing Substitute Products

In extending the product line of a business, one has to recognize that there will be some cannibalization when one product in the line may be substituted for another. For example, a business that offers both Yellow Page advertising and direct-mail advertising would find that there is a cross-elasticity of demand between the two of approximately +0.80. This means that if the business were to raise the price of Yellow Page advertising by 10 percent, the demand for direct mail would go up an estimated 8 percent, assuming no change in direct-mail prices. The cross-elasticity between these products and other media, such as newspaper, television, and radio advertisement, is less than +0.3. Thus, the rate of product substitution based on price change is much less.

Figure 8.12 shows the price elasticities and market shares for nine competing laundry detergents as well as their cross-elasticities.[11] The results of this empirical study illustrate the price elasticity of each brand of detergent as well as the cross-elasticity of competing substitutes. As shown, cross-elasticities are much higher for higher-share brands.

Pricing Complementary Products

Of course, products that are complements will also be affected by price change. Software and printers are products that complement personal computers. Therefore, the demand for these products varies with the price of personal computers. If the cross-elasticity between PCs and spreadsheet programs were –0.6, then for each one percent change in the price of PCs, there would be a 0.6 percent change in the demand for spreadsheet programs. Thus, if computer industry prices decreased by 10 percent, the demand for spreadsheet programs should go up by 6 percent. Conversely, if the price of personal computers were to increase by 10 percent, the demand for spreadsheet programs would decrease by 6 percent.

PROMOTION PRICING

The average price elasticity for consumer products has been estimated to be –1.76.[12] Promotional price elasticities are much greater for the four product categories shown in Figure 8.13.[13] The overall average promotional price elasticity for these products is –8.3, approximately three times their average price elasticity.

A promotional price elasticity of –8.3 means that a price promotion of a 10 percent discount should produce an increase in demand of over 80 percent, on average. These product categories are very price-sensitive, and promotional pricing is common. However, promotional price elasticity varies substantially among brands and product categories, depending on differences in market share and promotional activity.[14]

Brand	Share (%)	Wisk	Tide	Surf	Era	Solo	Cheer	Bold-3	All	Fab
Wisk	22.7	–1.37	0.31	0.37	0.23	0.11	0.12	0.09	0.08	0.07
Tide	21.5	0.33	–1.39	0.37	0.23	0.11	0.13	0.09	0.08	0.07
Surf	19.5	0.48	0.46	–1.91	0.33	0.16	0.16	0.12	0.11	0.09
Era	13.5	0.36	0.33	0.39	–1.57	0.11	0.12	0.10	0.08	0.07
Solo	5.9	0.36	0.34	0.41	0.25	–1.78	0.13	0.11	0.10	0.07
Cheer	4.9	0.46	0.47	0.47	0.31	0.15	–2.20	0.12	0.13	0.09
Bold-3	4.4	0.49	0.44	0.49	0.34	0.18	0.16	–2.32	0.11	0.10
All	3.6	0.48	0.46	0.50	0.32	0.17	0.20	0.12	–2.36	0.10
Fab	3.6	0.50	0.50	0.49	0.33	0.16	0.17	0.14	0.12	–2.41
Elasticities: A 1 percent price change in the brand column creates the percent change in market share for each row of brands.										

Figure 8.12 ◆ **Price and Cross Price Elasticity of Competing Laundry Detergent Brands**

Product Category	Promotional Elasticity	Price Elasticity	Ratio of Deal to Price
Flour	−8.9	−2.1	4.2
Bathroom Tissue	−10.3	−3.2	3.2
Tuna	−8.7	−2.9	3.0
Margarine	−5.1	−2.8	1.9
Average	−8.3	−2.8	3.0

Figure 8.13 ◆ Price and Promotional Price Elasticities

Price Promotion Bundling Strategies

Price promotion bundling involves combining two or more complementary products and selling that bundle at promotion prices.[15] Consider a telecommunications company that offers a basic phone service along with the options of having voice mail and a hot line. Voice mail is priced at $5.50 per month and the hot line service at $5.00. The following table shows the maximum price each of four different customers would pay for each of these services and for both.

	Maximum Price Customers Will Pay (per month)		
Customer	Voice Mail	Hot Line	Both
A	$5.00	$3.50	$ 8.50
B	$5.50	$4.00	$ 9.50
C	$4.00	$5.00	$ 9.00
D	$3.50	$4.50	$ 8.00

Note that the current pricing strategy, with no bundling, attracts only one customer (B) to voice mail and only one customer (C) to hot line. The combined result is revenue of $10.50, as shown in Figure 8.14. Since each service costs the company $3.00 to provide, the total cost for both services is $6.00, and the gross profit is $4.50, as also shown in Figure 8.14.

Discount Price Strategy   A *discount price* strategy designed to attract all customers to at least one service would require a price of $5.00 per month for voice mail and a price of $4.50 per month for the hot line service. This strategy would attract both customer A and customer B to voice mail and customers C and D to the hot line service. This would result in total revenue of $19.00, a variable cost of $12.00, and a gross profit of $7.00, as shown in Figure 8.14.

Pure Bundling Strategy   A *pure bundling* price strategy would use the lowest total price a customer would pay for both services in an attempt to get all customers to buy both these services. Thus, the pure bundling price would be $8.00 (the price customer D would pay for the combination of services). A price of $8.00 per month should attract all four customers to buy both services. This would result in total revenue of $32.00, to variable cost of $24.00 and a gross profit of $8.00, as also shown in Figure 8.14.

Price Strategy	Price (per month)			Services Purchased	Sales Revenue	Variable Cost	Gross Profit
	Voice Mail	Hot Line	Both				
No Bundling	$5.50	$5.00	–	2	$10.50	$ 6.00	$4.50
Discount Only	$5.00	$4.50	–	4	$19.00	$12.00	$7.00
Pure Bundling	–	–	$8.00	8	$32.00	$24.00	$8.00
Mixed Bundling	$5.00	$4.50	$9.00	6	$27.50	$18.00	$9.50

Figure 8.14 ◆ Performance Impact of Price Bundling

Mixed Bundling Strategy A *mixed bundling* price strategy is designed to offer both discount prices and a bundled price at levels that will attract customers from each segment. Offering a discount price of $5.00 for voice messaging and $4.50 for hot line as well as a bundled price for both services of $9.00 accomplishes this objective. Customers B and C are attracted to the bundled price for both services since they are available at or below what these customers would pay for both. Customer A will find the bundled price of $9.00 is too high, but will purchase voice mail at the discounted price of $5.00. Customer D will also find the bundled price of $9.00 too high but will purchase the hot line service at the discounted price of $4.50. As Figure 8.14 illustrates, this mixed bundling price strategy will result in total revenue of $27.50 (less than pure bundling), but a gross profit of $9.50, highest of these alternative pricing strategies.

NEW PRODUCT PRICING

In competitive markets, new products need to be priced on the basis of customer needs and price sensitivity, product positioning (differentiation), and the likely competitive environment. In some instances, the strength of a business's product positioning relative to competition and the sustainability of that product-price position are strong enough to warrant a price premium and still attract customers. In other instances, the business may expect very aggressive price competition and diminished differentiation, and, in response, pursue a very aggressive low-price, high-volume new product-price strategy. There will also be instances in which a business may price at competitive levels as new competitors enter the market with modestly differentiated products.

Skim Pricing

In some situations, a business may hold a proprietary product advantage relative to competition because it holds a patent or the product has a unique capability. In such a case, the business may pursue a premium price strategy while still delivering superior customer

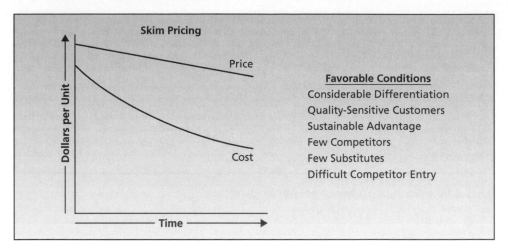

Figure 8.15 ◆ Skim Pricing

value until competition can match its source of competitive advantage. For example, many prescription drugs are patented. Under the protection of a patent, the holder may charge higher-than-normal prices. During this period, the business is able to create a *price umbrella* because the competition cannot match the business's relative advantage, as shown in Figure 8.15.

But under what conditions is a skim pricing strategy likely to work? As shown in Figure 8.15, when a business has a considerable, and sustainable, differentiation advantage in a quality-sensitive market that has few competitors and is difficult for competitors to enter, a *skim pricing* strategy is viable for new product pricing. When feasible, a skim pricing strategy allows a business to systematically penetrate markets as it adds production capacity. As the demand for a high-priced segment is saturated, price can be lowered to systematically attract more customers until prices reach a level affordable to most potential customers.

Penetration Pricing

At the other end of the price spectrum, a business may pursue a penetration pricing strategy in order to preempt competition and build a large share and volume advantage. For example, Compaq Computer was an early entry in the personal computer market. Compaq priced aggressively to build market share in a market where all computer manufacturers could offer the same product. In these instances, product differentiation is minimal, customers are price-sensitive, there are many competitors or substitutes, and competitor entry is easy, as outlined in Figure 8.16. The price leader can often both gain an early cost advantage with a large volume and charge lower prices, discouraging competitors from entering the market.

A cost leadership position can enable a business to use penetration pricing to build market share and discourage competition from either entering the market or staying in the market. In this situation, the share leader is simply further down the cost curve and is able to price at a lower level and still maintain a desirable contribution margin. Thus,

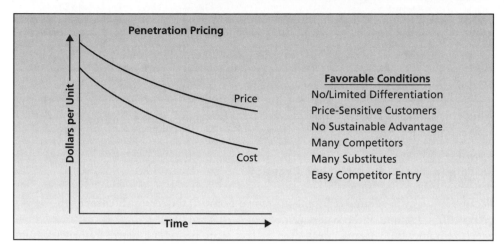

Figure 8.16 ◆ **Penetration Pricing**

when cost reduction is volume-sensitive and product differentiation is minimal, a penetration pricing strategy may be a viable path to market leadership and profitable growth.

PRICING STRATEGIES AND BREAK-EVEN ANALYSIS

Break-even analysis is generally viewed as an accounting concept, but it is extremely useful in evaluating the profit potential and risk associated with a pricing strategy, or any marketing strategy. The purpose of this last section is to examine, from a marketing viewpoint, the usefulness of break-even volume and break-even market share.

Price and Break-Even Volume

For a given price strategy and marketing effort, it is useful to determine the number of units that need to be sold in order to break even (produce a net profit equal to zero). For example, consider the situation shown next, in which a business produces a unit margin of $100 and incurs fixed expenses (marketing and direct operating expenses) of $9 million. It would take annual sales of 90,000 units to break even. Of course, if the manufacturing capacity were only 80,000 units per year, this project would result in a loss.

$$\text{Net Profit} \atop \text{(before taxes)} = [\text{Volume} \times (\text{Unit price} - \text{Unit variable cost})] - \text{Marketing} \atop \text{Expenses} - \text{Operating} \atop \text{Expenses}$$

$$0 = [\text{Volume} \times (\$200 - \$100)] - \$3 \text{ million} - \$6 \text{ million}$$

$$\text{Volume} = \frac{\$3 \text{ million} + \$6 \text{ million}}{\$200 - \$100} = \frac{\$9 \text{ million}}{\$100} = 90,000 \text{ units}$$

Break-even volume is the volume needed to cover fixed expenses on the basis of a particular margin per unit. Although break-even volume can be estimated graphically, as illustrated in Figure 8.17, it can be computed more directly with the following formula:

$$\text{Break-Even Volume} = \frac{\text{Fixed Expenses}}{\text{Margin per Unit}}$$

The lower the break-even volume is relative to manufacturing capacity or expected sales volume, the greater the profit potential.

Price and Break-Even Market Share

Because break-even volume is an unconstrained number, the reasonableness of the break-even volume requires additional considerations. Because market share is constrained between zero and 100 percent, break-even market share provides a better framework from which to judge profit potential and risk. To compute break-even market share requires only that we divide the break-even volume by the size of the target market, as shown next.

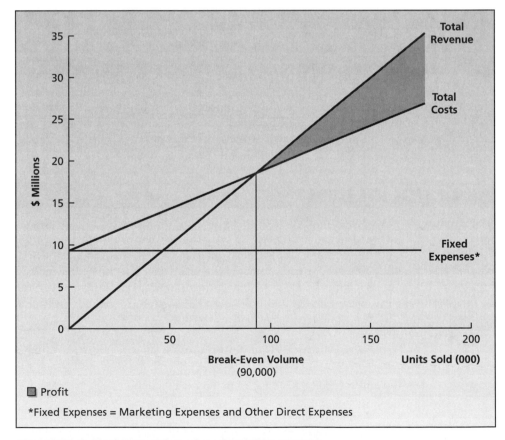

Figure 8.17 ◆ Break-Even Volume for a Given Price Strategy

$$\text{Break-Even Market Share} = \frac{\text{Break-Even Volume}}{\text{Market Demand}} \times 100$$

If the market demand for a product were one million units per year, then the break-even market share would be nine percent when the break-even volume is 90,000 units. If the business's target share is 10 percent, then the risk of a loss is greater because the break-even share is close to the target share. Or, put another way, this business decision would feel a lot better if the break-even share were three percent and target share 10 percent. In a situation in which the break-even share is higher than 10 percent, the assessment of profit potential and risk is very easy.

SUMMARY

Pricing is a critical part of customer value and business profitability. If prices are high, it is great for margins but could result in a low customer volume if perceived benefits are less than perceived price. In competitive markets where product differentiation is feasible, market-based pricing presents a pricing logic designed to deliver high levels of customer value and business profitability.

Market-based pricing starts with customer needs, competitors' positions, and the business's product positioning, and works backward to margin. By contrast, a cost-based pricing approach starts with the cost of the product and a desired margin and works forward to a market price. Cost-based pricing can lead to under- and overpricing in markets in which differentiation is possible. However, in markets in which differentiation is minimal and customers are price-sensitive, cost-based pricing can be a viable approach to pricing.

To enhance purchasing, a business could establish a reference price that is higher than the business's price position. This can be done by using competitors' prices, putting higher-priced products in higher-quality segments, ordering the presentation of a product line, or creating a flagship product with a very high reference price.

Product line price decisions are also complicated by cross-elasticity. The price elasticity of demand for a given product may signal a particular price strategy. When cross-elasticity exists between products, a business needs a more careful analysis of profit impact. The demand for products that are substitutes will change in the direction of the price change of the substitute. The demand for complementary products will change inversely to a price change in a complementary product.

Promotional price elasticities are much higher than nonpromotion price elasticities. The full profit impact of a price promotion requires a business to evaluate profit impact over a time span that includes periods before and after the price promotion. Forward consumer buying during a promotion, inventory depletion before a promotion by retailers, and forward buying by retailers lower demand in adjacent nonpromotional periods. This effect lowers the overall contribution of the promotional strategy.

New product pricing creates a unique opportunity to build a price umbrella and to skim price. Skim pricing works when the new product is highly differentiated, not easily copied, and sold to a quality-sensitive market, and when competitor entry and intensity are not serious threats. When the opposite conditions exist, a penetration strategy may be needed in order to build a cost advantage. Finally, because price affects margin and a certain level of fixed expenses is needed to achieve a certain level of market penetration, a

APPLICATION PROBLEM: MICROSOFT WINDOWS 95

In the late nineties, the U.S. government brought an antitrust lawsuit against Microsoft. Professor Richard Schmalansee, an economics professor at the Massachusetts Institute of Technology, defended Microsoft Windows' 90 percent market share. In his testimony, Professor Schmalansee provided the following insights:

Schmalansee disclosed that "the company had sold 125 million copies of Windows 95 for more than $7 billion—an average price of $56." Schmalansee also estimated "that if Microsoft could increase the price of Windows by 5 percent, it could raise its pretax revenues by $173 million. A 10 percent increase would earn the company an additional $345 million." Schmalansee asked, "Why would a profit-driven firm, not known for leaving money on the table, pass up such easy money?" "No one," he suggested, "could possibly conclude that Microsoft enjoys the quiet life of a monopolist."[15]

Questions

For Internet discussion, go to www.prenhall.com/phbusiness.

1. How many copies of Windows would Schmalansee estimate to be sold if Microsoft increased its price by five percent? How many copies would have been sold if Microsoft had raised the price 10 percent?

2. What is the price elasticity at a five percent higher price? At a 10 percent higher price?

3. On the basis of the estimated price elasticities, what would a monopolist do with respect to price?

break-even analysis is useful in assessing profit potential and risk. However, break-even volume, although a useful target, is not as useful in risk assessment as break-even market share. Because market share is constricted between zero and one (100 percent), it provides a relative index by which risk can be judged. Break-even market share enables a business to gauge profit potential and risk by the difference between target share and the break-even market share.

MARKET-BASED LOGIC AND STRATEGIC THINKING

1. How has the Gap addressed the price sensitivity of different clothing customers?
2. Why might GE Aerospace use cost-based pricing instead of market-based pricing in developing a bid for a U.S. Air Force contract?
3. How would an earthmoving equipment manufacturer with superior productivity price its product using economic value?
4. How would you approach pricing the Lexus sport-utility vehicle? What elements of perceived value would be important in developing a market-based price?
5. How does the three-segment–based price strategy for cellular phones described in the text contribute to the customer value in each segment?
6. Is Compaq pursuing a cost-based pricing strategy in the personal computer market? Why? What is the underlying pricing logic that supports Compaq's pricing strategy?
7. How would you advise a large shipping company to price requests for shipping?

8. How should a low-priced car manufacturer set its reference price? How would setting the reference price for an expensive luxury car differ?

9. Why do realtors generally first take you to homes that are more expensive than you can afford?

10. In 1998, Compaq Computer sold 12 million PCs at an average price of $2,500 with a 25 percent margin. What would the price elasticity have to be to allow the company to cut prices by 5 percent and increase total contribution?

11. If coffee and doughnuts were both price elastic and also cross-elastic complements, with the margin on doughnuts being much higher, how would you vary prices to increase overall profitability?

12. What factors would you want to consider in evaluating profitability if you were a beverage manufacturer and going to engage in a price promotion?

13. How would Dell Computer use competitive bid pricing in responding to an insurance company's request for a quote on 1,000 PCs of a certain type?

14. Which pricing strategy would you have recommended for Gillette's Mach3 razor: skimming, competitive, or penetration? What factors and assumptions influence your choice of new product price strategies?

15. Why is break-even market share potentially more valuable to a marketing manager than break-even volume?

NOTES

1. A. Cleland and A. Bruno, *The Market Value Process* (San Francisco: Jossey-Bass, 1996): 106; D. Kirkpatrick, "The Revolution at Compaq Computer," *Fortune* (December 14, 1992):80–88.

2. Ibid.

3. Michael Morris and Gene Morris, *Market-Oriented Pricing* (Lincolnwood, IL: NTC Business Books, 1990):93–100.

4. California Technology Stock Letter (February 4, 1999):4.

5. Thomas Nagle and Reed Holder, *The Strategy and Tactics of Pricing* (Upper Saddle River, NJ: Prentice Hall, 1995):199–206.

6. K.N. Rajendran and Gerard Tellis, "Contextual and Temporal Components of Reference Price," *Journal of Marketing* (January 1994):22–34.

7. Casey Donoho, "Purchase Price and Order of Price Presentation." Doctoral dissertation, University of Oregon, 1991.

8. Gerald Smith and Thomas Nagle, "Financial Analysis for Profit-Driven Pricing," *Sloan Management Review* (Spring 1994):71–84.

9. R. Dolan and H. Simon, *Power Pricing* (New York: Free Press, 1996):222–41.

10. J. Lambin, *Advertising, Competition and Market Conduct in Oligopoly Over Time* (Amsterdam: North Holland-Elsevier, 1976).

11. R. Bucklin, G. Russell, and V. Srinivasan, "A Relationship between Market Share Elasticities and Brand Switching Probabilities," *Journal of Marketing Research* (February 1998):99–113.

12. Gerard Tellis, "The Price Elasticity of Selective Demand: A Meta-Analysis of Econometric Models of Sales," *Journal of Marketing Research* (November 1988):331–41.

13. Robert Blattberg and Scott Neslin, *Sales Promotion Concepts, Methods, and Strategies* (Upper Saddle River, NJ: Prentice Hall, 1990):356.

14. Ruth Bolton, "The Relationship between Market Characteristics and Promotional Price Elasticities," *Marketing Science* (Spring 1989):153–69.

15. R. Dolan and H. Simon, *Power Pricing:* 222–45.

16. Ted Bridis, "Witness Says Price for Windows Cheap," *The Oregonian* (January 22, 1999):B2.

chapter 9

Marketing Channels and Sales Systems

The personal computer market is made up of many different types of customers, as shown in Figure 9.1. Each type of PC customer has distinct needs, buying behaviors, and purchase amounts. As a result, a variety of marketing channels has emerged. Dell Computer has exclusively used a *direct channel system,* which relies on a combination of a large direct sales force, a heavily advertised direct channel system, and on-line marketing, which is expected to be producing half of Dell's sales by the year 2000.

Compaq Computer, on the other hand, has a more complex channel system. Although Compaq uses *direct, mixed,* and *indirect channel systems,* it relies most heavily on its indirect and mixed systems. However, in response to customer needs and Dell's success with on-line marketing, Compaq added on-line marketing to its direct channel system. Although Compaq was the market share leader throughout most of the 1990s, to hold its share leadership position, Compaq has to be sensitive to customer needs and emerging channel preferences.

CHANNEL SYSTEMS

The combination of distribution channel and sales effort creates a particular channel system and way to reach a target customer. Both are necessary, and the two are interrelated. As a result, we will refer to any combination of channel and sales effort as a *channel system.* For Compaq Computer, several different channel systems (unique combinations of channel and sales efforts) were used to reach different target market customers, as outlined in Figure 9.1. Dell Computer used three direct channel systems. The objective of any combination of channel and sales effort is:

> A channel system that reaches the target customer's desired point of purchase, with the service level sought by target customers, while producing an effective sales opportunity for the business in a cost-efficient manner.

Given the trade-offs between customer reach, required services, sales effectiveness, and cost, a business must give careful consideration to a variety of alternative channel systems. If an acceptable level of performance on any one of these factors cannot be achieved, the channel system will most likely fail. Thus, an important part of marketing's responsibility is to evaluate alternative channel systems in order to develop the most customer-effective and cost-efficient channel system for a given target market.

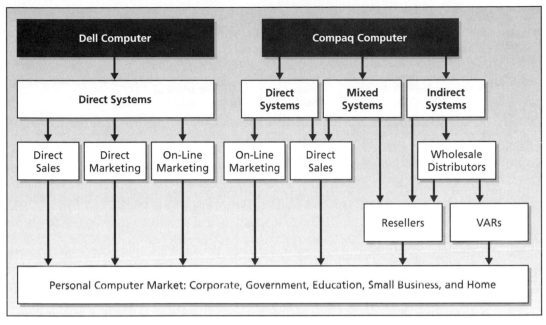

Figure 9.1 ◆ **Personal Computer Marketing Channels: Dell vs. Compaq**

There are three strategic benefits that motivate a business to effectively manage its channel systems:

- **Sales Growth:** Developing channel systems to reach and penetrate customer markets in order to create new sources of sales growth and profitability.
- **Competitive Advantage:** Building a channel system that creates an advantage relative to competitors, which makes market access or an equivalent marketing effort difficult for the competitors to achieve.
- **Customer Value:** Selecting and developing channel systems that enhance customer value in order to achieve higher levels of customer attraction, satisfaction, and retention.

Without an effective channel system, it would be difficult to build market share or to maintain a high market share position. A strong product position will not achieve a desired level of share penetration without a strong marketing effort, as illustrated in Figure 9.2. Distribution channels and sales systems are integral parts of the market share equation shown in Figure 9.2. The purpose of this chapter is to examine the various channel systems that can be used to reach customers and profitably grow the sales of a business.

ALTERNATIVE CHANNEL SYSTEMS

The first decision a business must make is whether to use a *direct, indirect,* or *mixed* channel system.[1] All things being equal, a business would generally prefer to sell and distribute directly to target customers, because this combination of channel and sales re-

Figure 9.2 ◆ **Product-Price Position, Marketing Effort, and Market Share**

sponsibility offers the most control and greatest potential for value-added sales and services. On the other hand, a business may not have the expertise or resources needed to fund and support a direct channel system and therefore might elect to reach target customers through an indirect channel system. A business may also need to use a combination of direct, indirect, and mixed channel systems in order to reach different target markets cost-effectively and to deliver the service level expected by target customers. These three channel systems are shown in Figure 9.3.

- **Direct Channel Systems:** Provide alternative direct channel and sales systems that require the business to retain ownership (title) of products sold and responsibility for delivery to customers and value-added functions desired by customers.
- **Indirect Channel Systems:** Provide varying degrees of sales and value-added functions while taking ownership and responsibility for delivery to target customers or other intermediaries.
- **Mixed Channel Systems:** Provide direct sales contact and technical support while the actual purchase is made at a channel intermediary who has taken title (ownership) of the products being sold.

Figure 9.3 ◆ **Alternative Channel Systems**

Direct Channel Systems

As illustrated in Figure 9.4, a direct approach can include a direct sales force, direct marketing, telemarketing, on-line marketing, manufacturer's representatives, sales agents, or brokers. In each case, the business retains *ownership* of the products and *responsibility* for sales, distribution, service, and collection of payment for products sold.

Although a direct sales force offers the best opportunity for sales communication and customer interaction, it is often too expensive to reach target customers with a direct sales approach. The cost of direct customer sales contact is both high and increasing. For example, the fully loaded cost (salary, benefits, and expenses) of a direct salesperson in many business-to-business markets can range from $100,000 to over $300,000 per year. Direct marketing, which includes direct mail and catalog sales, offers a less expensive alternative, but the opportunity for sales communications is more limited. Telemarketing provides a greater opportunity for a sales communication but is more labor-intensive and often more expensive than direct marketing. Emerging electronic marketing channels in home shopping and Internet computer-based purchasing are offering greater opportunities for customer interaction.[2] Finally, manufacturer's representatives, sales agents, and brokers can assume the selling responsibility for the business and are paid a sales commission only when a sale occurs. However, because commissioned sales agents work for several manufacturers, a large degree of control and service are potentially lost.

Figure 9.4 ◆ Alternative Customer Channel Systems

Indirect Channel Systems

Because using a direct channel system is often expensive, it limits the number of customers a business can profitably reach. As a result, many potential customers who buy in smaller purchase amounts cannot be profitably served with a direct channel system. In these situations, a business has to at least consider using indirect channel systems.

Indirect channel systems are inherently more complex, because they involve at least one intermediary who takes over both ownership of the product and the majority, if not all, of the control in both sales and distribution. As shown in Figure 9.4, an indirect channel system could include retailers, commercial distributors (also called dealers), full-function wholesalers, and specialty wholesalers.

Retailers take over the sales and point of purchase distribution in consumer markets, and distributors or dealers assume this responsibility in business-to-business markets. Compensation for their services is usually in the form of a discount off the customer selling price. This discount can range from 10 percent to over 50 percent.

Wholesalers offer an intermediate point of sales and physical distribution between a business and retailers or dealers. There are full-function wholesalers, who offer a full range of products and services (inventory, delivery, credit, and stocking), and limited-function wholesalers, who offer a limited range of products and services. For example, a cash-and-carry wholesaler does not deliver the product or offer credit. In most cases, the discount offered to wholesalers is less than that offered to retailers or dealers, because the range of services is considerably less.

VARs and OEMs are unique indirect channel system alternatives in that they buy products, directly or indirectly, add value to them, and resell them. These alternatives will be discussed at greater length in the discussion of business-to-business alternative channels.

Two-Tier Marketing Channels

In many consumer and business-to-business markets, two-tier indirect channel systems are common. In these indirect channels, end user prices are discounted twice, first to retailers and then to wholesalers. Shown in Figure 9.5 is a two-tier indirect channel system, the discount at each tier, and the manufacturer's index. For a sporting goods product, retailers require a 34.8 percent discount off the retail price index of 100, which yields a wholesale price index of 65.2. Wholesalers in this two-tier marketing channel require a

Business Sector	Price Index	Retailer Discount	Wholesale Price Index	Wholesaler Discount	Manufacturer Price Index
Furniture	100	38.9	61.1	27.7	44
Gasoline	100	19.8	80.2	15.7	68
Groceries	100	23.5	76.2	17.4	63
Sporting Goods	100	34.8	65.2	28.0	47
Liquor	100	21.6	78.4	23.6	60
Average	**100**	**27.7**	**72.3**	**22.5**	**56.4**

Figure 9.5 ◆ **Retailer and Wholesaler Price Discounts in a Two-Tier Channel System**

28 percent discount off their wholesale price, which yields a manufacturer's price index of 47. This means that the sporting goods manufacturer captures 47 percent of the customer price and the channel captures 53 percent. Obviously, this level of price discount would not be used if there were a more cost-efficient (equally effective) channel to the market.[3]

Mixed Channel Systems

In some instances, a combination of direct and indirect channel systems provides the best way to reach and serve target customers.[4] For example, many industrial and business-to-business firms use a direct sales force or manufacturers' representatives to perform the sales contact while localized dealers and distributors provide product availability, delivery, and service, as well as terms of payment.

Mixed channel systems are particularly important when products are fairly technical and localized availability and service are important. For example, Microsoft, Compaq Computer, and others have direct sales forces that call on large corporate accounts, often referred to as enterprise businesses. While the technical sales team works with the customer to create a desired customer solution, the local reseller of their products will handle the actual sales, delivery, and service.

Consumer Channel Systems

In consumer markets, businesses are likely to use indirect channel systems to effectively and cost-efficiently reach target customers. Innovations in direct marketing, on-line marketing, and wholesale shopping have opened new channel systems that may be equally attractive. Outlined in Figure 9.4 are the various channel systems typically used in consumer markets. As shown, there are both direct and indirect channel systems. In consumer markets, a direct channel system is less likely to be used. Direct marketing through consumer catalogs, direct-mail marketing, telemarketing, and electronic marketing have grown significantly in recent years and offer future growth opportunities with innovations in telecommunications. Catalog companies, such as Esprit, Eddie Bauer, and L.L. Bean, have had noteworthy success in recent years, whereas Mary Kay Cosmetics, Electrolux, and Amway have used a direct sales approach to reach target consumers. In each case, a different direct channel system is required to effectively meet customer needs and to produce acceptable levels of profitability. And, if there were a more efficient way to accomplish these objectives, it would be marketing's responsibility to find that alternative.

On-line marketing is an emerging direct consumer channel system that involves Internet computer-based purchasing and includes new businesses such as Amazon.com, Peapod, and Auto-By-Tel. These channel intermediaries buy their products from manufacturers and wholesalers and resell them through the Internet:

- Amazon.com is an on-line book retailer that purchases books from large book wholesalers and resells them on-line with next-day UPS delivery, if desired. Amazon.com also purchases and resells CDs.
- Peapod shoppers pay a monthly fee of $4.95 and 5 percent of the purchase price for groceries purchased on-line and delivered to the shoppers' home.

- Auto-By-Tel helps customers in their car purchase. They are an on-line broker that shops for the car and price the customer wants. In this case Internet shoppers do not directly pay Auto-By-Tel for this service. Rather, the dealers pay monthly fees for referrals of consumers who visit the Auto-By-Tel Web site.

Business-to-Business Channel Systems

Software manufacturers, such as Adobe, serve both consumer and business customers. As illustrated in Figure 9.6, these companies use a direct marketing channel to reach and serve large enterprises such as Fortune 500 companies. To reach medium-sized to smaller businesses and individual consumers, these manufacturers use on-line marketing as part of their direct channel, but, to a greater degree, they use an indirect channel to reach these customers. As shown in Figure 9.6, software producers will sell direct to large national chains, but they use independent, commissioned representatives to reach smaller independent retailers. Each of the channels has different levels of cost, control, sales contact, and ownership.

As stated earlier, most businesses would prefer to sell and distribute with a direct channel system. This provides a greater degree of control and specialized knowledge that can be customized for the end customer. Yet, for industrial products, such as the one illustrated in Figure 9.7 only 25 percent of sales are via direct channel systems.[5]

This percentage is partly the result of the cost of a business-to-business direct sales call, which ranges from $100 to over $300. In industrial markets, approximately 50 percent of all sales are derived from the combination of manufacturer's reps or sales agents

Figure 9.6 ◆ **Marketing Channels and Sales Systems Used to Reach Softwear Buyers**

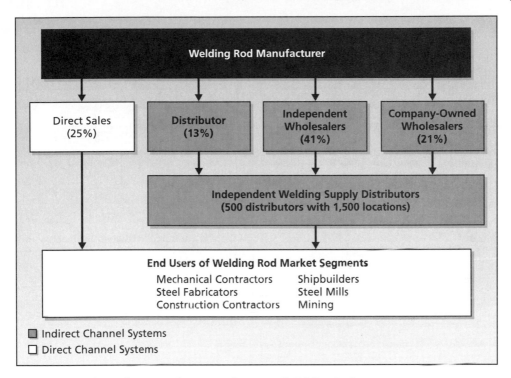

Figure 9.7 ◆ Channel Systems for a Manufacturer of Welding Rods

and industrial distributors. For many inexpensive industrial and commercial products, wholesalers are used. In some instances, as in hospital supply products, the large hospital supply wholesaler may sell directly to hospitals and other medical institutions.

Unique to the business-to-business market, as outlined in Figure 9.8, are VARs and OEMs. VARs purchase a variety of equipment from several manufacturers and package them as a system. A VAR often provides the total system, as well as specialized services, to help the customer learn, use, maintain, and upgrade the system. For example, a VAR in the agricultural market may purchase computers, printers, modems, fax machines, and telecommunications equipment from several manufacturers, along with specialized software, to help farmers with crop rotation, fertilizing, planting, and water requirements. The agricultural customers could buy all these products separately, but they prefer to purchase a complete (bundled) system that is customized to their specific needs.

An OEM is very similar but actually creates a new manufactured product. OEMs, such as Ford, IBM, or Caterpillar, buy component products from other manufacturers to incorporate into their products. For example, Ford does not manufacture tires; it purchases them from a tire manufacturer such as Firestone. Although Firestone operates primarily through company-owned retail tire stores, it also sell tires to automobile manufacturers, who provide another important, indirect channel sales opportunity. Likewise, IBM may buy disk drives from Seagate and computer chips from Intel, as well as make its own.

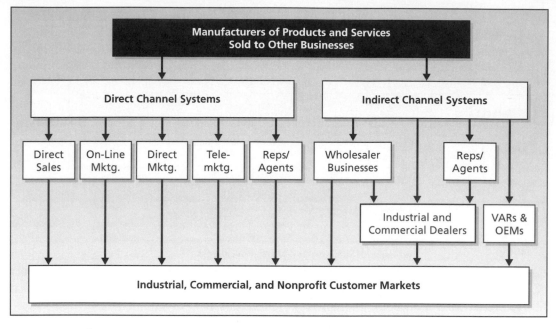

Figure 9.8 ◆ Alternative Business-to-Business Channel Systems

CHANNEL SYSTEMS THAT BUILD CUSTOMER VALUE

There are many alternative channel systems a business can use to reach target customers. To be successful, however, a channel system must enhance *customer value* by either increasing customer benefits or lowering customer cost of purchase, or both.

Delivering Product Benefits

Because many products are perishable or easily damaged, it is important to select a channel that will be able to deliver a business's product to target customers in the form that meets or exceeds customer expectations. In selecting a particular channel system, a business needs to consider how that channel system either enhances or detracts from the following product benefits:

- **Product Quality:** Can the channel system deliver the product or service with the quality level required and expected by target customers?
- **Product Assortment:** Can the channel system provide the range of products required in order to achieve a desired level of customer appeal?
- **Product Form:** Can the channel system provide the product, as it is needed, to both intermediaries and final customers?

In each case, a channel system is not a viable alternative if it cannot meet the product benefits sought by target customers.[6] Customers simply will not buy products that do not meet their buying needs. There are almost always competing alternatives, so customers will satisfy their buying needs by purchasing a competing product.

Delivering Service Benefits

Every channel has advantages and limitations with respect to service. The need for delivery, installation, training, technical support, repair, terms of payment, credit, and easy return are all service benefits that a business has to consider in selecting a particular channel system. To determine if a channel system is viable, a business has to consider the following questions with respect to a customer's service needs and expectations.

- **After-Sale Services:** What are the after-sale services that are critical to achieving total customer satisfaction with the product or service?
- **Availability/Delivery:** To what degree do customers benefit from quick access to goods or services and immediate delivery?
- **Transaction Services:** Can the channel system provide for the customer's credit needs, terms of payment, warranty, FOB pricing, and return of faulty products?

Each of these service benefits can be critical. A business with a better product may not achieve market success if it fails to provide the service benefits required by target customers. To be successful in meeting customer expectations, a business has to make the product available at the target customer's desired point of purchase. In addition, it must meet or exceed each of its customer's product and service requirements, whether this be the final customer or a channel intermediary.

Building Brand Image

It is important to carefully consider how a channel system will affect the image of a product or manufacturer. Hartman Luggage, for example, manufactures a high-quality line of luggage and has a certain image for quality. Hartman is very selective in choosing retailers who will support or enhance this brand image, as pointed out in Figure 9.9.

Likewise, Perfume de Paris manufactures and markets perfume at approximately one-third the price of Chanel and other higher-priced perfume products. It is important for Perfume de Paris to have its product sold through mass merchandisers who emphasize price, because mass merchandising is consistent with its target customer and product and price-positioning strategy.

Building Company Benefits

Overall benefits can be enhanced and contribute to building customer value with *relationship marketing*.[7] Direct channel systems offer the greatest opportunity for presenting product information, controlling the selling effort, and offering specialized selling skills. This opportunity to enhance the total benefits through personal relationships developed with customers or channel intermediaries can be very important. Strong customer-firm relationships produce high degrees of commitment by both parties, and high commitment has the potential to enhance customer value.

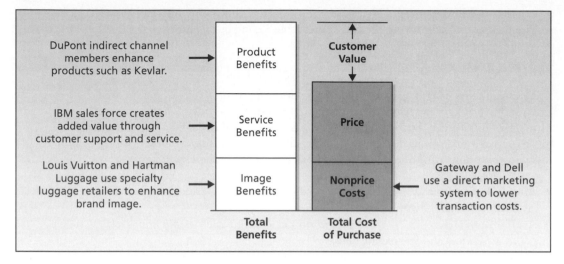

Figure 9.9 ◆ **How Channel Systems Contribute to Customer Value**

When a business cannot directly interact with target customers, it must take care in selecting a channel system that will be capable of fulfilling these customer relationships effectively.[8] For a given product and customer, this selection may require a certain level of product knowledge, sales and negotiation skills, call frequency, and follow-up with after-sales service. The bottom line is that any channel system is of little value if the sales interaction with the target customer is ineffective.

Improving Cost Efficiency

By making a product readily available, a business can lower a customer's transaction costs. Customers have preferred points of purchase. If a business does not make products readily available at these points of purchase, it inherently raises the cost of the transaction. For undifferentiated products, this type of transaction cost is high. Customers will not make the effort to purchase the product if it is not conveniently available. On the other hand, the more differentiated a product, and the greater its perceived value, the more willing the customer may be to incur this type of transaction cost.

Another way to affect customer value (total benefits less total costs) is to lower the cost of reaching customers. The more cost-efficient a channel system, the greater the opportunity to lower customer costs or to increase business profitability. An important marketing responsibility is to find and develop channel systems that are cost-efficient while still delivering the benefits sought by customers.

It is often assumed that the more intermediaries there are in a channel system, the higher the total cost of purchase. In general, that assumption is not true, or that channel system would not exist. Consider, for example, the channel system presented in Figure 9.10, in which 100 manufacturers each contact 20,000 retailers once a month. In this channel system, there is a monthly transaction cost of $50 for order placement, handling, delivery, and billing. The net result is an industry that has an overall channel system transaction cost of approximately $1.2 billion, as shown.

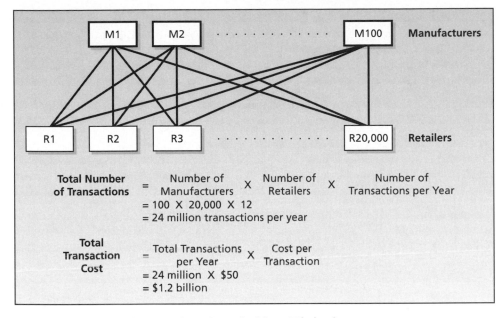

Figure 9.10 ◆ Transaction Costs in a Channel without Wholesalers

When an extra layer (wholesalers) is added to the channel system, each of the 100 manufacturers can now sell each month to wholesalers at a cost of $25,000 per month, as illustrated in Figure 9.11. This cost is much higher because a great deal more merchandise is handled and delivered each month. In this channel system, the wholesalers need to then distribute to the 20,000 retailers each month. Their cost is $750 per transaction, which is also considerably higher because wholesalers are shipping a variety of products, because they represent a large number of retailers. As shown, in this channel system the wholesaler lowers the annual transaction costs to $210 million, or approximately $1 billion less than the channel system without a wholesaler function.

Although a business generally builds customer value through a combination of product, service, and image benefits and the cost of acquiring these benefits (price and transaction costs), any given channel system can enhance or detract from the delivered customer value. Thus, selecting a particular channel system requires both careful consideration of the benefits sought by customers and the cost of delivering them through a particular channel system.

CHANNEL SYSTEMS AND COMPETITIVE ADVANTAGE

Customer contact is essential for any sale to occur. This contact can take many forms, whether direct or indirect. For direct channel systems, a business must have a certain number of salespeople to establish and maintain a certain level of contact. For indirect channel systems, a business must have a sufficient number of outlets, whether retail or wholesale. Either can be a source of competitive advantage when done in a manner that creates value for customers and relative advantage over competitors.

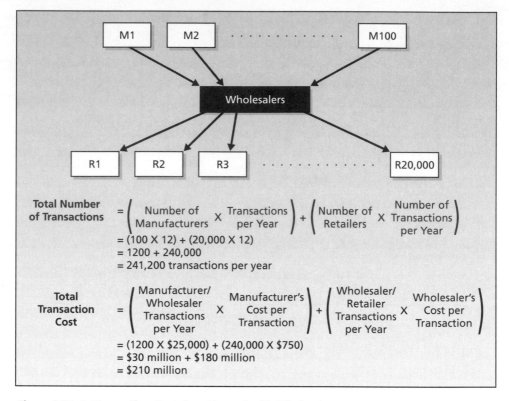

$$\text{Total Number of Transactions} = \left(\begin{array}{c}\text{Number of}\\\text{Manufacturers}\end{array} \times \begin{array}{c}\text{Transactions}\\\text{per Year}\end{array}\right) + \left(\begin{array}{c}\text{Number of}\\\text{Retailers}\end{array} \times \begin{array}{c}\text{Number of}\\\text{Transactions}\\\text{per Year}\end{array}\right)$$
$$= (100 \times 12) + (20{,}000 \times 12)$$
$$= 1200 + 240{,}000$$
$$= 241{,}200 \text{ transactions per year}$$

$$\text{Total Transaction Cost} = \left(\begin{array}{c}\text{Manufacturer/}\\\text{Wholesaler}\\\text{Transactions}\\\text{per Year}\end{array} \times \begin{array}{c}\text{Manufacturer's}\\\text{Cost per}\\\text{Transaction}\end{array}\right) + \left(\begin{array}{c}\text{Wholesaler/}\\\text{Retailer}\\\text{Transactions}\\\text{per Year}\end{array} \times \begin{array}{c}\text{Wholesaler's}\\\text{Cost per}\\\text{Transaction}\end{array}\right)$$
$$= (1200 \times \$25{,}000) + (240{,}000 \times \$750)$$
$$= \$30 \text{ million} + \$180 \text{ million}$$
$$= \$210 \text{ million}$$

Figure 9.11 ◆ Transaction Costs in a Channel with Wholesalers

Sales Force Advantage

When a direct channel system is selected as the best way to reach and effectively serve target customers, it is essential that a business have a sufficient number of salespeople. Assume that a business has 1,000 target customers and the required rate of customer contact for sales effectiveness and customer satisfaction is two customer visits per month. This translates into 24,000 customer contacts per year. Further assume that a salesperson in this particular industry can make three customer visits per day and has four days per week to make customer calls. This translates into a need for 38 salespeople.

If competitors have an average of only 20 salespeople, they cannot accomplish the same level of sales coverage. These competitors will either contact fewer customers or contact the same number of customers less frequently. In either case, the business with 38 salespeople is better able to reach more customers and better serve customers' needs, and both are sources of competitive advantage.

The quality of a business's sales force can also be a source of competitive advantage. A sales force with exceptional product knowledge and a strong market orientation is in a good position to serve target customer needs. Of course, the behavior and attitudes of the sales force are in part influenced by the market orientation of the business.[9] As a result, a business with a strong market orientation is in the best position to build customer relationships that enhance customer satisfaction and retention. The sales force is, in fact, creating a source of competitive advantage when this level of sales effort is valued by customers and cannot be matched by competitors.[10]

Sales Productivity

Businesses that have a high level of sales productivity can also develop a source of competitive advantage. A business with a more efficient sales force, in terms of sales per salesperson, will have a lower cost per sale than a less productive business with the same sales revenue. An efficient sales force translates into higher levels of profitability per sales dollar and a source of competitive advantage.

But how does a business develop high levels of sales productivity? Businesses with high-quality products, broad lines of related products, and efficient sales administrative systems produce high levels of sales per salesperson. High-quality products are easier to sell than are low-quality products, and they often have premium prices. A broad product line provides more sales opportunities per sales call. And the use of computers and other telecommunications systems has been shown to improve sales administrative efficiency and to allow for more time with customers.

Distribution Advantage

For markets in which indirect channel systems are the dominant channel system used to reach target customers, share of distributor outlets can be directly linked to market share. As shown in Figure 9.12, generally the higher a drug store's outlet share, the higher its market share. Empirical studies have shown that the relationship between outlet share and market share is nonlinear and generally S-shaped, as shown in Figure 9.13. A small distributor share produces proportionately smaller market shares. However, as outlet share grows, market share grows at a faster rate until it exceeds outlet

North American Drug Store Chains	Sales ($ billions)	Market Share (%)	Number of Stores	Outlet Share (%)	Sales per Store ($ millions)
Walgreen	$13.4	23	2,363	14	$ 5.67
Rite Aid	11.8	20	3,963	23	2.97
CVS	11.1	20	3,909	23	2.84
Eckerd	8.8	15	2,786	17	3.16
American Drug Stores	5.2	9	882	5	5.93
Longs Drug Stores	2.8	5	337	2	8.40
Shoppers Drug Mart	2.8	5	801	5	3.52
Jean Coutu	1.2	2	483	3	2.38
Phar-Mor	1.1	2	104	1	10.38
Medical Shoppe Int'l.	1.0	2	1,236	7	0.84
Total/Average	$59.2	100%	16,864	100%	$ 3.51

Figure 9.12 ◆ Drug Store Chain Market Share vs. Outlet Location Share

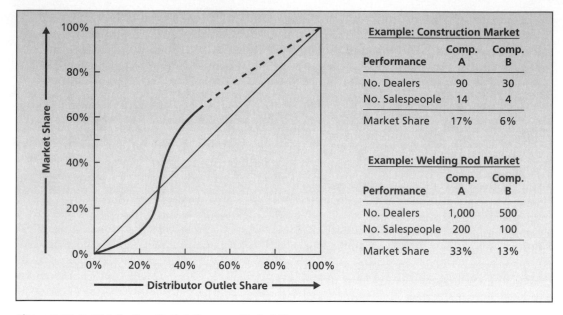

Figure 9.13 ◆ **Distribution Outlet Share vs. Market Share**

share. Then, as outlet share continues to increase, the rate of market share growth decreases.

There are only a few cases in which very high outlet and market shares have been observed. The lower part of the curve, below a 50 percent outlet share, is well-documented.[11] But, because market share must equal 100 percent when outlet share equals 100 percent, the upper half of the curve in Figure 9.13 can be extrapolated with some confidence. Recognizing this relationship, for markets in which indirect retail or dealer channel systems are required to reach and serve target customers, businesses with dominant distribution shares have a source of competitive advantage. Why? Because in any given market, there is a finite number of distributors, and fewer good ones. The business that dominates this channel system can control market access by blocking market entry because the number of available distributors or retailers is limited.

PROFIT IMPACT OF ALTERNATIVE CHANNEL SYSTEMS

Several aspects of profitability come into play in determining the profitability of any channel system. Consider for example a manufacturer who sells 10 million units per year of industrial lubricant in a market in which it has a 5 percent market share. The business currently sells its lubricants to independent wholesalers for $1.50 per unit, as shown in Figure 9.14. The wholesalers mark up the price of these lubricants 50 percent to $2.25 to achieve a 33.3 percent margin. Supply house distributors, in turn, mark up the price to $3 to achieve a 25 percent margin. The manufacturer's variable cost per unit is $0.90. In addition, the producer spends $3.5 million on fixed marketing expenses for advertising, selling, and administrative expense. With this channel system and marketing ex-

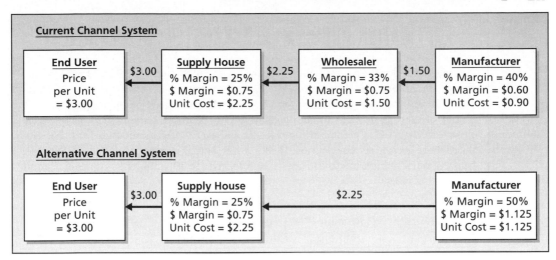

Current Channel System

End User		Supply House		Wholesaler		Manufacturer
Price per Unit = $3.00	$3.00	% Margin = 25% $ Margin = $0.75 Unit Cost = $2.25	$2.25	% Margin = 33% $ Margin = $0.75 Unit Cost = $1.50	$1.50	% Margin = 40% $ Margin = $0.60 Unit Cost = $0.90

Alternative Channel System

End User		Supply House		Manufacturer
Price per Unit = $3.00	$3.00	% Margin = 25% $ Margin = $0.75 Unit Cost = $2.25	$2.25	% Margin = 50% $ Margin = $1.125 Unit Cost = $1.125

Figure 9.14 ◆ Alternative Channel Systems for Industrial Lubricants

pense, the business is able to achieve a 5 percent market share and $2.5 million in net marketing contribution, as shown below:

$$\begin{array}{l}\text{Net} \\ \text{Marketing} \\ \text{Contribution}\end{array} = \left[\begin{array}{l}\text{Market} \\ \text{Demand}\end{array} \times \begin{array}{l}\text{Market} \\ \text{Share}\end{array} \times \left(\begin{array}{l}\text{Revenue per} \\ \text{Customer}\end{array} - \begin{array}{l}\text{Variable Cost} \\ \text{per Customer}\end{array}\right)\right] - \begin{array}{l}\text{Marketing} \\ \text{Expenses}\end{array}$$

$$= [200 \text{ million} \times 0.05 \times (\$1.50 - \$0.90)] - \$3.5 \text{ million}$$

$$= [10 \text{ million} \times \$0.60] - \$3.5 \text{ million}$$

$$= \$2.5 \text{ million}$$

At this point, management might ask, "What is an alternative channel system worth?" To answer this question, we need to compute the net marketing contribution of an alternative channel system and compare it with the business's current net marketing contribution.

Assume that the lubricant manufacturer feels that it could capture more margin and maintain the same market share by selling and distributing direct to the supply houses, as illustrated in Figure 9.14. The business estimates that this channel system would raise its variable cost per unit to $1.125 and would require twice the marketing budget ($7 million). These numbers translate into a net marketing contribution of $4.25 million, as shown below, $1.75 million greater than the current net marketing contribution.

$$\text{Net Marketing Contribution} = [200 \text{ million} \times 0.05 \times (\$2.25 - \$1.125)] - \$7 \text{ million}$$

$$= [10 \text{ million} \times \$1.125] - \$7 \text{ million}$$

$$= \$4.25 \text{ million}$$

Thus, the value of this alternative channel system would be $1.75 million, the increase in net marketing contribution that it would provide.

APPLICATION PROBLEM: BLOCKBUSTER ENTERTAINMENT

The video rental market is large and still growing. In 1998, there were 28,000 retail outlets that produced total sales revenues of $13 billion, an average of $468,000 per outlet. The industry is very fragmented, with the top 10 video rental companies accounting for only 30 percent of sales and outlet locations. Blockbuster Entertainment, however, is the clear market share leader, with 21.7 percent of the revenues and a 17.9 percent outlet share, and it produces above-average revenue per store ($562,264 vs. market average of $468,000). The table below outlines the revenues and market shares for the top 10 video rental companies in the U.S. market in 1998.

Company Name	Revenues (millions)	Number of Outlets	Revenue per Outlet	Market Share (%)	Outlet Share (%)
Blockbuster Ent.	$ 2,831	5,035	$562,264	21.7	17.9
Hollywood Ent.	287	851	337,250	2.2	3.0
Movie Gallery Inc.	254	972	261,312	2.0	3.5
West Coast Video	230	531	433,145	1.8	1.9
Video Update Inc.	84	308	272,727	0.65	1.1
Movies Inc.	82	223	367,713	0.65	0.8
Family Video	36	84	428,571	0.03	0.3
Blowout Ent.	30	200	150,000	0.02	0.7
Easy Video	21	38	552,632	0.016	0.14
Video Galaxy	20	31	645,161	0.016	0.11
All other	9,125	19,727	462,564	70.2	70.5
Total/Average	**$13,000**	**28,000**	**$468,000**	**100%**	**100%**

Questions

For Internet discussion, go to www.prenhall.com/phbusiness.

1. Create a graph of market share vs. outlet share (see Figure 9.13) using the data above. On the basis of the graph produced, explain how outlet share contributes to market share.

2. What factors would contribute to an above-average revenue per outlet for Blockbuster? How could a small share competitor such as Video Galaxy produce the highest revenue per outlet among the top 10 video rental businesses?

3. By early 1999, Blockbuster had grown to 6,000 stores with the acquisition of several smaller competitors. Assuming Blockbuster is able to maintain the same revenue per store, what would be an estimate of its total sales revenue and market share (assuming no change in market demand)? Also, explain how Blockbuster's outlet share would have changed.

SUMMARY

Regardless of how attractive a business's products or services may be, if the business cannot reach target customers with a desired level of services, it has little chance of marketing success. Customers have product and service requirements along with preferences of where to buy. Likewise, a business has image requirements and the need for sales effectiveness and cost-efficiency. To be successful, a channel system must meet both customer and business requirements.

The biggest decision is whether to use a direct or an indirect channel system. In a direct system, the business retains ownership of its products and is responsible for many of the selling, delivery, warehousing, and transaction activities. Direct channel systems include direct selling, direct marketing, telemarketing, and the use of manufacturer's reps and sales agents. An indirect system takes ownership of the product and varying degrees of responsibility for selling, warehousing, delivery, and transaction activities. Indirect systems include different combinations of wholesalers and retailers in the consumer market. In the business-to-business market, indirect systems can also include different combinations of wholesalers and dealers, value-added resellers (VARs) and original equipment manufacturers (OEMs).

In many instances, multitiered channel systems are more customer-effective and cost-efficient than direct systems. Thus, the belief that having more intermediaries in a channel system pushes up the cost, and, therefore, the price of a product is not true. If a more efficient system were available, marketers would find it. However, rarely is one channel and sales system sufficient to reach all target customers. And, the greater a business's market coverage, with either a direct or an indirect system, the greater its market share. Thus, an important part of a profitable marketing strategy is a well-thought-out and well-managed channel system strategy.

MARKET-BASED AND STRATEGIC THINKING

1. Why is it advantageous to view a combination of sales and channels of distribution as a channel system?
2. How has the use of a direct channel system helped Dell Computer grow over the last 10 years?
3. How has Compaq Computer's channel system contributed to its growth over the last 10 years?
4. What is the difference between a direct and an indirect channel system? Why might a business use both?
5. What is a mixed channel system? Why would Microsoft's Office suite be marketed with a mixed channel system to large business customers?
6. What are the various direct sales and channel systems that could be used in the consumer market? How do they differ from the business-to-business market?
7. What role do on-line channel systems play in the way we buy airline tickets and stocks?
8. Explain why sporting goods producers often use a two-tier indirect channel system. (See Figure 9.5.)
9. What role do VARs play in business-to-business markets? How do they enhance customer value?
10. How does the use of multiple channel systems affect the growth of a business?
11. How does the use of a channel system either enhance or detract from customer value? What specific factors need to be considered in selecting one channel system over another?
12. Why can a channel system be a source of competitive advantage?

13. What are some of the ways a channel system can be a source of advantage and contribute to a higher market share?
14. How can increased sales force quality and sales force productivity be developed into a source of competitive advantage?
15. How would you go about determining the profit impact of an alternative channel system?

NOTES

1. Kasturi Rangan, Melvyn Menezes, and E.P. Maier, "Channel Selection for New Industrial Products: A Framework, Method and Application," *Journal of Marketing* (July 1992):69–82.
2. R. Oliva, "Painting with Business Marketers' Web Palette," *Marketing Management* (Summer 1998):50–53.
3. *Annual Statement Statistics* (Robert Morris Agency, 1996).
4. F. Cespedes and R. Corey, "Managing Multiple Channels," *Business Horizons* (July–August 1990):72.
5. Robert Haas, *Industrial Marketing Management: Text and Cases,* 4th ed. (Northridge, CA: Kent, 1989), 239; and Michael Morris, *Industrial and Organizational Marketing* (Old Tappan, NJ: Macmillan, 1988):489–523.
6. Niraj Dawar and Philip Parker, "Marketing Universals: Consumers' Use of Brand Name, Price, Physical Appearance, and Retailer Reputation As Signals of Product Quality," *Journal of Marketing* (April 1994):81–95.
7. James Anderson and James Narus, "A Model of Distributor Firm and Manufacturer Firm Working Partnerships," *Journal of Marketing* (January 1990):42–58.
8. David Morris, "What's Old Is New in Relationship Marketing," *Marketing News* (February 1994):4, 8; and Robert Robicheaux and James Coleman, "The Structure of Marketing Channel Relationships," *Academy of Marketing Science* (Winter 1994):38–51.
9. Judy Siguaw, G. Brown, and Robert E. Widing, "The Influence of Market Orientation of the Firm on Sales Force Behavior and Attitudes," *Journal of Marketing Research* (February 1994):106–16.
10. Robert Ping, "Does Satisfaction Moderate the Association between Alternative Attractiveness and Exit Intention in a Marketing Channel?" *Academy of Marketing Science* (Fall 1994):364–71.
11. Gary Lilien, Philip Kotler, and K. Moorthy. *Marketing Models,* (Upper Saddle River, NJ: Prentice Hall, 1992):434–38; P. Hartung and J. Fisher, "Brand Switching and Mathematical Programming in Market Expansion," *Management Science* (August 1965):231–43; and Gary Lilien and Ambar Rao, "A Model for Allocating Retail Outlet Building Resources across Market Areas," *Operations Research* (January–February):1–14.

chapter 10

Marketing Communications and Customer Response

Gardenburger is a leading producer of meatless burgers, with distribution in over 35,000 food service outlets, 30,000 retail grocery stores, natural food outlets, and club store locations. Although widely distributed, Gardenburger felt it had to move its awareness and interest beyond the "healthy" niche market to the average consumer.[1] To accomplish that goal, the $90 million company spent $1.5 million on one commercial aired during the final episode of the television sitcom *Seinfeld* (see Figure 10.1). The following week, sales were 414 percent higher than sales for the same week one year earlier. Overall,

Figure 10.1 ◆ Gardenburger Television Ad Story Board

Gardenburger spent about $17 million, almost 19 percent of sales, on 1,500 television spots and 20 magazine print ads. According to one industry analyst, "The advertising clearly paid off. They're getting good response to new products, more shelf space, and a higher repeat purchase rate."[2]

MARKETING COMMUNICATIONS

The first job of a marketing communication is to build awareness: to inform customers of a business's products. Second, marketing communications need to continually reinforce messages in order to maintain awareness. Third, it is often the job of a marketing communication to motivate a target customer to take action. Thus, there are three fundamental marketing communications objectives, any one of which can be the focus of a particular marketing communication.

- **Build Awareness:** Build a level of awareness with respect to important information about the organization and its products and/or services.
- **Reinforce the Message:** Sustain a desired level of retention with respect to image, key benefits, and name recognition over time.
- **Stimulate Action:** Motivate target customers to take a specific action in a relatively short time.

Because message reinforcement and action can come only after a reasonable level of awareness, businesses need to first build awareness and comprehension before moving on to other marketing communications objectives.

MARKETING COMMUNICATIONS AND CUSTOMER RESPONSE

Building awareness, comprehension, and interest in a business's products are major steps in the hierarchy of customer response. As illustrated in Figure 10.2, there is a hierarchical set of customer response effects. If a marketing communication fails to create target customer awareness, the first stage in the hierarchy, none of the customer response effects that follow are possible. In this example, 37 percent of the target market will not be reached with the marketing communication and will therefore not have a chance to comprehend, become interested in, form intentions, or take action.

Of the 63 percent of the customers who are aware of the business's marketing communication, 54 percent can accurately recall the important content (comprehension). This means that 29 percent (the 46 percent who don't comprehend, out of the 63 percent who are aware) are removed from further customer response because they do not fully comprehend the marketing communication content. Thus, the combination of target customers lost due to lack of awareness (37 percent) and insufficient message comprehension (29 percent) is 66 percent.

Of those target customers who are aware of and adequately comprehend the marketing communication, 77 percent express an interest in the product and its benefits, leaving 23 percent who are uninterested and creating a lost customer response of approximately 8 percent. Of those who are interested, 68 percent intend to take a desired action.

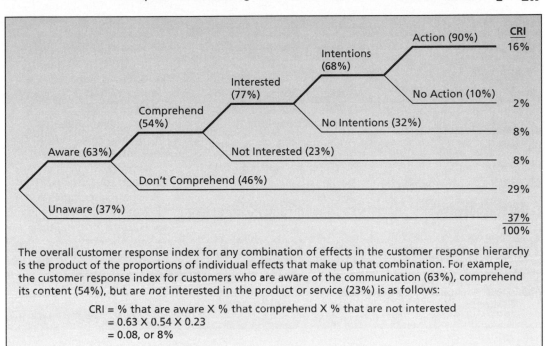

The overall customer response index for any combination of effects in the customer response hierarchy is the product of the proportions of individual effects that make up that combination. For example, the customer response index for customers who are aware of the communication (63%), comprehend its content (54%), but are *not* interested in the product or service (23%) is as follows:

CRI = % that are aware X % that comprehend X % that are not interested
= 0.63 X 0.54 X 0.23
= 0.08, or 8%

Figure 10.2 ◆ Marketing Communications and Customer Response Index

However, those who are interested, but not sufficiently motivated to take action, create another loss in customer response of 8 percent.

Finally, target customers who are aware, comprehend, are interested, intend to take action, and take the desired action produce a customer response of 16 percent. Target customers who intend to take action, but do not, create an additional loss of potential customer response of 2 percent. In order to achieve a higher overall level of customer response, a business would need to improve its performance at specific stages in the customer response hierarchy in which the business has not performed well.

STRATEGIES TO INCREASE CUSTOMER RESPONSE

The potential causes of low levels of customer response in the customer response hierarchy are outlined in Figure 10.3. Marketing communications play a major role in low levels of awareness and comprehension. Low levels of awareness can be caused by poor media selection, insufficient message frequency (repetition), or poor ad copy. Low levels of comprehension can also be the result of insufficient frequency or poor ad copy. Correcting these problems is essential to improving overall customer response.

For example, assume that for the situation presented in Figure 10.2, the business developed a more effective marketing communications strategy that increased awareness from 63 percent to 75 percent. This increase would translate into a potential increase in customer response index (CRI), from 16 percent to 19 percent.

Poor Response	Marketing Problem	Underlying Cause
Low Awareness	Marketing Communications	• Poor Media Selection • Insufficient Frequency • Poor Ad Copy
Poor Comprehension	Marketing Communications	• Insufficient Frequency • Poor Ad Copy
Low Interest	Product Positioning	• Insufficient Benefits • Weak Value Proposition • Poor Ad Copy
Low Intentions	Price and Transaction Cost	• High Price • Need for Low-Cost Trial • High Switching Cost
Low Purchase Level	Distribution and In-Store	• Not Readily Available • Hard to Find In-Store • Insufficient Sales/Service

Figure 10.3 ◆ Marketing Causes of Low Levels of Customer Response

$$\text{CRI (current)} = 0.63 \times 0.54 \times 0.77 \times 0.68 \times 0.90 = 0.16$$
$$\text{CRI (improved)} = 0.75 \times 0.54 \times 0.77 \times 0.68 \times 0.90 = 0.19$$

Assume, also, that the comprehension of its marketing communication was increased because of improved ad copy from 54 percent to 67 percent. The combined effects of increased awareness and comprehension increase the overall CRI from 16 percent to 24 percent, as illustrated.

$$\text{CRI (improved)} = 0.75 \times 0.67 \times 0.77 \times 0.68 \times 0.90 = 0.24$$

A well-positioned product with an attractive customer value (perceived benefits that are greater than perceived costs) and a strong marketing (channel) system will still not achieve full marketing success without a good marketing communications program. If target customers are unaware of a product's benefits, cost, and value, there is little opportunity for purchase.

For example, Johnson Controls is a Fortune 100 business that serves a variety of markets, one of which is the commercial building services market. Johnson Controls has achieved an excellent reputation among customers. However, a market research study revealed a low level of awareness in the commercial building services market; customers mentioned Johnson Controls with disappointing frequency when asked to identify suppliers of this service.[3]

In response to this information, Johnson Controls developed the "Classic Buildings" marketing communication illustrated in Figure 10.4. These print ads were run in *Forbes, Fortune, Business Week,* and the *Wall Street Journal,* each of which reached building and facilities managers (the target customers) in Fortune 1000 businesses. Nine months after the campaign, measurements were made. Unaided recall of Johnson Controls had increased by 30 percent. The marketing communication effort increased company awareness and helped presell the company. Both effects contributed to an increase in sales.

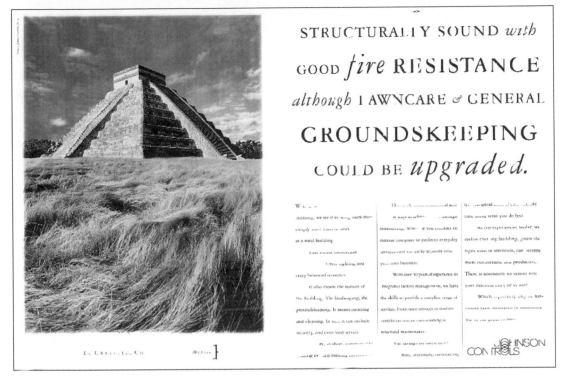

Figure 10.4 ◆ Johnson Controls' "Classic Buildings" Print Ad

BUILDING CUSTOMER AWARENESS AND COMPREHENSION

Creating awareness among a large number of people is not the objective of most marketing communications. The objective is to create awareness among and communicate effectively to *target customers*. A memorable advertisement that is well known among the general population will fail if it does not achieve a high level of awareness and comprehension among target market customers.

Media Selection and Customer Awareness

As outlined in Figure 10.3, target customer awareness and comprehension are affected by media selection, message frequency, and ad copy. To effectively reach target customers, a business has to have a good understanding of their media habits. Do they watch television, and, if they do, which programs? Do they listen to the radio, and, if they do, which stations and at what time? Which newspapers and which sections of the newspaper do they read? Which magazines do they subscribe to? How do they go to work, with respect to exposure to outdoor signage? Do they use the Yellow Pages; are they Internet users or cable TV shoppers, or do they respond to direct-mail advertising? All these questions must be answered in order to purchase the combination of media that will effectively reach as many target customers as economically possible.

A key measure of effective media selection is *target market reach*. Target market reach *is the percentage of target customers who will be exposed to the business's message given a certain combination of media.* For example, a golf ball manufacturer wants to reach golfers. To do so, the manufacturer might advertise in print media such as *Golf Digest, Golf Magazine*, the *Wall Street Journal*, and *Business Week* and on television during golf tournaments. Through this combination of media, the manufacturer might, for example, be able to reach 63 percent of the golfers it considers target customers for its golf balls.

To get a target market reach greater than 63 percent would require the manufacturer to add media that reach target customers not reached with the current combination of media. If the incremental reach were more expensive than the incremental economic benefit derived from reaching these target customers, then the business would not seek to go beyond its current level of target customer reach.[4]

Message Frequency and Customer Awareness

Once a business has found the right combination of media to effectively reach target customers, the next question becomes how often the business needs to expose target customers to its message in order to achieve a certain level of awareness. Using too few messages may prevent information from getting through to target customers and will probably result in low levels of awareness and comprehension. On the other hand, too many exposures could irritate target customers and potentially have an adverse effect on retained information and perceptions of the ad, product, or company.

For example, the frequency of print advertising by leading chemical companies affects the year-to-year change in ratings of company reputation, as shown in Figure 10.5. Leading chemical companies that advertise fewer than seven to 12 times per year in *Chemical and Engineering News (C&EN)* adversely affect their reputation, whereas those

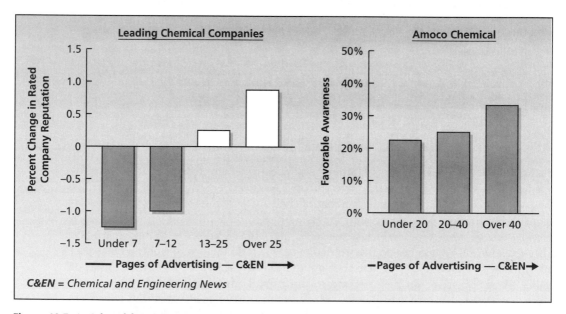

Figure 10.5 ◆ Advertising Frequency and Awareness in a Business-to-Business Market

at higher levels of frequency positively affect their reputations.[5] For Amoco Chemical, the level of favorable awareness steadily increased with the level of message frequency in *C&EN.*

If Amoco Chemical were to stop its marketing communications, over a relatively short time its level of awareness would diminish. Shown in Figure 10.6 are the results of a classic study on message frequency and awareness.[6] In a "concentrated frequency" strategy, 13 consecutive messages were exposed to target customers over 13 weeks. As shown, the message awareness steadily increased each week until it reached its highest level in week 13. However, after week 13, no more messages were exposed to target customers for the remainder of the year and, as shown, the message awareness decayed back down almost to zero. This marketing communications strategy would be appropriate for building awareness and comprehension for seasonal products, political candidates, and special events.

The same message was also sent to a different group of target customers once every four weeks throughout the year in a "distributed frequency" strategy. These target customers also received 13 message exposures, but they were spread out over the entire year. In the four-week period following each exposure, recall of the message decreased, but it did not go below the level prior to the last exposure. Hence, each additional exposure built from a higher base position. And, as shown, although this pattern of exposure frequency produced a

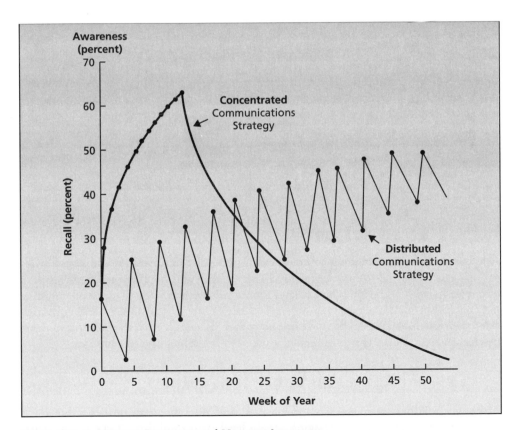

Figure 10.6 ◆ Message Frequency and Message Awareness

longer-lasting effect, it never reached the highest level of awareness produced by the concentrated frequency effort. This approach to marketing communications would be appropriate in building and maintaining target customer awareness and comprehension.

In Figure 10.6, target customers were exposed to each of the 13 messages sent. A more typical situation is one in which target customers are exposed to only a fraction of the messages sent. So, for most marketing communications, there are more messages sent than received, as illustrated here.

Number Recalled	Proportion Recalling	Weighted Average
0	0.10	0.00
1	0.10	0.10
2	0.10	0.20
3	0.10	0.30
4	0.15	0.60
5	0.20	1.00
6	0.15	0.90
7	0.05	0.35
8	0.05	0.40
Total	**1.00**	**3.85**

In this example, eight marketing communications were directed to target customers. Ten percent did not recall seeing any of these ads, while five percent recalled seeing all eight. A weighted average of this recall yields an average message frequency of approximately four. This means the average target customer was exposed to the business's marketing communication approximately four times during the exposure period even though eight communications were directed at the target market. In television advertising, the combined impact of message frequency and reach produces an index called *gross rating points* (GRPs). As shown below, a business with a 60 percent reach and a frequency of four produces an impact of 240 GRPs. This is a far better measure of advertising effectiveness than the dollars spent on advertising, because GRPs better measure how well the ad reached a target market and how often it was seen.

$$\text{Gross Rating Points} = \text{Reach} \times \text{Frequency} = 60 \times 4 = 240$$

Ad Copy and Customer Response

A highly memorable marketing communication that does not communicate the product and its benefits will fail to enhance interest in the product and will lower the overall level of customer response. Ad copy is best able to attract customers when it is based on customer needs and situations familiar to customers. It needs to integrate customer needs and situations with the product's benefits and business name.[7] If an ad is attractive but fails to create product interest, the ad copy is of limited value to the customer or to the business.

MESSAGE REINFORCEMENT

Although building awareness, comprehension, and interest are critical in achieving a high level of target customer response, these levels will diminish, as shown in Figure

10.6, if the message is not continually reinforced. Johnson Controls' marketing communications program improved ad awareness, but to hold or continue to grow a high level of awareness, a company would have had to continually keep the message in front of target customers.

Message Reinforcement and Pulsing

Maintaining a high level of awareness is expensive and requires new ad copy as the old copy begins to wear out. One approach to message reinforcement that maintains awareness, reduces copy wearout, and is cost-efficient is *pulsing*.[8] Pulsing involves the use of alternating exposure periods. An example of pulsing is a television advertisement that achieves 150 gross rating points over a four-week exposure period and is run in alternating four-week periods. As shown in Figure 10.6, a certain level of awareness is built up during a four-week exposure period; it then diminishes to some degree over the following four-week period in which there is no message exposure, and then awareness is built up again in a subsequent four-week exposure period.

If a business can maintain a desired level of awareness with pulsing, it can reduce the cost of advertising because there is no advertising expenditure in alternating nonexposure four-week periods. A secondary benefit of pulsing is that it reduces the potential for copy wearout due to overexposure to the same message. Because the marketing message is not seen on a continual basis, the ad copy's novelty and appeal wear out at a slower rate. Also, pulsing reduces the potential for overexposure, which can cause customer irritation and reduce ad effectiveness.

Heavy-Up Message Frequency

Because certain products can be purchased more readily at some times of the year than at others, a business may use a heavy-up exposure pattern to build higher levels of awareness, comprehension, and, it is hoped, interest in the advertised product or service. Figure 10.7 illustrates a heavy-up marketing communications program for a well-known brand that is consumed most heavily in the summer. Many other exposure patterns are possible, but in this example, the business elects to maintain a certain level of base awareness throughout most of the year and to heavy-up its message frequency just before and during the prime buying period for this product. The business could also combine a heavy-up strategy for its primary promotion period and a pulsing strategy throughout the rest of the year.

STIMULATING CUSTOMER ACTION

Quite often, simply informing target customers and maintaining awareness are not enough to stimulate customer action. More is needed, particularly for new products whose benefits cannot be fully realized until they have been tried. For example, advertising copy that attempted to explain the benefits of the Post-it Note was simply not taken seriously by target customers.[9] And after 18 months in four test markets, 3M's efforts to communicate the benefits of Post-it Notes led nowhere. A further complication was that 3M had a policy against giving away free goods on a new product introduction. The

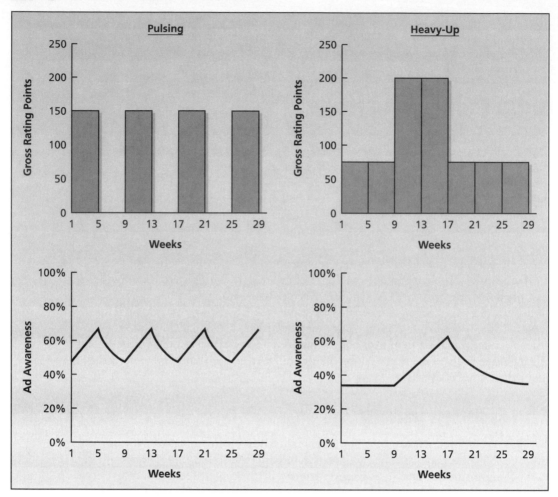

Figure 10.7 ◆ **Message Reinforcement Strategies**

marketing director opened a fifth test market to specifically get around the corporate policy and to generate trial purchase through a free sample program. This move enabled customers to discover the benefits of Post-it Notes by using them, and the product went on to be a great commercial success.

PUSH VS. PULL COMMUNICATIONS STRATEGIES

One almost always thinks of marketing communications as being directed toward customers, but an important aspect of marketing communications is communications directed toward channel intermediaries. Approximately one-third of marketing communications dollars is spent on customer advertising, and two-thirds on sales promotions. The largest portion of the sales promotion expense (37 percent of total spending) is spent on intermediary promotions, and the remaining portion (29 percent of total spending) on customer promotions. In total, approximately 63 percent of the marketing communications budget is spent on customers and 37 percent on intermediaries.

Customer-targeted marketing communications are *pull* type communications. The objectives of a pull-through marketing communication are to build awareness, attraction, and loyalty and to reduce search costs, as shown in Figure 10.8. When pull marketing communications are successful, customers will seek out certain products or services and, in essence, by the interest they create, pull the product through the channel. A pull strategy requires channel intermediaries to carry certain products or brands in order to attract and satisfy target customers.

Push communications are directed at channel intermediaries. The objective in this case is to motivate channel intermediaries to carry a particular product or brand and, in this way, make it more available to customers. When successful, push communications result in a wider range of availability, fewer stockouts, greater merchandising (shelf space), and a greater marketing effort than would have been achieved with little or no push communications.

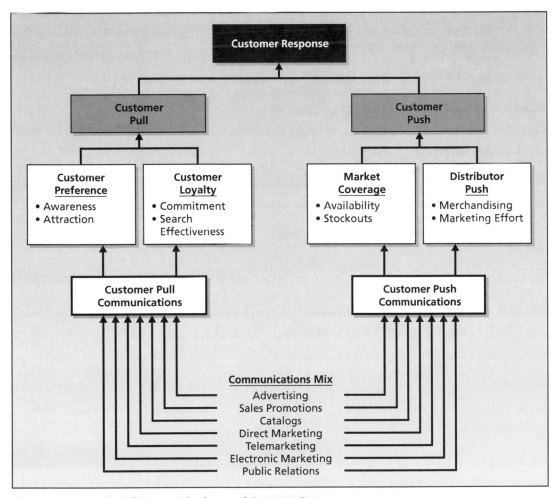

Figure 10.8 ◆ Push–Pull Communications and Customer Response

It is important, however, to understand that it is the combination of both push and pull marketing communications that creates the greatest impact on customer response and, therefore, market share gains.[10]

PULL COMMUNICATIONS AND CUSTOMER RESPONSE

As also shown in Figure 10.8, a wide range of alternative marketing communications can be used to create a communications mix designed to create customer pull.[11] To illustrate the power of media advertising, consider the fate of L&M cigarettes. Before cigarette advertising on television was banned, L&M had a 17 percent market share. After the ban, the decision was made to not advertise, because L&M management believed that other forms of advertising were ineffective. They were wrong, and today L&M is no longer on the market. The brand had good brand recognition and good customer pull. But, without continued reinforcement of the brand name and its positioning, it faded from customers' minds and, eventually, from the marketplace.

There are many forms of customer-directed sales promotions, such as coupons, rebates, sweepstakes, gifts, and rewards. When United Airlines initiated its Mileage Plus program, it changed how customers selected airlines and flights. Catalogs such as L.L. Bean, Eddie Bauer, Spiegel, and many others stimulate customer pull every month with mailings to targeted customers. Direct marketing and, more recently, electronic marketing on the Internet, take a similar, but even more customized, approach to creating customer pull in the marketplace.

Advertising Elasticity

The percent change in sales volume per one percent change in advertising effort is a measure of advertising elasticity. Although there are considerable variations among products and market situations, short-run advertising elasticities are relatively small when compared with price elasticities. A study of 128 advertising elasticities produced an average advertising elasticity of 0.22, with very few advertising elasticities greater than 0.5. This means that for every one percent change in advertising expenditures, there will be an estimated 0.22 percent change in volume sold.[12]

For instance a business with a sales volume of 200,000 units and a 0.22 advertising elasticity could estimate its sales to increase to a volume of 208,800 units with a 20 percent increase in advertising, as shown below.

$$\frac{\text{Sales}}{\text{Volume}} = \frac{\text{Current}}{\text{Volume}} \left[1 + \left(\text{Ad Elasticity} \times \frac{\text{Percent Change}}{\text{in Advertising}} \right) \right]$$

$$= 200,000 \times [1 + (0.22 \times 0.20)]$$

$$= 200,000 \times 1.044$$

$$= 208,800 \text{ units}$$

It is important to keep in mind that there are certain limits to what advertising can accomplish with respect to sales response at different stages of a product's life cycle. During the introductory stage, a business builds awareness, comprehension, and interest, but the market demand is small, and even when advertisements are very effective, only a limited volume and sales response are achievable.

The growth stage of a product's life cycle offers the greatest opportunity for sales gains using advertising. A business that does not invest in advertising during this phase is missing its best opportunity to grow sales, because advertising elasticities will be greatest during this period. However, as a market matures, there is less new volume coming into the market, and the effects of advertising on sales response begin to diminish. Finally, in declining markets, a business needs to cut back on advertising because dollars spent on advertising produce little, if any, sales response.

Advertising Carryover Effects

In addition to a short-run advertising impact on sales response, advertising also has been shown to have a long-run carryover effect. That is, the advertising effort made in a given period will produce some additional sales response in subsequent sales periods. Advertising carryover coefficients range from zero to less than one, with the average carryover coefficient equal to approximately 0.5.[13] This means that in the period immediately following the ad effort, a 0.50 sales effect from the previous period will carry over. In the second period, the carryover effect of 0.50 is squared, and 0.25 of the sales response produced two periods earlier occurs, and so on, as shown in Figure 10.9.

Recall the business with a short-run advertising elasticity of 0.22 that could expect a short-run increase of 80,000 units in sales revenue from a 20 percent increase in advertis-

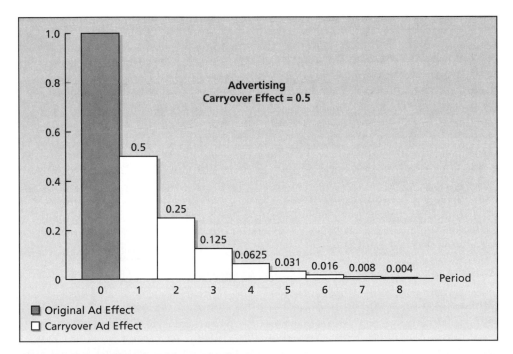

Figure 10.9 ◆ Media Advertising and Sales Carryover

ing expenditures. The total impact of this ad expenditure, using a 0.50 carryover effect, is approximately 160,000 units, as shown next. Thus, the overall sales response to the advertising effort would have been double the short-run effect as shown in Figure 10.10 and calculated below.

$$\frac{\text{Total Sales}}{\text{Effect}} = \frac{\text{Original Sales Effect}}{(1 - \text{Carryover Effect})} = \frac{80,000 \text{ units}}{(1 - 0.5)} = 160,000 \text{ units}$$

Direct Marketing Promotions

Database marketing makes customized direct-mail programs a viable opportunity to efficiently reach target customers and provide them with an incentive to take action. For example, consider a new sparkling wine, for which the producer direct mailed 100,000 known champagne consumers a $5 coupon good on the purchase of its sparkling wine. As shown in Figure 10.10, only 5 percent of the target customers responded by using the coupon. Of these 5,000 customers, 2,000 tried the new sparkling wine but did not repurchase; 1,000 used the coupon and became occasional buyers at the rate of one bottle per year; and 2,000 used the coupon and became regular purchasers at the rate of four bottles per year. Among the 95 percent who did not respond, 30 percent never opened the mailer and 65 percent opened it and were favorably impressed. Of these 65,000 customers, 5,000 purchased the product without the coupon at a later date. In total, 16,000 bottles of the new sparkling wine were purchased as a result of the direct-mail program, even though there was only a 5 percent initial response.[14]

*Regular customers purchase four times per year, and occasional customers once per year.

Figure 10.10 ◆ Customer Response to a Direct Marketing Promotion

Promotional Price Elasticity

The average price elasticity for consumer nondurable products is –1.76 according to a study of 367 brands.[15] However, the price promotion price elasticities for the three product categories shown in Figure 10.11 are considerably higher.[16]

Assume the market demand for sparkling wine is 10 million bottles per year and that a particular brand has a 4 percent market share resulting in a unit volume of 400,000 bottles. Without advertising, this brand should experience a promotional price elasticity of –10. Thus, a 5 percent price promotion should yield a 50 percent increase in unit volume, from 400,000 to 600,000, as shown below.

$$\text{Unit Volume} = (10 \text{ million} \times .04) \times [1 + (-10 \times -.05)]$$
$$= 400{,}000 \times 1.5$$
$$= 600{,}000 \text{ bottles}$$

By combining a price promotion with advertising, the promotional price elasticity can be further increased, as shown in Figure 10.11. For example, the promotion price elasticity of sparkling wine increases to approximately –14 with the support of an advertising campaign. This would produce an additional unit sales of 80,000 with a 5 percent price promotion.

$$\text{Unit Volume} = (10 \text{ million} \times .04) \times [1 + (-14 \times -.05)]$$
$$= 400{,}000 \times 1.7$$
$$= 680{,}000 \text{ bottles}$$

In all three cases shown in Figure 10.11, the promotional price elasticity increased significantly with the use of advertising. For cat litter, this effect was very dramatic, doubling

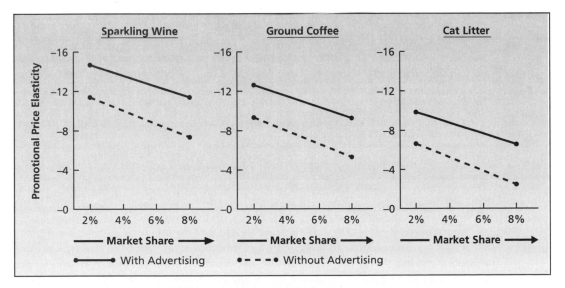

Figure 10.11 ◆ Promotional Elasticity and Advertising Support

promotional elasticities. It is also important to note that the promotional elasticities decreased with the increase in market share.

Recognizing the high level of price sensitivity to promotions and the tremendous short-run revenue gain that can be achieved from a price promotion, one can understand why many companies have increased their use of them. However, a marketing strategy that seeks profitable growth must also produce a higher net marketing contribution. Thus, it is important in market-based management to also assess the profit impact of a marketing communications effort.

PUSH COMMUNICATIONS AND CUSTOMER RESPONSE

Marketing communications directed at intermediaries are designed as push communications; they stimulate intermediaries to engage in aggressive customer promotion efforts. As seen in Figure 10.8, the objective of push communications is to build greater product availability and marketing effort. Businesses that are aggressive in rewarding and supporting channel intermediaries are able to obtain more market coverage (number of desired distributors) than are nonaggressive businesses. This support provides several mechanisms to deliver effective in-store merchandising and marketing efforts of a business's products.

Trade Promotions and Customer Response

Trade promotions designed to stimulate purchase are common among businesses who sell their products through intermediaries. Quite often, trade promotions involve price reductions to distributors or retailers. The idea is that the price incentive will motivate the intermediary to push the product.

For example, assume that a normal can of orange juice concentrate costs $1.49 and the manufacturer offers a $0.20 discount to encourage the retail trade to push the sale of frozen concentrate. Assume also that the normal sales level is 1 million cans per month; the retailer margin is normally $0.19 per can; the manufacturer's sales and distribution costs are $0.15 per can; and each unit costs $0.50 to produce. In nonpromotion months, the manufacturer would expect to make $650,000 in total contribution, as is shown below.

$$
\begin{aligned}
\text{Total Contribution (current)} &= \text{Current Volume} \times \left(\text{Retail Price} - \text{Retailer Margin} - \text{Sales and Distribution Cost} - \text{Unit Cost} \right) \\
&= 1,000,000 \times (\$1.49 - \$0.19 - \$0.15 - \$0.50) \\
&= 1,000,000 \times \$0.65 \\
&= \$650,000
\end{aligned}
$$

An important question for the manufacturer should be how much volume a trade promotion would have to produce to make a promotional period as profitable as a typical nonpromotion period. With the discount, the manufacturer's net promotional margin per unit drops to $0.45 per can. As shown below, the business would have to increase sales by 44 percent to 1.44 million cans in order to produce the same level of profitability.

$$\$650{,}000 \;=\; \frac{\text{Promotion}}{\text{Volume}} \times (\$1.49 - \$0.19 - \$0.15 - \$0.50 - \$0.20 \text{ discount})$$

$$\$650{,}000 \;=\; \frac{\text{Promotion}}{\text{Volume}} \times \$.045$$

$$\frac{\text{Promotion}}{\text{Volume}} \;=\; 1.44 \text{ million units}$$

Forward Buying and Customer Response

Trade promotions such as the one just described often result in forward buying by both customers and retailers. If the product is promoted effectively, customers will buy more during the promotion and will not have the same level of need in the following nonpro-

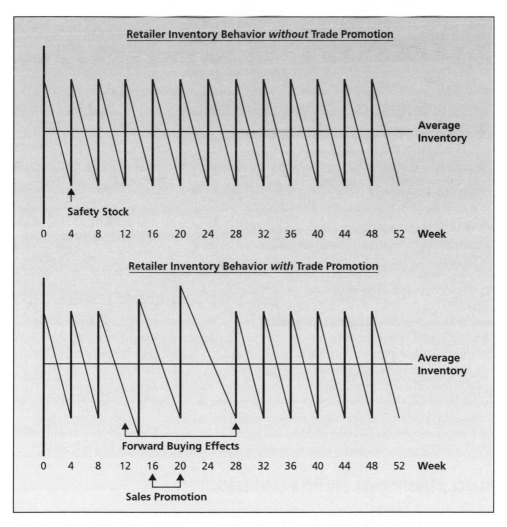

Figure 10.12 ◆ Retailer Inventories and Forward Buying on a Trade Promotion

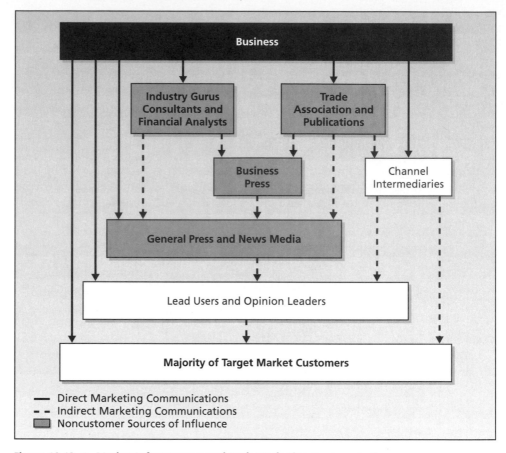

Figure 10.13 ◆ Market Infrastructure and Push Marketing Communications

motion period. The impact of customer forward buying was presented in chapter 8 with the discussion of price promotions.

Retailer forward buying involves less buying before the trade promotion as well as buying more than is needed during the promotion to take full advantage of the discounted price. These aspects of retailer trade promotion forward buying are illustrated in Figure 10.12, and the profit impact is presented in chapter 8 with the discussion of price promotions.

The net effect of forward buying is that retailers are able to buy at lower prices for a period much longer than the promotion. One study found that 80 percent of the products purchased by retailers were purchased at promotional prices. Buying at promotional prices, of course, greatly affects the manufacturer's profitability. This combination of customer stockpiling (customer forward buying) and deal-prone shopping (switching from one deal to another) makes it very difficult for manufacturers to make a profit on push sale promotions.[17]

Market Infrastructure and Push Communications

Figure 10.13 illustrates a communications market infrastructure that includes both end customers and intermediaries and nonmarket sources that influence them.[18] For example, marketing communications targeted at industry gurus, consultants, and financial analysts create secondary marketing communications that, in turn, influence the trade press, business press, and the general press. These nonmarket sources of influence, in turn, provide information to channel intermediaries and customers.

The solid lines in Figure 10.13 represent normal marketing communications targeted at customers or intermediaries. The dashed lines represent public relations–type communications that are targeted at individuals and institutions that influence customers and channel intermediaries. Some of these public relations communications are *primary* communications (from the company to the source of influence), and others are *secondary* communications (from one source of influence to another). Of course, one of the most important sources of secondary market communications is from lead users and opinion leaders who communicate by word of mouth to the larger market of target customers.

SUMMARY

Without an effective marketing communications program, a marketing strategy will fail. Target customers must be made aware of the product and its benefits, be continually reminded of these benefits, and stimulated to take action. Building awareness, message comprehension, and interest are essential phases in building a high level of customer response. The customer response index is a diagnostic tool to help a management team determine the sources of weakness in its marketing communications program.

To be effective and cost-efficient, a business's marketing communications must reach target customers and deliver an adequate level of message frequency to maintain desired levels of awareness, comprehension, and interest. Pulsing enables a business to use alternate exposure periods to more economically maintain customer awareness and interest while reducing the problem of ad copy wearout. Heavy-up efforts enable a business to build awareness and interest to higher levels during seasonal buying periods.

To build market share, a business needs both pull and push marketing communications. Pull marketing communications are targeted at customers with the intent of creating enough awareness and interest to motivate customers to demand the business's product. This customer demand creates market pull on intermediaries who, in turn, want the business's products to satisfy this customer demand. Push marketing communications are directed at intermediaries, with the intent of pushing the product through the channel. The objective of push communications is to create greater availability of, interest in, and access to the business's products.

Although the sales response to a marketing communication is difficult to estimate, the customer response index, advertising elasticity, advertising carryover effects, and promotional price elasticity provide systematic methods for estimating this response. However, sales response should not be the primary objective of a marketing communication. For marketing communications designed to increase sales, it is more important to estimate the profit impact of that promotion. Many sales promotions are not profitable, but businesses are forced into them to minimize losses.

In most markets, there is a marketing communications infrastructure that includes customers, intermediaries, and nonmarket sources of influence. Some push-through marketing communications are public relations–type communications directed at nonmarket sources of influence that, in turn, influence customers and intermediaries.

APPLICATION PROBLEM: GARDENBURGERS

The market demand for meatless burgers was approximately $225 million in 1997 and growing at 20 percent per year. International Research Institute (IRI) estimates from its household panel data that 6.8 million households bought meatless burgers in 1997. They also estimated that the meatless burger market would grow to 40 million households. Industry revenues were estimated to be $257 million in 1998 and to grow to $500 million by 2000 and $1 billion by 2005.

Gardenburger obtained a 35 percent market share with sales of approximately $90 million in 1998. To capture this share position, Gardenburger had made a bold move to build its brand name and legitimize the meatless burger market. Gardenburger spent $17 million in 1998 on media advertising, $1.5 million of which was spent one night on the final episode of *Seinfeld*. That show reached 76 million people, and the response was phenomenal. The week following the *Seinfeld* ad campaign the sales of meatless burgers increased 100 percent from the same week the year before, as shown below. Gardenburger's sales growth was up 414 percent from the same week a year earlier.

Category	1997	1998	Percent Change
Entire Market	$1.9 million	$3.8 million	100
Gardenburger	$370,000	$1.9 million	414

In addition to the *Seinfeld* campaign, Gardenburger spent $14 million on print and other TV advertising. This bought 1,500 TV spots and appearances in 20 magazines in an effort to build brand recognition, market share, and growth of the meatless burger market.

Questions

For Internet discussion, go to www.prenhall.com/phbusiness.

1. What was Gardenburger's cost per exposure (assuming all 76 million viewers saw the Gardenburger ad)? What percent of sales was Gardenburger spending on advertising?

2. Assuming the market growth was 20 percent from 1997 to 1998, what would Gardenburger's sales have been without the *Seinfeld* ad (assuming no other share growth)? What percentage of sales over projected sales actually occurred one year later?

3. What was the advertising elasticity for the Gardenburger *Seinfeld* ad campaign? How would you recommend evaluating the effectiveness of their overall marketing communications budget of $17 million?

MARKET-BASED LOGIC AND STRATEGIC THINKING

1. Why are customer awareness and message comprehension critical to the success of a marketing strategy?

2. How can interest in ad copy affect interest in a product and, subsequently, customer response?

3. When a business has an excellent marketing communications program and high intention to purchase, but a very low customer response, what kind of a marketing problem does it face?

4. When should a business use a combination of pulsing and heavy-up marketing communications?
5. Why is the message frequency for a marketing communication considerably lower than the number of messages sent?
6. Why will a business's market share be lower if it is not effective in both pull-through and push-through marketing communications?
7. At what stage of a product's life cycle is advertising elasticity likely to be highest?
8. How should the carryover sales effect of an advertising effort be used in evaluating the profit impact of the advertising effort?
9. What are the various behaviors that need to be tracked in order to evaluate the profit impact of a trade promotion?
10. How does the promotional price elasticity for a product change with advertising support? What effect does market share have on promotional price elasticity?
11. Why are the marketing communications infrastructure and public relations–type marketing communications important to the overall success of a marketing communications effort?
12. If advertising elasticity is so much smaller than promotional price elasticity, why should a business advertise?
13. How should a business use the advertising carryover effect in evaluating the sales response and profitability of a marketing communication?
14. Why are indirect sales promotions rarely profitable? If they are not profitable, why do manufacturers continue to offer them?
15. How does retailer forward buying affect trade promotion profitability?

NOTES

1. P. Stepankowsky, "Gardenburger Ad Campaign Shifts into Second Gear in Branding Push," *The Wall Street Journal* (May 4, 1999):A12.
2. C. Gonzales, "Gardenburger Returns to Profitability," *The Oregonian* (October 15, 1998):D1.
3. Betty Arndt, "Johnson Controls' 'Classic Buildings' Marketing Campaign—A Pre- and Post-Campaign Evaluation," in *Drive Marketing Excellence* (New York, Institute for International Research, 1994).
4. Peter Danaher and Roland Rust, "Determining the Optimal Level of Media Spending," *Journal of Advertising Research* (January–February 1994):28–34.
5. David Bender, Peter Farquhar, and Sanford Schulert, "Growing from the Top," *Marketing Management* (Winter/Spring 1996):10–19.
6. H. Zielske, "The Remembering and Forgetting of Advertising," *Journal of Marketing* (January 1959):140; and J. Simon, "What Do Zielske's Real Data Really Show about Pulsing," *Journal of Marketing Research* (August 1979):415–20.
7. Brian Wansink and Michael Ray, "Advertising Strategies to Increase Usage Frequency," *Journal of Marketing* (January 1996):31–46.
8. Vijay Mahajan, Eitan Muller, John E. Little, and Hugh Zielske, "Advertising Pulsing Policies for Generating Awareness of New Products," *Marketing Science* (Spring 1986):86–106.
9. Cliff Havener and Margaret Thorpe, "Customers Can Tell You What They Want," *Management Review* (December 1994):42–45.
10. David Reibstein, "Making the Most of Your Marketing Dollars," in *Drive Marketing Excellence* (New York: Institute for International Research, 1994).

11. Gary Lilien, Philip Kotler, and K. Moorthy, *Marketing Models* (Upper Saddle River, NJ: Prentice Hall, 1992):329–56.

12. Gert Assmus, John Farley, and Donald Lehmann, "How Advertising Affects Sales: Meta Analysis of Econometric Results," *Journal of Marketing Research* (February 1984):65–74.

13. Ron Schultz and Martin Block, "Empirical Estimates of Advertising Response Factors," *Journal of Media Planning* (Fall 1986):17–24.

14. Stan Rapp and Tom Collins, *Maximarketing* (New York: McGraw-Hill, 1987).

15. Robert Blattberg and Scott Neslin, *Sales Promotion Concepts, Methods and Strategies* (Upper Saddle River, NJ: Prentice Hall, 1990):356.

16. Albert Bemmaor and Dominique Mouchoux, "Measuring the Short-Term Effect of In-Store Promotion and Retail Advertising on Brand Sales," *Journal of Marketing Research* (May 1991):202–14.

17. Robert Blattberg and Alan Levin, "Modeling the Effectiveness and Profitability of Trade Promotions," *Marketing Science* (Spring 1987):124–46.

18. Regis McKenna, *The Regis Touch: New Marketing Strategies for Uncertain Times* (Reading, MA: Addison-Wesley, 1985).

part IV

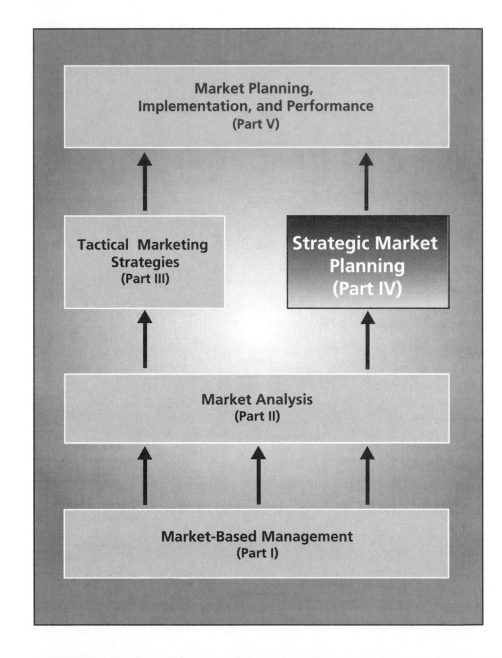

Strategic Market Planning

The concept is interesting and well-formed, but in order to earn better than a "C" grade, the idea must be feasible.

—Yale University professor's comments on Fred Smith's thesis proposing the overnight delivery service known today as FedEx

Strategic market planning sets the strategic direction for a business and plays a critical part in achieving a business's long-run objectives of sales growth, profit performance, and share position. Tactical marketing strategies (covered in part III) are more short-run, but essential to establishing desired target market positions and producing short-run growth and profit performance. Although each impacts growth, profitability, and share position, long-run marketing strategies set the strategic direction, and short-run target market positioning strategies provide the tactical marketing strategies needed to incrementally work toward long-run goals.

To facilitate the strategic market planning process, each product–market of interest is strategically assessed with respect to market attractiveness and position of competitive advantage. Using these two dimensions of strategic opportunity and position, in chapter 11 we will present a method of building a strategic market planning portfolio which would include all existing and potential product–markets.

The strategic market plans generated by the portfolio analysis can be either offensive or defensive. Offensive strategic market plans, presented in chapter 12, are growth-oriented plans built around share penetration or market growth of existing markets or plans to enter new existing or emerging markets. Offensive strategic market plans are critical to business growth and future market position and profitability.

Defensive strategic market plans, presented in chapter 13, are designed to protect market positions and profitability. Defensive strategic market plans can include protecting profitable market positions, reducing market focus to improve profitability, and harvesting and divestment strategies which will terminate with market exit. Defensive strategic market plans are critical to current share, sales, and profit performance.

chapter 11

Portfolio Analysis and Strategic Market Plans

The General Electric Company has evolved from having a relatively concentrated focus on electrical products to having a diverse portfolio of product–markets, as shown in Figure 11.1. Today, the GE portfolio includes light bulbs, household appliances, medical systems, plastics, transformers, jet engines, financial services, transportation equipment, steam turbines, and broadcasting. However, each product–market in the GE portfolio is under continuous review with respect to *share position, sales growth,* and *profit performance* in an effort to meet shareholder performance expectations. By the late 1990s, General Electric had created a market value (shares times price per share) of $360 billion, the largest of any U.S. company.

Successful companies such as General Electric, Coca-Cola, and Hewlett-Packard achieve year-after-year success with a great deal of strategic market planning.[1] These businesses are committed to serving shareholders, and this requires continuous review of current performance, new opportunities, and funding and investment decisions that contribute to a balance of short- and long-run performance. Product–market diversification is one aspect of portfolio analysis and strategic market planning.

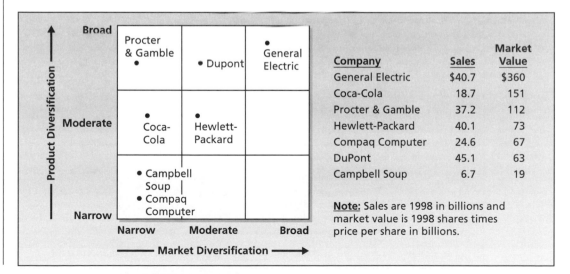

Company	Sales	Market Value
General Electric	$40.7	$360
Coca-Cola	18.7	151
Procter & Gamble	37.2	112
Hewlett-Packard	40.1	73
Compaq Computer	24.6	67
DuPont	45.1	63
Campbell Soup	6.7	19

Note: Sales are 1998 in billions and market value is 1998 shares times price per share in billions.

Figure 11.1 ◆ Product–Market Diversification

PRODUCT–MARKET DIVERSIFICATION

Diversification across product–markets adds two important advantages to the overall performance of a business. First, it reduces dependence on any single product–market. And second, by diversifying, a business can smooth overall performance with offsetting conditions created by the competitive conditions and product life cycles in different product–markets.

For example, Figure 11.2 illustrates the overall sales of a business that is diversified across different product–markets. In product–market A, its core market, sales are growing at an average rate of 1.5 percent per year, but this growth varies from year to year because of economic conditions and competitive forces. Because the business is also posi-

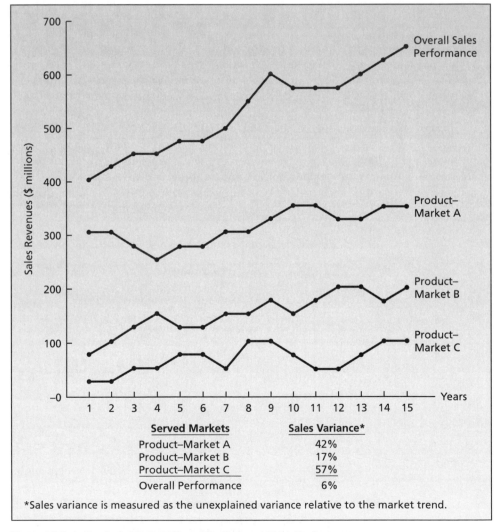

Served Markets	Sales Variance*
Product–Market A	42%
Product–Market B	17%
Product–Market C	57%
Overall Performance	6%

*Sales variance is measured as the unexplained variance relative to the market trend.

Figure 11.2 ◆ Product–Market Diversification and Sales Performance

tioned in two other, diversified product–markets, it is able to take advantage of offsetting product life cycles and competitive forces. Product–market B is growing at 4 percent per year and product–market C at almost 15 percent per year. Although sales in each of these two markets are much less than in the company's core market, product–market A, each contributes to overall sales growth and stabilizes performance.

The unexplained sales variance over the time period shown for product–market A is 42 percent, and for product–markets B and C, 17 and 57 percent, respectively. When the sales performances of all three markets are combined, the offsetting effects created by different competitive conditions and product life cycles produce more consistent growth, with only a 6 percent unexplained variance in the sales trend for the time period shown.

Product diversification provides one level of diversification. Obviously, the less dependent a business is on a single product, the less vulnerable it is to a major change in performance. For instance, Coca-Cola has a very broad line of beverage products that serves virtually all world markets. For Procter & Gamble, diversification goes further, as P&G has developed product positions in widely diversified consumer household product–markets. And General Electric, as discussed earlier, has expanded into a wide range of product–markets unrelated to its original electrical products.

Market diversification provides another way to achieve growth and risk reduction. DuPont, for example, has diversified across many markets that range from carpets to swimsuits and cookware with products such as Nylon, Dacron, Teflon, Lycra, Kevlar, and many others. This diversification has enabled DuPont to grow to a $50 billion company and yet not be dependent on any one product or market. In the early 1990s, US West split its company in two to better serve diverse markets. US West Communications remained in charge of the more mature core telecommunications businesses, while MediaOne Group was created to grow in high-technology markets. In the late 1990s, Hewlett-Packard did the same thing when it split its company into two companies, one an $8 billion test and measurement business and the other a $39 billion computer and imaging business. This split enabled HP to move faster in emerging computer and imaging markets without abandoning its core product–markets in test and measurement.

Although each product–market is going to experience periods of economic recession and growth, it is unlikely that *all* product–markets will experience the same conditions at the same time. Thus, participation in several diversified product–markets has the effect of offsetting economic conditions and product life cycle influences, thereby reducing the overall variability of business performance.

STRATEGIC MARKET PLANNING PROCESS

Each product–market in a business's portfolio in some way contributes to both the short-run and the long-run performance of the business. And, depending on current and future share position and performance, some product–markets will receive additional investment to grow or defend an important strategic market position. Other product–markets will be required to reduce focus in order to achieve a stronger competitive position and profit contribution with available resources. Still others may have resources withdrawn from them as a business begins to exit these product–markets. Because resources in any business are limited, a business needs a strategic market plan to carefully map out its future share position, sales growth, and profit performance. A strategic market plan sets the direction and provides guidelines for resource allocation.[2]

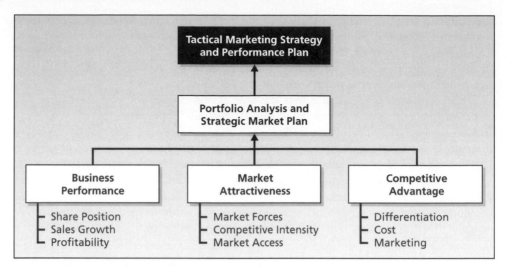

Figure 11.3 ◆ Strategic Market Planning Process

In order to specify a strategic direction for a product–market and to allocate resources to obtain desired short- and long-run performance, a business needs a *strategic market planning process*,[3] as outlined in Figure 11.3. The first step in this process is a careful assessment of current *business performance, market attractiveness,* and *competitive advantage* for each product–market a business wishes to consider over a three- to five-year strategic market planning horizon. With this information, the business can perform a *portfolio analysis* to better understand the current position of each product–market and its performance. On the basis of the portfolio position of each product–market, a *strategic market plan* can then be specified with respect to a desired set of performance objectives.

However, to make the strategic market plan actionable, the business has to develop a *tactical marketing strategy* in accordance with the strategic market plan and resources allocated. As the strategic market plan and a corresponding tactical marketing strategy are rolled out over a planning horizon, a *performance plan* outlines the short-run and long-run share position, sales growth, and profitability.[4] This chapter reviews the strategic market planning process and how it maps the short- and long-run performance of a business.

BUSINESS PERFORMANCE

Because each product–market can vary in attractiveness and competitive advantage, there can be a wide range of performance outcomes. The primary objective of a strategic market plan is to create a strategic direction and set of objectives for any product–market that affect three critical areas of business performance:

- **Share Position:** How will the strategic market plan contribute to the product–market's share and competitive advantage?
- **Sales Growth:** How much will the strategic market plan contribute to the business's sales revenue growth?

- **Profit Performance:** How will the strategic market plan affect short- and long-run profitability and contribute to shareholder value?

The strategic market plan for any given product–market is intended to produce results in all three areas of business performance. One of the primary objectives of a strategic market plan is to make explicit how the share position, sales revenue, and profit performance will change over time. For instance, a strategic market plan to *grow* share in a growing market will produce drastically different levels of performance than will a strategic market plan to *protect* market share in an increasingly competitive mature market.

MARKET ATTRACTIVENESS

The primary purpose of a strategic market plan is to provide a *strategic direction* from which to set performance objectives and guide the development of a tactical marketing strategy. This is an important step in the strategic market planning process, because it requires a careful examination of market attractiveness. This step allows us to compare the relative attractiveness of different product–markets using a common set of attractiveness criteria. To facilitate this step in the strategic market planning process, we need a systematic way to assess market attractiveness.

To assess and index the attractiveness of a product–market, a business must ask itself, "What factors make a market attractive or unattractive?" Factors that typically shape market attractiveness include market size, market growth, competition, margin potential, market access, and fit with the company's core capabilities. These factors can be meaningfully grouped into three dimensions of market attractiveness: *market forces, competitive intensity,* and *market access,* as shown in Figure 11.4.

Each of these three dimensions of market attractiveness can be weighted to reflect its importance in relation to the others. In the example presented in Figure 11.5, market forces and market access are each weighted as 30 percent of total importance, whereas competitive intensity is weighted a little more heavily at 40 percent. Each of the dimensions of market attractiveness is further broken down into factors that contribute to a particular aspect of market attractiveness. These factors are also weighted to represent their relative importance within a dimension.

Figure 11.4 ◆ Factors That Shape Market Attractiveness

When these and other factors that are considered to be important are weighted by their relative importance, an overall index for market attractiveness can be created, as illustrated in Figure 11.5. Special care should be taken to ensure that all the underlying forces that shape market attractiveness are adequately represented, on the basis of market and profit performance.[5]

In the example shown, each individual factor is also indexed from "very unattractive" to "very attractive" for a given product–market. This score (from 0 to 6) is multiplied by the factor weight to obtain a weighted individual factor attractiveness score. The sum of these individual scores for each dimension is computed and multiplied by the importance given that dimension. For example, market size is assigned 40 percent of relative importance within the market forces dimension and is given a rating of 6: very attractive. This results in a score of 240 (40 × 6) for this factor. This score is added to the scores of the other factors in this dimension to arrive at a total factor-weighted score of 370. This is multiplied by 0.30, the relative importance (weight) assigned to market

Market Attractiveness Factor	Relative Importance	Not 0	1	Attractive 2	3	4	Very 5	6	Overall Score
Market Forces									
Market Size	40%							X	240
Growth Rate	30%			X					60
Buyer Power	20%			X					40
Customer Loyalty	10%				X				30
	100%								370
Competitive Intensity									
Number of Competitors	30%				X				90
Price Rivalry	30%			X					60
Ease of Entry	20%						X		100
Substitutes	20%					X			80
	100%								330
Market Access									
Customer Familiarity	20%							X	120
Channel Access	40%						X		200
Sales Requirements	30%					X			120
Company Fit	10%							X	60
	100%								500

Market Attractiveness	Relative Weight	Factor Score	Overall Score	Maximum Score	Percent of Max.
Market Forces	0.30	370	111	180	62%
Competitive Intensity	0.40	330	132	240	55%
Market Access	0.30	500	150	180	83%
	1.00	1200	393	600	66%

Figure 11.5 ◆ Indexing the Market Attractiveness of a Market

forces, to produce a weighted overall score of 111 (62 percent of maximum), as shown in Figure 11.5.

When this process is completed for each of the market attractiveness factors and dimensions, an overall score of 393 is obtained. But, because different markets may have fewer or more factors and different dimension weights, the maximum score for different product–markets can vary. Therefore, to maintain comparability, the maximum possible score is derived, and the overall market attractiveness score is determined, as a percent of the maximum. In this example, the maximum score is 600, and the overall index market attractiveness score is 66 percent.

COMPETITIVE ADVANTAGE

The process of developing a multifactor index of competitive advantage follows the same procedure. The first question is, "What makes one business strong, with respect to competitive advantage, and another weak?" In answering this question, many businesses will arrive at a list of factors that determine competitive advantage that can be categorized into three dimensions of competitive advantage: *cost advantage, differentiation advantage,* and *marketing advantage.* Each of these drivers of competitive advantage also has underlying forces that shape the business's competitive advantage,[6] as shown in Figure 11.6.

Each of the three dimensions of competitive advantage is assigned a relative weight, just as was done in determining market attractiveness. And, as with market attractiveness, for each of the underlying factors, the relative importance within the dimension must be determined, as illustrated in Figure 11.7. Each factor must be assessed with respect to the competitive advantage of the business in its existing market or the potential position in new markets under consideration.

As shown in Figure 11.7, the competitive forces that shape a differentiation advantage for this business are relatively strong at 68 percent of maximum, while its competitive advantage with respect to marketing advantage is weak at 23 percent of maximum. Overall, the business is midrange in terms of competitive advantage, with a score of 52 percent.

Figure 11.6 ◆ Determinants of Competitive Advantage

Competitive Advantage Factors	Relative Importance	Way Behind 0	1	Equal 2	3	4	Way Ahead 5	6	Overall Score
Differentiation Advantage									
Product Quality	50%						X		250
Service Quality	30%			X					60
Brand Image	10%						X		50
Relative Price	10%						X		50
	100%								410
Cost Advantage									
Unit Cost	40%					X			160
Transaction Cost	10%		X						10
Marketing Expenses	30%				X				90
Overhead Expenses	20%			X					40
	100%								300
Marketing Advantage									
Market Share	30%		X						30
Brand Awareness	10%			X					20
Distribution	30%			X					60
Sales Coverage	30%		X						30
	100%								140

Source of Competitive Advantage	Relative Weight	Factor Score	Overall Score	Maximum Score	Percent of Max.
Cost Advantage	0.40	300	120	240	50%
Differentiation Advantage	0.40	410	164	240	68%
Marketing Advantage	0.20	140	28	120	23%
	1.00	850	312	600	53%

Figure 11.7 ◆ Indexing a Business's Competitive Advantage

PORTFOLIO ANALYSIS AND STRATEGIC MARKET PLANS

When we combine the overall competitive advantage score with the overall market attractiveness score, we can create a product–market portfolio. Each product–market served by a business can be placed in a portfolio such as the one shown in Figure 11.8. Product–markets strong in market attractiveness and competitive advantage present the strongest portfolio position and best opportunity for profit performance.[7] Having product–markets in this position usually would lead to a strategic market plan to *invest to protect* this attractive position of advantage. For each combination of market attractiveness and competitive advantage, there is at least one strategic market plan to be considered,[8] as shown in Figure 11.8.

As shown in Figure 11.8, attractive product–markets are most likely to warrant an *of-*

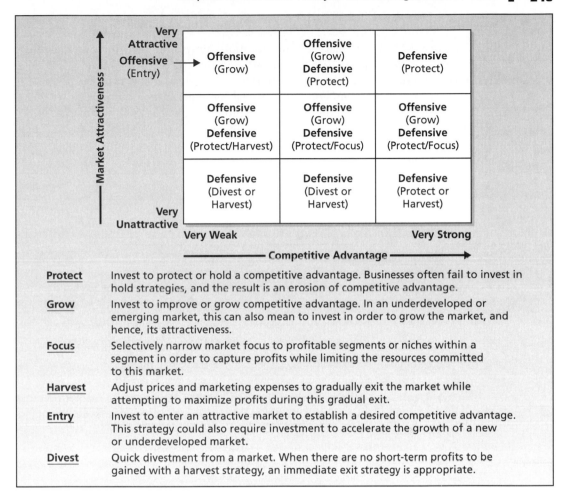

Figure 11.8 ◆ Portfolio Analysis and Strategic Market Plans

fensive strategic market plan. Strategic market plans can vary from improving a business's competitive advantage in attractive market situations to entering a new market. In addition, there may be opportunities to help develop or grow attractive emerging markets in which the business has the potential for a strong competitive advantage.

On the basis of a portfolio analysis and performance objectives, a business would select either an offensive or a defensive strategic market plan. First, with respect to performance objectives, offensive strategic market plans are geared to deliver above-average performance in the areas of sales growth, share position, and long-run profit performance. Defensive strategic market plans are important in producing short-run profit performance and protecting important share positions, while also contributing to long-run profit. Strategic market planning requires a careful balance of offensive and defensive strategic market plans in order to meet short-run profit objectives and investor expectations while investing in the business to protect important strategic positions, as well as developing stronger share positions in existing or new markets.

Offensive Strategic Market Plans and Performance Impact

Because offensive strategic market plans are more growth-oriented than are defensive plans, they are more likely to occur in attractive markets.[9] For example, consider Compaq Computer in the late 1990s. In 1997, Compaq was the share leader, with a 12.5 percent share in an 80 million unit personal computer market that was growing at a rate of 15 percent per year. Compaq's average selling price was $2,500, but market prices were eroding at a rate of 6 percent per year. Compaq's margins were holding at 25 percent of sales, and marketing expenses were 8 percent of sales. The combination of these factors produced the following level of performance.

$$\frac{\text{Sales}}{\text{Revenue}} = \frac{\text{Market}}{\text{Demand}} \times \frac{\text{Market}}{\text{Share}} \times \frac{\text{Price}}{\text{per Unit}}$$

$$\$25 \text{ billion} = 80 \text{ million} \times 0.125 \times \$2,500$$

$$\frac{\text{Marketing}}{\text{Expenses}} = \frac{\text{Sales}}{\text{Revenue}} \times \frac{\text{Percent Marketing}}{\text{Expenses}}$$

$$\$2 \text{ billion} = \$25 \text{ million} \times 0.08$$

$$\frac{\text{Net Marketing}}{\text{Contribution}} = \left(\frac{\text{Market}}{\text{Demand}} \times \frac{\text{Market}}{\text{Share}} \times \frac{\text{Price}}{\text{per Unit}} \times \frac{\text{Percent}}{\text{Margin}} \right) - \frac{\text{Marketing}}{\text{Expenses}}$$

$$\$4.25 \text{ billion} = 80 \text{ million} \times 0.125 \times \$2,500 \times 0.25 - \$2 \text{ billion}$$

An offensive strategy to grow market share to 14 percent in a growing market presents a bigger strategic challenge. This strategic market plan would require more resources. Assuming resources are available and the same assumptions hold, we could estimate the following year's performance impact of this strategy as shown below.

$$\frac{\text{Sales}}{\text{Revenue}} = \frac{\text{Market}}{\text{Demand}} \times \frac{\text{Market}}{\text{Share}} \times \frac{\text{Price}}{\text{per Unit}}$$

$$\$30.3 \text{ billion} = 92 \text{ million} \times 0.14 \times \$2,350$$

$$\frac{\text{Marketing}}{\text{Expenses}} = \frac{\text{Sales}}{\text{Revenues}} \times \frac{\text{Percent Marketing}}{\text{Expenses}}$$

$$\$2.4 \text{ billion} = \$30.3 \text{ billion} \times 0.08$$

$$\frac{\text{Net Marketing}}{\text{Contribution}} = \left(\frac{\text{Market}}{\text{Demand}} \times \frac{\text{Market}}{\text{Share}} \times \frac{\text{Price}}{\text{per Unit}} \times \frac{\text{Percent}}{\text{Margin}} \right) - \frac{\text{Marketing}}{\text{Expenses}}$$

$$\$5.2 \text{ billion} = (92 \text{ million} \times 0.14 \times \$2,350 \times 0.25) - \$2.4 \text{ billion}$$

If an offensive strategic market plan to grow share to 14 percent were successfully implemented, sales revenues in 1998 would have grown by $5 billion to $30.3 billion. More important, net marketing contribution would have increased by $950 million. Overall, this strategy would have contributed to an increased share position, sales growth, and growth in profits.

Defensive Strategic Market Plans and Performance Impact

Defensive strategic market plans are designed to protect important strategic market positions and to be large contributors to short-run cash flow and profit performance. As shown in Figure 11.8, defensive strategic market plans are most likely to occur in attractive markets with strong competitive advantage or in unattractive markets with weak levels of competitive advantage.

Defensive strategic market plans involve protecting or reducing the market scope within existing markets,[10] as shown in Figure 11.9. Defensive strategic market plans can also involve harvesting or divesting market share positions in existing markets.[11] As such, defensive strategic market plans are less likely to generate significant sales revenue growth except for a defensive strategy to protect (hold) share in a growing market. However, defensive strategic market plans are critical sources of short-run cash flow and profit performance and, in many ways, define the business's current level of share, sales, and profit performance.

A great number of other factors may come into play in selecting one strategic market plan over the other, but let's look at an estimate of Compaq Computer's 1998 performance while using a defensive strategic market plan to protect market share in a growing market. Using the same assumptions already made for market growth, price erosion, margin, and marketing expenses, a defensive Compaq Computer strategic market plan to protect market share would produce the following estimate of 1998's performance.

$$\frac{\text{Sales}}{\text{Revenue}} = \frac{\text{Market}}{\text{Demand}} \times \frac{\text{Market}}{\text{Share}} \times \frac{\text{Price}}{\text{per Unit}}$$

$$\$27 \text{ billion} = 92 \text{ million} \times 0.125 \times \$2,350$$

$$\frac{\text{Marketing}}{\text{Expenses}} = \frac{\text{Sales}}{\text{Revenue}} \times \frac{\text{Percent Marketing}}{\text{Expenses}}$$

$$\$2.2 \text{ billion} = \$27 \text{ billion} \times 0.08$$

Figure 11.9 ◆ Offensive and Defensive Strategic Market Plans

$$\begin{matrix} \text{Net Marketing} \\ \text{Contribution} \end{matrix} = \left(\begin{matrix} \text{Market} \\ \text{Demand} \end{matrix} \times \begin{matrix} \text{Market} \\ \text{Share} \end{matrix} \times \begin{matrix} \text{Price} \\ \text{per Unit} \end{matrix} \times \begin{matrix} \text{Percent} \\ \text{Margin} \end{matrix} \right) - \begin{matrix} \text{Marketing} \\ \text{Expenses} \end{matrix}$$

$$\$4.6 \text{ billion} = (92 \text{ million} \times 0.125 \times \$2,350 \times 0.25) - \$2.2 \text{ billion}$$

As shown above, a defensive strategic market plan to protect market share would yield an estimated $2 billion increase in sales revenue and a $350 million increase in net marketing contribution. Although many factors could keep these goals from being met, this strategy, if successfully implemented, would also succeed in protecting a share position, growing sales revenue, and increasing net marketing contribution.

During 1998, Compaq elected to pursue an offensive strategic market plan to grow market share. The actual results were a 14.5 percent market share, $31 billion in sales revenues, and an increase of $1.16 billion in net marketing contribution. However, this level of share growth in a growing market did not occur without a carefully designed and successfully implemented tactical marketing strategy.

TACTICAL MARKETING STRATEGY AND PERFORMANCE PLAN

A *strategic market plan* is a long-term strategy with a three- to five-year time horizon and specific performance objectives. A *tactical market strategy* is a short-term marketing strategy with a one-year time horizon. A tactical marketing strategy needs to be reviewed each year with respect to changing market conditions and adjusted accordingly to achieve the long-run performance objectives of a strategic market plan. In some instances, market conditions may change to the degree that the strategic market plan needs to be reassessed to determine if it remains the best long-run plan to achieve the business's performance objectives in a particular product–market.

Tactical Marketing Strategy

Given a specific strategic market plan, a detailed tactical marketing strategy needs to be developed. This means the development of a marketing mix strategy with respect to product positioning, price, promotion, and place. The degree to which the performance objectives of a strategic market plan are achieved is dependent on the effectiveness of the tactical marketing strategy designed to support this strategic market plan.

For example, Intel's strategic market plan to enter the low-end personal computer market required a different tactical marketing strategy from Intel's strategic market plan to defend its high share position in more expensive microprocessors. Each required different types of products and pricing to achieve a position that would be attractive to target customers relative to competitors' product-price positions.

The strategic market plan sets the strategic direction and provides broad guidelines for resource allocation. However, the tactical marketing strategy is the workhorse that has to succeed for the strategic market plan to achieve both short- and long-run performance objectives. The right strategic market plan with the wrong tactical marketing strategy will not normally produce desired levels of performance.

Performance Plan

The performance objectives and conditions under which a business would use either an offensive or a defensive strategic market plan are very different. As outlined in Figure 11.10, offensive strategic marketing plans are geared to deliver above-average performance in the areas of sales growth, improved share position, and long-run profit performance. Defensive strategic market plans are important in producing short-run profit performance and protecting important share positions while also contributing to long-run profit performance and strategic position.

Offensive strategic market plans require investment for growth, which limits short-run profit performance while building sales revenue and improving share position. In the long run, growth-oriented marketing strategies will shift from an offensive strategic market plan to a defensive strategic market plan. As shown, defensive strategic market plans are key sources of short-run profit performance but are not major contributors to sales revenue growth or long-run share and profit performance.

For example, consider Zi-Tech Acoustics, a $250 million engineering acoustics business. It manufactures and markets a variety of acoustic products to four distinct markets. Figure 11.11 illustrates the market share, sales revenues, and net marketing contribution for the company and in each of the four product–markets it serves. A portfolio analysis based on market attractiveness and competitive advantage produced the product–market portfolio illustrated in Figure 11.12. Also shown in Figure 11.12 is a new market opportunity (M5) uncovered in the strategic market planning process. This analysis, along with the current performance with regard to share position, sales revenue, and net marketing contribution led to the strategic market plans outlined in Figure 11.12 and described below.

- **Market 1** is a mature market in which Zi-Tech will strive to *protect share* to protect a net marketing contribution that produces over 50 percent of the overall net marketing contribution.

Performance Objective	Impact on Business Performance			
	Some	Moderate	Considerable	Substantial
Offensive Strategic Market Plans				
Short-run Profit Performance	X	X		
Short-run Share Position	X	X		
Long-run Profit Performance			X	X
Long-run Share Position			X	X
Long-run Sales Revenue Growth			X	X
Defensive Strategic Market Plans				
Short-run Profit Performance			X	X
Short-run Share Position			X	X
Long-run Profit Performance		X	X	
Long-run Share Position	X	X		
Long-run Sales Revenue Growth	X	X		

Figure 11.10 ◆ **Performance Objectives and Strategic Market Plan**

Market-Based Performance	Market 1	Market 2	Market 3	Market 4	Overall Company
Market Growth	3%	0%	17%	–5%	7%
Market Demand (000 customers)	800	1000	1200	1500	4500
Market Share	23%	13%	7%	12%	13%
Customer Volume	184	130	84	180	578
Revenue per Customer	$420	$450	$660	$325	$432
Sales Revenue (millions)	$ 77.3	$ 58.5	$ 55.4	$ 58.5	$250
Variable Cost per Customer	$250	$300	$440	$300	$305
Margin per Customer	$170	$150	$220	$ 25	$127
Total Contribution (millions)	$ 31	$ 19.5	$ 18.5	$ 4.5	$ 73.5
Marketing and Sales (millions)	$ 9	$ 7	$ 6.5	$ 7.5	$ 30
Net Marketing Contribution	$ 22	$ 12.5	$ 12.0	–$ 3	$ 43.5

Figure 11.11 ◆ Zi-Tech Acoustics' Current Performance: Share, Sales, and Net Marketing Contribution

- **Market 2** is mature, and management feels that a strategy to *reduce Zi-Tech's market focus* on more profitable segments would yield greater profits.
- **Market 3** is attractive and growing. These conditions led to a strategic market plan to invest to *grow market share.*
- **Market 4** is unattractive and declining; its competitive advantage is average. A *harvest strategy* would be designed to make a positive net marketing contribution in the short run but to be completely out of the market in five years.
- **Market 5** is a new market opportunity uncovered by the strategic market planning

Figure 11.12 ◆ Zi-Tech Portfolio Analysis and Strategic Market Plan

Figure 11.13 ◆ Strategic Market Plan and Performance Objectives

process. Zi-Tech would like to *enter this market.* It will involve losses for the first couple of years, but by year 5, Zi-Tech hopes to produce a positive net marketing contribution in market 5.

For each market plan, a set of performance objectives was created, as outlined in Figure 11.13. As shown, in the current year, Zi-Tech produced sales of $250 million in four product–markets. Three of the four product–markets were profitable, and the overall net marketing contribution was $43.5 million. On the basis of the strategic market plans and performance objectives created for each product–market, Zi-Tech hopes to grow overall sales by $100 million to $350 million in four to five years. More important, the Zi-Tech performance plan projects net marketing contribution to grow from $43.5 to $65 million in four to five years.

If this strategic market plan is successful, Zi-Tech will have improved its strategic position in served markets while growing sales and profits over a five-year period. In chapter 16 we will look more closely at how this plan translates into shareholder value. However, a 40 percent increase in sales revenues and a 49 percent increase in net market contribution should contribute positively to the net profit and shareholder value.

SUMMARY

Strategic market planning is a process. It is a process that involves assessing the current situation with respect to market attractiveness and competitive advantage along with business performance with respect to share position, sales revenues, and profitability. This type of assessment is made for each product–market served by the business and for new market opportunities the business may want to consider.

APPLICATION PROBLEM: FLX-100

Fluid Life Corporation (FLC) is a small business that developed and patented a product called FLX-100 that extends the life of metal-working fluids. This market includes 250,000 potential customers, of whom 90,000 use products of this type. FLX-100 has a 2 percent share of this market with sales of $19.5 million. FLC's margin is 33 percent of sales and its marketing expenses are 19.2 percent of sales. This results in a net marketing contribution of $2.75 million. However, the company has been unable to further penetrate this market because it has limited financial resources and limited experience in marketing. To obtain a loan to finance this business opportunity, FLC's bank required a marketing plan that would delineate the company's market objectives and projected profit performance.

With the help of a marketing consultant, FLC was able to segment the FLX-100 market into two needs-based market segments. Segment A consisted of more sophisticated and experienced customers, many of whom were already using a product of this type. Segment B consisted of many more potential customers but these customers were much smaller, less experienced, and less likely to have used this type of product. The consultant also created a portfolio analysis (shown below) that was based on the overall market attractiveness and the competitive advantage of each market segment.

Working with the consultant, the FLC management team agreed that focusing on Segment B would be more attractive in terms of market penetration and profitable growth. Although FLC had sales in both segments, its strategic market plan was to harvest its position in Segment A and focus on penetrating Segment B. Summarized in the Profit Plan below is the performance plan for each segment over the next three years.

Portfolio Analysis

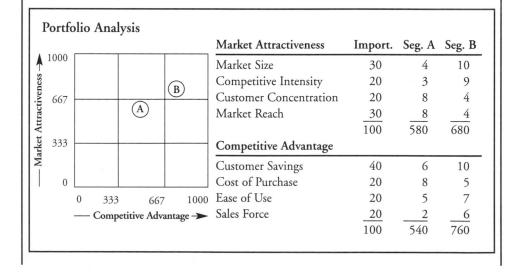

Market Attractiveness	Import.	Seg. A	Seg. B
Market Size	30	4	10
Competitive Intensity	20	3	9
Customer Concentration	20	8	4
Market Reach	30	8	4
	100	580	680
Competitive Advantage			
Customer Savings	40	6	10
Cost of Purchase	20	8	5
Ease of Use	20	5	7
Sales Force	20	2	6
	100	540	760

Profit Plan

Area of Performance	Segment A				Segment B			
	Current	1	2	3	Current	1	2	3
Market Potential (000)	50	50	50	50	200	200	200	200
Market Demand (000)	40	40	42	45	50	60	80	100
Market Share	**2%**	**1%**	**0.5%**	**0%**	**3%**	**5%**	**8%**	**10%**
Customer Volume (thousands)	0.8	0.4	0.21	0	1.5	3.0	6.4	10
Revenue/Customer (000)	$15	$16	$17	$18	$5	$5	$5	$5
Total Revenues (mil)	**$12**	**$6.4**	**$3.6**	**$ 0**	**$7.5**	**$15.0**	**$ 32**	**$ 50**
Margin	33%	33%	33%	33%	33%	33%	33%	33%
Total Contribution (mil)	$ 4	$2.1	$1.2	$ 0	$2.5	$5.0	$10.7	$16.7
Marketing Expense (mil)	$ 3	$0.5	0.1	0	$0.75	$2.25	$ 4.9	$ 7.5
Net Mktg. Contribution (mil)	**$ 1**	**$1.6**	**$1.1**	**$ 0**	**$1.75**	**$2.75**	**$ 5.8**	**$ 9.2**

Questions

For Internet discussion, go to www.prenhall.com/phbusiness.

1. How would you present the proposed strategic market plan to the financial officer of the bank being asked for a loan with respect to share position, sales growth, and profit performance?

2. What would be your estimate of the performance impact of a strategic market plan to protect share in Segment A while increasing share in Segment B from three percent to 10 percent?

3. What level of market share would FLC have to obtain in Segment B in year three in order to produce a break-even level of performance (i.e., zero net marketing contribution)?

From this assessment, a portfolio analysis is created based on two dimensions of performance: market attractiveness and competitive advantage. Each dimension is created with an index based on several underlying forces that shape it. Market attractiveness is indexed with respect to market forces (market size, growth, buyer power, etc.), competitive intensity (number of competitors, substitutes, price rivalry, etc.), and market access (customer familiarity, channel access, sales force requirements, etc.). Competitive advantage is indexed with respect to cost advantage (unit cost, transaction costs, marketing expenses, etc.), differentiation advantage (product quality, service quality, brand image, etc.), and marketing advantage (market share, brand awareness, channel control, etc.). A strategic market plan is specified for each product–market the business serves or would like to consider entering in the future, based on the product–market's position in the portfolio.

The strategic market plan is a long-run, three- to five-year, strategic market objective that involves share position but has corresponding implications for short- and long-run sales revenue growth and profit performance. Strategic market plans can be "offensive" or "defensive." Offensive strategic market plans involve market penetration strategies to grow share position, sales, and long-run profitability. Defensive strategic market plans involve protecting share, sales, and profits or harvesting strategies to exit markets while maximizing short-run profits. The combination of strategic market plans (one for each product–market) results in an overall view of how the business will grow with respect to share, sales, and profits.

Although the strategic market plan for a given product–market sets short- and long-run goals with respect to market share, sales revenues, and profits, it does not specify how this performance will be achieved. Therefore, for each strategic market plan there needs to be a corresponding tactical marketing plan. The tactical marketing plan is a marketing mix strategy (product, price, place, and promotion) and resource allocation (marketing budget) that specifies the tactical details of how a given strategic market plan will be achieved. On the basis of these marketing tactics and the marketing budget, a three- to five-year forecast of market share, sales revenues, and net marketing contribution, a performance plan is created.

MARKET-BASED LOGIC AND STRATEGIC THINKING

1. How does the level of product–market diversification affect sales growth and performance consistency?
2. Why would the overall variation in sales revenues over a 10-year period be different when comparing General Electric and Compaq Computer?
3. What is meant by the "strategic market planning process"?
4. How is a strategic market plan different from a strategic market planning process?
5. How would you assess the attractiveness of a new consumer product–market for Procter & Gamble? Be specific as to what factors you would include in building an index of market attractiveness for a Procter & Gamble consumer market.
6. How would you assess the competitive advantage Procter & Gamble would have in a new consumer product–market? Be specific as to what factors you would include in building an index of competitive advantage for a Procter & Gamble consumer market.
7. Using the information provided below, create a portfolio analysis and specify a strategic market plan for a business that serves three product–markets.

Product–Market	Share	Sales (millions)	Market Attractiveness	Competitive Advantage
A	10%	$20	20	40
B	33%	$50	75	80
C	5%	$10	85	15

8. Using the information presented in question 7 and the added information below, create a three-year performance plan with respect to market share and sales revenues for each product–market, given the strategic market plan specified below. Also create a projection of overall sales for each year of the three-year planning horizon.

Product–Market	Strategic Market Plan	Share Objective	Market Demand (mil)	Market Growth
A	Reduced Focus	5%	$200	5%
B	Protect Share	33%	$150	7%
C	Grow Share	10%	$200	20%

9. Under what conditions would a business specify an offensive strategic market plan?
10. Under what conditions would a business specify a defensive strategic market plan?
11. What role do offensive and defensive strategic market plans play in the short- and long-run performance of a business?
12. How would the sales and profit performance over a three-year period differ between a business with only defensive strategic market plans and a business that has only offensive strategic market plans? Why is it important to have a balance of offensive and defensive plans?
13. Why is a tactical marketing plan for each strategic market plan an important part of the strategic market planning process?
14. How does a manager develop a tactical marketing plan and marketing budget to achieve a specific strategic market plan?
15. How would the tactical marketing plan and marketing budget for a strategic market plan to grow market share (offensive) differ from those of a reduced focus strategic market plan to reduce share?
16. How does a business create a forecast of its future performance based on the strategic market plans for each product–market it intends to serve over a given planning horizon?

NOTES

1. Michael Treacy and Fred Wiersama, *The Discipline of Market Leaders* (Reading, MA: Addison-Wesley, 1995).
2. Some analysts believe the guidelines of the market plan may lead to a strategic advantage. See David A. Garvin, "Leveraging Processes for Strategic Advantage," *Harvard Business Review* (September–October 1995):77.
3. Roger A. Kerin, Vijay Mahajan, and P. Rajan Varadarajan, *Strategic Market Planning* (Boston: Allyn and Bacon, 1990).
4. Frances V. McCrory and Peter G. Gerstberger, "The New Math of Performance Measurements," *Journal of Business Strategy* (March–April 1992):33–38.
5. Kasturi Rangan, Melvyn Menezes, and E.P. Maier, "Channel Selection for New Industrial Products: A Framework, Method and Application," *Journal of Marketing* (July 1992):69–82.
6. L. W. Phillips, D.R. Chang, and R.D. Bussell, "Product Quality, Cost Position, and Business Performance: A Test of Some Key Hypotheses," *Journal of Marketing* 47 (January 1983):26–43.
7. Michael E. Porter, *Competitive Advantage* (New York: Free Press, 1986).

8. David Aaker, "Formal Planning System," in *Strategic Market Management* (New York: Wiley, 1995):341–53.

9. Thomas Powell, "Strategic Planning As Competitive Advantage," *Strategic Management Journal* 13 (1992):551–58; Scott Armstrong, "The Value of Formal Planning for Strategic Decisions: Reply," *Strategic Management Journal* 7 (1986):183–85; and Deepak Sinha, "The Contribution of Formal Planning to Decisions, " *Strategic Management Journal* (October 1990):479–92.

10. William K. Hall, "Survival Strategies in a Hostile Environment," *Harvard Business Review* (September–October 1980):75–85.

11. Kathryn Rudie Harrigan, *Strategies for Declining Businesses* (Lexington, MA: Lexington Books, 1980); and Kathryn Rudie Harrigan and Michael E. Porter, "End-Game Strategies for Declining Industries," *Harvard Business Review* (July–August 1983):111–20. Also see Katheryn Rudie Harrigan, *Managing Maturing Businesses* (New York: Lexington Books, 1988).

chapter 12

Offensive Strategic Market Plans

Coca-Cola's chairman, Douglas Ivester, believes that Coca-Cola is "the perfect growth company." This assertion may be questioned by some, given Coca-Cola's commanding 50 percent share of the worldwide carbonated soft drink market. However, Ivester explains that Coca-Cola represents only a 2 percent *share of stomach* on a worldwide basis. This point is further driven home in Coca-Cola's annual report, which features 47 empty Coke bottles and one full one. This way of thinking has enabled Coca-Cola to grow its volume at the rate of 7 to 8 percent, while PepsiCo, its chief rival, is growing unit volume at the rate of 1 percent per year.

Clearly, the Coca-Cola chairman is challenging his company to think *offensively* and find ways to grow Coca-Cola's share of the beverage market. Many businesses, such as Coca-Cola, Microsoft, America Online, Dell Computer, and Intel experienced considerable growth in the 1990s. To grow, these businesses have had to utilize a variety of strategic market plans that range from market share penetration to development of completely new products and markets. In every case, their strategic market plans have had to address three basic performance objectives.

- **Share Position:** How will the strategic market plan contribute to the business's share position in served markets?
- **Sales Growth:** To what degree will the strategic market plan contribute to sales growth?
- **Profit Performance:** How will the strategic market plan impact short-run and long-run profit performance?

Because resources are limited, a business needs a strategic market plan to carefully map out its future growth and profit performance.[1] Every strategic market plan a business develops will in some way affect both short-run and long-run business performance in each of the three areas of performance identified above. And, depending on the situation, some will be *offensive* and some will be *defensive* strategic market plans.

Offensive strategic market plans are more often growth-oriented and, therefore, more likely to occur in the growth stage of a product–market life cycle,[2] as shown in Figure 12.1. Offensive strategic market plans are designed to produce sales growth, improve share position, and future profit performance. Defensive strategic market plans are more likely to occur in the latter stages of a product–market life cycle and are often designed to protect important share positions and be large contributors to short-run sales revenues and profits. This chapter examines various offensive strategic market plans, and chapter 13 will present various defensive strategic market plans.

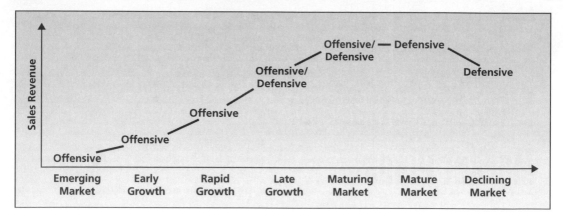

Figure 12.1 ◆ Product Life Cycle and Offensive and Defensive Marketing Strategies

OFFENSIVE STRATEGIC MARKET PLANS

The combination of market attractiveness and competitive advantage creates a portfolio position for any given product–market.[3] As shown in Figure 12.2, attractive markets are most likely to warrant an offensive strategic market plan to improve competitive advantage and share position when the business's competitive advantage is average or below. These offensive strategic market plans can range from entering a new market with no established share position to growing the competitive advantage and market share in existing product–markets. In addition, there may be the opportunity to use an offensive strategic market plan to help grow (make more attractive) an emerging or underdeveloped market in which the business has established a strong position of advantage.

Of the five cells in which an offensive strategic market plan could be used, three (with

Figure 12.2 ◆ Selecting between Offensive and Defensive Marketing Strategies

average market attractiveness) could also use a defensive strategic market plan. In these portfolio positions, more information would be needed before one could select between an offensive or a defensive strategic market plan. For example, it may be that an offensive strategic market plan is warranted, given the business's sources of relative advantage. On the other hand, a defensive strategic market plan to protect the current position may be the best alternative in achieving desired performance objectives. Or perhaps the business should narrow its market focus and attempt to minimize investment and capture more profits.

Fundamentally, offensive strategic market plans are geared for growth and inherently involve strategies to penetrate or grow existing markets or to enter or develop new markets, as summarized in Figure 12.3. There is a wide range of potential offensive strategic market plans.[4] However, a logical place to start is with offensive strategies within *existing markets*. Because the business has already established a working knowledge of customers and competitors and has resources in place to serve existing markets, it should seek to leverage its existing market position with an offensive strategic market plan to further penetrate and develop the product–markets it already serves.

MARKET PENETRATION STRATEGIES

As shown in Figure 12.3, there are four fundamental offensive strategic market plans that can be used to grow a business's penetration of an existing market. These strategic market plans range from share penetration to growing market demand in markets served by the business.

Strategies to Grow Market Share

There are many factors that affect a business's ability to grow market share and profitability.[5] One consideration is share potential. To what degree has the business achieved its share potential? And what factors need to be managed to grow share in a given product–market? Each is an important consideration in developing an offensive strategic market plan to grow market share.

Figure 12.3 ◆ Offensive Strategic Market Plans

Market Share Penetration   In chapter 3, we introduced the idea of a Share Development Index (SDI). This is the ratio of actual market share to share potential. The share potential of a business is based on what that business believes it should be able to achieve with a successful tactical marketing strategy, given the strength of its competitive advantage and marketing effectiveness in a given product–market. For example, in the case presented below, a business estimates that it should perform at a 90 percent level in product awareness, 50 percent in product preference, 80 percent in intentions to purchase, 80 percent in product availability, and 70 percent in rate of purchase. Performing at these levels would produce a potential market share index of approximately 20 percent.

$$\begin{array}{l} \text{Market} \\ \text{Share} \\ \text{Potential} \end{array} = \frac{\text{Product}}{\text{Awareness}} \times \frac{\text{Product}}{\text{Preference}} \times \frac{\text{Purchase}}{\text{Intentions}} \times \frac{\text{Product}}{\text{Availability}} \times \frac{\text{Purchase}}{\text{Rate}}$$

$$= 0.90 \times 0.50 \times 0.80 \times 0.80 \times 0.70$$

$$= 20.2\%$$

If a business's actual market share were 8 percent, the business would be underperforming and, hence, would have a Share Development Index of 40.

$$\text{Share Development Index} = \frac{\text{Current Market Share}}{\text{Market Share Potential}} = \frac{8\%}{20\%} \times 100 = 40$$

This means that the business has achieved only 40 percent of its potential market share. Therefore, there is an opportunity to grow market share with a market penetration strategy.

To grow share, a business would have to examine each of the areas of performance with respect to its expected versus its actual market performance. For instance, the business in the example expects to achieve a 90 percent target market product awareness. If its actual target market awareness were only 67 percent, this performance gap would prevent this business from reaching its full market share potential. Thus, to grow share when it is at less than its full potential, this business would need to examine key performance gaps in its market share response.

There is also the possibility that a business has reached its share potential but feels it can still expand its market share position with a new strategic market plan. For example, product improvements that are able to shift product preference from 50 percent to 70 percent would raise the market share potential (index) from 20.2 percent to 28.2 percent in the example presented. Of course, to achieve this level of share penetration, the business would have to adequately communicate and deliver these product improvements to the full satisfaction of target customers.

Market Share Change   Market shares change as a result of market forces, a business's competitive position, and marketing effort, as illustrated in Figure 12.4. Although there is a wide range of market share change forces occurring in any given market, the net result is some rate of market share change based on the collective influences of these forces that shape market share change.

Market forces that shape market share change are generally beyond the control of a business. Market growth, size of shares, and competitor entry all create market forces that tend to lower market share, whereas competitor exit contributes to market share gains.[6] As a result, a silent strategic market plan with respect to either improved competi-

Figure 12.4 ◆ Fundamental Forces That Affect Market Share Change

tive position or marketing effort is likely to result in share loss. To grow share, a business needs to more than offset share erosion forces with changes in competitive position or marketing effort, or both.

One way to offset market forces that tend to erode share is for a business to improve its competitive position. Each of the factors that affects a business's competitive position also indirectly affects market share. However, in order to *gain* share with the use of any of these positioning variables, a business needs to increase its *relative* advantage: its position relative to key competitors.

For example, if a business were to improve its product quality, we would assume that this change would contribute to a market share gain. However, if the business's competitors were improving their product quality at a faster rate, then the business's *relative* product quality would actually go down and its market share would be expected to go down as well. Thus, to gain market share, a business has to improve its *relative* competitive advantage on one or more of the positioning variables shown in Figure 12.4 and discussed in chapters 7 and 8.

Marketing effort also affects market share change, as discussed in chapters 9 and 10. In a growing market with more customers and competitors entering the market, a business needs to expand its marketing effort in order to protect or gain share. For example, a business with $150 million in sales and 50 salespeople would have a sales productivity of $3 million per salesperson. If total market demand were $600 million, the business would have a 25 percent market share. Let's assume that as more customers enter the market, demand grows to $750 million in three years. To *protect* share, the business would need to increase its sales force to at least 62 salespeople or increase the sales productivity of its present 50 salespeople. To *grow* share with a sales force effort, the business would need more than 62 salespeople at the current sales productivity of $3 million per salesperson.

Strategies to Grow Customer Purchase

As a business approaches 100 percent of its Share Development Index, additional growth, based on market share gains, becomes increasingly difficult. Up to this point, share gains have been based on correcting ineffective tactical marketing strategies, improving competitive position, or adding to a business's marketing effort. However, there is also the opportunity to grow revenues with existing customers by growing revenue *per* customer. For example, McDonald's once sold a limited product line of hamburgers, french fries, and drinks. With product line extensions in hamburgers, chicken and fish sandwiches, and a line of breakfast products, McDonald's has been able to grow the average dollars spent at McDonald's by customers who already were McDonald's customers. Of course, these line extensions also attracted new customers to the fast-food industry and drew new customers from competing fast-food businesses.

Businesses with well-known names, such as Kodak, Nike, Honda, IBM, and Disney, are able to introduce line extensions that leverage the awareness and image already created by their company reputation.[7] When Honda entered the lawn mower market in the early 1990s, the Honda lawn mower was immediately perceived by many customers as reliable and of high quality. These perceptions were created by Honda's success in automobiles, motorcycles, and other motorized products. The high level of name awareness also greatly assisted the company's quick penetration of this market. Many lawn mower customers were already owners of other Honda products. This level of awareness led Honda to build a growth strategy around the volume of Honda products purchased by existing Honda customers. This strategy is aptly expressed in Honda's marketing objective: "Our goal is to have five Hondas in every garage."

Obviously, few, if any, Honda customers would purchase five Honda automobiles. But the Honda offensive strategic market plan is to capture the Honda car owner's purchase of lawn mowers, recreational vehicles (motorcycles, snowmobiles, jet skis, all-terrain vehicles, outboard motors), and portable motors and generators. In this way, Honda is growing its business by building the total ownership of Honda products among existing customers. A business's existing customer pool is a customer franchise that offers considerable opportunity for within-market sales growth.

Revenue per customer can also be built with a strategy to build price premiums. Businesses that enhance their products by adding value-added services or building a superior reputation for quality can charge higher prices than competing businesses and still maintain a superior customer value. General Electric's turbines command a price premium relative to competing turbines around the world. This premium is based on superior product quality, engineering and installation services, and a reputation for innovation and technology in the area of turbine design and development. In this way, GE is able to attain a higher revenue per customer than many competing turbine manufacturers.

Strategies to Enter New Customer Segments

Another offensive growth strategy within existing markets is to develop a strategic market plan to enter a new customer segment within an existing market.[8] For example, as the personal computer market has grown, the under $1,000 personal computer segment has emerged. Intel, which did not have a product suitable for this segment, saw competitors such as Advanced Micro Devices take the lead in the under $1,000 segment. With demand in this segment growing faster than in any other segment, Intel responded with a new product designed for the price-performance needs of the segment. As shown in Figure 12.5, the Celeron chip provided PC manufacturers a low-cost Intel microprocessor for this segment. This offensive strategic market plan provided a new source of sales revenues and profitability for Intel.

Figure 12.5 ◆ **Intel New Segment Entry Strategy**

Strategies to Grow Market Demand

At any given point in time, the number of customers in a market is finite. New customer growth strategies can focus on growing market demand by bringing new customers into a market. In chapter 3, we introduced the concept of a Market Development Index. This index is simply a ratio of current market demand to market potential, the maximum number of customers possible for a particular geographic market scope. For example, the Market Development Index for the wireless phone market in the United States is approximately 33. This means that there are many potential customers who have not entered the market for various reasons. And, since market share battles often lead to price erosion, a strategy to grow market demand may offer an offensive strategic market plan to grow share, sales, and profits.

$$\begin{array}{c} \text{Market} \\ \text{Development} \\ \text{Index} \end{array} = \frac{\text{Current Market Demand for Wireless Phones}}{\text{Market Potential for Wireless Phones}} \times 100$$

$$= \frac{60 \text{ million customers}}{180 \text{ million customers}} \times 100$$

$$= 33.3$$

But how does a business actually attract new customers and grow market demand? As shown in Figure 12.6, there are basically five market forces that limit market demand from reaching its full potential. Each of these forces must be addressed in strategic market plans to grow either the entire market or a specific segment within the market. Marketing communications efforts can be used to address awareness and comprehension of benefits for the wireless phone market.

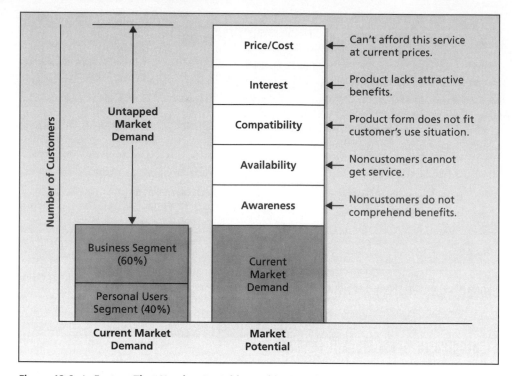

Figure 12.6 ◆ Factors That Need to Be Addressed in Growing the Market Demand for Wireless Phones

Improving availability is a matter of adding more cell sites in geographic areas where potential demand justifies the investment. On the other hand, compatibility is more likely to be a product issue. To improve use compatibility, wireless providers have to better understand how customers use wireless phones and design products to better serve those use situations. For example, a contractor on a construction site may need a more durable phone, whereas a salesperson may need more features to enhance sales productivity. Finally, because the cost of service, and not the initial cost of a phone, prevents many potential customers from entering the market, some wireless phone service providers have developed special usage rate pricing programs that make the price of service adjustable, based on level of usage. The net effect of these efforts is a new market demand of over 25,000 new customers per week.

NEW MARKET ENTRY STRATEGIES

At some point, every business needs to examine growth opportunities outside the existing markets it serves.[9] This need can occur for three fundamental reasons: (1) the number of attractive market opportunities within existing markets may be limited; (2) new market opportunities outside existing markets are simply more attractive in terms of meeting the business's overall performance objectives; and (3) a move to new markets helps diversify a business's sources of profitability and, hence, reduces variation in performance.[10]

As shown in Figure 12.3, there are four fundamental *new market entry* offensive strategic market plans. New market entry strategies can include entry into established related markets (similar to markets served by the business) and diversified markets (unrelated to markets served by the business), or entry into less established new emerging markets or markets with considerable undeveloped market potential. Entry into established markets (related or diversified) offers existing market demand along with existing competitors. Entry into less established markets requires development of market demand but often in the absence of competition.

Related New Market Entry Strategies

K2 is best known as a ski manufacturer. Over a 10-year period, K2 steadily increased its share of the American ski market until it became the market share leader by the mid-1990s. The American ski market is also mature, and opportunities for sales revenue growth through either market growth or increased market share are limited. This situation led K2 to a related new market entry strategy into the snowboard and in-line skate markets. K2 hopes to achieve significant sales revenue growth over the next 10 years as a result of the new market entry strategy.

K2's entry into these two related customer markets enables it to leverage its brand name awareness, reputation for quality, manufacturing and design expertise, and, in some instances, its existing marketing channel and sales systems. Each of these factors offers a variety of potential cost and marketing efficiencies.

There are instances in which entry into a new market can be blocked. Market entry can be very difficult because of the cost of entry, technology requirements, or a lack of market access. In the telecommunications industry, these difficulties have led to many mergers, joint ventures, and strategic alliances among telecommunications, computer, and cable TV companies. In each case, partner companies provided related market expertise and leverage. By blending the strengths of businesses from two related markets, these new entities become potentially more complete businesses from which to build and market products that more completely serve and fulfill customer needs.

Diversified New Market Entry Growth Strategies

Westinghouse acquired CBS in the mid-1990s. The week before, Disney acquired ABC. The Disney acquisition was a *related* new market entry strategy in which Disney could leverage its name, reputation for quality, and creative and production expertise. The Westinghouse acquisition was an *unrelated* new market entry strategy that moved Westinghouse into the increasingly attractive communications market. Disney was leveraging its strength along with new market access. Westinghouse was redefining itself by acquiring CBS in the hope of reshaping its competitive advantage in an increasingly attractive market. However, both of these businesses were pursuing new sources of market share, sales growth, and profit performance.

One of the primary advantages of a diversified new market entry strategy is reduced market dependency, because most markets go through temporary periods of expansion and contraction. For example, the residential construction market is a slow-growth market that fluctuates considerably with economic conditions. A manufacturer of earth-moving equipment for this market could reduce the magnitude of swings in performance by entering a diversified market, such as mining or agriculture, unrelated to the residential construction market. In this way the performance of the business could be subject to smaller variations in overall business performance.

An additional advantage to market diversification is reduced vulnerability. If a business derives the bulk of its performance from one type of market, a major change in that market could threaten the company's performance, and, potentially, its survival. In the mid-1970s, the National Cash Register Corporation (NCR) was focused primarily on the cash register market and had over an 80 percent share of this market. When competitors entered with a new cash register technology, NCR's market share began to decline rapidly. In less than six years, its share had shrunk to less than 25 percent, and the company's survival was threatened.

Thus, there are three good reasons a business might pursue a diversified new market entry strategy:

- **New Source of Growth:** New market diversification offers the potential of adding to the business's sales growth and profit performance.
- **Smoother Performance:** New market diversification offers customer diversification, which can reduce the magnitude of swings in sales and profit performance.
- **Reduced Vulnerability:** New market diversification reduces market dependence and vulnerability, which better protects the business's performance and, in some instances, its survival.

Although these are important benefits, many businesses have failed to perform effectively in diversified markets and have retreated to their core markets. Mobil's acquisition of Montgomery Ward, Coca-Cola's acquisition of Columbia Pictures, and General Motors' acquisition of Data Information Services were each unsuccessful diversified new market strategies. In each case, the new market opportunities went too far from the marketing and business expertise and experience of the acquiring company. On the other hand, Phillip Morris's acquisition of the Miller Brewing Company, Pepsi's acquisition of Kentucky Fried Chicken, and Motorola's move into wireless communication products each provided the advantages identified above while still leveraging their marketing and business expertise.

Strategies to Enter New Emerging Markets

As depicted in Figure 12.3, a business can grow by entering new emerging markets into which customers have not yet entered. Although considerably risky with respect to profit performance, this strategy can enable a business to establish an early leadership position in the market. From this position, a business can influence product positioning and market growth.

High-technology markets have rapidly emerging market demand and relatively short product and market life cycles. Businesses in these markets need to move quickly to capitalize on emerging new market opportunities or they will completely miss this opportunity for growth.[11] The pioneer in these emerging new markets has the potential to achieve a competitive advantage if it can sustain its advantage in these early stages of market development.[12] When pioneers can establish a *dominant design,* a standard emerges that followers must follow in order to compete.[13] For example, VHS prevailed over Beta as the design standard in the early evolution of the VCR market.

As the market emerges, *"early followers"* enter the market. Early followers emulate the dominant design and enter the market after letting the pioneer invest in developing the technology, establishing the design standard, and initiating market development. Many Japanese companies use an early follower strategy. Microsoft's entry into the Internet market was as an early follower. CompuServe, Prodigy, and America Online established a dominant position, but as the market developed, Microsoft entered the market and capitalized on emerging new market demand.

With rapid market growth, many customers are attracted to the market, and customer use and experience grow. It is during this phase of market development and growth that segments begin to form as customer needs become more salient and numerous. This growth attracts more competitors, many of whom will fill niche markets to serve the unique needs of a subset of customers.[14] This is a critical point for market leaders in emerging markets to develop multisegment solutions. Businesses that remain narrowly focused will see their market shares erode as new competitors deliver more attractive value propositions. Market pioneers who can sustain a market leadership position through this phase of market development are in the best position to achieve high levels of performance.[15]

Strategies to Develop New Market Potential

Apple Computer's initial entry into the personal computer market was a market growth strategy that focused on the enormous *untapped market potential* of the personal computer market. Apple's philosophy was to bring computing power to the masses. The company's original positioning strategy for Macintosh was: "Only a few have the expertise to operate computers. . . . Introducing Macintosh, for the rest of the world."

In the beginning, they had very few competitors because they were addressing a market ignored by the major computer manufacturers. Only after Apple legitimized this market did competitors begin to flow to this untapped market.

Global markets such as China, India, and Africa make up over half the world population, yet many of the products manufactured for the United States, Western Europe, and more affluent Asian countries have not been formulated for these markets. Constraints due to price, use compatibility, and availability create a large untapped new market potential for many products.

For example, many products need electricity, yet rural areas of underdeveloped countries cannot use electrical products because they do not have electricity. A company such as General Electric, which makes gas turbines for jet engines, has already adapted that expertise to enable a business (called a co-generator) to produce its own electricity and sell any excess to local utilities during periods of excess supply. GE has the capability of building electricity production on a small scale, thereby bringing many of its electrical products to consumers in remote locations around the world.

A growth strategy to develop an untapped new market potential has both high risk and the potential for high return.[16] Because the market is undeveloped, the cost of development can be significant even with a very good customer solution. On the other hand, with few competitors, if any, a business has the opportunity to pioneer a portion of the market largely ignored by competitors. With a "first-mover" advantage, there is the potential to own the market until other competitors venture to enter.

Area of Performance	Share Penetration Strategy		Market Development Strategy	
	First Year	In 5 Years	First Year	In 5 Years
Market Demand	600,000	600,000	20,000	200,000
Market Share	15%	20%	80%	50%
Market Growth Rate	3%	3%	158%	158%
Target Volume	90,000	120,000	16,000	100,000
Revenue per Customer	$ 450	$ 450	$ 950	$ 450
Total Revenue (millions)	$40.5	$54.0	$15.2	$45.0
Variable Cost per Customer	$ 250	$ 250	$ 650	$ 200
Total Variable Costs (millions)	$22.5	$30.0	$10.4	$20.0
Margin per Customer	$ 200	$ 200	$ 300	$ 250
Total Contribution (millions)	$18.0	$24.0	$ 4.8	$25.0
Marketing Expenses (millions)	$7.0	$10.0	$ 6.0	$12.0
Net Marketing Contribution (millions)	$11.0	$14.0	–$ 1.2	$13.0

Figure 12.7 ◆ Alternative Offensive Strategic Market Plans

EVALUATING OFFENSIVE STRATEGIC MARKET PLANS

A market-based business will often find that it has more market opportunities than it has resources to fund. In that case, the business will have to prioritize strategic market opportunities on the basis of its performance objectives. A business with a short-run need for better profit performance would be inclined to select the share penetration strategy, shown in Figure 12.7, rather than a long-run market development strategy. The share penetration strategy is expected to produce $14 million in net marketing contribution in five years. The share penetration strategy offers immediate profit performance and a reasonable level of sales revenue and profit growth.

On the other hand, a business with a good cash position, but facing stagnant growth in maturing markets, might pursue the market development strategy presented in Figure 12.7. This offensive strategy would produce a $1.2 million negative net marketing contribution in the first year of a new market development strategy. However, in five years, this strategy would be expected to produce $13 million in net marketing contribution. Although riskier, this new market development strategy could provide this business needed growth and market diversification in an attractive market. Thus, the selection of one offensive strategic market plan over another depends on the business's short-run profit needs, strategic position and resources, and opportunities for growth.

SUMMARY

Businesses have a short-term obligation to investors to meet their financial promises of growth and performance. At the same time, they have an obligation to investors and employees to carve out a set of marketing strategies that will improve the position of the business in the long run. The purpose of strategic market planning is to examine the market attractiveness and competitive advantage of each market served by a business. On the basis of an assessment of this position, a strategic market objective is developed and resources are allocated accordingly. To accomplish these performance objectives, a business generally needs a combination of offensive and defensive strategic market plans.

Offensive strategic market plans are more growth-oriented and can be broken down into four strategies that address existing markets and four that focus on new market opportunities. Existing markets and current customers offer the most logical place to initiate growth-oriented offensive strategies. When market share is underdeveloped, share penetration offers a very good growth opportunity. Likewise, product line extensions that can be marketed to existing customers provide growth without substantial additions to marketing expenses. New customer opportunities within existing markets can be addressed with strategies to enter new segments within existing markets or to grow segment or market demand.

New market offensive strategies center around markets with market entry opportunities as well as emerging and undeveloped markets. New market entry into related markets is often pursued as a way of leveraging brand name recognition, channel systems, or manufacturing synergies. Related new market entry offers the least risk, whereas diversified new market entry offers a better opportunity to reduce vulnerability due to changing market conditions. Early entry into emerging markets and development of untapped new market opportunities offer tremendous growth potential but are high risk in terms of profit performance and the time it takes to achieve a high level of profit performance.

APPLICATION PROBLEM: COMPAQ COMPUTER

In 1997, Compaq Computer sold approximately 10 million personal computers. At that time, the market was 80 million PCs and growing at 15 percent per year. This market was projected to be 150 million units by 2002. Compaq's average selling price was approximately $2,500. Overall, PC prices were eroding at the rate of 6 percent per year. Compaq's margin was 25 percent, and marketing expenses were 8 percent of sales.

Questions

For Internet discussion, go to www.prenhall.com/phbusiness.

1. Estimate the volume, sales revenues, and net marketing contribution of a protect (hold) market share strategy for Compaq in 2001, given the following: assume the market will continue to grow at 15 percent; price erosion will continue at 6 percent; margin will remain at 25 percent; and marketing expenses will remain at 8 percent of sales.

2. Assuming the same market growth and margins, evaluate a share penetration strategy in which Compaq would price aggressively by lowering prices at the rate of 10 percent per year in an effort to gain a 17.5 percent market share by 2001. Contrast the profit impact of this strategy with the results presented in question 1.

3. Using the net marketing contribution estimated for the protect share strategy in question 1, estimate how much market share Compaq would have to obtain to produce the same level of net marketing contribution if marketing expenses were increased from 8 percent to 10 percent of sales. Would this be a more profitable strategy than the strategies in questions 1 and 2?

MARKET-BASED LOGIC AND STRATEGIC THINKING

1. What is the difference between offensive strategic market plans and defensive strategic market plans?
2. Explain why a business might shift from an offensive strategic market plan to a defensive strategic market plan over the life cycle of a particular product.
3. How can a business meet short-run growth and profit performance targets and still invest in strategic market plans that are focused on long-run objectives with respect to share position, sales growth, and profit performance?
4. How would a Nike offensive strategy to grow market penetration differ from a strategy to grow customer purchases (revenue per customer) in the under-18 female athlete market?
5. Hewlett-Packard entered the low-priced printer market with a new brand name (Apollo). Explain the logic of this offensive strategic market plan and how it is likely to affect HP performance.
6. Microsoft has developed a product called *Meeting Pro* to help facilitate the running of small business meetings. Although this is a value-added software product, Microsoft offers this product at no cost to Windows users. Explain how this is an offensive market penetration strategy.
7. Why are offensive strategic market plans crucial for the long-run success of a business? What kind of offensive strategies could McDonald's use to ensure future growth in sales and profits?
8. Microsoft has developed a joint venture with Sony to develop an on-line alternative to the telephone. What type of offensive marketing strategy best describes this joint venture, and what would the expected short- and long-run performance objectives be?
9. How does a market penetration strategy to grow market share differ from a strategy to enter a new segment in the same market?
10. Why is a marketing strategy to grow customer purchases (revenue per customer) potentially more profitable than many other offensive marketing strategies?
11. Why would a business first pursue offensive marketing strategies to increase market share or grow revenue per customer rather than other offensive marketing strategies?
12. What forces limit new customer growth within existing markets? How could a business grow market demand by addressing these forces?
13. What are the important differences between a related new marketing strategy and a diversified new marketing strategy?
14. When would a business pursue a diversified new market entry strategy?
15. What is the advantage of growing market demand in a new, emerging market?

NOTES

1. David Aaker, "Portfolio Analysis," *Strategic Market Management,* (New York: Wiley, 1995):155–69.
2. Bernard Catry and Michel Chevalier, "Market Share Strategy and the Product Life Cycle," *Journal of Marketing* (October 1974):29–34.
3. Philippe Haspeslagh, "Portfolio Planning: Uses and Limits," *Harvard Business Review* (January–February 1982):58–73; and S. Robinson, R. Hichens, and D. Wade, "The Directional Policy Matrix Tool for Strategic Planning," *Long-Range Planning* (June 1978):8–15.

4. David Aaker, "Growth Strategies," *Strategic Market Management* (New York: Wiley, 1995):238–59.

5. David Szymanski, Sundar Bharadwaj, and Rajan Varadarajan, "An Analysis of the Market Share-Profitability Relationship," *Journal of Marketing* (July 1993):1–18; and C. Davis Fogg, "Planning Gains in Market Share," *Journal of Marketing* (July 1994):30–38.

6. Charles Lillis, James Cook, Roger Best, and Del Hawkins, "Marketing Strategies to Achieve Market Share Goals," in *Strategic Marketing Management,* ed. H. Thomas and D. Gardner (New York: Wiley, 1985).

7. Daniel Sheinen and Bernd Schmitt, "Extending Brands with New Product Concepts: The Role of Category Attribute Congruity, Brand Affect and Brand Breadth," *Journal of Business Research* (September 1994):1–10.

8. Gary Hamel and C. K. Prahalad, "Seeing the Future First," *Fortune* (September 5, 1994):64–70.

9. Edward Roberts and Charles Berry, "Entering New Business: Selecting Strategies for Success," *Sloan Management Review* (Spring 1985):3–17.

10. Richard Rumelt, "Diversification, Strategy and Profitability," *Strategic Management Journal* 3 (1982):359–69.

11. G. Stalk Jr., "Time: The Next Source of Competitive Advantage," *Harvard Business Review* (July–August 1988):41–51; and Thomas Robertson, "How to Reduce Market Penetration Cycle Times," *Sloan Management Review* (Fall 1993):87–96.

12. William Robinson and Claes Fornell, "Sources of Market Pioneer Advantage in Consumer Goods Industries," *Journal of Marketing Research* (August 1985):305–17; and William Robinson, "Sources of Market Pioneer Advantages: The Case for Industrial Goods Industries," *Journal of Marketing Research,* 25 (1988):87–94.

13. Roger Best and Reinhard Angelmar, "Strategies for Leveraging Technology Advantage," in *Handbook on Business Strategy* (New York: Warren, Gorham and Lamont, 1989):2.1–2.10.

14. Vijay Mahajan, Subhash Sharma, and Robert Buzzell, "Assessing the Impact of Competitive Entry on Market Expansion and Incumbent Sales," *Journal of Marketing* (July 1993):39–52.

15. Glen Urban, T. Carter, S. Gaskin, and Z. Mucha, "Marketing Share Rewards to Pioneering Brands: An Empirical Analysis and Strategic Implications," *Management Science* 32 (1986):635–59.

16. Igal Ayal and Jehiel Zif, "Market Expansion Strategies in Multinational Markets," *Journal of Marketing* (Spring 1979):84–94.

chapter 13

Defensive Strategic Market Plans

Historical share leaders such as General Motors, AT&T, IBM, and others have been under attack in their core markets for some time. For each, a loss on one share point is considerable in terms of sales revenues, net profits, and cash flow. Relatively new share leaders such as Intel, Cisco Systems, and Microsoft face the same challenge. These businesses, like other *share defenders* are engaged in a battle to protect their share in the markets they serve.[1]

Intel is the worldwide market leader in the microprocessor market. Over the past several years Intel has maintained an 85 percent share of a market growing at 15 to 20 percent per year. A strategic market plan to *protect market share* would provide continued growth in sales revenues despite anticipated price erosion. As shown in Figure 13.1, a *protect share* strategy, along with a strategy to improve margins, yields an increase in total contribution over the five-year planning horizon. Intel's cost of marketing, sales, and administration has historically been 12 percent of sales. Taking this into account yields a projected net marketing contribution that will increase by $4.9 billion from 1997 to 2002. This increase will, in turn, contribute to increased earnings and shareholder value over the same time horizon.

Businesses in less attractive markets or businesses with fewer resources may be forced to *reduce share* in an effort to find a more profitable combination of market share and profitability. Others may be forced to exit markets slowly, with a *harvest* strategy, or quickly, with a *divestment* strategy. Each *defensive strategy* is intended to maximize or protect short-run profits or to minimize short-run losses. This chapter examines defensive

Area of Performance	1997	1998	1999	2000	2001	2002
Market Demand (millions)	83	109	133	155	183	214
Market Share	85%	85%	85%	85%	85%	85%
Unit Volume (millions)	71	93	113	132	155	182
Average Selling Price	$ 240	$ 210	$ 190	$ 182	$ 175	$ 168
Sales Revenues (billions)	$17.1	$19.5	$21.5	$24.0	$27.1	$30.6
Percent Margin	60%	57%	50%	52%	55%	55%
Total Contribution (billions)	$10.3	$11.1	$10.8	$12.5	$14.9	$16.8
Marketing Expenses (billions)	$ 2.1	$ 2.3	$ 2.6	$ 2.9	$ 3.3	$ 3.7
Net Marketing Contribution (billions)	$ 8.2	$ 8.8	$ 8.2	$ 9.6	$11.6	$13.1

Figure 13.1 ◆ Intel Strategy to Protect Microprocessor Market Share

strategic market plans and the role they play in achieving the short- and long-run performance objectives of a business.

DEFENSIVE STRATEGIC MARKET PLANS

A key part of Intel's long-run performance relies on its ability to successfully implement a *protect share* strategy in the microprocessor market. Any degree of share erosion will lower unit volume, sales revenues, and net marketing contribution. However, a defensive strategy to protect share should not be misinterpreted to mean a *hold resources constant* strategy. To protect share in a market growing at 15 to 20 percent a year, Intel will have to continue its roll-out of new products and add to its marketing budget. Not doing either would almost guarantee erosion of Intel's market share position in the microprocessor market.

In general, businesses in high share positions in growing or mature markets will use defensive strategic market plans to maintain cash flow that supports short-run profit performance and shareholder value. Without these defensive strategic market plans and their profitability, businesses would face a difficult short-run situation in terms of profit performance and also would lack the resources to invest in growth-oriented offensive market opportunities.

For example, consider the business situation presented in Figure 13.2. Currently, the business is in four markets, one of which is losing money. The first market (M1) is a ma-

Figure 13.2 ◆ Strategic Market Planning and Performance

turing market in which this business holds a high-share position. The business's strategic market plan for this market is to protect this high-share position. The second market (M2) is a slow-growth market in which this business's strategic market plan is to grow share. The third market (M3) is a high-growth market in which the business's strategic market plan is to protect its share position. Market four (M4) is losing money and has been determined to be unattractive. The strategic market plan for this market is to harvest share and maximize short-run profits as the business systematically exits the market. A fifth strategic market plan is to enter an attractive emerging market (M5) in which the business will lose money initially but will be a good source of future growth, improved share position, and long-run cash flow.

With these five market-based management strategies, this business hopes to grow revenue and profits with a series of strategic moves to *protect, grow,* or *harvest* market share.[2] Each strategic market plan plays an important role in the business's short- and long-run sales and profitability. Figure 13.3 summarizes defensive strategic market plans.

PROTECT MARKET STRATEGIES

The primary goal of a defensive strategic market plan is to protect profitability and key strategic share positions. This goal translates into a combination of defensive strategic market plans. As shown in Figure 13.4, certain portfolio positions based on market attractiveness and competitive advantage lead to more than one defensive strategic market plans. A defensive strategic market plan designed to protect a desired share position can lead to a *protect share, reduced focus, harvest,* or *divest* defensive strategic market plan. In all cases, these defensive marketing strategies are focused on maximizing short-run profits and protecting or improving the overall strategic position of a business.

Protect Market Share

Many share leaders have market shares in excess of 50 percent. However, the conditions under which they have to defend their share position can be drastically different. For example, Campbell Soup has a 60 percent share position in a mature American soup market; Gillette has a 70 percent share and is the share leader in the razor and blade market,

Figure 13.3 ◆ Defensive Strategic Market Plans

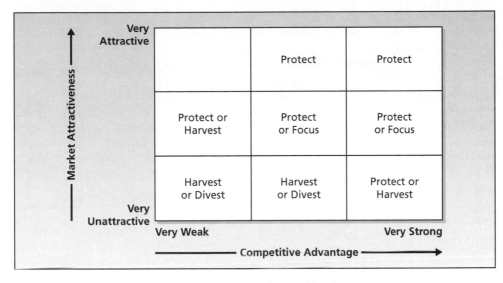

Figure 13.4 ◆ Portfolio Positions and Defensive Strategic Market Plans

which is also mature; and Kodak has more than a 60 percent share of the American film market. Their defensive strategies in slow-growth mature markets will be very different from those of businesses with high shares in fast-growth markets. Intel, with an 85 percent share in the fast-growing computer market, and Microsoft, with a 90 percent share in the rapidly developing software market, will each have to exert greater marketing efforts to protect high-share positions while their markets are still experiencing rapid growth. However, each has the same fundamental objective: *protect market share.*

Protecting Share in Growth Markets

Growth markets require a much greater marketing effort and investment in new products to protect a share leadership position than do mature markets. The faster the market grows, the more marketing resources needed to protect share. If a business does not invest to protect share in a growth market, its market share is almost certain to decline. Thus, growing markets create a much greater potential for share loss than do slow-growth markets. Hence, the resources needed to offset the effects of growth with a defensive strategic market plan to protect share must be much greater.

In the Profit Impact of Marketing Strategies (PIMS) database, the average business will experience approximately a –0.4 percent annual rate of market share change per one percent of market growth rate. This means that a business in a market growing at 10 percent a year will experience a 4 percent rate of share erosion if the effects of market growth are not offset by a defensive strategic market plan. Using this average, a business with a 20 percent market share in a market growing at a rate of 10 percent per year would experience an estimated share loss of almost 4 share points in five years if it did nothing to offset the negative impact of market growth. Of course, if the market were growing at 15 percent per year, the business would experience a much faster rate of share erosion, as shown in Figure 13.5.

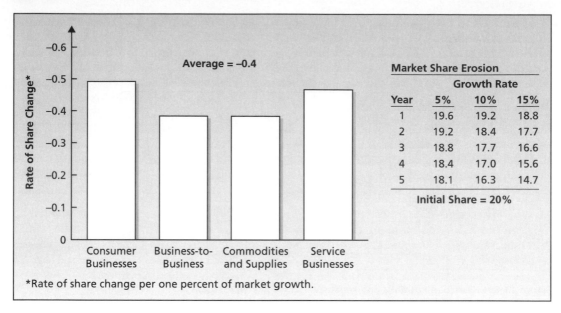

Figure 13.5 ◆ **Market Growth Rate and Share Erosion**

Although the effects of market growth on market share change are likely to be different among industries, these differences are relatively small in reasonably diverse areas of business, as also shown in Figure 13.5. Thus, the impact of market growth on market share erosion is fairly uniform among different areas of business.

Protecting a High-Share Position

Market share leaders such as Eastman Kodak, Campbell Soup, and Cisco Systems have strong share positions that generate considerable sales revenues and profits that directly affect the financial performance of these businesses. Hence, defensive marketing strategies to protect these high-share positions are critical to short-run profit performance and provide a major source of cash for investment in offensive marketing strategies for future growth and profit performance.

It is hard to imagine how having a large market share could be a handicap with respect to protecting market share. However, in the PIMS database, we consistently find an inverse relationship between market share change and size of market share. As shown in Figure 13.6, the average PIMS business would experience approximately a –0.08 percent rate of market share change per 1 percent of current market share.

This means that a business with a 30 percent market share would experience a –2.4 percent annual rate of share loss, which would lead to a 26.5 percent share loss in five years. A business with a 10 percent market share would never really feel this effect, because the size of its market share is much smaller, and its share would erode only to an estimated 9.6 percent in five years.

Thus, high-share businesses have to invest considerably more to protect share independently of other share-eroding market forces such as market growth, competitor entry, or competitor strategies. As one begins to comprehend the impact high share and high market growth rate have on eroding market share, one can better understand the market share losses experienced by Eastman Kodak, IBM, AT&T, General Motors, and other high-share businesses. And, as it is on market growth, the impact of size of market share on the rate of market share change is fairly consistent among diverse areas of business in the PIMS database, as illustrated in Figure 13.6.

To successfully defend high-share positions, businesses need to continuously improve their competitive advantage and marketing effort. Share leaders that make temporary cuts in marketing to improve short-run profit only hurt next year's profits with a reduced market share. Thus, share leaders must remain committed to (1) new product development, (2) efforts to improve product and service quality at a rate faster than the competition, and (3) fully supporting the marketing budgets needed to protect a high-share position.[3]

Protecting a Follower Share Position

Of course, not everyone can be a market share leader. Illustrated in Figure 13.7 are four market structures, each presenting *followers* in a different market share position. A business that is second in market share, but a close follower (Market II in Figure 13.7), has an interesting strategic market decision to consider. Does this follower challenge the leader with an offensive share penetration strategy? Or does it protect its share position and maximize the profits that can be extracted from that share position? Depending on the strength of the share leader, the share leader's commitment to defending its share position, and the follower business's resources and short-run profit needs, either strategic market plan could be pursued. But what does a successful defensive follower strategy look like?[4]

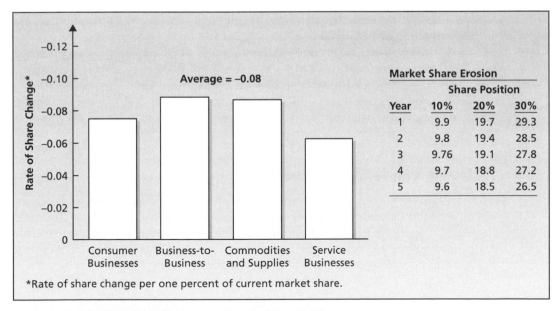

Figure 13.6 ◆ **Market Share Erosion and Current Share Position**

Figure 13.7 ◆ Market Structure and Share Position

Figure 13.8 profiles the average follower (number two share) business in the PIMS database that has achieved above-average profitability and the average follower business with below-average profit performance. With respect to competitive advantage, profitable share followers have higher relative product quality, which helps support higher levels of customer value, price, and unit margin. However, they also invest more aggressively in marketing as a percentage of sales as well as on a relative basis when compared with competitors. These effects produce a slightly higher share, which contributes to a higher level of capacity utilization.

These businesses also invest more in research and development as a percentage of sales. This investment translates into a higher level of technological advantage that most likely can be traced back to higher relative product quality. Thus, profitable followers protect their number two share position with investments in both R&D and marketing. As pointed out earlier, without these types of investments, a business could not protect a share position, even in relatively slow-growth markets.

Protecting a Niche Share Position

The strategic decision to engage in a long-run offensive or defensive strategic market plan has to also be made by *niche* share businesses. For example, niche share businesses depicted in Figure 13.7 may elect to pursue an offensive strategic market plans to challenge share leaders. Or, perhaps the market situation would lead a business to pursue a defensive strategy to protect a profitable niche market. In many ways, a niche business is simply the share leader in a more narrowly defined market. Thus, share leaders, followers, and niche businesses could each pursue defensive strategies to protect their market share positions.

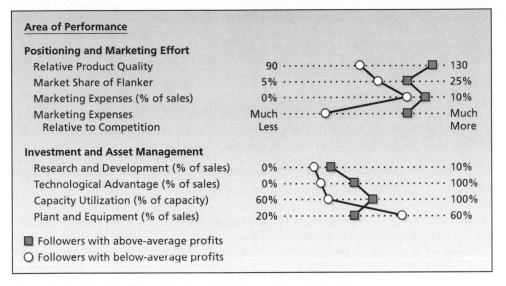

Figure 13.8 ◆ Successful vs. Unsuccessful Follower Share Strategies

A business that pursues a niche strategic market plan could be a small business with limited resources or a large business that has pursued a reduced focus strategy within a larger market and still achieves high levels of profitability.[5] For whatever reason, the business could develop a dominant position in a niche market but still have an overall share of the market that is relatively small when compared with the share leader. However, within its market niche, it is the share leader and has the same needs as share leaders in defending its share position.

Shown in Figure 13.9 are average profiles for profitable high-share and profitable low-share businesses. If you examine these two profiles closely, you will notice that there are only two areas of commonality: relative product quality and relative sales force expense.

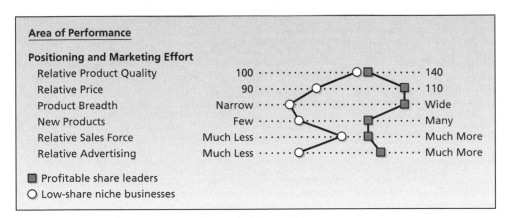

Figure 13.9 ◆ Marketing Strategies for Profitable Share Leaders and Profitable Low-Share Businesses

Having above-average product quality and above-average customer contact and market coverage are key success factors for both profitable high-share businesses and profitable low-share businesses.

However, to achieve above-average levels of profitability, low-share niche businesses need to *focus* in order to keep expenses low.[6] Their niche focus is most evident in their narrow product line, limited new product effort, and limited advertising effort relative to competitors. In addition, relative prices are slightly below the average relative price index of 100. With an average relative price near 96, and relative product quality close to 123, these successful niche businesses create an attractive customer value as shown below:

$$\text{Customer Value} = \text{Relative Benefits} - \text{Relative Price}$$

$$+27 = 123 - 97$$

As shown in Figure 13.10, low-share niche businesses with above-average customer value are more profitable. As a matter of fact, a low-share business with above-average customer value is more profitable than a high-share business with below-average customer value. Thus, an important component of success for niche share businesses is above-average customer value and sales coverage with a careful product focus.

Building Customer Retention

Protecting a valued share position is certainly a defensive strategy that is at the core of many successful businesses. However, the profit impact of holding a 30 percent market share can be quite different for high and low levels of customer retention.

For example, assume that two businesses each produce $400 of margin per customer the first year, but this margin grows by $25 per year for each year the customer is re-

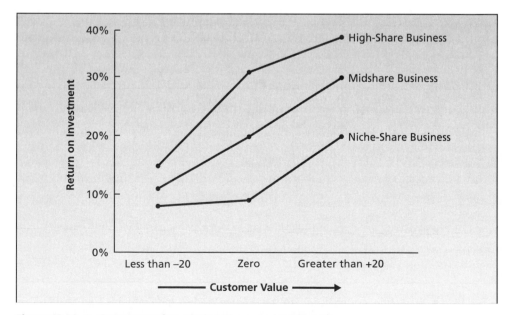

Figure 13.10 ◆ **Customer Value, Market Share, and Profitability**

tained. Further assume that each business spends $500 to acquire a new customer and $100 per year to retain a customer. As shown in Figure 13.11, the business with a 75 percent customer retention will retain the average customer for four years, whereas an 80 percent customer retention will keep the average customer for five years. That's an extra $199 in discounted net cash flow.

This analysis demonstrates how a business that is able to build a higher level of customer retention can be more profitable than another business, both with the same market share. Whether a high-share market leader, a share follower, or a low-share niche business, a business can build profits with a defensive strategy to protect share while building customer retention.

Reduced Market Focus

As shown earlier in Figure 13.4, a business may find itself in a portfolio position that can lead to more than one defensive strategic market plan. Should the business invest to strengthen its competitive advantage, allocate resources to protect its share position, or reduce its focus position within a market to maximize profitability? All can be viable strategic market plans depending upon different market and business conditions.

A decision to pursue a *reduced focus* defensive strategy would be most appropriate when:

> there are not sufficient resources to invest to protect the current share position or when greater levels of profitability can be derived from a narrower, more selective choice of target customers.

Thus, a reduced market focus prescribes a defensive strategic market plan that involves narrowing market focus and trimming market share in an effort to improve profit performance. This approach may produce a reduction in revenue and marketing budget but higher levels of profitability as a percentage of sales.[7] As shown in Figure 13.12, the whole idea of a reduced focus is to become more efficient. In this illustration, a mass market approach is less efficient than a reduced market focus in terms of marketing pro-

75% Customer Retention*				80% Customer Retention*			
Year	Net Cash	Discount Factor	Value	Year	Net Cash	Discount Factor	Present Value
0	−$500	1.000	−$500	0	−$500	1.000	−$500
1	+$300	0.870	+$261	1	+$300	0.870	+$261
2	+$325	0.756	+$246	2	+$325	0.756	+$246
3	+$350	0.658	+$230	3	+$350	0.658	+$230
4	+$375	0.572	+$215	4	+$375	0.572	+$215
5	0	0.497	0	5	+$400	0.497	+$199

Net Present Value @ 15% = +$452   Net Present Value @ 15% = +$651

* Customer Life = 1 / (1 − Customer Retention)

Figure 13.11 ◆ Profit Impact of Customer Retention Strategy

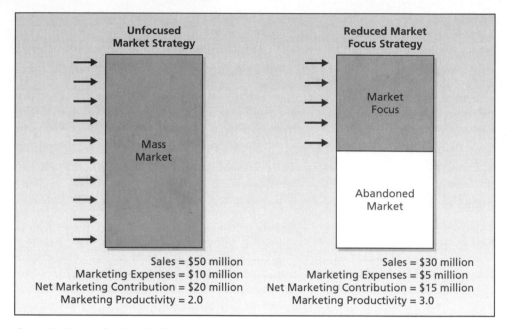

Figure 13.12 ◆ **Selective Market Focus, Marketing Resources, and Marketing Productivity**

ductivity. Although sales and profits are reduced, a reduced focus is able to improve marketing productivity from $2 of net contribution per $1 of marketing budget to $3. Thus, this business had to get smaller to become more efficient in producing profits.

EXIT MARKET STRATEGIES

Portfolio positions that warrant a defensive strategic market plan to exit from a market can lead to a *harvest* (slow exit) marketing strategy or to a *divestment* (fast exit) strategic market plan, as depicted in the portfolio model shown in Figure 13.4. When there are additional profits to be made with a slow exit, a harvest strategy can be a good source of short-run profits. If a business were losing money in a given market, it might be more inclined to pursue a quick market exit strategy and divest its share position as quickly as possible. In this case, a divestment strategy also improves short-run profits by eliminating a source of negative cash flow. Each of these defensive strategic market plans involves some aspect of market share management. However, unlike offensive strategic market plans, many of which are focused on growing market share, defensive strategic market plans are focused on protecting or pruning market share.

Harvest Price Strategy

The combination of unattractive markets and weak competitive advantage translates into both weak strategic position and potentially weak profit performance.[8] When a reduced focus strategy cannot produce desired levels of performance, an exit strategic market plan warrants consideration. However, rather than divest a share position and exit quickly, there are often good short-run performance opportunities offered by systematically rais-ing prices and reducing marketing expenses.[9]

For example, consider the business situation, outlined in Figure 13.13, that faced a chemical business.[10] Two of five product lines were not covering their marketing ex-penses. With respect to portfolio position, the business had an average competitive ad-vantage in an increasingly unattractive market. Senior management felt the best strategy would be to divest the business by selling it. However, they could not find a buyer, so they pursued a *harvest price* strategy.

The prices of silicon pigments, primary products, and special products were immedi-ately raised 10 to 19 percent. At the same time, the prices of basic colors and color en-hancers were raised 10 percent and then another 10 percent in six months. These changes resulted in an overall price increase of 22.5 percent for basic colors and 25 percent for color enhancers. In addition, marketing expenses were modestly reduced. The initial customer reaction was what was expected. There was an immediate reduction of 14 to 18 percent in the volume of silicon pigments, primary products, and special products. The customer exit for basic colors and color enhancers, with more aggressive price increases, was even greater, as the volume for these two product lines decreased by 33 and 35 percent, respectively.

However, after 18 months, customer defection subsided. And, as shown in Figure 13.14, the increased prices offset some of the lost volume, as sales revenues decreased from $183 million to $170 million. More important, however, each of the product lines now produced a positive net marketing contribution. The overall net marketing contri-bution more than doubled, from $16 million to $36.1 million.

After attaining this level of performance, the business was successful in finding a buyer. One might wonder why the company would not retain the business after it be-came profitable. First, this level of profitability was still below the company average and, hence, a drain on overall profits and shareholder value. But more important, this was an unattractive market, and the business wanted to redirect these resources into a better strategic market opportunity.

Area of Performance	Silicon Pigments	Primary Products	Special Products	Basic Colors	Color Enhancers	Overall Total
Market Demand (millions)	100	167	154	96	556	
Market Share	10%	12%	13%	26%	9%	
Unit Volume (millions)	10	20	20	25	50	125
Unit Price	$4.50	$2.80	$1.60	$0.80	$0.60	
Sales Revenue (millions)	$ 45	$ 56	$ 32	$ 20	$ 30	$ 183
Unit Variable Cost	$3.50	$2.00	$1.30	$0.70	$0.54	
Unit Margin	$1.00	$0.80	$0.30	$0.10	$0.06	
Total Contribution (millions)	$10.0	$16.0	$ 6.0	$ 2.5	$ 3.0	$37.5
Marketing Expenses (millions)	2.0	7.0	5.0	3.0	4.5	21.5
Net Marketing Contribution (millions)	$ 8.0	$ 9.0	$ 1.0	–$ .5	–$ 1.5	$16.0

Figure 13.13 ◆ **Chemical Business Product Line Performance**

Area of Performance	Silicon Pigments	Primary Products	Special Products	Basic Colors	Color Enhancers	Overall Total
Market Demand (millions)	100	167	154	96	556	
Market Share	8.6%	10.3%	10.7%	17.1%	6.0%	
Unit Volume (millions)	8.6	17.2	16.5	16.4	33.3	92
Unit Price	$4.95	$3.20	$1.90	$0.98	$0.75	
Sales Revenue (millions)	$42.6	$55.0	$31.4	$16.1	$25.0	$ 170
Unit Variable Cost	$3.50	$2.00	$1.30	$0.70	$0.54	
Unit Margin	$1.45	$1.20	$0.60	$0.28	$0.21	
Total Contribution (millions)	$12.5	$20.6	$ 9.9	$ 4.6	$ 7.0	$54.6
Marketing Expenses (millions)	2.0	7.0	4.5	2.0	3.0	18.5
Net Marketing Contribution (millions)	$10.5	$13.6	$5.4	$ 2.6	$ 4.0	$36.1

Figure 13.14 ◆ Chemical Business Product Line Performance

Harvest Resource Strategy

In many instances a business may not be able to raise prices as a strategy to harvest share while maximizing short-run profits. A soft drink manufacturer's prices are difficult to alter in the end market. In such a case, a business can reduce the marketing resources it devotes to that product and its market share position. For example, Slice is a low-share soft drink with minimal marketing support. Its market share is less than 5 percent of the lemon-lime soft drink segment and well behind Sprite, which has a 56 percent segment share. While Pepsi has examined different ways to either revitalize the brand or reposition it, its market share remains relatively stagnant. By not supporting Slice, the company is maximizing what profits it can take as Slice slowly exits the market.

In heavily advertised consumer goods markets, share erosion can be rather dramatic with major reductions in advertising budget. From the PIMS database, one can learn that the rate of share change is affected by the rate of change in advertising budget. For example, shown below is the rate of share loss for a consumer product that experienced a 25 percent reduction in advertising budget for each of three consecutive years. As shown, in this case, a 10 percent market share would erode to 9.6 percent in three years.

$$\text{Market Share (3 years)} = \text{Market Share } (1.00 + [0.05 \times \text{Change in Advertising Budget}])^3$$
$$= 10\% \times (1.00 + [0.05 \times -0.25])^3$$
$$= 10\% \times (1.00 - 0.0125)^3$$
$$= 10\% \times .96$$
$$= 9.6\%$$

When advertising budgets are very large, this can be a significant savings. As long as the product has an adequate profit margin, a business could improve short-run profits as it reduces marketing expenses and slowly loses market share. The profits taken in the short run from the harvested product would normally be reallocated to a more attractive product–market in which the business hopes to build a stronger share position and desired levels of profit.

Divest Market Strategies

One of most difficult decisions any business faces is the decision to quickly sell off (divest) an unattractive product. In some instances, these are products that the company was built on, and it is difficult to let them go. In other cases, they are major investments that are hard to kill because of the money spent and the commitment made to make them successful ventures. As a result, businesses hang on to unattractive market positions with weak or average competitive advantage far too long.

Figure 13.15 shows the porfolio of General Electric's clock and timer products as it existed in the late 1970s. Many of the products were in unattractive markets or had a weak competitive advantage, or both. GE divested the businesses shown and invested in the two that were in more attractive market positions. Eventually, these product–markets were also divested because they did not match the overall performance objectives of the company.

To divest a share position, a business can either find a buyer for the business or simply close down the operation and sell its assets. The desired choice, in most instances, is to find a buyer. Selling generally yields a greater return and preserves the employment of those working in the business.

A divestment strategy, although desired, may sometimes not be feasible. For example, a business that has a 20-year commitment to produce a critical component for a government missile cannot easily exit the product–market; it has a responsibility to supply that product for the duration of the contract. Likewise, producers of pharmaceuticals or other life-supporting products may have a difficult time divesting a share position for either le-

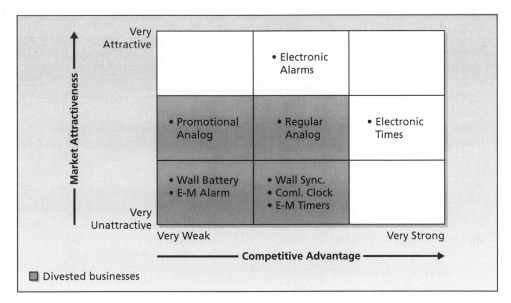

Figure 13.15 ◆ General Electric Divestment Strategy for Unattractive Product–Markets

gal or ethical reasons. Also, a simple divest share position when no buyer is available can be difficult.

SELECTING A DEFENSIVE STRATEGIC MARKET PLAN

Consider a business in a market with below-average market attractiveness and average competitive advantage that is making $25 million in net marketing contribution, as shown in Figure 13.16. This is a reasonably good profit performance, but an average competitive advantage in an unattractive market does not warrant an offensive strategic market plan to grow share. However, the share position is profitable enough to keep and, hence, a harvest market defensive strategy may not be appropriate. The choices left for this business are a *protect share* strategy and a *reduced focus* strategy.

If the business elected to pursue a protect share strategy, it would have to invest in marketing and other business activities such as research and development to maintain its 30 percent share. Given these assumptions, it is estimated that the business could maintain sales revenues of $240 million over the next three years. A protect share strategy would produce $30 million in net marketing contribution. With marketing expenses also equal to $30 million, a protect share strategy would yield a marketing productivity equal to 1.0.

The alternative defensive strategic market plan would be to reduce focus. This strategy would purposefully reduce the business's market share from 30 percent to 20 percent. However, the selective market focus strategy would yield a higher average price and unit margin and would require less in marketing expenses. The net result would be a $60 million reduction in sales revenue but an increase in net marketing contribution of $10, to $40 million. With marketing expenses of $20, this strategy also resulted in a market productivity of 2.0, twice that of the protect share strategy.

Overall, a business faces many market situations and a well-defined set of business objectives. Some performance objectives are short-run, others are long-run. Recognizing its

	Estimated Performance in Three Years	
Area of Performance	Protect Share Strategy	Reduced Focus Stragegy
Market Demand (000)	2,000	2,000
Market Share	30%	20%
Unit Volume (000)	600	400
Unit Price	$400	$450
Sales Revenues (millions)	$240	$180
Unit Variable Cost	$300	$300
Unit Margin	$100	$150
Total Contribution (millions)	$60	$60
Marketing Expenses (millions)	30	20
Net Marketing Contribution (millions)	**$30**	**$40**

Figure 13.16 ◆ Selecting between Two Defensive Marketing Strategies

performance objectives and its positioning in each of its markets, the business must put together a set of strategic market plans that will meet its performance objectives. Businesses will generally need a combination of offensive and defensive strategic market plans. Whereas offensive strategic market plans are geared for growth and improving share position, defensive strategic market plans are important sources of short-run profits and important in defending strategic share positions. Hence, both are needed and play key roles in meeting a business's performance objectives.

SUMMARY

Businesses have a short-term obligation to investors to meet their financial promises of growth and profit performance. At the same time, they have an obligation to investors and employees to carve out a set of strategic market plans that will improve the position of the business in the long run. The primary purpose of a defensive strategic market plan is to protect key strategic share positions while managing defensive positions to produce short-run growth and profits to meet the business's performance objectives.

Defensive strategic market plans play a critical role in the short-run profit performance of a business and in the protection of key strategic share positions that will support future profit performance. Strategically important share positions require a defensive strategic market plan to protect share position. This can include a protect share position in attractive markets in which a business has an average to strong competitive advantage. A protect market position defensive strategy can also include a strategy to improve customer retention, which, while maintaining a share position can have a dramatic impact on profits with little or no change in sales revenue. A business may also use a reduced market focus strategy to more narrowly focus its resources in an effort to better defend a desired share position and improve the profits derived from this market.

To protect market share requires much more than a business-as-usual marketing effort. Market forces such as market growth rate, market share size, and competitor entry each create share-eroding forces that can cause share to decrease if not offset with improved competitive advantage or increased marketing effort. Declines in relative competitive advantage in the areas of new product sales, product quality, and service quality can also contribute to market share erosion. And decreases in marketing effort in the areas of sales force and marketing communications will adversely affect defensive strategic market plans designed to protect an important share position.

In situations in which a business is in either an unattractive market or has weak competitive advantage, it may elect to use an exit strategic market plan. If the business is profitable and capable of producing good short-run profits, a harvest strategy would be used. A harvest strategy could involve raising prices or reducing marketing resources or both. This type of defensive strategic market plan enables a business to slowly exit a market while maximizing short-run profits.

On the other hand, if a business is losing money or would like to free up resources at a faster rate, a divest strategy would be more appropriate. A divest strategy would normally seek to sell the business in order to maximize the value derived from the assets and goodwill created by the business. If there are no buyers, a business may simply have to use an accelerated harvest strategy. In some instances, a business may be prevented from exiting a share position because of legal or ethical considerations. Finally, companies tend

APPLICATION PROBLEM: AMAZON.COM

In 1997, Amazon.com produced sales of approximately $150 million and a net loss after taxes of $29 million. However, with a 35 percent share in a rapidly growing market, Amazon.com seems well positioned to grow sales revenues and achieve a desired level of profit performance. The market for on-line purchase of books was approximately $430 million in 1997 but was projected to grow to over $1.5 billion by 2001. The full market potential for on-line book buying is estimated at $9 billion.

The average book price was $12 in 1997. This results in an estimated product volume of 12.5 million books. Amazon.com achieves a 20 percent profit margin on its sales.

Questions

For Internet discussion, go to www.prenhall.com/phbusiness.

1. What would Amazon.com's sales and total contribution be by 2001 if it were successful in implementing a "protect share" strategy and the on-line book market grew to the projected level of $1.5 billion?

2. Using the market share erosion caused by market growth (see Figure 13.5), estimate Amazon.com's market share in the year 2001 if this effect was not offset by the marketing resources needed to hold share in a growing market.

3. Amazon.com's fixed expenses (marketing and overhead) were approximately $58 million in 1997. If these total fixed expenses were to increase to $100 million in the year 2001, what level of market share would Amazon.com need to break even?

to hold on far too long to businesses that should be divested. Holding on too long restricts the resources available to invest in offensive marketing strategies designed to improve sales revenue growth, share position, and future profit performance.

MARKET-BASED LOGIC AND STRATEGIC THINKING

1. How do defensive marketing strategies contribute to a business's performance objectives (sales growth, share position, and profit performance)?
2. What are the differences between defensive marketing strategies and offensive marketing strategies?
3. Why is it more difficult to protect market share in a high-growth market than in a slow- or no-growth market?
4. Why do share leaders have to work harder than share followers to protect share?
5. What are some of the key aspects of performance that would enable a share follower to achieve the same level of profits as share leaders?
6. What aspects of positioning and marketing effort can be managed to achieve a high profit with a reduced focus niche market strategy?
7. Why should a reduced focus niche strategy with above-average customer value deliver above-average profits?
8. How do defensive marketing strategies contribute to the long-run share position and profit performance of a business?

9. Compare defensive marketing strategies to protect a share position with strategies to exit a share position in terms of their contributions to short-run profit performance and the overall share position of the business.
10. Why would a business pursue a reduced market focus strategic market plan?
11. What is the primary objective of a reduced market focus strategic market plan?
12. Under what conditions would a business select an exit marketing strategy over a protect share position strategy?
13. When should a business pursue a harvest marketing strategy, and how could that strategy affect short-run profit performance?
14. When should a business pursue a divest marketing strategy, and how could that strategy affect short-run profit performance?
15. Why would businesses in harvest or divest share portfolio positions continue to support the businesses rather than harvest or divest them?

NOTES

1. Donald Potter, "Strategy to Succeed in Hostile Markets," *California Management Review* (Fall 1994):65–82.
2. Sidney Schoeffer, "Market Position: Build, Hold or Harvest," PIMS Letter No. 3 (1978):1–10.
3. Philip Kotler and Paul Bloom, "Strategies for High-Market Share Companies," *Harvard Business Review* (November–December 1975):63–72.
4. Donald Clifford and Richard Cavanagh, *The Winning Performance: How America's High- and Mid-Size Growth Companies Succeed* (New York: Bantam Books, 1985).
5. Carolyn Woo and Arnold Cooper, "The Surprising Case for Low Market Share," *Harvard Business Review* (November–December 1982):106–13.
6. Robert Linneman and John Stanton Jr., "Mining for Niches," *Business Horizons* (May–June 1992):43–51.
7. Robert Hamermesh and Steven Silk, "How to Compete in Stagnant Industries," *Harvard Business Review* (September–October 1979):161–68.
8. V. Cook and R. Rothberg, "The Harvesting of USAUTO?" *Journal of Product Innovation Management* (1980):310–22.
9. Kathryn Rudie Harrigan, "Strategies for Declining Businesses," *Journal of Business Strategy* (Fall 1980):27.
10. George Seiler, "Colorful Chemicals Cuts Its Losses," *Planning Review* (January–February 1987):16–22.

part V

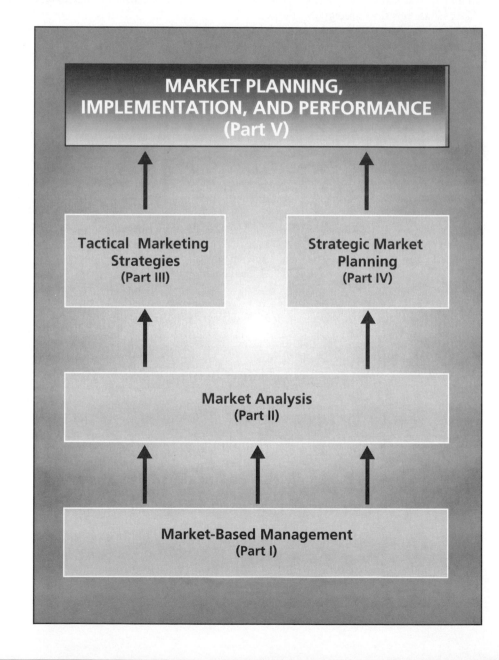

MARKET PLANNING,
IMPLEMENTATION, AND PERFORMANCE
(Part V)

Tactical Marketing Strategies
(Part III)

Strategic Market Planning
(Part IV)

Market Analysis
(Part II)

Market-Based Management
(Part I)

Market Planning, Implementation, and Performance

It is better to be prepared for an opportunity and not have one than to have an opportunity and not be prepared.

—Whitney Young Jr.

Given a specific strategic market plan and performance objectives, a tactical marketing strategy and marketing plan must be developed and successfully implemented in order to move a business toward its planned performance objectives. Chapter 14 presents a process and structure for developing a marketing plan.

Chapter 15 addresses implementation of a marketing plan and the various forces that affect the success or failure of a marketing plan. Ownership, commitment, performance measurement, adaptation, and resource allocation are important aspects of market-based management and successful implementation. Process market metrics such as customer awareness, customer perceptions of performance, trial usage, and customer satisfaction are key market-based performance metrics that are tracked, along with end-result metrics that generally measure profit performance.

Finally, it is important that those in responsible marketing positions understand how marketing strategies individually and collectively affect net profit, cash flow, investment, and, ultimately, shareholder value. Chapter 16 carefully illustrates how each aspect of a marketing strategy ripples through the organizational maze of financial accounting to affect each aspect of profitability and, ultimately, shareholder value. Regardless of a business's assets, technology, and financial leverage, *there is only one source of positive cash flow, and that is the customer; everything else is expense.*

chapter 14

Building a Marketing Plan

Stericycle, Inc. is in the business of recycling medical waste. It provides a safe, cost-effective, and environmentally friendly method for health care providers to dispose of their medical waste. In 1997, Stericycle was the second largest provider of medical waste management services in the United States, with seven treatment facilities and over 43,000 customers.

By that time, Stericycle had achieved sales of $46.2 million and a total contribution of $12.2 million, as shown in Figure 14.1. The sales revenues, revenue per customer, and percent margin were radically different in the two segments served by Stericycle. The core segment is made up of hospitals, many of which have their own waste disposal incinerators. Because of their size, hospitals in the core segment produce an average customer revenue of $35,000 per year. The alternate care segment includes the offices of physicians, dentists, and veterinarians. This segment produces an average customer revenue of $530 per year. However, the percent margin in the alternate care segment is seven times greater and the market is growing at a faster rate. By 2002, medical waste disposal is projected to be a $1.5 billion market, of which the alternate care segment will be approximately $1 billion.

With limited resources and multiple market opportunities, Stericycle needs to build a marketing plan that will address both these segments in a way that capitalizes on opportunities to grow sales and profits in a growing market. The purpose of this chapter is to do just that. We will first look at the process of building a marketing plan within the context of the market served by Stericycle, and then we will build a sample marketing plan for Stericycle, using publicly available information.

Area of Performance	Core Segment	Alternate Care Segment	Company Total	Market Demand ($ billions)
Market Demand (customers)	10,000	630,000	640,000	
Market Share	6.8%	6.72%	6.72%	
Customer Value	680	42,320	43,000	
Revenue per Customer	$35,000	$530	$1,075	
Sales Revenues (millions)	$23.8	$22.4	$46.2	
Percent Margin	6.7%	47.3%	26.4%	
Margin per Customer	$2,345	$250	$284	
Total Contribution (millions)	$1.6	$10.6	$12.2	

Figure 14.1 ◆ Stericycle Segment Demand, Sales, and Total Contribution

CREATIVITY VS. STRUCTURE

The market planning process is a delicate balance of creativity and structure. The opportunity to think creatively and explore market issues outside the realm of day-to-day business is an important part of developing a proactive marketing plan. On the other hand, a marketing plan has to have enough structure to ensure that it is comprehensive and accurate and that marketing strategies, resources, and performance objectives are credibly linked to the market situation.

Developing a marketing plan is similar to painting a picture. The creative use of light and color can make a picture interesting and appealing, but without some degree of form that adds meaning to the composition the picture may be intriguing but confusing. On the other hand, all form and no creative expression would yield a sterile picture. The same is true for a marketing plan; both creative insight and structure are necessary to paint a meaningful picture of the market situation, marketing strategy, and logic-based path that leads to desired performance objectives.

Although a marketing plan is intended to help a business systematically understand a market and develop a strategy to achieve a predetermined set of strategic market objectives, there is a paradox between having no marketing plan and having a highly formalized marketing plan.[1] A business with no marketing plan completely forgoes the opportunity to uncover key market insights that are a direct result of the market planning process. At the other extreme, businesses with highly formalized processes often evolve to a level of filling out forms as a basis for a marketing plan.[2]

Both extremes diminish the opportunity to uncover meaningful market insights. What is needed is an *open system* that encourages exploration and creative insight and, at the same time, has a structure that ensures comprehensiveness and completeness. With an open system, marketing planners should act as facilitators in the planning process rather than as developers of a marketing plan.[3] As facilitators, they facilitate acquisition of information, coordinate schedules, manage progress, and ensure that the business's mission, customers, and goals do not get lost in the planning process. Although there are recognizable organizational hurdles, in general, businesses that use a formal planning process are more likely to achieve improved performance than are businesses that have no formal plan.[4]

BENEFITS OF BUILDING A MARKETING PLAN

A good marketing plan is an essential part of a proactive market orientation. Businesses with a strong market orientation are in continuous pursuit of customer, competitor, and market intelligence and work cross-functionally to create value-added customer solutions. While these activities are ongoing, however, there are important benefits that result directly from the process of developing a marketing plan, as well as the successful *implementation* of the marketing plan.

Identifying Opportunities

It is not the plan, but the process, that helps a business uncover new opportunities and recognize important threats. With a systematic evaluation of the market and internal capabilities, there is the opportunity to step back from day-to-day tactical marketing decision making and take a broader, more comprehensive view of the market and business situation.[5] K2, a ski manufacturer, for example, has become the market share leader in the American market for skis. A systematic evaluation of the American ski market showed that it was a mature market and that additional share penetration would be difficult. However, while performing this situation analysis, K2 was led to more fully recognize the emerging markets in snowboards and in-line skates. This discovery, in turn, led to new market entry strategies that are intended to provide new growth, a more diversified strategic position, and new sources of profit.

Leveraging Core Capabilities

As K2 aggressively enters the snowboard and in-line skate markets, it will be able to leverage its brand name and awareness in closely related markets. K2 will also be able to leverage existing manufacturing and engineering expertise, as well as sales and distribution systems that currently serve the American ski market. Thus, an important benefit to a carefully thought-out marketing plan is the greater utilization of existing assets, business and marketing systems, and unique capabilities.

Focused Marketing Strategy

Most markets are complex aggregates of many smaller markets and market *segments*. These segments can be broken down further into smaller market *niches*. Without a good marketing plan, a business could find itself vaguely positioned in a variety of market segments. This position results in going in all directions in the search for customers and not really being able to fully satisfy any of them.

A good marketing plan will delineate target customers such that the positioning strategy can be customized around the needs of the target segment and the marketing effort can be directed at these target customers. In this way, the marketing plan helps bring target customers into clearer focus. Charles M. Lillis, CEO of MediaOne Group, once stated: "I will know when our businesses have done a good job in market segmentation and planning when they can tell me who we should *not* sell to."

Resource Allocation

A well-defined target market focus is also cost-efficient. If you do not know who your customers are, you are going to spend a lot of time and money informing people who are not likely to buy, regardless of your marketing efforts. Or, if they do buy, they will be difficult to retain because your value proposition cannot deliver the customer satisfaction they desire. A good marketing plan will be more productive; it will take fewer dollars to accomplish performance objectives because there are fewer resources wasted on nontarget customers.

Performance Roadmap

A good marketing plan also provides a roadmap for both marketing strategy and expected performance. The marketing plan maps a business's projected market share, sales revenue, and profits over a specified planning horizon. This may sound like a fairly easy task, but the business world is complex, with many factors affecting the situation, strategy, and resources needed. Market conditions are complicated and constantly changing with respect to customer needs, competitor structure and strategies, and the environment within which the market operates. In addition, market information is often incomplete or inaccurate or both.

The environment *within* a business can also make the market planning process difficult. Marketing strategies are often driven internally by short-run profit objectives rather than by market-based performance objectives. Further, resources are often not allocated on the basis of strategy needs and performance objectives, but by organizational needs, political processes, and short-run need for profits. These factors and others make meaningful marketing plans difficult to develop and successfully implement.

BUILDING A MARKETING PLAN: PROCESS AND LOGIC

A good marketing plan is the result of a systematic, creative yet structured, process that is designed to uncover market opportunities and threats that need to be addressed in order to achieve performance objectives. As illustrated in Figure 14.2, the development of a marketing plan is a *process,* and each step in the process has a structure that enables the marketing plan to evolve from abstract information and ideas into a tangible document that can easily be understood, evaluated, and implemented. This section is devoted to an in-depth discussion of each step in this process.

Step I: Situation Analysis

The marketing planning process outlined in Figure 14.2 starts with a detailed *situation analysis* of the market and business with respect to current market forces, the business's competitive position, and its current performance. The primary purpose of a detailed situation analysis is to uncover key performance issues that normally might go unnoticed in day-to-day business operations. First, we need to go deeper into the market and business situation with respect to understanding customer needs, competition, and channel systems, as well as business positioning, margins, and profitability, as outlined in Figure 14.3. A thorough situation analysis is required to uncover the key issues that affect performance.

The best place to start the situation analysis is with market demand. After a detailed analysis of market demand, we may find that the market is fully developed or that the total demand is small relative to the business's size and needs for growth. When this is the case, there may be little reason to go further in building a marketing plan for this product–market. Thus, an important place to start the analysis of a particular product–market situation is with an examination of the current market demand, maximum market potential, market growth rate, and factors limiting growth.

For example, the analysis of the market demand for medical waste recycling shown in Figure 14.4 would provide an excellent opportunity for Stericycle to grow sales revenues over the next five years. Market demand in dollar value was projected to grow by 50 percent. However, just as important in this situation analysis would be how the dollar value of the market demand is projected to shift to the alternate care segment. While the dollar

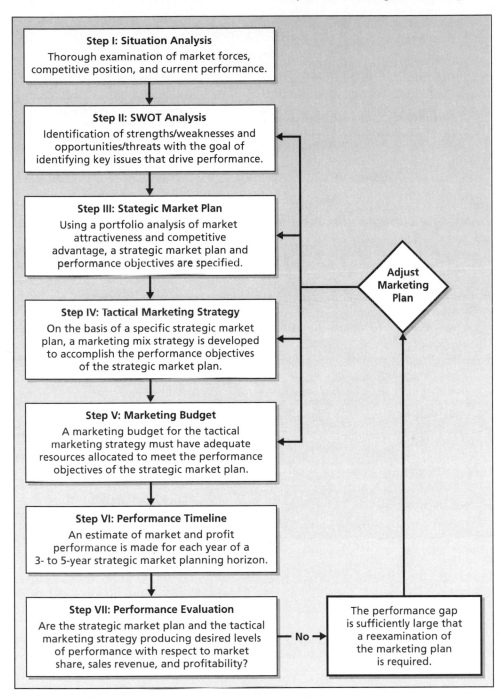

Step I: Situation Analysis
Thorough examination of market forces, competitive position, and current performance.

Step II: SWOT Analysis
Identification of strengths/weaknesses and opportunities/threats with the goal of identifying key issues that drive performance.

Step III: Stategic Market Plan
Using a portfolio analysis of market attractiveness and competitive advantage, a strategic market plan and performance objectives are specified.

Step IV: Tactical Marketing Strategy
On the basis of a specific strategic market plan, a marketing mix strategy is developed to accomplish the performance objectives of the strategic market plan.

Step V: Marketing Budget
A marketing budget for the tactical marketing strategy must have adequate resources allocated to meet the performance objectives of the strategic market plan.

Step VI: Performance Timeline
An estimate of market and profit performance is made for each year of a 3- to 5-year strategic market planning horizon.

Step VII: Performance Evaluation
Are the strategic market plan and the tactical marketing strategy producing desired levels of performance with respect to market share, sales revenue, and profitability?

Adjust Marketing Plan

— No →

The performance gap is sufficiently large that a reexamination of the marketing plan is required.

Figure 14.2 ◆ The Process of Building a Marketing Plan

Figure 14.3 ◆ **Major Components of a Situation Analysis**

value in the core segment is projected to grow, it is projected to grow at a much slower rate in the alternate care segment. Both these observations (derived from the situation analysis) would be critical in shaping a strategic market plan and tactical marketing strategies for both segments of the medical waste recycling market.

Recognizing a good opportunity for growth and the segment differences uncovered in this portion of the situation analysis, Stericycle could further examine the needs and buying behavior of each segment to more completely understand the market situation. As shown

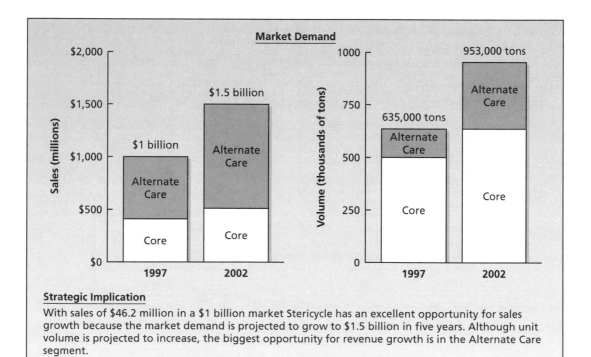

Figure 14.4 ◆ **Situational Analysis: Medical Waste Market Demand**

MARKET SEGMENTATION			
Segment Profile Factors	**Core**	**Alternate Care**	**Total Market**
Value Driver	Cost of Service	Value-Added Service	
Primary Benefits	Low Price	Training and Support	
Price Sensitivity	High	Low	
Firmographics	Hospitals	Health Care Offices	
Waste Management Expertise	Above Average	Poor	
Number of Customers	10,000	630,000	640,000
Revenue per Customer	$35,000	$530	$1,075
Margin per Customer	$2,345	$250	$284
Percent Margin	6.7%	47.3%	26.4%
Waste Volume (tons)	490,000	145,000	635,000
Waste Volume per Customer	98,000 lb	460 lb	1984 lb
Price per Pound	$0.41/lb	$2.06/lb	$0.79/lb
Margin per Pound	$0.03/lb	$0.87/lb	$0.45/lb

Strategic Implications
The core segment has fewer, more price-sensitive customers but offers a much higher revenue and margin per customer. The alternate care segment, while less price-sensitive, yields a much lower margin per customer even though the percent margin is quite attractive.

Figure 14.5 ◆ Situation Analysis: Medical Waste Segments

in Figure 14.5, these segments are quite different in primary needs, price sensitivity, and experience in managing medical waste. There are also important differences in customer buying and, as a result, significant differences in revenue and margin per customer. These insights are a key part of the situation analysis. Without them, the business is likely to follow an internal strategy based on experience and management perceptions of market needs.

To complete this phase of the market planning process, we must comprehensively examine each of the situational forces outlined in Figure 14.3. When a comprehensive representation of the situation analysis is complete, it is time to move on to identifying and prioritizing *key issues* that affect the business's performance objectives (share position, sales growth, and profit performance).

Step II: SWOT Analysis and Key Performance Issues

The *SWOT analysis* is critical in summarizing key strengths and weaknesses, as well as opportunities and threats. It is important in this process that there be a strong linkage between the situation analysis and the SWOT analysis. These must be interconnected, not separate and distinct, parts of the market planning process. The steps that follow will be only as good as the situation analysis and key performance issues that are uncovered in the situation and SWOT analyses.

Perhaps the most difficult and elusive part of a marketing plan is the identification of key performance issues. A *key performance issue* is a problem or unaddressed opportunity that is an underlying cause that limits market or profit performance or both.

In the process of sorting out key issues, it is useful to classify them as strengths and weaknesses or opportunities and threats. This is what is called a SWOT analysis. Shown in Figure 14.6 is a SWOT analysis derived from a situation analysis of the medical waste recycling market and Stericycle's position and performance in it. As shown, there are several strengths, weakness, opportunities, and threats that Stericycle needs to recognize in building a marketing plan for the medical waste recycling market. It is important that the business also understand the degree to which each of these key issues affects key performance metrics. Because the key issues will be the primary guideline to developing a tactical marketing strategy, it is important that these issues be carefully specified and articulated. This step in the market planning process is critical in terms of the marketing strategy to be developed and the potential impact it has on performance.

Step III: Strategic Market Plan

On the basis of the insights derived from the situation analysis and SWOT analysis, a *strategic market plan* must be developed. The primary purpose of a strategic market plan is to provide a *strategic direction* from which to set performance objectives and guide the development of a tactical marketing strategy.[6] This is an important step in the market planning process because it requires a careful examination of market attractiveness and the business's competitive advantage based on the information provided in the situation analysis.

STRENGTHS	WEAKNESSES	**KEY ISSUES**
Recognized Leader in Service	High Cost of Marketing	**New Customer Growth** will require more marketing budget until full-share penetration.
Technology Advantage	Growth Limited to Capacity	
Room to Grow (Excess Capacity)	Low Margins in Core Segment	**Market Focus** is important because we have limited capacity.
Established Marketing Systems	Poor Productivity in Alt. Care	
OPPORTUNITIES	THREATS	**Supply and Pricing:** reduced competition and short supply should favor higher prices.
Growing Market Demand	Increased Government Regulation	
Market Restructuring	Price Competition in Alt. Care	
Attractive Industry Dynamics	Efforts of Major Competitors	
Competitor Exit		

Strategic Implications
The key issues can be directly linked to current positioning and performance. To the degree these issues are addressed in the marketing plan, Stericyle has the potential to achieve above-average levels of profitable growth.

Figure 14.6 ◆ **SWOT Analysis: Stericycle Medical Waste Recycling Business**

By analyzing the forces that shape market attractiveness and competitive advantage, the business can create a product–market portfolio. Each product–market opportunity can be placed in the portfolio, as shown in Figure 14.7. On the basis of the relative portfolio position, a long-run market share objective must be specified for each product–market.[7] The alternate care segment is in a very attractive market with an average position of advantage. It represents the stronger strategic position and best opportunity for profit performance. This analysis and current performance indicate that an offensive strategic market plan to grow market share is appropriate.

The core segment is less attractive but is still above average in overall market attractiveness and competitive advantage. However, in this segment, a defensive reduced focus strategic market plan is more appropriate given limited resources and the profit potential of this segment.

Step IV: Tactical Marketing Strategy

The next step in the marketing planning process is the development of a *tactical marketing strategy* to put the strategic market plan into effect. Although the overall marketing strategy to protect, grow, reduce-focus, harvest, enter, or exit a market position is set by the strategic market plan, more-specific tactical marketing strategies need to be developed for each of the key performance issues. Each element of a tactical marketing strategy is a specific response to a key performance issue that exists within the context of the market situation. Thus, specific marketing strategies developed will be only as good as the key performance issues uncovered as an output of the situation analysis.

For example, given a strategic market plan of reduced focus for the core segment, Stericycle would need to develop a specific tactical marketing strategy. Outlined in Figure 14.8 is one approach to the marketing tactics that could be used to implement and achieve the performance objectives specified by the strategic market plan.

Figure 14.7 ◆ Stericycle Strategic Market Plan: Portfolio Analysis

CORE SEGMENT STRATEGY: REDUCED FOCUS	
Value Proposition	*Stericycle Medical Waste Management—For Hospitals Who Value Superior Service and Unquestionable Safety*
Positioning Strategy	Above-average customer service, training, and technical support priced 10 to 20 percent higher than competition in the core market. Stericycle will also provide an Excel-based software program for customers to track their waste management activities.
Channel System	Account managers who are highly trained in business and waste management technology will call on Stericycle customers once a month. They will provide training when needed as well as annual financial analysis and client review.
Share Objective	Decrease number of price-sensitive customers using modest price increases. This move is expected to erode market share from 6.8 percent to 5 percent. We will not actively seek new customers, but we will watch for opportunities to take on new core customers attracted to our value proposition.

Figure 14.8 ◆ Stericycle Core Segment Strategy

Note that the tactical marketing strategy presented in Figure 14.8 is in direct response to key performance issues and is not vague. It is clear in its approach to addressing these issues and gives specific details with respect to target share, positioning, pricing, channel system, and the value proposition to be used in target market communications. This level of detail is required in order to evaluate the market and profit impact of this tactical marketing strategy. A separate tactical marketing strategy will also have to be developed for the alternate care segment on the basis of its strategic market plan, key performance issues, and performance objectives. This tactical marketing strategy is presented in the complete Stericycle Marketing Plan later in this chapter.

Step V: Marketing Budget

Resources need to be allocated in a *marketing budget* based on the strategic market plan and the tactical marketing strategy. Without adequate resources, the tactical marketing strategies cannot succeed, and, as a consequence, performance objectives cannot be achieved. One cannot expect to grow share in the growing alternate care segment without additions to the marketing budget. A reduced focus in the core segment should require fewer resources than a share growth strategy with respect to the marketing budget.

Specifying a marketing budget is perhaps the most difficult part of the market planning process. Although specifying the budget is not a precise process, there must be a logical connection between the strategy and performance objectives and the marketing budget.

There are three ways to build a marketing budget that is based on a specific strategic market plan and the tactical marketing strategy designed to achieve the target level of performance. Each is briefly described below with respect to Stericycle.

- **Top-Down Budget:** A new marketing budget based on projected sales objectives is determined, using past marketing expenses as a percentage of sales.
- **Customer Mix Budget:** The cost of customer acquisition and retention and the combination of new and retained customers are used to derive a new marketing budget.
- **Bottom-Up Budget:** Each element of the marketing effort is budgeted for specific tasks identified in the marketing plan.

Stericycle's marketing expenses in 1997 were $10.7 million, and total sales were $46.2 million. Thus, marketing budget as a percentage of sales was 23.2 percent. This is a relatively high percentage of sales for a marketing budget, but Stericycle is in a rapid-growth phase. If Stericycle's sales objective was $54 million in 1998, then, using a "top-down" approach, they would budget $12.5 million in marketing expenses (23.2 percent of $54 million).

Because each market segment has different customer acquisition and retention costs as well as vastly different numbers of customers, the "customer mix" approach is probably more appropriate for Stericycle. Several assumptions (made here, not made by Stericycle) result in the following estimate of Stericycle's acquisition and retention costs for each segment:

Market Segment	Acquisition Cost per Customer	Number of New Customers	Retention Cost per Customer	Number of Customers Retained
Core	$3,500	300	$700	380
Alternate Care	$385	20,000	$80	22,300

$$\text{Marketing Budget} = \left(\text{Acquisition Cost per Customer} \times \text{Number of New Customers}\right) + \left(\text{Retention Cost per Customer} \times \text{Number of Customers Retained}\right)$$

$$\text{Marketing Budget (Core)} = (\$3,500 \times 300) + (\$700 \times 380)$$
$$= \$1,050,000 + \$266,000$$
$$= \$1,316,000$$

$$\text{Marketing Budget (Alternate Care)} = (\$385 \times 20,000) + (\$80 \times 22,300)$$
$$= \$7,700,000 + \$1,784,000$$
$$= \$9,484,000$$

This would be the budget for each segment for 1997. If, in 1998, Stericycle maintained a 95 percent retention and sought only to replace lost customers in the core segment, it would need a marketing budget of $571,200, as estimated below.

$$\text{Marketing Budget (Core)} = \left(\text{Percent to Replace} \times \text{Customer Base} \times \text{Cost to Replace}\right) + \left(\text{Percent Retained} \times \text{Customer Base} \times \text{Cost to Retain}\right)$$

$$= (0.05 \times 680 \times \$3,500) + (0.95 \times 680 \times \$700)$$
$$= \$119,000 + \$452,200$$
$$= \$571,200$$

If Stericycle's strategy in the alternate care segment is to replace lost customers (assuming a 95 percentage retention) and add 20,000 new customers as it did the year before, its estimated marketing budget will be $11.73 million, as shown below.

$$
\begin{aligned}
\text{Marketing Budget} \atop \text{(Alternate Care)} &= \{\$385 \times [(0.05 \times 42{,}300) + 20{,}000]\} + (\$80 \times 0.95 \times 42{,}300) \\
&= \$8{,}514{,}275 + \$3{,}214{,}800 \\
&= \$11{,}729{,}075
\end{aligned}
$$

Overall, a customer mix approach would result in a marketing budget of $12.3 million to retain a customer base of 680 in the core segment and to grow the customer base in the alternate care segment by 20,000 customers.

A "bottom-up" approach would require specifying each marketing task and the amount needed to accomplish it given a particular strategic market plan and tactical marketing strategy. For example, we can estimate the bottom-up marketing budget for the core segment strategy to hold market share as follows:

$800,000	**Sales Force** (10 salespeople to make monthly calls on 646 existing customers and develop 34 new accounts per year. Average cost per salesperson including salary, benefits, and sales expenses is $80,000 per year.)
$50,000	**Inside Sales** (Two people for order processing, invoicing and accounting)
$50,000	**Customer Literature** (Safety tips and technical information)
$50,000	**Technical Support** (One inside technical support person to assist sales force)
$50,000	**Marketing Communications** (print ads run in hospital trade magazines)
$1,000,000	**Core Segment Marketing Budget**

As shown above, a bottom-up marketing budget provides for 10 direct salespeople, two inside salespeople, one technical support person, order processing, customer literature, and marketing communications print advertising. Each item has a specific objective and cost based on the core segment strategy specified and the volume of customers that is expected to be served based on this strategy. Of course, a bottom-up marketing budget for the alternate care segment would be much more complex, and much larger, given a strategy to grow the number of customers from 42,300 to 62,300.

When the new resources required are added to the existing base, a total budget for the marketing plan can be systematically derived. This bottom-up approach to setting the marketing budget is directly tied to a specific marketing strategy and performance objectives. Deviation from the resources required should be reconciled with the tactical marketing strategy and the intended impact on performance. If insufficient resources are available to fund a proposed tactical marketing strategy, then the strategy must be revised to reflect how the available resources will be used to achieve a desired, though reduced, level of performance in share, sales, and profitability.

Step VI: Performance Timeline

Given an adequate allocation of resources, a *performance timeline*, is critical in depicting performance levels for external market metrics and internal operating metrics over the planning horizon. This step must make explicit the timing of specific performance objectives (share position, sales revenue, and profit performance) so that the success or failure of the marketing plan can be evaluated. Performance metrics include external market metrics, such as customer awareness, customer satisfaction, product availability, perceptions of product and service quality, and market share, as well as internal profit performance metrics, such as sales revenues, contribution margins, total contribution, and net marketing contribution.

A Stericycle performance plan to "reduce customer share" in the core segment and to "grow customer share" in the alternate care segment is outlined over a five-year time frame in Figure 14.9. As shown, each segment strategy has different levels of expected performance with respect to customer share, sales growth, and net marketing contribution. This performance plan estimates that if the strategic market plan and tactical marketing strategy are successful, Stericycle's overall customer share should grow to approximately 20 percent and that sales revenues should more than double. More important, net marketing contribution is projected to grow from $1.4 million to $34.5 million. Beyond this point, the marketing budget should decrease if Stericycle's customer share objective is attained, because the cost of new customer acquisition would be focused entirely on replacing lost customers.

The degree to which these estimates of projected performance are credible is directly related to the credibility of the key performance issues, strategic market plans, marketing strategies, and marketing budgets made to support specific tactical marketing strategies. If these linkages are not credible, then the numbers presented in the performance impact assessment are open to question.

Step VII: Performance Evaluation

Step VII, *performance evaluation,* is an ongoing monitoring of market and profit performance and comparisons with the performance timeline. If the marketing plan fails to meet the desired performance objectives specified as part of the strategic market plan, then the marketing plan has to be reevaluated with respect to all inputs used in the market planning process, as shown in Figure 14.2. These performance gaps require the business to consider several options. One is to reexamine the pricing, customer and channel discounts, unit costs, and the marketing budget to determine if, in fact, there are opportunities to improve performance.

A second alternative is to reexamine the entire marketing plan. Both the situation and the key performance issues would be reviewed to see if there were alternative tactical marketing strategies that would work better in achieving the desired performance objectives. Whichever the case, a credible marketing strategy must be linked to the market situation, key performance issues, and available resources and then linked to projections of external market metrics and internal profit metrics.

And of course, a final option may be to refrain from pursuing this market opportunity further. It may be that none of the alternative marketing strategies considered can deliver, with credibility and confidence, the desired level of performance. When this is the case, the business is better off abandoning this market opportunity and allocating its resources and management time to other market opportunities.

SAMPLE MARKETING PLAN

To facilitate a better understanding of a marketing plan and the benefits of building one, a sample marketing plan for Stericycle is presented at the end of this chapter. The infor-

Area of Performance	1997	1998	1999	2000	2001	2002
Core Segment						
Market Demand						
(number of customers)	10,000	10,000	10,000	10,000	10,000	10,000
Market Share (% of customers)	6.8%	6.0%	5.0%	5.0%	5.0%	5.0%
Number of Customers	680	600	500	500	500	500
Average Revenue per Customer	$35,000	$38,000	$40,000	$42,000	$44,000	$46,000
Sales Revenues (millions)	$ 23.8	$ 22.8	$ 20.0	$ 21.0	$ 22.0	$ 23.0
Percent Margin	6.7%	14.0%	18.0%	22.0%	24.0%	25.0%
Total Contribution (millions)	$ 1.6	$ 3.2	$ 3.6	$ 4.6	$ 5.3	$ 5.8
Marketing Budget (millions)	$ 1.3	$ 0.5	$ 0.5	$ 0.5	$ 0.5	$ 0.5
Net Marketing Contribution (millions)	$ 0.3	$ 2.7	$ 3.1	$ 4.1	$ 4.8	$ 5.3
Alternate Care Segment						
Market Demand						
(number of customers)	630,000	630,000	630,000	630,000	630,000	630,000
Market Share (% of customers)	6.72%	10.0%	13.0%	16.0%	18.0%	20.0%
Number of Customers	42,320	63,000	81,900	100,800	113,400	126,000
Average Revenue per Customer	$ 530	$ 570	$ 600	$ 650	$ 700	$ 750
Sales Revenues (millions)	$22.4	$35.9	$49.1	$65.5	$79.4	$94.5
Percent Margin	47.3%	47.3%	47.3%	47.3%	47.3%	47.3%
Total Contribution (millions)	$10.6	$17.0	$23.2	$31.0	$37.5	$44.7
Marketing Budget (millions)	$ 9.5	$12.0	$13.2	$15.0	$14.4	$15.5
Net Marketing Contribution (millions)	$ 1.1	$ 5.0	$10.0	$16.0	$23.1	$29.2
Overall Stericycle Performance						
Market Share	6.7%	9.9%	12.9%	15.8%	17.8%	19.8%
Sales Revenues (millions)	$46.2	$58.7	$69.1	$86.5	$101.4	$117.5
Percent Margin	26.4%	34.4%	38.8%	41.2%	42.2%	42.9%
Total Contribution (millions)	$12.2	$20.2	$26.8	$35.6	$ 42.2	$ 50.5
Marketing Budget (millions)	$10.8	$12.5	$13.7	$15.5	$ 14.9	$ 16.0
Net Marketing Contribution (millions)	$ 1.4	$ 7.7	$13.1	$20.1	$ 27.9	$ 34.5

Figure 14.9 ◆ Performance Plan: Sample Stericycle Marketing Plan

mation used to construct the sample marketing plan shown here was taken from information publicly available in 1997 and 1998. All assumptions, inferences, analyses, and recommendations are mine, not Stericycle's.

Because of space limitations, not all of the supporting assumptions, analyses, and interpretations of the information are presented.

Step I: Situation Analysis

As shown in Figure 14.2, the first step in building a marketing plan is a situation analysis, which encompasses external and internal forces that shape market attractiveness, competitive position, and current performance with respect to share position, sales revenues, and profitability. Described below are the various situational forces I used in building the situation analysis. As shown in the sample marketing plan, each important aspect of the current situation is presented in one page and the implications it has for strategy development are discussed. Outlined below is a brief summary of the situation analysis, the first seven pages of the sample marketing plan.

- **Market Demand:** Presents the current and future level of market demand as well as Stericycle segment sales.
- **Market Segmentation:** A profile of each segment served by Stericycle with respect to segment needs, size, and growth rates, as well as revenue and margin per customer.
- **Industry Analysis:** Summarizes the industry forces that shape segment attractiveness and profit potential and presents and overall index of industry attractiveness for each.
- **Market Share and Customer Retention:** Presents Stericycle's current level of market share penetration and identifies the major forces that shape Stericycle penetration of this market.
- **Competition and Market Restructuring:** Presents a summary of the current competition and how the competitive landscape of this market will be restructured over the next five years.
- **Channel Systems and Marketing Budget:** Illustrates the channel systems used to reach target segments and the breakdown of the marketing budget with respect to the cost of customer acquisition and retention.
- **Market and Profit Performance:** Presents the market share, customer retention, and lifetime value of each segment as well as sales, margins, and profits currently obtained from each segment.

Although more aspects of the situation and greater detail could have been developed and presented, these situational forces and their respective strategy implications provide us the basis to identify key issues that affect performance, which is the next step in the process of building a marketing plan.

Step II: SWOT Analysis

The SWOT analysis is a summary of the key strategy implications uncovered in the situation analysis. The various strategy implications are categorized as a strength or weakness or an opportunity or threat so they can be more fully comprehended. Then, from this SWOT analysis, the most important issues need to be identified and described more completely. Among the strategy implications presented in the SWOT analysis, these are the issues that are believed to have the greatest impact on future performance. Thus, it is important that these strategic issues be highlighted and become a central focus of the strategy to be developed. For the Stericycle sample marketing plan, the following is a brief description of the SWOT analysis that is presented on page 8 of the sample marketing plan.

- **SWOT Analysis and Key Issues:** Summarizes the strategic implications uncovered in the Stericycle situation analysis and identifies key issues to be addressed in the strategies to be developed.

Recognizing both the information presented in the situation analysis and the strategy implications derived in the SWOT analysis, we next must develop a strategic market plan for each segment.

Step III: Strategic Market Plan

Stericycle faces two market opportunities, one in the core segment and the other in the alternate care segment. Because the resources in most businesses are limited and market opportunities vary in market attractiveness and potential for competitive advantage, a strategic market plan needs to be specified for each market segment. This process is described below and presented on pages 9 and 10 of the sample Stericycle marketing plan.

- **Strategic Market Assessment:** Market attractiveness and competitive advantage criteria are specified and weighted with respect to importance. On the basis of these criteria, each market segment is assessed and indexed with respect to market attractiveness and competitive advantage.
- **Portfolio Analysis:** A product–market portfolio is created based on the market attractiveness and competitive advantage for each market segment.
- **Strategic Market Plan:** On the basis of the portfolio position, situation analysis, SWOT analysis, and resources, a strategic market plan is specified for each segment.

The strategic market plan for each segment sets a strategic direction and implicitly specifies the short- and long-run performance expectations for each segment. The next step in building a marketing plan is to develop a tactical marketing strategy for each target market.

Step IV: Tactical Marketing Strategy

The strategic market plan for each segment and the situation forces presented in the situation analysis were used to develop the tactical marketing strategy for each market segment, presented on pages 11 and 12 of the sample Stericycle marketing plan.

- **Core Segment Strategy: Reduced Focus:** The tactical marketing mix strategy (product, price, promotion, and place) recommended for this segment is a defensive strategy that is consistent with the strategic market plan specified for this segment and the situational forces presented in the situation analysis.
- **Alternate Care Segment Strategy: Share Penetration:** The tactical marketing mix strategy recommended for this segment is an offensive strategy to aggressively build market share. As such, the marketing mix is quite different from the one specified for the core segment.

Tactical marketing strategies provide the level of detail required to allow resource allocations in the marketing budget and to subsequently build a performance plan.

Step V: Marketing Budget

Producing a marketing budget is a critical step in building a marketing plan and one most businesses do not do a very good job on. Up to now the process of building a marketing plan was relatively free of risk and economic consequences. Now, it is time to resource each strategic market plan and supporting tactical marketing strategy with a marketing budget. If this is not done correctly, the whole effort is subject to a higher probability of failure. The "customer mix" approach was used to develop the marketing budget that is summarized and presented on page 13 of the sample Stericycle marketing plan.

- **Resource Allocation and Marketing Budget:** On the basis of the market share objectives of each segment strategy and the respective cost of new customer acquisition and retention of existing customers, a marketing budget was created for each market segment over a five-year planning horizon.

The marketing budget for each segment is consistent with the market share objective for each segment over the next five years. Naturally, the core segment, with a reduced focus strategy, will require less marketing budget than the alternate care segment, which hopes to more than triple its market share over the next five years.

Step VI: Performance Timeline

The last page of the sample Stericycle marketing plan is a performance timeline. The plan outlines for each segment how market share, sales revenues, margins, marketing expenses, and profitability will evolve over the five-year planning horizon. A brief description is provided below and shown on page 14 of the sample marketing plan.

- **Performance Timeline:** The current performance with respect to market share, sales, margin, marketing expense, and net marketing contribution is reported for each segment. Then, on the basis of the strategic market plan and tactical marketing strategy for each segment, a five-year performance timeline is projected.

The performance timeline represents a close reconciliation between situation, strategy, and resource allocation. To the degree that this reconciliation is done accurately, the performance timeline provides a legitimate roadmap from which actual performance can be evaluated as the marketing plan is implemented over time.

Step VII: Performance Evaluation

The sample marketing plan built for Stericycle represents a strategic roadmap for navigation of two specific segment strategic market plans and tactical marketing strategies. As shown in Figure 14.2, after the marketing plan has been implemented, performance gaps are likely to emerge because of changing market conditions and the effectiveness of proposed marketing tactics. Addressing these performance gaps as they occur is a critical part of the marketing planning process. Modifying, adapting, and even abandoning the strategy for a segment are all part of the process of building and implementing a marketing plan. The next chapter is devoted specifically to successful implementation of a marketing plan.

SUMMARY

A marketing plan is a roadmap. It carefully outlines where a business is, its desired destination (objectives), and the conditions it will face in its efforts to reach that destination.

APPLICATION PROBLEM: STERICYCLE, INC.

The core segment marketing manager for Stericycle felt that the company was making a mistake by not pursuing a greater share of this segment. He reasoned that, although the percent margin was lower in the core segment, the revenue per customer was much higher. This combination of factors produces a higher dollar margin per customer and much higher level of marketing productivity (net marketing contribution per dollar of marketing budget). On the basis of this logic, the core segment marketing manager argued it would be more profitable to "grow share" in the core segment and "hold share" in the alternate care segment.

In response, the senior management team thought it would be a good idea to examine this alternative strategic market plan. Using the Stericycle Marketing Plan presented in this chapter, evaluate a five-year marketing strategy based on an alternative strategic market plan outlined below.

- Hold the current (1997) share and customer volume position in the alternate care segment. Assume Stericycle maintains a 95 percent customer retention and replaces lost customers each year to maintain its 1997 share and customer volume.
- Grow share in the core segment to 20 percent assuming Stericycle maintains a 95 percent customer retention.

In doing this analysis use the same price strategies as originally proposed in each tactical marketing strategy but restructure the marketing budget for each market segment on the basis of this alternative strategic market plan.

Questions

For Internet discussion, go to www.prenhall.com/phbusiness.

1. What would be the total contribution produced by each segment strategy in year 5? To what degree is this strategy better or worse than the original strategic market plan with respect to these performance objectives?
2. How much net marketing contribution is produced by each segment strategy in year 5? To what degree is this strategy better or worse than the original strategic market plan with respect to these performance objectives?
3. Is this strategic market plan superior to the one discussed in this chapter?

Understanding the market situation reveals a set of key issues that need to be addressed in order to reach the desired destination. Situation analysis and identification of key performance issues are key inputs to the marketing plan designed to accomplish a business's objectives.

The strategies developed in a marketing plan will not necessarily succeed just because they have been laid out. Resources in the form of people and money need to be allocated to implement strategies. If adequate resources are not available, attainment of a business's objectives may not be possible, and marketing strategies will have to be revised or abandoned. Thus, the process of developing a marketing plan is not that much different from planning an extensive vacation; it is just much more complex.

There are many benefits to a good marketing plan. The process of market planning can lead a business to discovery of new market opportunities, to better utilization of assets and capabilities, to a well-defined market focus, to improved marketing productivity, and to a baseline from which to evaluate progress toward goals. There is a planning paradox, however. It goes without saying that those with no marketing plans severely restrict themselves in achieving benefits, but it is also true that those with too highly formalized marketing plans may also minimize their potential of achieving benefits. The business with no marketing plan will not see the market around them and the opportunities and threats that need to be addressed while pursuing a market objective. Businesses with highly formalized plans can evolve to merely filling in forms and can thereby miss the opportunity to understand the subtler aspects of the market.

The development of a marketing plan involves process and structure, creativity and form. The process begins with a broad view of market opportunities that encourages a wider consideration of many market opportunities. For each market opportunity, a strategic market objective is set, based on market attractiveness and competitive advantage attained or attainable in the market. For each market to be pursued, a separate situation analysis and marketing plan is required. The situation analysis enables the business to uncover key issues that limit performance. These key performance issues are the basic guidelines from which marketing strategies are developed. Each aspect of the strategy must be scrutinized with respect to the market situation, key issues, strategies to address those issues, and the resources needed to achieve specific performance objectives. With the marketing strategy and budget set, an estimate of market and financial performance metrics must be projected over a specified time frame. If the marketing plan fails to produce desired levels of performance, the marketing strategy needs to be reexamined.

MARKET-BASED LOGIC AND STRATEGIC THINKING

1. Why is a roadmap for a family vacation a good metaphor for the process of developing a marketing plan? What are the similarities and differences?
2. How would the process of developing a marketing plan help Stericycle achieve a higher level of sales growth and profitability?
3. Why would a business with a strong market orientation do a better job in situation analysis than a business with a poor market orientation?
4. How could businesses engaged in no market planning or in highly formalized market planning both miss meaningful market insights?

5. How would a business with a sound market planning process differ from a business with no marketing plan in the following:

   Discovering opportunities

   Leveraging existing systems, assets, and core capabilities

   Implementing a market-focused strategy

   Allocating resources

   Planning performance

6. Why does the first step in the market planning process involve a situation analysis?

7. What is the role of a SWOT analysis in the market planning process? What is the role of key issues in the SWOT analysis?

8. For each product–market opportunity, how is a strategic market plan determined?

9. How does the strategic marketing plan for a given product–market influence the tactical marketing strategy for that product–market?

10. How are key performance issues identified in the SWOT analysis used in selecting a strategic market plan and building a tactical marketing strategy?

11. Why is the development of a marketing budget so important to the success of the marketing plan?

12. What are the various ways one could develop a marketing budget for a given strategic market plan and supporting tactical marketing strategy?

13. How should the resources needed to support a marketing plan be logically linked to the key issues, marketing strategies, and expected performance?

14. What is the purpose of the performance plan? What role should it play in the successful implementation of a marketing plan?

NOTES

1. David Aaker, "Formal Planning System," *Strategic Market Management* (New York: Wiley, 1995), 341–53.

2. Arie Rijvnis and Graham Sharman, "New Life for Formal Planning Systems," *Journal of Business Strategy* (Spring 1982):103.

3. Henry Mintzberg, "The Fall and Rise of Strategic Planning," *Harvard Business Review* (January–February 1994):107–14; and Benjamin Tregoe and Peter Tobia, "Strategy versus Planning: Bridging the Gap," *Journal of Business Strategy* (December 1991):14–19.

4. Thomas Powell, "Strategic Planning As Competitive Advantage," *Strategic Management Journal* 13 (1992):551–58; Scott Armstrong, "The Value of Formal Planning for Strategic Decisions: Reply," *Strategic Management Journal* 7 (1986):183–85; and Deepak Sinha, "The Contribution of Formal Planning to Decisions," *Strategic Management Journal* (October 1990):479–92.

5. Philip Kotler, *Marketing Management: Analysis, Planning, Implementation and Control,* 7th ed. (Upper Saddle River, NJ: Prentice Hall, 1991), 62–72.

6. Gary Hamel and C. K. Prahalad, "Strategic Intent," *Harvard Business Review* (May–June 1989):63–75; and Michael Treacy, and Frederic Wiersema, "Customer Intimacy and Other Value Disciplines," *Harvard Business Review* (January–February 1993):84–93.

7. Rajan Varadarajan, "Product Portfolio Analysis and Market Share Objectives: An Exposition of Certain Underlying Assumptions," *Journal of the Academy of Marketing Science* (Winter 1990): 17–29.

STERICYCLE MARKETING PLAN

Stericycle is a distant share follower in a growing market that is rapidly consolidating as competitors are forced to exit the market. The purpose of this marketing plan is to delineate a marketing strategy to grow Stericycle's market share threefold and thereby grow sales revenues, profits, and shareholder value.

Lundquist College of Business
University of Oregon

Roger J. Best
Professor of Marketing

CONTENTS

SITUATION ANALYSIS 1
  Market Demand 1
  Market Segmentation 2
  Industry Analysis. 3
  Market Share and Customer Retention 4
  Competition and Market Restructuring 5
  Channel Systems and Marketing Budget 6
  Market and Profit Performance 7
SWOT ANALYSIS 8
MARKETING STRATEGY and PERFORMANCE PLAN 9
  Strategic Market Assessment. 9
  Portfolio Analysis and Strategic Market Plans 10
  Core Segment Strategy: Reduced Focus 11
  Alternate Care Segment Strategy: Share Penetration 12
  Resource Allocation and Marketing Budget 13
  Performance Plan and Timeline. 14

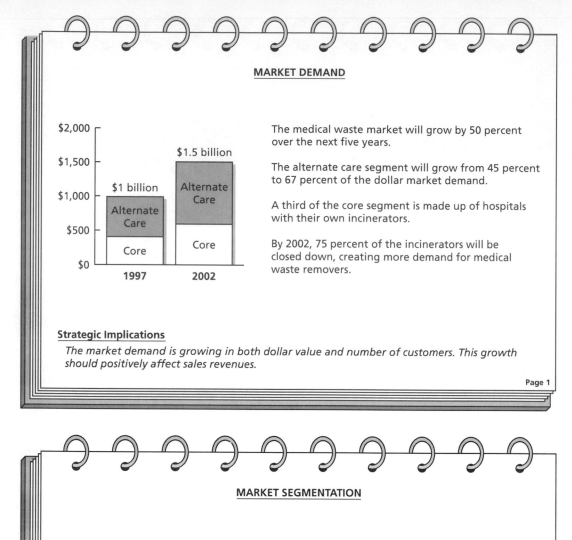

MARKET DEMAND

$2,000

$1,500

$1 billion

$1.5 billion

$1,000

Alternate Care

Alternate Care

$500

$0

Core

Core

1997   2002

The medical waste market will grow by 50 percent over the next five years.

The alternate care segment will grow from 45 percent to 67 percent of the dollar market demand.

A third of the core segment is made up of hospitals with their own incinerators.

By 2002, 75 percent of the incinerators will be closed down, creating more demand for medical waste removers.

Strategic Implications

The market demand is growing in both dollar value and number of customers. This growth should positively affect sales revenues.

MARKET SEGMENTATION

Strategic Profile	Core	Alternate Care	Segment Analysis
Primary Benefits	Low Cost	Service	
Price Sensitivity	High	Low	
Firmographics	Hospitals	Health Care Offices	The core segment is more
Management Expertise	Very Good	Poor	concentrated, buys in larger
Need for Training	Minimal	Expensive	amounts, and is more price
			sensitive than the alternative
Number of Customers	10,000	630,000	care segment.
Revenue per Customer	$35,000	$530	
Margin per Customer	$2,345	$250	
Percent Margin	6.7%	47.3%	
Segment Growth Rate	3%	8.5%	

Strategic Implications

The alternate care segment is less price sensitive and offers a better percent margin, but the core segment offers a higher dollar margin per customer.

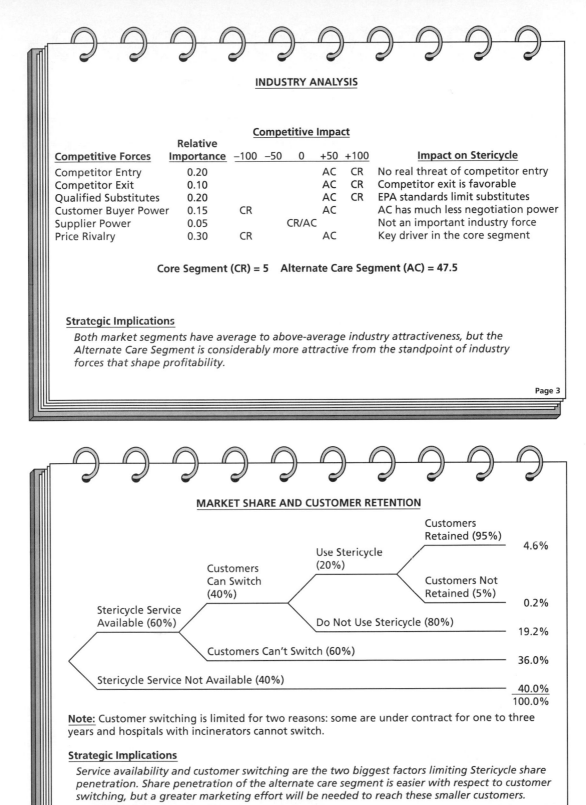

INDUSTRY ANALYSIS

Competitive Impact

Competitive Forces	Relative Importance	−100	−50	0	+50	+100	Impact on Stericycle
Competitor Entry	0.20				AC	CR	No real threat of competitor entry
Competitor Exit	0.10				AC	CR	Competitor exit is favorable
Qualified Substitutes	0.20				AC	CR	EPA standards limit substitutes
Customer Buyer Power	0.15		CR		AC		AC has much less negotiation power
Supplier Power	0.05			CR/AC			Not an important industry force
Price Rivalry	0.30		CR		AC		Key driver in the core segment

Core Segment (CR) = 5   Alternate Care Segment (AC) = 47.5

Strategic Implications

Both market segments have average to above-average industry attractiveness, but the Alternate Care Segment is considerably more attractive from the standpoint of industry forces that shape profitability.

Page 3

MARKET SHARE AND CUSTOMER RETENTION

Stericycle Service Available (60%)
- Customers Can Switch (40%)
  - Use Stericycle (20%)
    - Customers Retained (95%) — 4.6%
    - Customers Not Retained (5%) — 0.2%
  - Do Not Use Stericycle (80%) — 19.2%
- Customers Can't Switch (60%) — 36.0%

Stericycle Service Not Available (40%) — 40.0%

100.0%

Note: Customer switching is limited for two reasons: some are under contract for one to three years and hospitals with incinerators cannot switch.

Strategic Implications

Service availability and customer switching are the two biggest factors limiting Stericycle share penetration. Share penetration of the alternate care segment is easier with respect to customer switching, but a greater marketing effort will be needed to reach these smaller customers.

Page 4

COMPETITION and MARKET RESTRUCTURING

Competitors	No. of Competitor Locations			Market Share ($)		
	1997	2000	2003	1997	2000	2003
Incinerators						
Large Hospital	460	380	300	20%	17%	13%
Medium Hospital	690	400	150	10%	7%	3%
Small Hospital	1,100	600	100	3%	3%	1%
Browning-Ferris Industries	30	32	35	20%	?	?
Stericycle Inc.	7	8	10	7%	?	?
Regional Competitors	50	30	15	40%	?	?
Total Number of Competitors	2,337	1,570	785	100%	100%	100%

Strategic Implications

The market is going under a complete restructuring that will lessen the number of incinerator competitors (substitutes) and drastically reduce the number of regional competitors. This level of consolidation should favor Stericycle's ability to build market share during this period.

CHANNEL SYSTEMS and MARKETING BUDGET

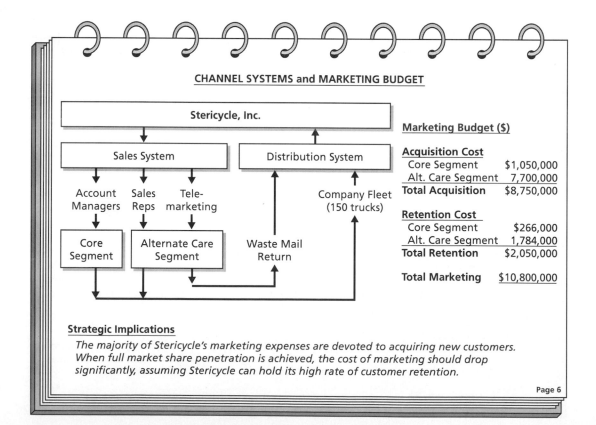

Marketing Budget ($)

Acquisition Cost
Core Segment	$1,050,000
Alt. Care Segment	7,700,000
Total Acquisition	$8,750,000

Retention Cost
Core Segment	$266,000
Alt. Care Segment	1,784,000
Total Retention	$2,050,000

Total Marketing $10,800,000

Strategic Implications

The majority of Stericycle's marketing expenses are devoted to acquiring new customers. When full market share penetration is achieved, the cost of marketing should drop significantly, assuming Stericycle can hold its high rate of customer retention.

MARKET and PROFIT PERFORMANCE

Market Performance Metrics	Core	Alt. Care	Company	Performance Drivers
Stericycle Market Share	6.7%	6.8%	6.8%	
Acquisition Cost per Customer	$3,500	$375	$421	
Retention Cost per Customer	$700	$80	$86	
Customer Retention	95%	95%	95%	The lifetime value of
Lifetime Value (15%)	$6,790	$678	$818	← core customers is much
Revenue per Customer	$35,000	$530	$1,075	greater.

Profit Performance Metrics	Core	Alt. Care	Company	
Sales Revenue (millions)	$23.1	$23.1	$46.2	
Percent Margin	6.7%	47.3%	26.4%	The dollar margin per
Margin per Customer	$2,345	$230	$282	← customer in the core
Total Contribution (millions)	$1.6	$10.6	$12.2	segment is much greater.
Marketing Expenses (millions)	$1.0	$9.8	$10.8	
Net Marketing Cont. (millions)	$.6	$.8	$1.4	← Each segment produces a marketing profit.

Strategic Implications

Although the Alternate Care customer offers a higher percent margin, the actual dollar margin per customer is approximately one-tenth that of a core customer. Both have a high rate of retention, but the lower dollar margin per alternate care customer results in lower lifetime value (net present value).

SWOT ANALYSIS

STRENGTHS	WEAKNESSES
Recognized Leader in Service Technology Advantage Room to Grow (Excess Capacity) Established Marketing Systems	High Cost of Marketing Growth Limited to Capacity Low Margins in Core Segment Poor Productivity in Alt. Care
OPPORTUNITIES	THREATS
Growing Market Demand Market Restructuring Attractive Industry Dynamics Competitor Exit	Increased Government Regulation Price Competition in Alt. Care Increased Market Focus of Major Competitors

KEY ISSUES

New Customer Growth will require more marketing budget until full-share penetration.

Market Focus is important because we have limited capacity.

Supply and Pricing: reduced competition and short supply should favor higher prices.

Strategic Implications

The key issues can be directly linked to current positioning and performance. To the degree these issues are addressed in the marketing plan, Stericycle has the potential to achieve above average levels of profitable growth.

STRATEGIC MARKET ASSESSMENT

Market Attractiveness	Imp.	1	2	3	4	5	Competitive Advantage	Imp.	1	2	3	4	5
Market Size (volume)	30				AC	CR	Market Share	40	AC/CR				
Market Growth	10	CR		AC			Service Advantage	30		CR			AC
Sustainable Margins	30	CR			AC		Technology Advantage	20			CR/AC		
Industry Analysis	20			CR	AC		Reputation for Quality	5				CR	AC
Market Reach	10	AC		CR			Marketing System	5					CR/AC

Market Attractiveness	Competitive Advantage
Core Segment (CR) = 330 (66%)	Core Segment (CR) = 240 (48%)
Alt. Care Segment (AC) = 410 (82%)	Alt. Care Segment (AC) = 340 (68%)

Strategic Implications

Both market segments have above-average market attractiveness and competitive advantage, but the alternate care segment is higher in both and is considerably stronger with respect to competitive advantage.

PORTFOLIO ANALYSIS and STRATEGIC MARKET PLANS

Strategic Market Plan

Core: Reduced Focus

Reduce focus to profitable segment customers while modestly reducing segment market share from 6.8 percent to 5 percent.

Alternative Care: Market Penetration

Allocate resources to gain market share in alternate care segment from 6.7 percent to 20 percent over five years.

Strategic Implications

The portfolio analysis yields two strategic market plans. In the core segment, Stericycle should focus on high margin customers and give up share to do so. In the alternate care segment, Stericycle should invest to achieve market share penetration.

CORE SEGMENT STRATEGY: REDUCED FOCUS

Value Proposition   *For Hospitals That Value Superior Service and Unquestionable Safety*

Positioning Strategy   Above-average customer service, training, and technical support priced 10 to 20 percent higher than the major competitor in the core segment. To enhance this service, Stericycle will provide an Excel-based software program for customers to track their waste management activities.

Channel System   Account managers who are highly trained in business and waste management technology will call on hospital customers once a month. They will provide training when needed as well as annual financial analysis and client review.

Share Objective   Decrease the number of price-sensitive customers with price increases. This move is expected to erode market share from 6.8 percent to 5 percent. We will not actively seek new customers, but we will watch for opportunities to take on new core customers attracted to our value proposition.

ALTERNATE CARE SEGMENT STRATEGY: SHARE PENETRATION

Value Proposition   *Helping Health Care Professionals Safely Manage Medical Waste*

Positioning Strategy   Above-average customer service, training, and technical support priced 10 to 20 percent higher than competitors in the alternate care segment. To further facilitate a position of customer service, Stericycle will offer a 24-hour hot-line for waste management problems.

Market System   Company reps will call on new accounts while telemarketing will be used to maintain monthly contact to manage customer service, ensure customer satisfaction, and identify opportunities to increase revenue per customer. A technical support team will be created to deliver training and to perform on-site waste management studies.

Share Objective   Grow customer share from 6.7 percent to 20 percent with value-added medical waste recycling services and training.

RESOURCE ALLOCATION and MARKETING BUDGET

Core Segment	1997	1998	1999	2000	2001	2002
Market Share	6.8%	6.0%	5.0%	5.0%	5.0%	5.0%
Number of Customers	680	600	500	500	500	500
Retention Cost (millions)	$0.3	$0.5	$0.5	$0.4	$0.4	$0.4
Acquisition Cost (millions)	$1.0	$0.0	$0.0	$0.1	$0.1	$0.1
Marketing Budget (millions)	$1.3	$0.5	$0.5	$0.5	$0.5	$0.5
Alternate Care Segment						
Market Share	6.72%	10.0%	13.0%	16.0%	18.0%	20.0%
Number of Customers	42,320	63,000	81,900	100,000	113,400	126,000
Retention Cost (millions)	$1.76	$3.18	$4.73	$6.15	$7.57	$8.51
Acquisition Cost (millions)	$7.74	$8.78	$8.49	$8.85	$6.79	$7.03
Marketing Budget (millions)	$ 9.5	$12.0	$13.2	$15.0	$14.4	$15.5
Overall Marketing Budget (millions)	**$10.8**	**$12.5**	**$13.7**	**$15.5**	**$14.9**	**$16.0**

Strategic Implications

To accomplish the market share goals prescribed by each segment strategic market plan and to cover the costs of customer acquisition and retention, the current marketing budget of $10.8 million will have to increase to $16 million in five years.

PERFORMANCE PLAN and TIMELINE

Core Segment	1997	1998	1999	2000	2001	2002
Number of Customers	680	600	500	500	500	500
Revenue per Customer	$35,000	$38,000	$40,000	$42,000	$44,000	$46,000
Sales Revenue (millions)	$ 23.8	$ 22.8	$ 20.0	$ 21.0	$ 22.0	$ 23.0
Percent Margin	6.7%	14.0%	18.0%	22.0%	24.0%	25.0%
Total Contribution (millions)	$ 1.6	$ 3.2	$ 3.6	$ 4.6	$ 5.3	$ 5.8
Marketing Budget (millions)	$ 1.3	$ 0.5	$ 0.5	$ 0.5	$ 0.5	$ 0.5
Net Marketing Contribution (millions)	$ 0.3	$ 2.7	$ 3.1	$ 4.1	$ 4.8	$ 5.3
Alternate Care Segment						
Number of Customers	42,320	63,000	81,900	100,800	113,400	126,000
Revenue per Customer	$ 530	$ 570	$ 600	$ 650	$ 700	$ 750
Sales Revenue (millions)	$22.4	$35.9	$49.1	$65.5	$79.4	$94.5
Percent Margin	47.3%	47.3%	47.3%	47.3%	47.3%	47.3%
Total Contribution (millions)	$10.6	$17.0	$23.2	$31.0	$37.5	$44.7
Marketing Budget (millions)	$ 9.5	$12.0	$13.2	$15.0	$14.4	$15.5
Net Marketing Contribution (millions)	**$ 1.1**	**$ 5.0**	**$10.0**	**$16.0**	**$23.1**	**$29.2**

Strategic Implications

The proposed strategic and tactical market plans and their respective share goals are intended to increase overall sales to $117.5 and the net marketing contribution from $1.4 million in 1997 to $34.5 million in five years.

chapter 15

Strategy Implementation and Performance Metrics

A successful marketing plan will provide a business with the roadmap it needs to pursue a specific strategic direction and set of performance objectives. However, this is just a plan; it does not guarantee that the desired performance objectives will be reached any more than having a roadmap guarantees the traveler will arrive at the desired destination. The marketing plan must now be successfully implemented.

A manufacturer of electric utility equipment engaged in an extensive market segmentation project in an effort to revitalize its sales and profitability. The effort revealed several market segments, all of which were reachable and judged to be attractive. A multi-segment strategy was developed with separate segment strategies for each market segment. However, the sales force was divided into three sales regions and had not been part of the segmentation study and strategy development. The marketing manager knew that without their support and commitment this marketing strategy would fail.

To successfully implement this strategy, the marketing manager had to sell the strategy to three regional sales vice presidents. Two of the VPs agreed to implement the strategy, but one elected not to become involved. The results, shown in Figure 15.1, illustrate the importance of effective strategy implementation. In the two sales regions in which the marketing strategy was implemented, sales increased by 18 percent and 12 percent, in a market in which total demand declined by 15 percent. By contrast, there was only a 3 percent sales gain in the sales region that did not implement the marketing strategy.

To achieve marketing success and reach target performance objectives, a business needs a good marketing plan and a well-executed implementation of the plan. A good marketing plan without a dedicated implementation effort will fail. This chapter will cover the forces that affect implementation of a strategy and a marketing plan, the importance of performance metrics, and the mechanics of a marketing plan variance analysis.

FORCES THAT SHAPE SUCCESSFUL STRATEGY IMPLEMENTATION

Even if a flawless marketing plan could be developed, there would still be no guarantee that the marketing strategy and marketing plan would succeed in meeting the desired performance metrics. The marketing plan must still be successfully implemented. It is very difficult to implement a poor marketing plan; but it is still possible to fail to implement a good marketing plan. Shown in Figure 15.2 are three major forces that con-

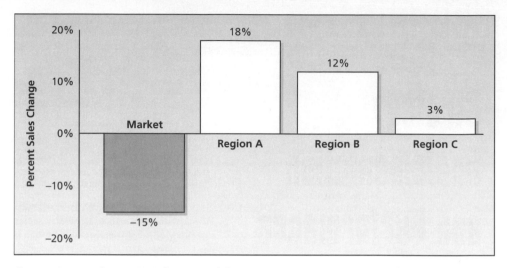

Figure 15.1 ◆ Sales Impact of a Successful Strategy Implementation

tribute to success or failure in implementing a marketing plan. As shown, each of these major forces has specific factors that contribute to the degree to which that force either positively or negatively affects the implementation of the marketing plan. Collectively, these factors will shape the behavior and organizational structure in a way that facilitates successful implementation.[1]

Owning the Marketing Plan

Perhaps the most common reason a marketing plan fails is a lack of *ownership*. If people do not have an ownership stake and responsibility in the marketing plan, it will be business as usual for all but a frustrated few. As shown in Figure 15.2, the ownership of a market plan can be enhanced with *detailed action plans, a champion and ownership team, compensation based on performance metrics,* and *top management involvement.*

Figure 15.2 ◆ Successful Implementation of a Marketing Plan

Detailed Action Plans   The development and use of detailed action plans may be the single most effective market management practice in determining the success of a marketing plan. A detailed action plan involves each aspect of the marketing strategy, but in greater detail with respect to specific actions that have to occur for the marketing plan to be implemented. Figure 15.3 outlines how a particular tactical marketing strategy within a marketing plan will be implemented. In this case, the strategy is broken down into five important action items, each of which must occur for this aspect of the marketing plan to succeed. As shown, for each of the five action items specified, an individual is assigned a specific responsibility, a measure or goal is delineated, and a time frame within which the action item should be completed is agreed upon.

Any number of action items could be added to this action plan, but the important point is that significant elements of this strategy have specific ownership. In this way individuals have ownership and are accountable for implementing a portion of the marketing plan. Assigning responsibility enables a business to break the "business as usual" routine and fosters successful implementation of the marketing plan.

Champion and Ownership Team   Whereas laying out individual responsibilities in the detailed action plan is a way to get a wide range of people involved in implementation, every successful marketing strategy has a *champion:* a person who is devoted to the successful implementation of the marketing strategy and marketing plan. And, although there is nothing wrong with having a single owner or champion, the creation of an *ownership team* can leverage the unique talents of multiple people and exert more organizational leverage than a single individual.[2] With a champion and an ownership team in place, the implementation process can stay on track even when some members of the team are gone for extended periods of time because of business trips, training programs, sickness, or vacations.

Compensation   Most people respond to financial rewards. Tying the compensation of those principally responsible for implementation of the marketing plan to performance metrics increases the incentive to successfully implement the marketing plan. Compensation can be tied to both external market metrics and internal financial metrics, which will be discussed later in this chapter.

Marketing Strategy To create adequate end user product availability, 80 manufacturers' reps and five missionary salespeople will be used to sell and distribute our product to 5,000 industrial supply houses.

No.	Action Item	Responsibility	Measure	Time Frame*
1.	Identify target supply houses and establish contracts.	P. Elliot	5,000 Dealers	12 months
2.	Contact manufacturer reps.	T. Smith	80 Reps	6 months
3.	Hire missionary sales force.	P. Wilson	5 People	3 months
4.	Develop rep training program.	S. Bradley	Program Pilot	6 months
5.	Develop dealer training program.	R. Otto	Program Pilot	6 months

* From time of implementation.

Figure 15.3 ◆ Detailed Action Plan for a Channel Strategy

Market metrics are most important in the early stages of marketing plan implementation. Market metrics such as end-customer awareness and interest, product availability, and trial are market behaviors that must occur before financial metrics such as sales revenue, total contribution, net marketing contribution, and net profit can occur. The overall goal of compensation tied to market metrics is to create motivation and responsibility.

Management Involvement   Senior managers must stay committed to their involvement with the marketing plan and to their review of its progress. When top managers lessen the time available to review the marketing plan and performance, they send an implicit signal of lack of interest and support. This signal weakens the motivation of the ownership team and the chance for successful implementation.

Supporting the Marketing Plan

Though there are potentially many factors that could affect the degree to which a business is committed to a marketing plan, *time to succeed, resource allocation, communication,* and *skills to succeed* are critical.[3]

Time to Succeed   In many instances, commitment to a marketing plan weakens when financial performance is not on track. Without meaningful market metrics, a business may pull support for a marketing plan without knowing why it is not working. It may be that the marketing strategy and plan are very good, but implementation has been poor. It may also be that the market metrics are on target but that it simply may take more time for financial metrics to respond to desired or target levels.

Time to succeed will, in part, depend on the marketing strategy and the nature of the market opportunity. A share penetration strategy in an existing market should take less time to succeed than a strategy to enter a new market that is undeveloped. In either case, the time to succeed, along with market metrics that signal progress, are important aspects of commitment to the marketing plan and successful implementation.

Resource Allocation   If the process and structure of marketing planning are followed as described in chapter 14, the marketing plan should be allocated sufficient resources with respect to personnel and funding. If less than the required resources are reserved for the marketing plan, the chances for success are greatly reduced. Of course, if the resources needed are not systematically determined in the marketing planning process, it is even more likely that the marketing plan will be underresourced. (It is rare that marketing plans are overresourced.) Thus, an important step in successful implementation is to ensure that the resources needed are fully committed to support implementation of the marketing plan.

Communication   It is difficult to get support either *internally,* within the company, or *externally,* from the market, if the marketing plan and its strategic intent are not aggressively communicated. Although senior management and the market management team are likely to fully understand the logic and tactics of the marketing plan, others—in sales, customer support, manufacturing, and finance—may not understand the strategic objectives and marketing strategy being implemented. As a result, these employees, who may play key roles in successful implementation, will continue in a business-as-usual mode of operation. To facilitate communication and understanding, some businesses have created videos for employees describing strategic market objectives and the marketing strategy.

Internal communication of a marketing plan, including the specific role individuals within the business play with respect to the market plan, is critical. To the degree possible, these job functions should be integrated into detailed action plans, as described earlier. In this way, key individuals understand their roles and responsibilities in the successful implementation of the market plan.

External communication of the marketing plan is also critical. Each of the following groups must be made aware of different aspects of the marketing plan:

- **Target Customers:** Need to be made aware of the benefits of the product, the value proposition, and where the product can be acquired.
- **Channel Intermediaries:** Need to understand target customers, their profit potential, and inventory, sales, and service requirements.
- **The Trade Press:** Needs to be informed as to product benefits and availability of the product.
- **Market Influencers:** Must be informed. These could include consultants, financial analysts, or others who influence customers and channel intermediaries.
- **The General and Business Press:** Must receive news releases that can further communicate the market plan to potential customers, distributors, and investors.

Of course, the extent to which external market communications are engaged depends on the nature of the marketing strategy and product. A new product made to more effectively treat metal-working fluids in small machine shops would not interest most consumers, the general press, or even the business press. However, trade press publishers, consultants, the EPA (Environmental Protection Agency), and others may be interested in promoting awareness of a new product that greatly reduces the problems of disposal of hazardous waste, lowers the cost of disposal, and improves working conditions.

Required Skills   Do those implementing the marketing plan have the required skills to effectively implement the marketing plan?[4] For example, a bank wanting to improve customer satisfaction and retention may have to do some training to communicate new policies and customer-oriented employee attitudes. Two of the five action items detailed in Figure 15.3 involved training. For that marketing strategy to succeed, it was essential that manufacturers' reps and distributors were trained with respect to product knowledge, service requirements, how to sell the product, and how to explain the value derived from this product. Without a training effort, this strategy would likely not succeed.

In many instances, even members of the management team may need additional training to successfully implement the marketing plan. A business implementing a program to get more new product sales may need to provide some management training on the new product. Without the necessary skills, the management team might produce a meaningful objective but have no way of successfully accomplishing it.

Adapting the Marketing Plan

The marketing planning process does not stop when marketing plan implementation begins; it continues through strategy implementation. As do all systems, a marketing plan needs to be adapted to survive changing or unanticipated conditions. To survive, as well as to succeed, the marketing plan needs to be *adaptive*. Four factors that contribute to the adaptive nature of a marketing plan are *continuous improvement, feedback measurements, persistence,* and *adaptive roll-out* of the marketing plan.

Continuous Improvement   A marketing plan that is not adapted to unexpected or changing market conditions will fail. Because market conditions are complex and changing, a business must be flexible in modifying its marketing plan to adapt to the changing market conditions. In many instances, these may be small changes, made in order to more finely tune the business's marketing strategy and value proposition. However, in some cases, a major shift in marketing strategy may be required.

The term *adaptive persistence* has been attributed to the success of many Japanese marketing strategies. One of Japanese management's greatest assets is their ability to adapt when a marketing plan is not working and to stick with it—to *persist*. The whole concept of continuous improvement is implicit in Japanese marketing plan implementation. While the marketing plan sets the direction and provides the initial roadmap, once it is in place, the flexibility to adapt is an important aspect of continuous improvement.

Feedback Measurements   An essential element of any adaptive system, whether mechanical, electrical, or human, is feedback. Mechanical, electrical, and human systems have built-in sensors and feedback systems. Management systems also require measurements to provide a mechanism for feedback. Measurements of process-oriented market metrics play the role of a sensor in a marketing plan feedback system. These measurements signal the status of the marketing plan with respect to progress toward end-result metrics such as sales, market share, total contribution, and net profit.

Key process metrics that provide leading signals as to the success of the marketing plan and implementation include:

- Customer awareness, interest, intentions to buy, trial, and repeat purchase.
- Intermediary market coverage, interest, support, and motivation.
- Business responsiveness to customer inquiries and problems.

Each of these market metrics has to reach an effective level of performance before financial metrics can begin to perform. The importance of market metrics is twofold. First, they provide an early signal as to the progress of the marketing plan. If market metrics are behind target performance levels specified in the marketing plan, then financial metrics and profit performance will be slower to materialize than projected. Second, the market metrics provide a signal as to which aspect of the marketing plan is not working. Is it the channel system, the communications strategy, or the product-price positioning strategy that is the cause of poor market performance? Each of these could trigger different strategies designed to better adapt the marketing plan to market conditions.

Persistence   One of the great traits of Japanese managers is their inherent ability to adapt and persist throughout the implementation of the marketing plan. Rarely have Japanese marketing strategies worked initially. However, Japanese marketing managers remain committed to the strategic market objective and persist by adapting their market plans. Quite often, their marketing strategies need to be modified, but it is their determination to make them work that underlies the secret of their market success.

On the other hand, American managers are often quick to drop a marketing strategy and plan when it meets the first bit of resistance. Perhaps expectations of performance have been overstated—or time to succeed misspecified. Whichever the case, marketing strategies developed in a corporate office often lack the realism of the marketplace and may need to be adapted during implementation. Without a high degree of management persistence, there is little chance of successful implementation, particularly when aspects of the marketing plan need to be modified.

Adaptive Roll-Out There are many benefits to a regional roll-out as opposed to a nationwide launch, and it signals a business's marketing strategy to competitors as effectively. First, fewer resources are required in a small-scale regional launch of a marketing plan than in a nationwide launch. Second, problems with distributors, marketing communications, and product positioning can more readily be addressed and corrected on a small scale. Third, if the marketing plan is more effective than planned, additions can be made to production capacity without the potential of stockout and the loss of opportunities to capture customers when they want to buy. Fourth, even for a marketing plan that is tracking as planned on a regional basis, additional marketing insights will result that can be opportunistically integrated into the marketing plan as full marketing plan implementation is pursued. And fifth, the financial metrics generated from a successful roll-out signal long-run profit potential and can be used to help fund the full introduction. Because of these benefits, many foreign competitors have used regional roll-outs upon entering the American market.

Many American businesses, however, do not want to take the time to engage in a corrective roll-out of a marketing plan. However, it is rare that a marketing plan will succeed as conceived on paper. At risk are customers and distributors who might lose interest in the business's value proposition when it is ineffectively presented. In addition, the cost of a full market introduction when things go wrong is enormous, even when customers and distributors are retained through the repositioning period.

Assessing Marketing Plan Implementation

No single factor presented in Figure 15.2 will make or break the successful implementation of a marketing plan. However, when the sum of these factors is adequately addressed, the chances for successful marketing plan implementation are greatly improved. Shown in Figure 15.4 is a summary of these factors and a profile of a business that worked to improve its marketing plan implementation. Although this business did not perform well on every factor, it performed much better than it had in past efforts. This level of implementation effort, along with a good marketing strategy and marketing plan, will enable the business to achieve a market success well beyond planned performance, and in a much shorter time than expected.

At the heart of successful implementation of a marketing plan is a business's market orientation. The greater the degree to which the business has built a market-based organization, the more likely is successful marketing plan implementation.[5] A market-based business with a strong customer focus and competitor orientation that works well across functions has a greater level of market sensitivity and urgency from which to both develop and implement a marketing plan.

Owning the Plan
- Detailed Action Plan   None ▣ _ _ _ _ ❑ Extensive
- Ownership   None _ ▣ _ _ _ ❑ Champion
- Compensation   None _ ▣ ❑ _ _ Performance-based
- Management Involvement   None _ _ _ ▣ _ ❑ _ High

Supporting the Plan
- Time to Succeed   Inadequate _ ▣ _ ❑ _ _ _ Sufficient
- Resource Allocation   Insufficient _ ▣ _ ❑ _ _ _ Sufficient
- Communication Effort   None _ ▣ _ _ ❑ _ _ Thorough
- Required Skills   Poor _ _ ▣ _ ❑ _ _ Exceptional

Adapting the Plan
- Continuous Improvement   None _ ▣ _ _ _ ❑ _ Ongoing
- Feedback Metrics   None ▣ _ _ ❑ _ _ _ Extensive
- Persistence   None _ _ ▣ _ ❑ _ _ Relentless
- Roll-out   Full Launch _ ▣ _ ❑ _ _ _ Roll-out

▣ Past Efforts
❑ Current Efforts

Figure 15.4 ◆ **An Assessment of Marketing Plan Implementation**

MARKET METRICS AND FINANCIAL PERFORMANCE

No matter how efficient a business's production operations, how expert its R&D, or how wise its financial management, if the customer doesn't buy or rebuy a business's products or services, the marketing plan will fail. As shown in Figure 15.5, market-based marketing strategies are designed to deliver customer satisfaction and retention. The degree to which a marketing strategy is successful will be first detected by market metrics that track customer satisfaction, retention, and perceptions of value; only subsequently will success or failure be observed in financial performance in the form of gains in revenue, total contribution, net profit, and cash flow. And, as shown in Figure 15.5, ultimately the results of a marketing strategy will affect shareholders in the form of earnings growth and expectations of improved future earnings.

The best the investment community can do is to report financial performance and expectations based on what the business says future performance will be. However, a business managed by a market-based management system is better able to detect and report future success by tracking market metrics, many of which *lead* changes in financial performance.

For example, an increase in the percentage of dissatisfied customers may not result in an immediate decrease in sales or net profits. First, dissatisfied customers often give a business a chance to correct the source of their dissatisfaction. Remedying problems quickly and meaningfully can often translate into improved customer loyalty. Second, it often takes time for customers to make a change in product or supplier. Thus, there is often a time lag between customer dissatisfaction (a market metric) and sales decline (a financial metric).

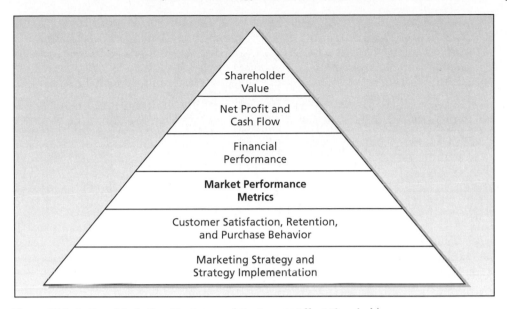

Figure 15.5 ◆ How Marketing Strategy and Customers Affect Shareholders

To illustrate the importance of market metrics in market-based management and its profit impact, consider the example in Figure 15.6. In period I, the business had no customer dissatisfaction and net profits of $5 million on sales of $50 million. The total variable cost was $25 million and fixed expenses were $20 million. In period II, 10 percent of the business's customers became dissatisfied. In this example, however, the business did not have a market-based metric that tracked customer dissatisfaction. Thus, there would be no reason for concern because sales and profits were at a normal and expected level.

In period III, dissatisfied customers began to leave the business, and sales slowly declined. During this period, all fixed expenses remained the same, but there was less profit margin produced, and, hence, both sales and profits were down. The business took action in period IV by cutting marketing expenses in proportion to lost net income with the goal of returning net profits to their previous level. But sales were still down, and, in period V, the business created a task force to investigate the problem. The task force found that the customers that had been lost had left because of a particular source of dissatisfaction.

In period VI, the business restored the marketing budget and added budget to correct the problem and to replace lost customers. There were no immediate sales gains, and net profit decreased because of the increased expenses. However, finally, in period VII the business was back to where it had been in period I; no customer dissatisfaction, sales of $50 million, and net profits of $5 million.

That sequence of events could easily have occurred over three to five years. But a market-based business would have detected the problem in period II and would have immediately made corrections to restore customer satisfaction and retain its customer base. If the problem had been detected and corrected in period II, net profits over the seven periods would have totaled $35 million. The total in Figure 15.6 is $25 million. In other words, there was $10 million less in profit to reinvest in the business and contribute to earnings. In this way, stockholder value was diminished.

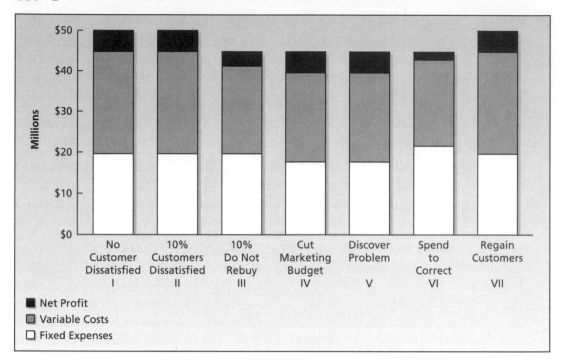

Figure 15.6 ◆ Customer Behavior, Market Metrics, and Profit Performance

The purpose of this example is twofold: First, it points out the importance of market metrics that track customer behavior (remember, customers are the only source of positive cash flow). Second, it demonstrates that many market metrics are leading indicators of financial performance and an important market-based management tool that should contribute to better financial performance.

PROCESS VS. END-RESULT MARKET METRICS

The primary purpose of using market metrics is to maintain ongoing measures of market performance. And, because many market metrics precede financial performance, using them is critical to strategy implementation and financial performance. However, not all market metrics are leading indicators of business performance. There are *process market metrics* and *end-result market metrics*.[6] Both are important, but process market metrics are particularly important because they are also leading indicators of financial performance.[7] End-result market metrics correspond more closely to internal financial performance metrics.

Process Market Metrics

Customer awareness, interest, product trial, customer satisfaction and dissatisfaction, along with perceptions of relative product quality, service quality, and customer value, all serve as process market metrics and leading indicators of end-result performance.

Changes in each, positive or negative, precede actual changes in customer behavior. As a result, these in-process measures of customer thinking and attitude are important leading indicators of financial performance.

For example, perhaps customers are satisfied, but their perceptions of the value they derive from your product, relative to competing alternatives, is steadily diminishing. You may well have done nothing wrong to dissatisfy customers; the competition may have simply improved in delivering customer value based on a combination of total benefits and total cost. However, the net effect is that customer perceptions of the value created by your product have diminished. This change, in turn, opens the door to competitors' products that your customers may be inclined to try or purchase.

The whole purpose of process market metrics is to track customer perceptions and attitudes that precede changes in customer behavior and financial performance. For example, customer satisfaction is a process metric of considerable importance with many alternative measures.[8] As shown in Figure 15.7, measures of customer satisfaction can be broken down into different classifications. Very satisfied customers are loyal and buy in considerable amounts.[9] Merely satisfied customer are less loyal and more easily switch to competitors' products. Dissatisfied customers, of course, are likely to leave, although those who complain can be retained but remain vulnerable until their source of dissatisfaction is adequately addressed. However, very few (less than 10 percent) dissatisfied customers complain,[10] and of those who do not complain, the majority stop buying from the business. And, because most dissatisfied customers do not complain, a business may not know it has a problem. Eventually, these customers leave, and to maintain sales and profits, the business has to attract new customers. Businesses that use measures of customer satisfaction effectively have a process metric that enables them to take corrective action in order to avoid adverse effects on financial performance.

Thus, a market-based business with several process market metrics will detect early adverse changes in customer attitudes and perceptions. With an early warning signal, the market-based business can take corrective action before customers alter their purchase behavior. Without process market metrics, this problem may go undetected and unresolved until after declines in financial performance, as was illustrated in Figure 15.6.

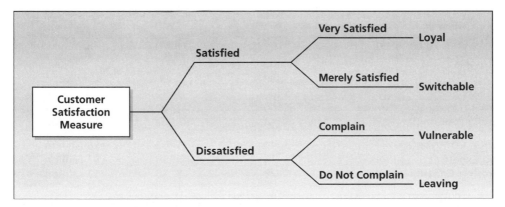

Figure 15.7 ◆ Customer Dissatisfaction and Customer Exit

End-Result Market Metrics

End-result market metrics include market share, customer retention, and revenue per customer. Each of these metrics occurs simultaneously with financial performance metrics. However, each provides a different set of performance diagnostic insights. For example, let's assume sales revenues are increasing and ahead of forecast, and financial performance is also better than expected. Most businesses would feel pretty good about their performance. However, if end-result performance metrics show that the business is losing market share in a growing market, and poor customer retention is masked by new customer growth, there should be concern. Without end-result market metrics, the business has only an internal measure of performance.

Even for a business that is not losing market share, poor customer retention has a powerful impact on financial performance, as illustrated in Figure 15.8. In this example, a business with a 20 percent market share and a 90 percent level of customer retention produces 24 percent more net marketing contribution than the same business with an 80 percent customer retention.

Because existing customers generally spend more than new customers and the cost of serving an existing customer is less than that of acquiring and serving a new customer, the margin per customer is generally different. In this example, an existing customer produces $300 of margin per year, whereas a new customer results in a net loss of $100 per year. Retaining a larger percentage of existing customers improves total contribution and net marketing contribution even when an additional $1 million is added to marketing expenses for a customer retention program. Overall, the assets increase a little because

Business Performance	80% Retention	90% Retention	Performance Gain
Customer Demand	1,000,000	1,000,000	None
Market Share	20%	20%	None
Customer Volume	200,000	200,000	None
Revenue per Customer	$460	$480	+$ 20
Total Revenue (millions)	**$ 92**	**$ 96**	+$4 Million
Retained Customers	160,000	180,000	+20,000
Revenue per Customer	$500	$500	None
Cost per Customer	$200	$200	None
Margin per Customer	$300	$300	None
Total Contribution (millions)	**$ 48**	**$ 54**	+$6 Million
New Customers	40,000	20,000	–20,000
Revenue per Customer	$300	$300	None
Cost per Customer	$400	$400	None
Margin per Customer	–$100	–$100	None
Total Contribution (millions)	**–$ 4**	**–$ 2**	+$2 Million
Overall Total Contribution	$ 44	$ 52	+$8 Million
Marketing Expenses	$ 15	$ 16	+$1 Million
Net Marketing Contribution	**$ 29**	**$ 36**	+$7 Million

Figure 15.8 ◆ Customer Retention Is a Key End-Result Market Metric

higher revenues result in proportionately higher accounts receivable. However, return on assets still increases from 18 percent to over 30 percent.

Thus, the combination of market share, customer retention, and revenue per customer provides a totally different picture of performance than financial performance metrics. Both financial and market metrics are important, and each provides a different insight into business performance and successful implementation of a marketing plan.

VARIANCE ANALYSIS OF A MARKETING PLAN

The primary objective of process market metrics is to provide a set of diagnostic leading indicators that signals a business when a marketing plan is not working. End-result metrics, such as sales, total contribution, net marketing contribution, and net profit are, of course, key measures of growth and financial performance. And, while the process market metrics provide an insight into marketing plan performance, a variance analysis of the end-result financial performance is equally valuable in developing corrective action when a marketing plan falls short of planned performance.[11]

The basic marketing profitability equation for marketing managers is net marketing contribution.

$$\text{Net Marketing Contribution} = \left[\text{Market Demand} \times \text{Market Share} \times \left(\text{Price per Unit} - \text{Variable Cost per Unit} \right) \right] - \text{Marketing Expenses}$$

Recognizing these marketing performance parameters, a marketing plan requires that the business estimate a specific level of:

- **Market Demand:** Size of the target market(s).
- **Market Share:** Level of market penetration based on the marketing strategy.
- **Price:** Market-based price designed to achieve a desired product position and customer value.
- **Variable Costs:** All product costs, transportation costs, and sales costs that vary with each unit sold.
- **Marketing Expense:** Marketing budget needed to achieve a certain level of market penetration.

From these estimates, an estimate of net marketing contribution is made. And, at some future point, an actual level of net marketing contribution is achieved, based on the actual performance of these five marketing parameters. When there is a major difference between the actual net marketing contribution and the level projected in the marketing plan, a business must reconcile the overall difference in an effort to determine the major causes of the performance gap.

For example, consider a business that has a marketing plan that is projected to produce $420,000 in net marketing contribution in year 1 of the marketing plan. However, the actual performance falls $86,800 short. What is the primary cause of this shortfall in performance? As shown in Figure 15.9, there are performance differences between planned and actual volume (V_p vs. V_a), margin (M_p vs. M_a), and marketing expenses (ME_p vs. ME_a). While the actual net marketing contribution was $86,800 less than that estimated in the marketing plan, the volume sold was higher than planned, and the unit margin was lower and marketing expenses higher. The portion of the difference between the marketing plan and actual performance attributable to marketing expenses is easily determined by the differences between planned and actual marketing expenses. However, variance in volume and the margin are related to other performance factors and create a more complex source of variance between planned and actual performance.

As illustrated in Figure 15.9, a variance in volume can be due to a difference between planned and actual market demand or a difference between planned and actual market share or both. In this example, a positive volume variance of $29,000 ($10 planned margin per unit multiplied by 2,900 more units sold) resulted from the net of a market demand variance that contributed $75,000 (30,000 greater actual demand than planned multiplied by the planned market share of 25 percent, which would result in 7,500 more units sold at the planned $10 margin per unit) and a market share variance of −$46,000 (the 2 percent shortfall in actual versus planned market share multiplied by the actual market demand of 230,000, which results in 4,600 fewer units sold at the planned margin of $10). Thus, the positive volume variance is actually the result of a higher-than-expected level of market demand and lower-than-planned market share penetration, and, despite this apparent positive outcome, a closer look at the market share strategy is warranted.

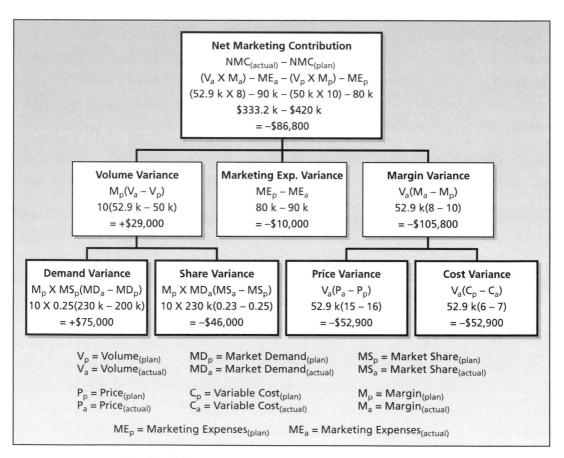

Net Marketing Contribution

$NMC_{(actual)} - NMC_{(plan)}$

$(V_a \times M_a) - ME_a - (V_p \times M_p) - ME_p$

$(52.9 \text{ k} \times 8) - 90 \text{ k} - (50 \text{ k} \times 10) - 80 \text{ k}$

$\$333.2 \text{ k} - \$420 \text{ k}$

$= -\$86,800$

Volume Variance

$M_p(V_a - V_p)$

$10(52.9 \text{ k} - 50 \text{ k})$

$= +\$29,000$

Marketing Exp. Variance

$ME_p - ME_a$

$80 \text{ k} - 90 \text{ k}$

$= -\$10,000$

Margin Variance

$V_a(M_a - M_p)$

$52.9 \text{ k}(8 - 10)$

$= -\$105,800$

Demand Variance

$M_p \times MS_p(MD_a - MD_p)$

$10 \times 0.25(230 \text{ k} - 200 \text{ k})$

$= +\$75,000$

Share Variance

$M_p \times MD_a(MS_a - MS_p)$

$10 \times 230 \text{ k}(0.23 - 0.25)$

$= -\$46,000$

Price Variance

$V_a(P_a - P_p)$

$52.9 \text{ k}(15 - 16)$

$= -\$52,900$

Cost Variance

$V_a(C_p - C_a)$

$52.9 \text{ k}(6 - 7)$

$= -\$52,900$

$V_p = \text{Volume}_{(plan)}$ $MD_p = \text{Market Demand}_{(plan)}$ $MS_p = \text{Market Share}_{(plan)}$
$V_a = \text{Volume}_{(actual)}$ $MD_a = \text{Market Demand}_{(actual)}$ $MS_a = \text{Market Share}_{(actual)}$

$P_p = \text{Price}_{(plan)}$ $C_p = \text{Variable Cost}_{(plan)}$ $M_p = \text{Margin}_{(plan)}$
$P_a = \text{Price}_{(actual)}$ $C_a = \text{Variable Cost}_{(actual)}$ $M_a = \text{Margin}_{(actual)}$

$ME_p = \text{Marketing Expenses}_{(plan)}$ $ME_a = \text{Marketing Expenses}_{(actual)}$

Figure 15.9 ◆ Reconciling Marketing Plan Performance Gaps

The margin variance in this example is similarly made up of more than just one factor. The overall margin variance of –$105,800 can be broken down into a price variance of –$52,900 (52,900 actual units sold multiplied by $1 per unit lower actual price than planned) and a cost variance of –$52,900 (actual units sold multiplied by $1 greater costs than planned).

The basic profitability equation for marketing management is net marketing contribution. However, by decomposing variances into their more basic elements, a marketing manager is better able to correct areas of poor performance and make adjustments to the market plan to more accurately forecast the following year's marketing plan profitability. In this example, some insights the marketing manager could gain would be:

- If market demand had not been greater than expected, the performance gap in net marketing contribution would have been even greater.
- If the business had gained its planned market share penetration, the net marketing contribution shortfall would have been less than one-half what it was.
- Higher unit cost, lower unit price, and higher-than-planned marketing expenses each contributed to a lower-than-planned net marketing contribution.

With this information, the marketing team can review both pricing and variable costs to determine if the marketing strategy should be changed. Of course, this variance analysis could be extended to fully reconcile differences between actual and planned net profit by including nonmarketing fixed business and overhead expenses.

A situation in which profits are below expectations is likely to draw the attention of senior management. But, what about a situation in which there is no difference between planned and actual net marketing contribution, volume sold, or marketing expenses, as illustrated in Figure 15.10? Why worry? The marketing plan is obviously on track. A finance-oriented business would note that the price per unit was actually $10 higher than planned and would likely investigate the cost increase. However, a finance-oriented business would rarely look beyond volume to understand variances in market demand and market share.

Area of Performance	Marketing Plan	Actual	Variance
Market Demand (units)	1,000,000	1,250,000	+250,000
Market Share	25%	20%	–5%
Volume	250,000	250,000	0
Price per Unit	$450	$460	+$ 10
Revenue (millions)	$112.5	$115	+$2.5
Cost per Unit	$200	$210	+$ 10
Contribution Margin	$250	$250	0
Total Contribution (millions)	$62.5	$62.5	0
Marketing Expenses (millions)	$15.0	$15.0	0
Net Marketing Contribution	**$47.5**	**$47.5**	0

Figure 15.10 ◆ **Profit Impact and Variance from Marketing Plan**

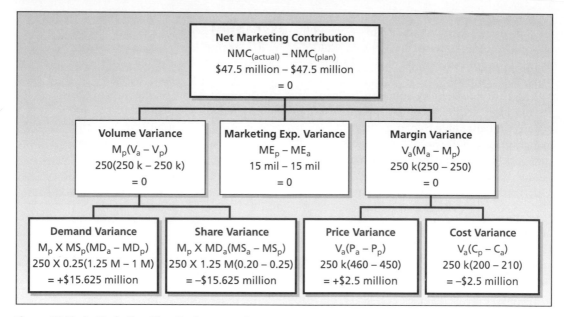

Figure 15.11 ◆ Marketing Plan Performance Gaps

A market-based business that tracks market demand and market share would discover that there *were* major deviations from the marketing plan and that the marketing plan was *not* working as intended. The variance analysis presented in Figure 15.11 illustrates the effects of the market demand and market share differences between the marketing plan and the actual results. This information alerts the business to the fact that there is indeed a performance gap with regard to market share.

A business that does not track market metrics such as market share and market demand will rarely discover that its marketing plan is not working as intended. With this analysis, we would expect a market-based business to recognize higher-than-expected market demand and to determine what needs to be done to achieve the target share of 25 percent. Although the variances in price and cost have a smaller impact on net marketing contribution, they are still important enough to reconcile as the business revises its marketing strategy and marketing plan for the subsequent year.

SUMMARY

Developing a sound marketing plan is only the first half of achieving market success. The marketing plan must be successfully implemented. Without ownership, support, and adaptation, the marketing plan will fail. Detailed action plans, a market plan champion or ownership team, performance-based compensation plans, and top management involvement contribute to ownership of the marketing plan and provide a better chance for successful implementation.

Successful marketing plan implementation also requires time to succeed, sufficient resources, communication, and skills. In addition, numerous unanticipated problems and

APPLICATION PROBLEM: STERICYCLE, INC.

The Stericycle Marketing Plan presented in chapter 14 includes a projected performance timeline for 1998. It is summarized below. The actual results for 1998 were much better than projected in the marketing plan performance timeline. Using the information below, perform a variance analysis (as outlined in Figure 15.9) to reconcile the differences between the planned and actual performance for 1998 and to better understand how different aspects of performance drove an above-expected level of net marketing contribution in 1998.

Area of Performance	1998 Plan	1998 Actual	Performance Gap
Market Demand (customers)	630,000	630,000	0
Market Share	10.1%	11.1%	+1%
Customer Volume	63,600	70,000	+6,400
Revenue per Customer	$923	$910	−$13
Sales Revenues (millions)	$ 58.7	$ 63.7	+$ 5.0
Cost per Customer	$605.4	$620	+$14.6
Margin per Customer	$317.6	$290	−$27.6
Total Contribution (millions)	$ 20.2	$ 20.3	+$ .1
Marketing Expenses (millions)	$ 12.5	$ 13.9	+$ 1.4
Net Marketing Contribution (millions)	$ 7.7	$ 6.4	−$ 1.3

Questions

   For Internet discussions go to www.prenhall.com/phbusiness.

1. Which areas performed better than planned, and how did each contribute to 1998 net marketing contribution?

2. Which areas performed below plan, and how did each affect the 1998 net marketing contribution?

3. What changes in the original performance timeline would you recommend in making a revised forecast for 1999 net marketing contribution?

obstacles will arise during implementation. These require that marketing plans be adaptive. Continuous efforts to improve the marketing plan, based on feedback measures, are an important part of successful implementation. In addition, businesses that are persistent in adapting their marketing plan have a greater chance for success. And a regional roll-out of the marketing plan provides a less expensive venue for adapting the marketing plan.

   Performance metrics play a key role in marketing plan implementation. There are market performance metrics and financial performance metrics. Market metrics are external measures of market performance such as awareness, customer satisfaction, and market share. Financial performance metrics are internal measures of performance such as unit margin, net profit, and return on investment. Market performance metrics, however, include both process metrics and end-result metrics. Customer awareness, perceived performance, and customer satisfaction are process performance metrics that occur ahead of end-result performance metrics such as sales, market share, net profit, and return on investment. Process market metrics play an important role in the early signaling of the success or failure of a marketing plan and its implementation effort.

Finally, it is useful to systematically determine which aspects of a marketing plan are contributing to any variance between the marketing plan and actual performance. Variance decomposition is an accounting technique that can be used to decompose differences between planned and actual performance into variances in market demand, market share, price, unit cost, and marketing expenses. In some situations, deviations from the marketing plan may not be apparent without this decomposition of the variances between the marketing plan and actual performance. The discovery of negative variances and recognition of less obvious positive variances can enable a business to focus on improving key weaknesses and thereby improve performance beyond the level projected in the marketing plan.

MARKET-BASED LOGIC AND STRATEGIC THINKING

1. Why is implementation as important as marketing plan development in achieving market success?
2. How do detailed action plans contribute to individual ownership of a marketing plan?
3. Why does a marketing plan need a champion or an ownership team?
4. How should a business tie compensation to successful implementation of a marketing plan?
5. Why is time to succeed an important element of commitment to a marketing plan?
6. What kind of signal is management sending when it does not have time to review a marketing plan and its performance?
7. What is meant by persistence in terms of commitment? What is meant by the term *adaptive persistence* as it is often used to describe the Japanese style of marketing plan implementation?
8. Why are continuous improvement and feedback measures important aspects of successful marketing plan implementation?
9. What are the advantages and disadvantages of a regional roll-out of a marketing plan?
10. What role do resources, organizational communications, and training play in the support and successful implementation of a marketing plan?
11. Why are performance metrics important?
12. What is the difference between a market performance metric and a financial performance metric?
13. Why are process metrics an important part of the implementation process? What is the relationship between process metrics and end-result metrics?
14. What is variance decomposition? How would it help in the successful implementation of a marketing plan?

NOTES

1. Nigel Piercy and Neil Morgan, "The Marketing Planning Process: Behavioral Problems Compared to Analytical Techniques in Explaining Marketing Plan Credibility," *Journal of Business Research* 29

(1994):167–78; and Nigel Piercy, *Marketing Organization: An Analysis of Information Processing, Power and Politics* (Chicago: George Allen & Unwin, 1985).

2. Robert Ruekert and Orville Walker Jr., "Marketing's Interaction with Other Functional Units: A Conceptual Framework and Empirical Evidence," *Journal of Marketing* (January 1987):1–19.

3. William Egelhoff, "Great Strategies or Great Strategy Implementation—Two Ways of Competing in Global Markets," *Sloan Management Review* (Winter 1993):37–50.

4. Thomas Bonoma, *The Marketing Edge: Making Strategies Work* (New York: Free Press, 1985).

5. George Day, "Building a Market-Driven Organization," *Market-Driven Strategy* (New York: Free Press, 1990), 356–76.

6. George Cressman, "Choosing the Right Metric," *Drive Marketing Excellence* (November 1994), Institute for International Research, New York.

7. Robert Kaplan and David Norton, "The Balanced Scorecard—Measures That Drive Performance," *Harvard Business Review* (January–February 1982):71–79.

8. Robert Peterson and William Wilson, "Measuring Customer Satisfaction: Fact or Artifact," *Journal of the Academy of Marketing Science* 20 (1992):61–71.

9. Thomas Jones and Earl Sasser Jr., "Why Satisfied Customers Defect," *Harvard Business Review* (November–December 1995):88–99; Frederick F. Reichheld and W. Earl Sasser Jr., "Zero Defections: Quality Comes to Services," *Harvard Business Review* (September–October 1990): 106–11; and Frederick F. Reichheld, "Loyalty-Based Management," *Harvard Business Review* (March–April 1993):64–73.

10. Patrick Byrne, "Global Logistics: Only 10% of Companies Satisfy Customers," *Transportation and Distribution* (December 1993); and Tom Eck, "Are Customers Happy? Don't Assume," *Positive Impact* (July 1992):3.

11. James Hulbert and Norman Toy, "A Strategic Framework for Marketing Control," *Journal of Marketing* (April 1977):12–20; V. K. Kirpalani and Stanley Shapiro, "Financial Dimensions of Marketing Management," *Journal of Marketing* (July 1973):40–53; and John Shank and Vijay Govindarajan, *Strategic Cost Analysis* (Burr Ridge, IL: Irwin, 1989):99–112.

chapter 16

Profit Impact of Market-Based Management

Businesses such as Disney, IBM, MBNA, Nordstrom, Ritz-Carlton, and Xerox have one thing in common, customer satisfaction. It is the core value that drives their business cultures and the marketing strategies that evolve. These businesses are also highly profitable, and for some time they have created value for customers, employees, and shareholders.

HOW TO OVERWHELM CUSTOMERS AND SHAREHOLDERS

The process starts with a strong market orientation and a passion for customer satisfaction, as illustrated in Figure 16.1. Although there are many ways to better serve cus-

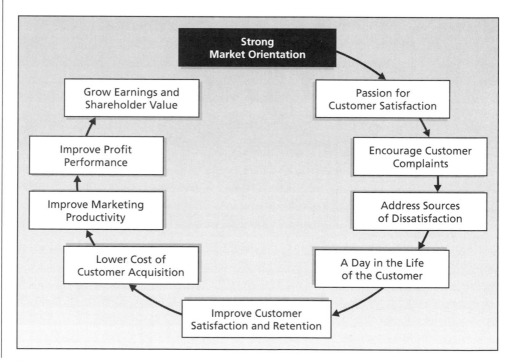

Figure 16.1 ◆ **How to Overwhelm Customers and Shareholders**

344

tomers in a effort to improve customer satisfaction, a business with a passion for customer satisfaction will start with its dissatisfied customers by encouraging them to complain.

Encouraging customer complaints is easier said than done. Most customers don't complain for a variety of good reasons. A market-based business will develop proactive customer satisfaction programs and systems to encourage customer complaint and will measure its success with the rate at which they hear from dissatisfied customers. Capturing customer complaints provides a wonderful opportunity to discover and address sources of dissatisfaction. The most effective and lowest-cost customer research any business will ever engage in is hearing from dissatisfied customers.

However, a business with a passion for customer satisfaction will go further to understand customer needs, frustrations, and opportunities to create customer solutions that build higher levels of customer satisfaction. A *day in the life of a customer* is one way to further discover ways to build customer satisfaction. A day in the life of a customer is a *process-focused,* not *product-focused,* effort to understand how customers acquire, use, and replace products, and the sources of frustration that occur in these processes. The outputs of this effort are customer solutions designed to enhance customer satisfaction and improve customer retention, as shown in Figure 16.1.

With higher customer retention, a business can lower its cost of customer acquisition and improve marketing productivity. Recall, a common rule of thumb is that it is five times more expensive to replace a customer than to retain one. Thus, higher customer retention means that fewer dollars of marketing budget are needed to maintain a certain level of market share. These gains drop to the bottom line, which contributes directly to improved net profits and shareholder value. In this last chapter we make explicit the relationship between customer satisfaction and profitability and shareholder value, but also, in a broader sense, we demonstrate how every marketing strategy affects profits, and shareholders.

CUSTOMER SATISFACTION AND PROFITABILITY

To manage this process, a business must first understand its levels of customer satisfaction, dissatisfaction, complaint recovery, and customer retention, as well as the cost of customer acquisition. Figure 16.2 presents the current customer situation for AirComm, a wireless telecommunications business.

As shown in Figure 16.2, AirComm has achieved a 75 percent level of customer satisfaction, which here translates into an 80 percent customer retention, given the rate at which AirComm recovers customer complaints and resolves dissatisfaction. At current levels of performance, 25 percent of AirComm's customer base is dissatisfied, but the business hears from only 10 percent of these dissatisfied customers. When AirComm *does* recover a customer complaint, it is able to retain 80 percent of these dissatisfied customers. The business loses 87 percent of those dissatisfied customers it *does not* hear from. Of course, this level of customer complaint recovery contributes to AirComm's overall level of customer retention.

At this level of customer satisfaction and retention, AirComm produces a net profit of $50 million on sales of $500 million, a 10 percent return on sales. As shown in Figure 16.3, the major driver of profitability is percentage of retained customers. At an 80 percent level of customer retention, AirComm's retained customers produce $120 million in

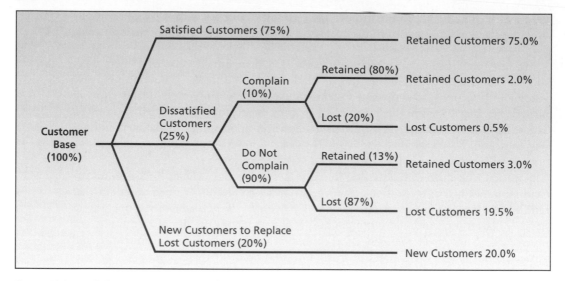

Figure 16.2 ◆ AirComm Customer Satisfaction and 80 Percent Customer Retention

net marketing contribution, while customers who are lost and those who replace them produce a combined net marketing contribution of –$30 million.

Improving customer retention to 90 percent would improve overall net profits by $20 million, with no change in sales revenue. Retained customer profitability would improve modestly, but the greatest gain in profitability would be due to a lower cost of new customer acquisition. As shown in Figure 16.4, the return on sales is 14 percent with 90 percent retention, a healthy increase over the 10 percent return at the 80 percent level of customer retention.

Area of Performance	Retained Customers	Lost Customers	New Customers	Overall Performance
Number of Customers	800,000	200,000	200,000	1,200,000
Revenue per Customer	$500	$300	$200	
Total Revenue (millions)	$400	$ 60	$ 40	$500
Variable Cost per Customer	$300	$200	$150	
Margin per Customer	$200	$100	$ 50	
Total Contribution (millions)	$160	$ 20	$ 10	$190
Marketing Expenses (millions)	$ 40	$ 10	$ 50	$100
Market Exp. per Customer	$ 50	$ 50	$250	
Net Marketing Contribution (mil)	**$120**	**$ 10**	**–$ 40**	**$ 90**
Operating Expense (millions)				$ 40
Net Profit (before taxes) (millions)				$ 50
Return on Sales				**10.0%**

Retention Cost = $50 per Customer; Acquisition Cost = $250 per Customer.

Figure 16.3 ◆ AirComm Profitability at 80 Percent Customer Retention

Area of Performance	Retained Customers	Lost Customers	New Customers	Overall Performance
Number of Customers	900,000	100,000	100,000	1,100,000
Revenue per Customer	$500	$300	$200	
Total Revenue (millions)	$450	$ 30	$ 20	$500
Variable Cost per Customer	$300	$200	$150	
Margin per Customer	$200	$100	$ 50	
Total Contribution (millions)	$180	$ 10	$ 5	$195
Marketing Expenses (millions)	$ 54	$ 6	$ 25	$ 85
Marketing Exp. per Customer*	$ 60	$ 60	$250	
Net Marketing Contribution (mil)	**$126**	**$ 4**	**–$ 20**	**$110**
Operating Expense (millions)				$ 40
Pretax Net Profit (before taxes) (millions)				$ 70
Return on Sales				**14.0%**

* Marketing expenses focused on customer retention were increased by 20% (from $50 to $60 per customer) in an effort to improve customer satisfaction and achieve 90% retention.

Figure 16.4 ◆ AirComm Profitability at 90 Percent Customer Retention

HOW MARKETING STRATEGIES AFFECT PROFITABILITY

A passion for customer satisfaction is one way a market-oriented business builds superior profits. Businesses with a strong market-orientation see current and potential customers as key sources of profitability, cash flow, and earnings. Customers, products, and assets are all important parts of business and business success, but only one produces money. Each is an important aspect of a business, and each needs to be managed on a day-to-day basis for a business to be efficient and profitable. However, financial reports and product-line income statements often dominate the thinking of a business that lacks a market orientation. Products will come and go; assets will be purchased and consumed; but *the customer is the only enduring asset a business has.* Keeping in mind that the customer is the only source of positive cash flow, it is the responsibility of those in marketing to understand how customers affect a business and its profitability.[1] This section addresses these issues in an attempt to bring into greater focus customers and the importance of their role in contributing to the profits of a business.

Customer Volume

Recognizing the *customer* as the primary unit of focus, a market-based business will expand its focus to customers and markets, not just products or units sold.[2] This is an important strategic distinction because there is a finite number of potential customers, but a large range of products and services can be sold to each customer. And, as shown below, a business's volume is its customer share in a market with a finite number of customers at any point in time, not the number of units sold.

$$\text{Customer Volume} = \text{Market Demand (customers)} \times \text{Market Share (percentage)}$$

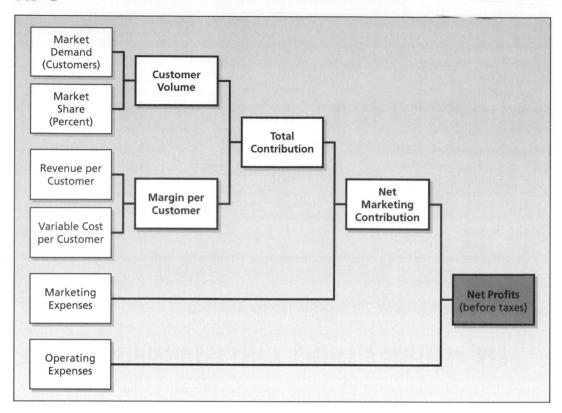

Figure 16.5 ◆ **A Customer-Based Model of Net Profits (before Taxes)**

Figure 16.5 presents an overall flow chart of how market-based net profits are derived. Customer volume, at the top of this diagram, is derived from a certain level of customer market demand and a business's share of that customer demand. Without a sufficient volume of customers, net profit will be impossible to obtain. Marketing strategies that affect customer volume include marketing strategies that:

- Attract new customers to grow market share
- Grow the market demand by bringing more customers into a market
- Enter new markets to create new sources of customer volume

Each of these customer-focused marketing strategies affects net profits, invested assets, cash flow, and, as we will show later, shareholder value. Thus, a key component of profitability and financial performance is customer purchases and the collective customer volume produced. Without customer purchases, there is no positive cash flow or potential for net profits or shareholder value.

Margin per Customer

When customers decide to purchase an assortment of products and services from a business, the result is a certain revenue per customer. And, of course, a corresponding set of variable costs that go into each purchase and sales transaction must be taken into account to determine margin per customer:

$$\frac{\text{Customer}}{\text{Margin}} = \frac{\text{Revenue}}{\text{per Customer}} \times \frac{\text{Variable Cost}}{\text{per Customer}}$$

This measure of customer profitability, as shown above and in Figure 16.5, could be computed on a transaction basis, monthly or annually. The bottom line is that a business has to make a positive margin per customer or it will produce no profits and, therefore, no shareholder value. In many instances, new customers may produce a small or negative customer margin. Over time, we would expect a business to manage its marketing strategies so as to increase customer margin. If it does not, it has several alternatives to consider, one of which is to not continue to serve that customer as part of the business's marketing strategy. In general, marketing strategies designed to improve margin per customer can include marketing strategies that:

- Grow revenue per customer by product line extensions
- Grow revenue per customer by adding services that enhance customer value
- Improve margin per customer with improved products and services for which the customer is willing to pay a premium price
- Develop more cost-efficient marketing systems that lower variable sales and transactions costs
- Eliminate customers that are not able to produce an acceptable level of customer margin

As shown in Figure 16.5, *revenue per customer* and *variable cost per customer* come together to produce a certain level of *margin per customer*. Because the customer is the primary unit of focus of market-based management, it is the business's responsibility to develop marketing strategies that systematically build customer volume and customer margin.

Total Contribution

Ultimately, whether tracking product revenues and variable product costs or tracking customer volume and margin per customer, the end result will be a total contribution produced by the marketing strategies that have been developed and implemented. Once again, *both approaches* are needed in managing different aspects of a business. However, those in marketing should be more concerned with a customer perspective and how to develop marketing strategies that affect both customers and the total contribution of the business.

$$\frac{\text{Total}}{\text{Contribution}} = \frac{\text{Customer}}{\text{Volume}} \times \frac{\text{Customer}}{\text{Margin}}$$

As shown in Figure 16.5, the total contribution produced by a marketing strategy is the product of the customer volume it produces and customer margin derived from customer purchases. The total contribution produced by a marketing strategy is an important component in the profitability equation because from this point forward only expenses are introduced. Hence, building market-based strategies that increase total contribution is an important priority in developing marketing strategies that deliver profitable growth.

Net Marketing Contribution

All marketing strategies require *some* level of marketing effort to achieve a certain level of market share. Expenses associated with sales effort, market communications, customer service, and market management are required to implement a marketing strategy designed to obtain a certain customer volume. The cost of this marketing effort is shown in Figure 16.5 as *marketing expenses* and must be deducted from the total contribution to produce a *net marketing contribution.* This is the net contribution or dollars produced after the marketing expenses are deducted from the total contribution produced.

$$\text{Net Marketing Contribution} = \text{Total Contribution} - \text{Marketing Expenses}$$

In effect, this is how the marketing function contributes to the business's profits. If the marketing team develops a marketing strategy that fails and, therefore, lowers net marketing contribution, then that marketing strategy has, in effect, lowered the net profits of the business.

Marketing strategies are generally designed to affect total contribution, whether by increasing market demand, market share, or revenue per customer or by decreasing variable cost per customer. The net marketing contribution equation should make it clear that such strategies are profitable only if the increase in total contribution exceeds the increase in marketing expenses required to produce that increase in total contribution. That is, for a marketing strategy to improve profits for the business, it has to improve net marketing contribution.

Net Profit (before Taxes)

Although marketing strategies contribute to net profits through net marketing contribution, net profits (before taxes) of a business are generally beyond the control of the marketing function or the marketing management team. Marketing strategies produce a certain level of net marketing contribution from which all other business expenses must be deducted before a net profit is realized, as illustrated in Figure 16.5. These operating expenses include fixed expenses, such as human resources management, research and development, and administrative expenses, and other operating expenses, such as utilities, rent, and fees. In most instances, there would also be allocated corporate overhead, which includes company expenses such as legal fees, corporate advertising, and executive salaries.

$$\text{Net Profit (before taxes)} = \text{Net Marketing Contribution} - \text{Operating Expenses}$$

However, there are instances when a marketing strategy can affect operating expenses. For example, a strategy to improve a product to attract more customers and build market share could involve research and development expenses to develop the new product.

HOW MARKETING STRATEGIES AFFECT ASSETS

Most businesses do not consider the impact marketing strategies have on a business's investment in assets. As will be demonstrated, the assets of a business are indirectly affected by marketing strategies. We will limit our discussion to accounts receivable, inventory, and fixed assets. These assets normally account for the majority of a business's investment in assets.

Investment in Accounts Receivable

We frequently do not think about the effect a marketing strategy can have on accounts receivable. Accounts receivable is the money owed a business and varies in proportion to sales revenues and customer payment behavior. As sales revenues increase or decrease, there will be a corresponding change in accounts receivable. In addition, customer payment behavior will determine the time customers take to pay for what they have purchased. For example, if customers take an average of 45 days to pay their bills, for approximately 12.5 percent of a year (45 divided by 365) customers are holding the business's money. If annual sales were $100 million, the accounts receivable would be approximately $12.5 million at any point in time.

$$\frac{\text{Accounts}}{\text{Receivable}} = \frac{\text{Sales}}{\text{Revenues}} \times \frac{\text{Percent Days}}{\text{Outstanding}}$$

$$= \$100 \text{ million} \times 0.125 \ (12.5\%)$$

$$= \$12.5 \text{ million}$$

To put this in marketing terms, accounts receivable is a function of customer volume, revenue per customer, and customer payment behavior. When we state this relation in terms of marketing strategy, we can express accounts receivable in the following way:

$$\frac{\text{Accounts}}{\text{Receivable}} = \frac{\text{Customer}}{\text{Volume}} \times \frac{\text{Revenue per}}{\text{Customer}} \times \frac{\text{Percent Days}}{\text{Outstanding}}$$

$$= 20,000 \times \$5,000 \times 0.125 \ (12.5\%)$$

$$= \$12.5 \text{ million}$$

In this form, one can readily see how strategies that affect customer volume and revenue per customer also affect accounts receivable. In addition, the selection of target customers could be based partly upon their bill-paying behavior. Thus, a business may avoid customers who are slow payers, thereby lowering the level invested in accounts receivable. For example, about 3 percent of residential phone customers are labeled "movers and shakers." These are customers who run up large telephone bills but move on and shake loose before paying their bills. If these customers could be identified early, it would be wise to avoid them when possible.

In addition, a business's service quality also affects how fast customers pay their bills (and, hence, the level of accounts receivable). For example, consider how customer service affects the following customer payment behavior:[3]

- Eight out of 10 Fortune 500 companies report that the level of customer service they receive affects their decision to pay a bill on time.
- More than half of the Fortune 500 companies withhold payment from suppliers when they are dissatisfied with the level of service they have received.

Thus, a business with a strong market orientation and commitment to service quality and customer satisfaction is likely to be paid faster than businesses that deliver lower levels of service quality or customer satisfaction. In this way, the market orientation of a business affects the business's investment in accounts receivable.

Investment in Inventory

Many businesses are required to carry large inventories to adequately serve target customers. Long production runs and uncertain market demand often require a business to maintain a certain level of finished goods inventory. There are also work-in-process inventories (partially finished goods) and raw materials inventories. All these inventories are assets with market values.

As with accounts receivable, the size and value of inventories vary with sales revenues and target customer purchase behavior. As such, inventory at any time is roughly equal to total cost of goods sold times a percentage of days of inventory on hand. The need to have inventory on hand to cover an average of 30 days of sales would equate to 8.2 percent days of inventory (30 days divided by 365 days in a year). If the manufactured cost of goods sold for a year is \$40 million, the average investment in inventory would be \$3.28 million, as shown here.

$$\frac{\text{Inventory}}{\text{Investment}} = \frac{\text{Total Cost}}{\text{of Inventory}} \times \frac{\text{Percent Days}}{\text{of Inventory}}$$

$$= \$40 \text{ million} \times 0.082 \ (8.2\%)$$

$$= \$3.28 \text{ million}$$

In terms of marketing strategy, the investment in inventory can be expressed as:

$$\frac{\text{Inventory}}{\text{Investment}} = \frac{\text{Customer}}{\text{Volume}} \times \frac{\text{Unit Cost}}{\text{per Customer}} \times \frac{\text{Percent Days}}{\text{of Inventory}}$$

$$= 200,000 \times \$200 \times 0.082 \ (8.2\%)$$

$$= \$3.28 \text{ million}$$

Once again, marketing strategies that affect market demand, market share, and the unit manufacturing cost will affect investment in inventory. Likewise, channel marketing strategies will affect investment in inventory. A shift from a direct sales and distribution system to a distributor channel system could lead to lower inventories as a business is able to shift inventory requirements to distributors and, hence, lower the business's investment in assets.

Investment in Fixed Assets

Fixed assets include investments in buildings, land, equipment, office furniture, and so on. Most of these assets are depreciated each year as business expenses, and, therefore, at least from a financial accounting point of view, lose value over time. However, the amount and value of fixed assets at any point in time is relative to sales volume. A marketing strategy to grow sales volume substantially in a growing market would typically require additional fixed assets to accommodate that volume increase.

Thus, fixed assets are a function of sales volume which, in turn, is a function of marketing strategies to grow customer volume or volume per customer or both. Most businesses have excess manufacturing capacity, which is a large component of fixed assets. A marketing strategy to grow volume, by growing customer demand or increasing customer market share, will increase capacity utilization. If the increased volume produced increases net profits, this marketing strategy will result in an overall increase in the business's return on assets, because no addition to assets was necessary. Naturally, in situations where fixed assets have to be added to accommodate growth, the investment in assets would be greater. A business that derives profits from an increase in volume has to have profits sufficiently large to produce a higher return on assets.

In general, most managers do not consider the impact of a marketing strategy on assets or return on assets. Although not scrutinized at this level, every marketing decision affects one or more of the return-on-asset components shown in Figure 16.6.

For example, consider a scanner manufacturer's marketing strategy to capture a significant share of the retail scanner market. The business knew that a major customer was price-sensitive and that competitors would price aggressively to get this customer's volume. Recognizing the importance of price, the scanner manufacturer offered a price lower than competing offers but required full payment within 10 days, with no cash discount. Unit margins were lower, but the large volume captured produced a large total contribution, and with a very minimal investment in accounts receivable, the business produced a much higher return on assets. The net result was a marketing strategy that produced higher net profits and a lower level of investment, each of which contributed to an increase in return on investment.

RETURN MEASURES OF PROFITABILITY

Accounting and financial measures of profitability include net profit, return on sales (ROS), return on assets (ROA), and return on equity (ROE). As shown below, net marketing contribution is a key driver of net profits. To grow net profits in any given year, a business has two fundamental options: lower operating expenses or grow net marketing contribution.

$$\underbrace{\begin{array}{c}\text{Net Profit} \\ \text{(after taxes)}\end{array} = \left[\left(\begin{array}{c}\text{Customer (new)} \\ \text{Volume}\end{array} \times \begin{array}{c}\text{Margin per} \\ \text{Customer (new)}\end{array} \right) - \begin{array}{c}\text{Marketing} \\ \text{Expenses}\end{array} \right]}_{\text{Net Marketing Contribution}} - \begin{array}{c}\text{Operating} \\ \text{Expenses}\end{array} - \begin{array}{c}\text{Interest} \\ \text{and Taxes}\end{array}$$

The three fundamental measures of profit performance—return on sales (ROS), return on assests (ROA), and return on equity (ROE)—are based on the net profit produced in any given period:

$$\text{Return on Sales (ROS)} = \frac{\text{Net Profit (after taxes)}}{\text{Sales}}$$

$$\text{Return on Assets (ROA)} = \frac{\text{Net Profit (after taxes)}}{\text{Assets}}$$

$$\text{Return on Equity (ROE)} = \frac{\text{Net Profit (after taxes)}}{\text{Equity}}$$

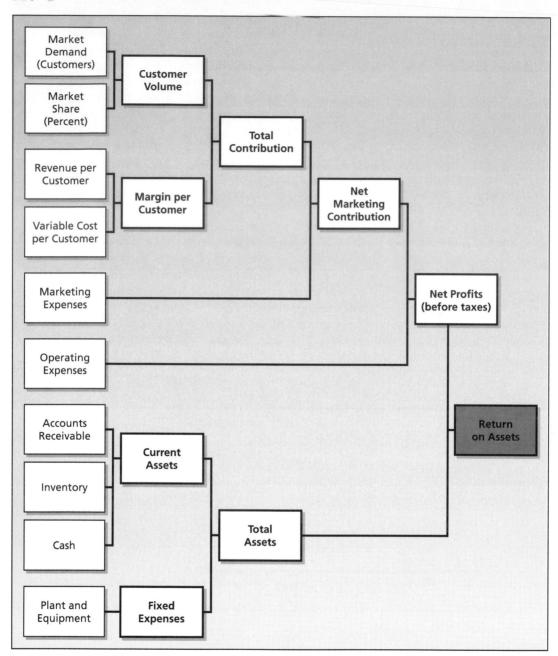

Figure 16.6 ◆ A Customer-Based Model of Return on Assets

The denominator in each case is directly or indirectly affected by market-based management, but the gains in these performance indexes are driven primarily by net profits. For example, as shown in Figure 16.7, the sales of Dell Computer in 1997 were $7.76 billion and net profit (after taxes) was $520 million, therefore the return on sales (ROS)

Area of Performance	1997	1998
Market Demand (millions)	79.5	91.5
Market Share	5.7%	7.9%
Unit Volume (millions)	4.53	7.23
Sales Revenues (billions)	$7.76	$12.33
Percent Margin	22.0%	22.6%
Total Contribution (billions)	$1.71	$ 2.79
Marketing, Sales, and Admin.	0.83	1.22
Net Marketing Contribution (billions)	**$0.88**	**$ 1.57**
Operating Expenses (billions)	0.13	0.20
Operating Income (billions)	$0.75	$ 1.37
Taxes and Other Income (billions)	0.23	0.43
Net Profit (billions)	$0.52	$ 0.94
Balance Sheet Information		
Total Assets (billions)	$2.99	$ 4.27
Liabilities (billions)	2.18	2.98
Equity (billions)	$0.81	$ 1.29
Return Measures of Performance		
Return on Sales (ROS)	6.7%	7.6%
Return on Assets (ROA)	17.3%	22.0%
Return on Equity (ROE)	60.0%	72.8%

Figure 16.7 ◆ **Dell Computer Profitability Performance**

was 6.7 percent. Dell's balance sheet figures show that its return on assets (ROA) was 17.3 percent and return on equity (ROE) was 60 percent. A key driver of this performance was a net marketing contribution of $880 million.

In 1998, Dell grew its market share from 5.7 percent to 7.9 percent in a market that grew from 79.5 million personal computers to 91.5 million. This level of market performance yielded a net marketing contribution of $1.57 billion. The gain in net marketing contribution contributed to an overall gain in net profits of $420 million. This level of performance increased ROS from 6.7 percent to 7.6 percent and ROA from 17.3 percent to 22 percent. Return on owners' equity (ROE) increased from 60 percent to 72.8 percent.

MEASURES OF SHAREHOLDER VALUE

Having demonstrated the importance of the customer and market-based management with respect to net profits, assets, and return measures of profit performance, we need to extend our discussion of how market-based management affects shareholder value.[4] To do so, we need to first develop a way of linking market-based management and net marketing contribution to profit performance and shareholder value.

Return measures of performance such as ROS, ROA, and ROE, present an aspect of profit performance. Although these are important, shareholder value is more closely associated with earnings per share, economic value-added,[5] and price-earnings ratio. Each of these is briefly described below, and illustrated in Figure 16.8, for AirComm at the 80 percent level of customer retention.

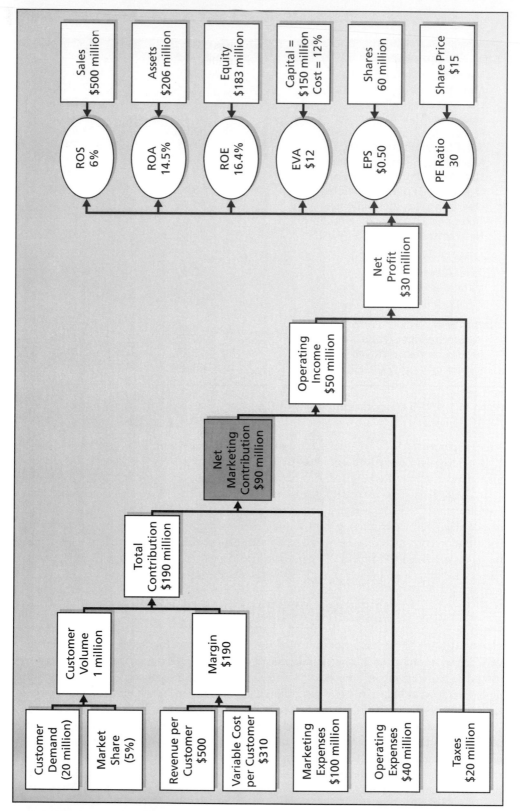

Figure 16.8 ◆ AirComm Financial Performance: 80 Percent Customer Retention

- **Earnings per Share (EPS):** Net profit (after taxes) divided by the number of shares. For AirComm, a net profit (after taxes) of $3 million and 6 million shares translates to $0.50 per share.
- **Economic Value-Added (EVA):** Net profit (after taxes) minus the business's capital investment times the cost of capital yields a measure of how much value it created by that level of net profit (earnings). For AirComm, a net profit (after taxes) of $30 million minus capital investment ($150 million) times the cost of capital (12 percent), yields an EVA of $12 million.
- **Price-Earnings (PE) Ratio:** The price of a share of stock divided by the earnings per share. For AirComm, the share price of $15 divided by its earnings per share of 0.50 yields a price-earnings (PE) ratio of 30.

A market-based strategy to improve customer retention from 80 to 90 percent would yield improved profit performance, as shown in Figure 16.9. Earnings per share would increase from $0.50 to $0.70, EVA would improve from $12 million to $24 million, and the price-earnings ratio would drop from 30 to approximately 21. Or, to maintain a price-earnings ratio of 30, share price would have to increase from $15 per share to $21 per share. Thus, businesses with a strong market orientation and passion for customer satisfaction and retention should deliver higher levels of profitability and shareholder value, even with no change in sales revenues.

MARKET-BASED MANAGEMENT

To be profitable, a business needs to achieve above-average market performance and operational performance.[6] In fact, market and operational performance are interrelated, as illustrated in Figure 16.10. A business with poor levels of customer satisfaction can expect sales to these customers to decline and the speed with which they pay their invoices to decrease. These business have to spend more marketing dollars in an effort to maintain a certain level of sales. The combination of these effects influences all aspects of financial performance shown in market and operational performance metrics.

The central theme of this book has been how a business can develop and deliver marketing strategies that:

- Deliver high levels of customer satisfaction and superior customer value.
- Improve market position, sales, and profitability.
- Improve earnings and shareholder value.

Market-based management, as shown in Figure 16.11, is at the base of a business with a strong market orientation. A strong market orientation translates into a strong customer focus, competitor orientation, and a team approach that cuts across organizational functions. The result is a market-based business that is in a strong position to develop and deliver market-based strategies designed to attract, satisfy, and retain customers. Implemented successfully across a wide range of market situations, a market-based approach to market management will deliver higher levels of profitability, cash flow, and shareholder value than will a cost-based approach.

One should never forget that the only source of positive cash flow is the customer. Without customers, technology, assets, and management are of little value. The job of a

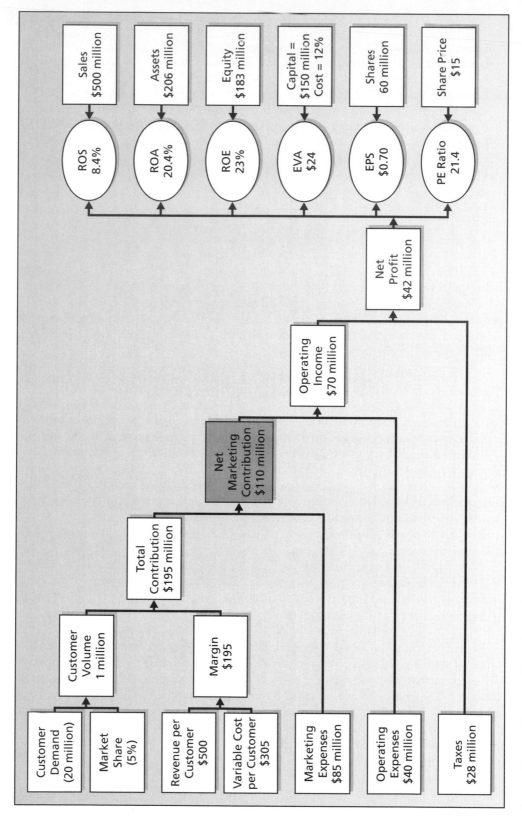

Figure 16.9 ◆ **AirComm Financial Performance: 90 Percent Customer Retention**

Figure 16.10 ◆ Market, Operational, and Profit Performance

market-based business is to understand customers, competition, and the market environment within the context of the business's technology, assets, and management capabilities and to render a market-based strategy that delivers superior levels of customer satisfaction, profitability, and shareholder value.

SUMMARY

Marketing strategies directly affect customers and sales revenues. However, they also affect margins, total contribution, and marketing expenses. These effects, in turn, lead to a net marketing contribution. Because operating and overhead expenses are beyond the control of marketing managers, net marketing contribution plays an important role in evaluating the profit impact of marketing strategies. Thus, throughout this book we have sought to determine the profit impact of a marketing strategy based on the level of net marketing contribution produced.

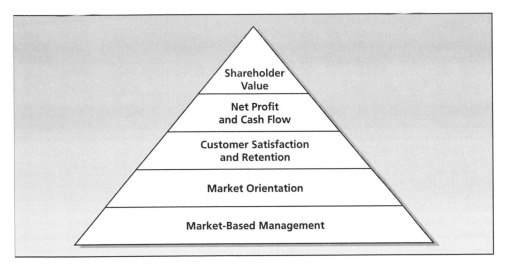

Figure 16.11 ◆ Market-Based Management and Shareholder Value

APPLICATION PROBLEM: STERICYCLE, INC.

At the end of chapter 14 we developed a marketing plan for Stericycle, Inc. The base year for the marketing plan was 1997. The marketing plan was for 1998 to 2002. Shown below are the actual results for 1997 and 1998. Using these data, create a market-based analysis of profitability like the one developed for Dell in Figure 16.7.

Area of Performance	1997	1998
Market Demand (customers)	630,000	630,000
Market Share	6.8%	11.1%
Customer Volume	43,000	70,000
Sales Revenues (millions)	$ 46.2	$ 63.8
Revenue per Customer	$1074.42	$910.00
Cost per Customer	793.00	620.00
Margin per Customer	$ 281.42	$290.00
Total Contribution	$ 12.1	$ 20.3
Marketing Expenses (millions)	10.7	13.9
Net Marketing Contribution (millions)	$ 1.4	$ 6.4
Overhead Expenses (millions)	0.0	0.0
Operating Income (millions)	$ 1.4	$ 6.4
Other Income and Taxes (millions)	0.0	1.0
Net Profit (millions)	**$ 1.4**	**$ 5.4**
Assets (millions)	$ 61.2	$ 70.7
Liabilities (millions)	16.2	19.2
Owners Equity (millions)	$ 45.0	$ 51.5
Shares (millions)	10.77	11.25
Earnings per Share	$ 0.13	$ 0.48

Questions

For Internet discussion go to www.prenhall.com/phbusiness.

1. What were the key factors driving the increase in net profit from 1997 to 1998?

2. How did the financial measures of performance change from 1997 to 1998? How are these changes related to the market-based forces identified in question 1?

3. How did Stericycle's share growth affect performance and shareholder value?

Marketing strategies also directly impact assets. Changes in sales produce corresponding changes in accounts receivable and inventory. Likewise, a major increase in volume based on a particular marketing strategy may require additional operating expenses and investment in fixed assets. Marketing strategies impact both the numerator of the ROA (return on assets) equation as well as the denominator. This presents a much broader view of the impact a marketing strategy has on a business's profitability.

The net marketing contribution for each product–market strategy contributes to both profit performance and shareholder value. Return measures of profit performance (ROS, ROA, and ROE) are driven by market performance and net marketing contribution. Shareholder measures of performance (earnings per share, EVA, and price-earnings ratio) are directly influenced by product–market performance and profitability.

Finally, it is the market orientation that is at the heart of market-based management. With a strong market orientation, a business will develop marketing strategies that are intended to attract, satisfy, and retain target customers. A market-based managed business should at the same time be evaluating alternative marketing strategies that contribute to the business's growth, short- and long-run profit performance and how to improve a business's strategic position. If successful, a market-driven business should deliver high levels of customer satisfaction, profitability, and shareholder value.

MARKET-BASED LOGIC AND STRATEGIC THINKING

1. Why is it important for those in responsible marketing positions to understand the profit impact of marketing strategies?
2. What should be the role of net marketing contribution in the development of a marketing strategy? Why is net profit often a misleading indicator of the profit impact of a marketing strategy?
3. How does a marketing strategy affect the assets of a business? Why should the accounts receivable and inventory change with a change in marketing strategy? When will the fixed assets change?
4. How does the net marketing contribution of a marketing strategy affect return on assets (ROA)?
5. How do investments in customer retention contribute to higher levels of profit performance?
6. Explain how the net marketing contribution of a marketing strategy affects return measures of profit performance.
7. How do changes in customer retention affect shareholder measures of performance such as earnings per share?
8. Explain how Dell Computer's market share gain in a growing personal computer market affected net marketing contribution, net profits, and return measures of performance.
9. Why should shareholders and Wall Street analysts be interested in a business's customer retention?
10. Why would two businesses with the same sales have different shareholder value if one had a 60 percent level of customer retention and the other 80 percent?
11. How would you use the net marketing contribution for each product–market to forecast earnings and earnings per share?
12. What role does net marketing contribution play in understanding the earnings level of a business?
13. How does the market orientation of a business affect customers, business performance, and shareholders?
14. Why should a market-oriented business with a passion for customer satisfaction produce higher levels of earnings per share and, therefore, have greater shareholder value than a business which is not market-oriented?

NOTES

1. Robert Kaplan and David Norton, "The Balanced Score Card—Measures That Drive Performance," *Harvard Business Review* (January–February 1992):71–79.
2. Eric Hardy, "The Forbes 500's Annual Directory," *Forbes* (April 22, 1996):232–78.
3. "Customer Service Impacts Cash Flow," *Positive Impact* (August 1993):5–6.
4. Sidney Schoeffler, "Impacts of Business Strategy on Stock Prices," PIMS Letter No. 20 (1980):1–9.
5. "Valuing Companies," *The Economist* (August 2, 1997):53–55; Eric Olsen and Thomas Rawley, "Stock Prices Performance: Corporate Agenda for the 1980s," *Journal of Accounting and Corporate Finance* (Spring 1987):3–15; Bill Birchard, "Mastering the New Metrics," *CFO: The Magazine for Senior Financial Executives* (October 1994); and Bill Barmhardt, "Chicago's Top 100 Companies," *Chicago Tribune* (May 15, 1995); Thomas Rawley and L. Edwards, "How Holt Methods Work for Good Decisions, Determine Business Value More Accurately," *Corporate Cashflow Magazine* (September 1993); and Bernard Reimann, "Stock Price and Business Success: What Is the Relationship?" *Journal of Business Strategy* (Summer 1987):38–50.
6. Robert Hayes, "Strategic Planning: Forward in Reverse," *Harvard Business Review* (November–December 1985):111–19.

"*For some reason, I became interested in watching the raindrops on the window. Two separate drops, pushed by the wind, merged into one for a moment and then divided again—each carrying with it a part of the other. Simply by that momentary touching neither was what it was before. And, as one went on to touch other raindrops, it shared not only itself, but what it had gleaned from the other.*"

—*Peggy Tabor Miller, in* Mary's Way

Though the words of this book may only touch you momentarily, it is my hope that they will have made a small difference, and will be shared with others.

—*Roger J. Best*

glossary

Acquisition cost. The marketing expense to acquire one new customer.

Advertising carryover effects. Sales occurring after the period in which an advertisement was run.

Advertising elasticity. The percent change in volume per 1 percent change in advertising expenditures.

Agents, brokers, and reps. Salespeople who work for a business on a commission basis.

Assets. Cash, accounts receivable, inventory, plant and equipment, and other assets.

Bottom-up marketing budget. A budget based on the cost of each specific marketing task needed to implement a tactical marketing strategy.

Brand equity. The attractiveness of a brand based entirely on its name and image.

Brand image. The perceived image of what a brand stands for in the mind of a target customer.

Brand personality. The personality a brand takes on based on human personality characteristics.

Break-even volume. The unit volume at which total sales equals total cost.

Break-even market share. The market share needed to reach break-even volume.

Channel system. A particular combination of distribution and sales.

Company benefits. The level of perceived benefit a customer attaches to a company or brand name.

Competitive advantage. A relative advantage one business has over another that is sustainable and translates into a benefit that is important to target customers.

Competitive benchmarking. Benchmarking a company outside your industry on a certain business practice in which the benchmark company is known for excellence.

Competitive bid pricing. Pricing a bid based on the historical success of past price-to-cost bid ratios and the competitive bid situation.

Competitive position. A business's position relative to a benchmark competitor's position with regard to price, product quality, delivery, new product sales, and so on.

Competitor analysis. Benchmarking a key competitor with respect to important areas of performance.

Competitor orientation. The degree to which a business tracks competitor's strategies and benchmarks its performance relative to competitors.

Cost advantage.   A sustainable lower cost relative to competition.

Cost-based pricing.   Pricing that is determined by a business's cost and margin requirements.

Cross price elasticity.   The percent change in volume in one product when the price is changed 1 percent in another product.

Customer focus.   The degree to which business seeks to understand customer needs and use situations, and to track customer satisfaction.

Customer life.   The number of purchase periods a customer is retained by a business.

Customer's lifetime value.   The net present value of cash flows produced over a customer's life.

Customer mix marketing budget.   A marketing budget based on the cost of new customer acquisition and retention.

Customer retention.   The percentage of customers retained from one purchase period to another.

Customer satisfaction.   The degree to which customers are satisfied or dissatisfied with a business, product, or specific aspect of a product or service provided by a business.

Customer value.   Total benefits minus the cost of acquiring those benefits.

Day in the life of a customer.   The process a customer goes through in acquiring, using, and disposing of a product.

Defensive strategic market plan.   A long-run plan to protect or exit a market position.

Differentiation advantage.   A sustainable product or service advantage that translates into a benefit important to target customers.

Direct channel system.   A channel system that retains ownership of the product and requires management of its sales, distribution, and customer service.

Discount rate.   A business's cost of capital.

Discount factor.   The net present value of $1.00 when discounted from a particular point in time and at a particular discount rate.

Distributors.   Intermediaries who take title (ownership) of a product and are responsible for its sale, distribution, and customer service.

Divest market strategy.   A defensive strategic market plan to exit a market by selling or closing down a business.

Earnings per share.   Net profits (after taxes) divided by the number of shares held by shareholders.

Economic value-added.   Net profits (after taxes) minus the product of a business's investment in capital assets times its cost of capital.

Economic value pricing.   Pricing to create a dollar savings for a customer based on a lower total life cycle cost when compared to a competitor's total life cycle cost.

Empathic design process. An observational approach to discovering customer problems, frustrations, and inconveniences in using your product.

End-result performance metrics. Performance metrics that occur at the end of a normal accounting period.

External performance metrics. Market performance metrics that track external performance with respect to market penetration, competitive position, and customer satisfaction.

Exit market strategies. Defensive strategic market plans that specify a market exit strategy that can range from immediate exit with a divestment strategy to a slow exit with harvesting strategy.

Firmagraphics. Characteristics used to describe a business such as size, financial position, years in business, type of business, number of locations, etc.

Flagship brand. The highest price and quality brand in a business's product line.

Flanker brand. A product extension of a business's core brand.

Forward buying. The practice of buying a greater volume of a product when it is on sale.

Grow market share strategy. A long-run offensive strategic market plan to grow market share.

Harvest market strategy. A defensive strategic market plan to slowly exit a market while maximizing profits.

Heavy-up message frequency. A period when a business increases its advertising effort.

Horizontal market opportunity. Market with closely related substitute products.

Indirect channel systems. Channels in which intermediaries take ownership of a business's product and the responsibility for its sale, distribution, and customer service.

Industry analysis. A structural analysis of a competitive environment based on competitor entry/exit, buyer/supplier power, substitutes, and competitive rivalry.

In-process performance metrics. Performance metrics that occur during a reporting period and precede end-result performance metrics.

Internal performance metrics. Performance metrics that are internal measures of a business's operations.

Margin per unit. The selling price of a product minus all the variable costs associated with producing, distributing, and selling the product.

Market analysis. An external analysis of market demand, customer needs, competition, distributors, and environmental forces that influence market demand and customer behavior.

Market attractiveness. The relative attractiveness of a market based on market forces, competitive environment, and market access.

Market-based management. The commitment of a strong market orientation and management of markets that strives to deliver superior customer value and profitability.

Market-based organization. A business organized around markets with market units as profit centers.

Market-based pricing.   Price is based on target customer need, competitors' product position, and the strength of a business's product, service, or brand advantage.

Market definition.   A specification of market scope that makes clear current and potential customers.

Market development index.   The ratio of current market demand to market potential (maximum market demand).

Market infrastructure.   Channel intermediaries and channel influencers that shape opinions and communicate information about a business and its products.

Market orientation.   The degree to which a business has a strong customer-focus and competitor orientation and works as a team across functions to develop and deliver a market-based strategy.

Market penetration strategies.   Offensive strategic market plans designed to further penetrate existing markets or enter new markets.

Market potential.   The maximum market demand that should occur when all potential customers have entered a market.

Market segmentation.   Grouping customers into segments on the basis of similar needs and differentiating demographic characteristics.

Market share.   The percentage of current market demand obtained by a business.

Market share index.   A hierarchy of market share factors (such as awareness, availability, interest, intention to buy, and purchase) that results in an estimate of market share.

Market vision.   A broad view of the market based on a fundamental customer need that goes beyond existing product solutions.

Marketing advantage.   A sustainable advantage over competitors in either channels of distribution, sales force, or marketing communications.

Marketing expenses.   All fixed expenses associated with selling, marketing, and managing of a marketing strategy targeted at a particular market.

Marketing mix.   A combination of the 4Ps (product, price, promotion, and place) designed for a specific target market.

Marketing planning process.   A process that starts with a situation analysis that leads to a specific strategic market plan, tactical marketing strategy, and marketing budget and results in a performance plan.

Marketing productivity.   Dollars of net marketing contributions produced by a strategy per dollar of fixed marketing expenses.

Mass customization.   An individualized marketing mix in which products, prices, promotion, and place are customized to the individual needs of a niche market or individual customers.

Mass market.   A market which is not segmented and all customers and potential customers are treated as one.

Message frequency.   The average number of times a target customer recalls seeing an advertisement in a given period of time.

Mixed channel systems.   A combination of direct and indirect channel systems in which a business and intermediary perform different functions with respect to sales, distribution, and customer service.

Multi-segment strategy.   Two or more separate and distinct marketing mix strategies (4Ps) that are created for different needs-based market segments.

Needs-based segmentation.   Market segmentation based on customer needs and/or the benefits they seek in satisfying a particular problem or buying situation.

Net marketing contribution.   The total contribution produced by a marketing strategy minus marketing expenses needed to produce it.

Net present value.   The value in today's dollars of a cash flow that occurs over time and is evaluated with a particular discount rate.

Net profit.   Sales revenues minus all expenses including taxes and interest.

New market entry strategies.   Offensive strategic market plans designed to enter new markets.

Niche market.   A small segment of a market which is often overlooked or ignored by large competitors.

Offensive strategic market plans.   Long-run plans (3 to 5 years) to penetrate markets or enter new market.

Operating expenses.   Overhead expenses that are not the direct result of marketing activities.

Operating income.   Sales minus all expenses before taxes and interest.

Penetration pricing.   A low price strategy to achieve a high market share/high volume position.

Perceived value pricing.   Pricing to create a greater customer value based on customer perceptions of product, service, company benefits, and the perceived cost of acquiring those benefits.

Perceptual mapping.   A display of competing products based on their relative substitutability and customer ideal products based on their strength of preference for each competing product.

Performance timeline.   A 3- to 5-year forecast of market and profit performance metrics.

Plus-one product positioning.   A product position that matches the performance features of competing products but offers one more important feature/benefit that is not offered by competitors.

Portfolio analysis.   An evaluation of a product, market, or business with respect to market attractiveness and competitive advantage.

Price-earnings ratio.   The price of a share of stock in a business divided by the business's earnings per share.

Price elasticity.   The percentage change in unit volume for a product per 1 percent change in price.

Price per unit. The selling price of a product or service.

Price premium. The dollar amount, or percentage, by which the price of a product exceeds competing products.

Prisoner's dilemma. A price situation in which businesses are forced to follow downward price moves by competitors to remain competitive.

Product benefits. The overall benefit a customer derives from the product performance and features.

Product bundling. Combining for sale two or more products at a total price that would be lower than the price paid if each product were purchased separately.

Product differentiation. The degree to which a business's product is meaningfully different and superior when compared by customers to competing products.

Product-focused. A business that is focused internally on product development and utilizes marketing primarily as an advertising and sales function.

Product life cycle. The life of a product as it progresses from introduction through growth, maturity, and decline.

Product line extensions. Products that are added to a product line under an umbrella brand which is well known and has an established reputation for quality.

Product line positioning. A planned sequence of alternative product offerings that differ in product performance and price.

Product-market diversification. The degree to which a business has different products across different markets.

Product positioning. The manner in which customers perceive a business's product features and price in comparison to competitors' product features and prices.

Product unbundling. Offering for sale an individual product that is normally sold as a product bundle.

Promotional price elasticity. The percent volume increase per 1 percent price decrease during a price promotion.

Protect market share strategy. A defensive strategic market plan in which a business develops a marketing strategy to protect/defend its competitive position and market share.

Pull communications. Marketing communications directed at end-user customers in an attempt to motivate target customers to seek a business's products (i.e., pull the products through the channel).

Push communications. Marketing communications directed at intermediaries in an attempt to motivate them to push a business's product through the channel in an effort to reach target customers.

Reduced market focus. A planned reduction in market share by reducing focus to a smaller number of customers.

Reference price. A price point used by customers to evaluate the price of competing products.

Relative cost.   A business's cost per unit relative to a competitor's cost per unit.

Relative market share.   A business's market share divided by the share of the market share leader competitor or next largest share competitor.

Relative new product sales.   The sales of new products introduced over the last three years divided by the new product sales produced by a competitor over the same time period.

Relative price.   A business's price divided by the price of a competitor or the average price of several competitors.

Relative product quality.   An overall relative index based on customer perceptions when comparing a business's product against a competitor's product on each aspect of product quality.

Relative service quality.   An overall relative index based on customer perceptions when comparing a business's service against a competitor's service on each aspect of service quality.

Retention cost.   The cost of retaining one customer over a given period of time.

Return on assets.   The net profit produced by a business divided by its total assets.

Return on equity.   The net profit produced by a business divided by its owner's equity.

Return on sales.   The net profit produced by a business divided by its total sales.

Sales revenue.   The price times the volume sold for each of the products sold by a company.

Service benefits.   The overall benefit a customer derives from the various components of service a business provides.

Share development index.   The percentage of current market demand obtained by a business.

Served market.   The target market to be served by the business.

Service differentiation.   The degree to which a business's service is meaningfully different and superior when compared by customers to competing products.

Share follower.   The business with the second largest market share in a given market.

Situation analysis.   An external analysis of market forces and internal analysis of business performance that are used to identify key performance issues and guide strategic market planning and development of tactical marketing strategies.

Skim pricing.   A high price position that attracts a limited number of customers but is sustainable because competitors cannot match the business's competitive advantage and value proposition.

Strategic market definition.   A broad definition of market demand that includes the business's served market and relevant substitute product–markets.

Strategic market planning.   The specification of a long-run (3- to 5-year) strategic market plan that will result in specific performance objectives with respect to market share, sales revenues, and profitability over the planning horizon.

Strategy implementation. The actions taken to implement, track, and adapt a tactical marketing plan derived from a specific strategic market plan.

SWOT analysis. A summary of strengths/weaknesses and opportunities/threats that are uncovered in a situation analysis.

Tactical marketing strategy. A one-year marketing mix strategy (4Ps) for a particular target market and specific strategic market plan.

Target market. A collection of customers that the business has decided to focus on in building a marketing mix strategy.

Team approach. The degree to which a business works across functions as a team in creating and delivering market-based customer solutions and implementation strategies.

Top-down marketing budget. A marketing budget based on a certain percentage of sales.

Total contribution. Total sales minus total variable cost of sales.

Trade-off analysis. Customer preferences for different combinations of price, product, service, and company benefits.

Two-tier marketing channel. A channel and sales system that involves two or more intermediaries.

Umbrella brand. A core brand that is well known and under which brand extensions can be easily introduced.

Unit volume vector. A projection of volume sold in 3 to 5 year based on different combinations of market growth and market share.

Untapped market opportunities. The gap between current market demand and market potential.

Value-added resellers. Intermediaries that buy products from several manufacturers and customize them for certain market applications.

Value map. A graph of relative performance and relative price.

Variable cost per unit. All of the variables costs associated with one unit sold.

Variance analysis. A reconciliation of planned vs. actual performance for each element of net marketing contribution.

Vertical market opportunities. Forward or backward integration along the supply chain that starts with raw materials and moves vertically through different stages of production, distribution, sales, and service.

Volume. The number of units sold for a particular product in a given period of time.

credits

CHAPTER 1

page 17, Figure 1.10: Adapted and reprinted by permission *Harvard Business Review* from "Zero Defections: Quality Comes to Services," by F.F. Reichheld and W. Earl Sasser, Jr. (September–October, 1990). Copyright © 1990 by the President and Fellows of Harvard College; all rights reserved.

CHAPTER 4

page 81, Figure 4.2: Ad courtesy of the Weyerhaeuser Corporation.   page 85, Figure 4.5: Adapted from Forbis, John, and Nitin, Mehta. "Value-Based Strategies for Industrial Products," *Business Horizons* (May–June, 1981) 32–42.   page 86, Figure 4.6: Ad courtesy of Sealed Air Corporation.   page 87, Figure 4.7: Ad courtesy of Rohm and Haas Company.

CHAPTER 5

page 117, Figure 5.10: Advertising and photo courtesy of DuPont.

CHAPTER 6

page 138, Figure 6.10: *Source:* PIMS Database, Strategic Planning Institute, Cambridge, MA.   page 138, Figure 6.11: Used with permission of US West Media Group.   page 141, Figure 6.14: *Source:* PIMS Database, Strategic Planning Institute, Cambridge, MA.   page 142, Figure 6.15: *Source:* Best, Roger J., Del I. Hawkins, and Charles M. Lillis, "Building a Value-Based Pricing Strategy," Working Paper (1994), University of Oregon.   page 143, Figure 6.16: *Source (left side): Marketing Models* by Kotler & Lilien, © 1992. Adapted by permission of Prentice-Hall, Inc., Upper Saddle River, NJ. *Source (right side):* PIMS Database, Strategic Planning Institute, Cambridge, MA.

CHAPTER 7

page 154, Figure 7.1: Ads courtesy of Loctite.   page 158, Figure 7.6: *Source:* Garvin, David. "Competing on Eight Dimensions of Quality," *Harvard Business Review* (November–December, 1987):101–105.   page 163, Figure 7.9: *Source:* PIMS Database, Strategic Planning Institute, Cambridge, MA.   page 167, Figure 7.11: *Source:* PIMS Database, Strategic Planning Institute, Cambridge, MA.

CHAPTER 9

page 210, Figure 9.13: *Marketing Models* by Kotler & Lilien, © 1992. Adapted by permission of Prentice-Hall, Inc., Upper Saddle River, NJ.

CHAPTER 10

page 215, Figure 10.1: Ad courtesy of Gardenburger.   page 219, Figure 10.4: Ad courtesy of Johnson Controls, Inc.   page 220, Figure 10.5: Adapted from Bender, David, Peter Farquhar, and Sanford Schulert. "Growing from the Top," *Marketing Management* (Winter/Spring, 1996):10–19.   page 221, Figure 10.6: *Source:* Zielske, H. "The Remembering and Forgetting of Advertising," *Journal of Marketing* (January, 1959):140.   page 225, Figure 10.8: Adapted from Reibstein, David. "Making the Most of Your Marketing Dollars," Drive Marketing Excellence, Institute for International Research, New York, NY, 1994.   page 229, Figure 10.11: *Source:* Bemmaor, Albert, and Dominique Mouchoux. "Measuring the Short-Term Effect of In-Store Promotion and Retail Advertising on Brand Sales," *Journal of Marketing Research* (May, 1991):202–214.

CHAPTER 13

page 280, Figure 13.5: *Source:* PIMS Database, Strategic Planning Institute, Cambridge, MA.   page 281, Figure 13.6: *Source:* PIMS Database, Strategic Planning Institute, Cambridge, MA.   page 383, Figures 13.8 and 13.9: *Source:* PIMS Database, Strategic Planning Institute, Cambridge, MA.   page 284, Figure 13.10: *Source:* PIMS Database, Strategic Planning Institute, Cambridge, MA.

index

ABC, 126

Access, market, 113, 142

Accounting systems, 37–39

Accounts receivable, investment in, 351–52

Acid test, segment strategy, 116–17

Acquisition costs, 84

Action plans, detailed, 327

Adaptation and the marketing plan, 329–31

Ad copy and customer response, 222

Adjacent segment strategies, 119

Advanced Micro Devices, 266

AdvanTech, 101

Advertising carryover effects, 227–28

Advertising elasticity, 226–27

Aesthetics, quality, 159

Affordability, restricting a market from reaching its full potential, 61–62

AirComm, 21, 345–47, 356, 358

Amazon.com, 201, 292

American Hospital Supply, 84, 162

America Online, 271

Amoco Chemical, 221

Amway, 201

Analysis, market, 53. *See also* Competitor analysis and competitive position; Customer analysis; Portfolio analysis and strategic market plans; Segmentation, needs-based market; Value creation, customer analysis and

break-even analysis and pricing strategies, 191–93

definition, market, 55–59

demand, market, 66–67

life cycle, product, 67–68

potential, market, 59–66

share and share potential, 68–74

situation analysis, 300–303, 311, 317–21

SWOT analysis, 303–4, 311–12, 321

unit volume vector, 74–75

Anheuser-Busch, 163–64

Apple Computer, 271

Articulated/unarticulated needs of served customers, 57

Assets, marketing strategies affecting, 350

accounts receivable, 351–52

fixed assets, 352–53

inventory, 352

return on assets, 353–55

Assurance and service quality, 160

AT&T, 11, 281

Attractiveness, market, 111–13, 245–47, 322

Auto-By-Tel, 202

Availability, product, 60, 71

Awareness

customer comprehension and, building, 219–22

product, 70

restricting a market from reaching its full potential, 59–60

Benchmarking, competitor, 130

analysis, competitor, 131, 133

differentiation, interbrand, 132

identifying business competitors, 131

intelligence, competitor, 133, 134

internal metrics important to, 126, 127

sample competitor analysis, 133–35

Xerox, 136

Benefit deficiency restricting a market from reaching its full potential, 60–61

Benefits *vs.* price, customer trade-off of, 97–100

Bid pricing, competitive, 180–82

Black & Decker, 154–55

Blockbuster Entertainment, 212

BMW, 131, 132

Bottom-up budget, 307

Brands, product

channels and sales systems, marketing, 205

differentiation, product, 131, 132, 160–61

marketing advantage, 144

perceived benefits and value creation, 92–93

Brands, product *(continued)*
   personality and value creation, 96–97
   reputation, 142
   umbrella branding, 164–65
Break-even analysis, and pricing strategies,
   191–93
Budget, marketing, 306–8, 313, 320, 322,
   324
Buick Regal, 131, 132
Bundling/unbundling products, 165–66,
   188–89
Business culture, shaping business market needs,
   108
Business market needs, 107–8. *See also*
   Segmentation, needs-based market
Business-to-business channel systems, 202–4
Buying power, customer, 128–29

Cadillac, division of General Motors, 16–17
Campbell Soup, 278, 280
Caterpillar, 203
CBS, 126
Champion and ownership team, 327
Change, as the only constant, 5–6
Channels and sales systems, marketing
   alternative channel systems, 197–204
   business-to-business channel systems,
     202–4
   competitive advantage, 207–10
   consumer channel systems, 201–2
   customer value, enhancing, 204–7
   Dell and Compaq Computer, 196–97
   direct channel systems, 199
   indirect channel systems, 200
   marketing advantage, 143
   mixed channel systems, 201
   profitability, 210–12
   two-tier marketing channels, 200–201
Cisco Systems, 280
Coca-Cola, 161, 241, 261
Cola wars of the 1980s, 55–56
Commitment to a marketing plan, 328–29
Commodity pricing, 179–80
Communications and customer response, marketing
   awareness and comprehension, building cus-
     tomer, 219–22

Gardenburger, 215–16, 234
   implementation and performance metrics,
     328–29
   message reinforcement, 222–24
   objectives, three, 216–17
   pull communications, 226–30
   push communications, 230–31
   push *vs.* pull communications strategies,
     224–26
   stimulating customer action, 223–24
   strategies to increase customer response,
     217–18
Company reputation, 92–93
Compaq Computer, 176, 196–97, 252, 273
Compensation, 327
Competitive intensity, 113
Competitor analysis and competitive position
   advantage, competitive, 126–27, 136–37,
     247–48
   benchmarking, competitor, 130–36
   channels and sales systems, marketing, 197,
     207–10
   cost advantage, 137–40
   differentiation advantage, 141–42
   industry analysis, 127–30
   industry forces, 126, 127
   marketing advantage, 142–44
   NewVector Consulting, 145–46
   penetration strategies, 320
   planning, strategic market, 247–48
   position, competitive, 126
   price and pricing strategies, 180–81,
     185–86
   Xerox, 135–36
Competitor orientation, 7
Complementary products, 186, 187
Complete solutions, developing, 63–64, 66
CompuServe, 271
Consumer channel systems, 201–02
Consumer market needs, forces that shape,
   106–7. *See also* Segmentation, needs-based
   market
Consumer Reports, 87–88
Continuous improvement, 330
Core capabilities, leveraging, 299
Core segment strategy, 306, 312, 323

Cost(s)
  acquisition, 84
  competitor analysis and competitive position, 137–40
  decomposition of a marketing plan, variance, 337–40
  disposal, 86–87
  efficiency, improving cost, 206–8
  maintenance, 85
  marketing cost advantage, 139–40
  overhead cost advantage, 140
  ownership, 85–86
  perceived benefits and value creation, 93–94
  price and pricing strategies, 175–76, 179–81
  strategies to lower variable, 42
  sustainers, cost-focused, 108
  transaction, 162, 208
  usage, 84–85
  value creation, customer analysis and, 84–87
  variable, 34, 42, 137–39
Creativity *vs.* structure in building a marketing plan, 298
Cross-functional teams, 7, 168–69
Customer analysis. *See also* Value creation, customer analysis and
  benefits, discovering customer, 79–83
  benefits and value, 82–83
  day in the life of a customer, 80
  empathic design process, 80–81
  understanding customer needs, 81–82
Customer mix budget, 307
Customer Retention Tree, 12, 13
Customer(s). *See also* Communications and customer response, marketing; Value creation, customer analysis and
  articulated/unarticulated needs of served, 57
  budget, customer mix, 307
  buying power, 128–29
  channel systems enhancing customer value, 197
  dissatisfied, 332–35
  growth, customer influences on market, 64–65
  lead, 63
  margin per customer, 348–49
  needs, 105. *See also* Segmentation, needs-based market
  overwhelming, 344–45
  penetration strategies, 265–66
  profitability and customer satisfaction, 345–47
  target, 329
  tradeoffs: benefits *vs.* price, 97–100
  volume, 347–48, 351–53
Customer satisfaction
  connectivity between market orientation/customer satisfaction/market-based management/profitability, 3
  dissatisfied customers, 10–11, 332–35
  exit, customer dissatisfaction and customer, 10–11
  measuring, 8–9, 21
  product impact of market-based management, 345–47
  profitability, 11–15
  retention, customer, 14–16, 284–85, 319, 356, 358
  selection, customer, 18
  underwhelming customers and shareholders, 6
  value of a customer, lifetime, 16–18
  wide-angle view of, 9

Database marketing, 228
DEC, 126
Decomposition of a marketing plan, variance, 337–40
Defensive strategic market plans
  Amazon.com, 292
  exit market strategies, 286–90
  Intel, 276
  offensive and, selecting between, 262–63
  performance, 251–52, 277–78
  portfolio analysis, 251–52
  protect market strategies, 278–86
  selecting, 290–91
Definition, market
  cola wars of the 1980s, 55–56
  served market definition, 58–59
  strategic market definition, 57
  vertical *vs.* horizontal market opportunities, 57–58
  vision, market, 56–57

Dell Computer
  channels and sales systems, marketing,
    196–97
  competitor analysis and competitive position,
    133, 135
  net marketing contribution, 47
  price and pricing strategies, 162, 180
Demand, market, 66–67. *See also* Share, market
  decomposition of a marketing plan, variance,
    337–40
  defensive strategic market plans, 251–52
  finite aspect of, 55
  growth, market/business, 40–41
  offensive strategic market plans, 250
  penetration strategies, 267–68, 318
  volume, customer, 347–48
Demographic influences shaping consumer mar-
    ket needs, 106
Demographic trap, 109–10
Desired level of response, 73
Detailed action plans, 327
DeWalt, 155
Differentiation, product, 157
  advantage, product, 141
  brands, 131, 132, 160–61
  positioning, product, 157–62
  price and pricing strategies, 161–62
  quality, 158–59
  reputation advantage, 142
  rivalry, competitive, 129
  service, 159, 160
  transaction costs, 162
Direct channel systems, 199, 201
Direct-mail programs, 228
Disney, 19, 269
Disposal costs, 86–87
Dissatisfied customers. *See* Customer satisfaction
Distributions advantage and channel systems,
    209–10
Distributor and market share, relationship be-
    tween, 143
Diversification across product-markets,
    242–43, 269–70
Divest market strategies, 289–90
Domino's Pizza, 10–11
DuPont, 84, 117
Durability and product quality, 159

Early adopters, 63–64
Earnings per share (EPS), 357
Eastman Kodak, 164, 279–81
Economic benefits and customer value creation
  acquisition costs, 84
  disposal costs, 86–87
  maintenance costs, 85
  ownership costs, 85–86
  price, low, 84
  six primary sources of economic value cre-
    ation, 83–84
  usage costs, 84–85
Economic value-added (EVA), 357
Economic value pricing, 177
Eddie Bauer, 201
Efficiency, strategies to increase market, 42
Elasticity, advertising, 226–27
Elasticity, price, 183–86, 229–30
Electrolux, 201
Emotional benefits and value creation, 95–97
Empathic design process, 80–81
Empathy and service quality, 160
Employee satisfaction, 18, 20, 22
End-result market metrics, 31, 32, 336–37
Entrepreneurs, growth-oriented, 108
Entry, barriers to market, 127
Equity, return on, 353–55
ESCO Corporation, 141
Espirit, 201
Exit market strategies
  barriers to market exit, 128
  dissatisfaction, customer, 10–11, 335
  divest market strategies, 289–90
  harvest price strategy, 286–87
  harvest resource strategy, 288–89
Expenses, marketing
  decomposition of a marketing plan, variance,
    337–40
  defensive strategic market plans, 251–52
  offensive strategic market plans, 250
  profitability, market-based measure of, 32–34
External *vs.* internal performance metrics, 30–31

FedEx, 141–42, 160
Feedback measurements, 330
Financial *vs.* market performance, 27–30
Firestone, 203

Firmographics, shaping business market needs, 107

Fixed assets, investment in, 352–53

Fixed expenses, 33

Flagship products, 182

Fluid Life Corporation (FLC), 256–57

Focused marketing strategy, 299

Follower share position, protecting a, 281–83

Ford, 203

Forward buying and customer response, 231

FP International (FPI), 86

Gap, market development, 64

Gap, The, 175

Gardenburger, 215–16, 234

Gates, Bill, 57

Gateway Computer, 96, 133, 135, 162

General Electric, 85–86, 241, 266, 271

General Motors, 16–17, 85, 126, 281

Gillette, 278

Gross rating points (GRPs), 222

Growth, market/business. *See also* Penetration
  strategies, market; Potential, market
  attractiveness, segment, 112
  cost, strategies to lower variable, 42
  demand, strategies to grow market, 40–41
  diversification across product-markets, 270
  efficiency, strategies to increase market, 42
  entrepreneurs, growth-oriented, 108
  life cycle, product, 67–68
  product influences on, 65–66
  profitability, marketing strategies designed to
    grow, 39–42
  protect market strategies, 279–80
  revenue per customer, strategies to increase,
    41
  share, strategies to increase market, 41

Hartman Luggage, 205

Harvest price strategy, 286–87

Harvest resource strategy, 288–89

Heavy-up message frequency, 223

Hewlett-Packard (HP), 70, 96, 136, 171, 241

Hitachi, 160–61

Honda, 82, 131, 132

Horizontal *vs.* vertical market opportunities,
  57–58

IBM, 20, 70, 126, 203, 281

Identification, segment, 111

Implementation and performance metrics, 325
  adapting the marketing plan, 329–31
  assessing marketing plan implementation,
    331–32
  decomposition of a marketing plan, variance,
    337–40
  metrics and financial performance, market,
    332–37
  owning the marketing plan, 326–28
  Stericycle, Inc., 341
  supporting the marketing plan, 328–29

Improvement, continuous, 330

Indirect channel systems, 200

Industry analysis
  buying power, customer, 128–29
  entry, barriers to market, 127
  exit, barriers to market, 128
  penetration strategies, 319
  prisoner's dilemma, 130
  product substitutes, 129
  rivalry, competitive, 129
  supplier selling power, 129

Industry forces and competition/competitive position, 126, 127

Inelastic price performance, 183–85

Influencers, market, 329

Information search, competitor, 134

Infrastructure and push communications, market, 231, 233

Innovation, new product, 166–67

Innovators and emerging markets, 63–64

In-process *vs.* end-result performance metrics,
  31, 32

Intel, 159, 266, 276

Intellectual property, costs incurred to
  create/maintain, 206–8

Intelligence, competitor, 133, 134

Intention to buy, 70–71

Intermediaries, market, 329

Internal *vs.* external performance metrics, 30–31

International Research Institute (IRI), 234

Internet computer-based purchasing, 201

Intuit, 80, 82

Inventory, investment in, 352

Ivester, Douglas, 261

Johnson Controls, 218–19

K2, 269, 299
Kellogg, 160
Knight, Phil, 57

Large segment strategy, 118–19
Lead customers, 63
Leadership, marketing, 18, 19–20
Lead segments in mainstream market, 64
Learning effects, 139
Leveraging core capabilities, 299
Lexus, 92, 96, 162
Life cycle, product, 67–68
Lifestyle influences shaping consumer market
    needs, 106–7
Lincoln Towncar, 131, 132
L.L. Bean, 201
Loctite Corporation, 85, 153–54
Long-run survival and a strong market orienta-
    tion, 6

Maintenance costs, 85
Management, market-based, 3, 328, 357–59.
    See also Profit impact of market-based man-
    agement; *individual subject headings*
Margin per customer, 348–49
Market access, 113, 142
Market analysis. *See* Analysis, market;
    Competitor analysis and competitive posi-
    tion; Customer analysis; Portfolio analysis
    and strategic market plans; Segmentation,
    needs-based market; Value creation, cus-
    tomer analysis and
Market definition. *See* Definition, market
Market demand. *See* Demand, market
Market development index (MDI), 62, 76
Market growth. *See* Growth, market/business;
    Potential, marketing
Market infrastructure and push communica-
    tions, 231, 233
Marketing cost scope effect, 139–40
Marketing mix, 69–70, 117
Marketing strategies, 151. *See also* Channels and
    sales systems, marketing; Communications
    and customer response, marketing; Price(s)
    and pricing strategies; Product positioning

Market orientation. *See also* Customer satisfac-
    tion; *individual subject headings*
advantage, marketing, 142–43
building a, 18
change as the only constant, 5–6
connectivity between market orientation/cus-
    tomer satisfaction/market-based manage-
    ment/profitability, 3
cost advantage, 139–40
employee satisfaction, 20, 22
knowledge, marketing, 18–19
leadership, marketing, 19–20
long and short-run benefits, 5–6
management characteristics, three, 6–7
profitability, 347–50
weak, underwhelming customers/shareholders
    with a, 6, 7
Market Share Index, 71–72. *See also* Share, mar-
    ket
Marriott, 160
Mary Kay Cosmetics, 201
Mass customization strategy, 122
Mass market strategy, 118
MBNA America, 12
McDonald's, 140, 266
Media selection and customer awareness,
    219–20
Mercedes, 121, 131, 132
Message frequency and customer awareness,
    220–22
Message reinforcement, 222–24
Metrics, market/performance
    dissatisfied customers, 332–34
    early stages of marketing plan implementa-
        tion, 328
    end-result, 336–37
    internal *vs.* external metrics, 30–31
    process, 334–35
Microsoft, 194, 271, 278
Mixed channel systems, 201
Moore's Law, 159
Multisegment strategies, 120, 121

**National Cash Register Corporation (NCR),
    270**
NBC, 126
NCR, 20, 22

Needs, customer/business market, 105–8. *See also* Segmentation, needs-based market

Nested hierarchy, 122

Net marketing contribution (NMC), 33–37, 47, 250, 337–40, 350

Net present value, 17–18

Net profit, 350

New customer segments, strategies to enter, 266–67

New market entry strategies, 268
   diversified, 269–70
   potential, strategies to develop new market, 271
   related, 269
   strategies to enter, 270–71

New product development
   cross-functional teams, 168–69
   Hewlett-Packard (HP), 171
   innovation, commitment to, 166–67
   inputs, process, 167–68
   outputs, process, 169–70
   price and pricing strategies, 189–91
   sales, 166
   testing, concept, 168, 170

NewVector Consulting, 145–46

Niche segment strategies, 122, 282–84

Nike, 96, 144

Nordstrom, 20, 160

Ocean Spray, 58

Offensive strategic market plans
   Coca-Cola, 261
   Compaq Computer, 273
   defensive and, selecting between, 262–63
   evaluating, 272
   new market entry strategies, 268–71
   penetration strategies, 263–68
   performance impact, 250
   portfolio analysis, 250

Old Navy, 175

On-line marketing, 201

Operating expenses, 33, 34

Opportunities, identifying, 298–99

Oregon Chai, 76

Organizations, market-based, 44–46

Orientation. *See* Market orientation

Original equipment manufacturers (OEMs), 200, 203

Overhead cost advantage, 140

Ownership, marketing plan, 326–28

Ownership costs, 85–86

Peapod, 201

Penetration strategies, market
   alternate care segment strategy, 312
   customer purchase, 265–66
   demand, market, 267–68, 318
   new customer segments, 266–67
   price and pricing strategies, 190–91
   rate of market growth, 63–64
   share, market, 263–65, 319, 323
   Stericycle, Inc., 317–24

Perceived benefits and value creation
   AdvanTech, 101
   benchmark competitors, 131
   company or brand benefits, 92–93
   cost of purchase, 93–94
   evaluating the degree of value created, businesses, 94–95
   overall customer benefits, 93
   price and pricing strategies, 177–78
   product benefits, 90–91
   service benefits, 91–92

Performance, market-based. *See also* Implementation and performance metrics
   accounting systems, 37–39
   defensive strategic market plans, 251–52, 277–78
   diversification across product-markets, 270
   evaluation, 309, 313–14
   financial *vs.* market performance, 27–30
   growth, profitable, 39–42
   measure of profitability, 32–39
   metrics, market/performance, 30–31, 332–38
   net marketing contribution, 33–37
   offensive strategic market plans, 250
   organizations, market-based, 44–46
   penetration strategies, 322–24
   plan, building a marketing, 299–300
   planning, strategic market, 244–45
   price elasticity, 183–86
   productivity, marketing, 43–44
   SWOT analysis, 303–4, 311–12
   tactical marketing strategy, 253–55

Performance, market-based *(continued)*
 timeline, 308–9, 313, 324
 value creation, customer analysis and, 87–90
Perfume de Paris, 205
Perrier, 92
Persistence, 330–31
Personality and value creation, 96–97
Philosophy, market-based management, 3
Place strategies, 69
Plan, building a marketing. *See also*
  Implementation and performance metrics
 benefits of, 298–300
 budget, marketing, 306–8
 creativity *vs.* structure, 298
 performance timeline/evaluation, 308–9
 process and logic, 300–9
 sample marketing plan, 309–13
 situation analysis, 300–303
 Stericycle, Inc., 297, 314, 317–24
 strategic market plan, 304–5
 SWOT analysis, 303–4
 tactical marketing strategy, 305–6
Planning, strategic market, 239, 304–5, 312.
  See also Defensive strategic market plans;
  Offensive strategic market plans; Portfolio
  analysis and strategic market plans
 attractiveness, market, 245–47
 competitive advantage, 247–48
 diversification across product-markets,
  242–43
 Fluid Life Corporation (FLC), 256–57
 performance, business, 244–45
 process, planning, 243–44
Plus-one product positioning, 162
Portfolio analysis and strategic market plans,
  248–49
 defensive strategic market plans and performance impact, 251–52
 offensive strategic market plans and performance impact, 250
 tactical marketing strategy and performance
  plan, 252–55
Positioning products. *See* Product positioning
Potential, market. *See also* Growth, market
 accelerating market growth, 64–66
 market development index, 62
 new market entry strategies, 271

 rate of market development, 63–64
 rate of market growth, three forces capturing,
  62–63
 share potential and market share management,
  72–73
 untapped market opportunities, 59–61
Present value table, 26
Press, general/business/trade, 329
Price(s) and pricing strategies
 break-even analysis, 191–93
 competitor analysis and competitive position,
  180–81, 185–86
 cost-based pricing, 175–76, 179–81
 customer trade-off: benefits *vs.* price, 97–100
 defensive strategic market plans, 251–52
 differentiation, product, 161–62
 elasticity, 183–86, 229–30
 harvest price strategy, 286–87
 market-based pricing, 175–79
 marketing mix, 69
 Microsoft, 194
 new products, 189–91
 offensive strategic market plans, 250
 price-earnings ratio, 357
 prisoner's dilemma, 130
 product line pricing, 186–87
 product positioning, 153, 154
 promotion pricing, 187–89
 pull communications and customer response,
  229–30
 reference price, 181–82
 relative price, 88–89
 value creation, customer analysis and, 83–84,
  88–90
Prisoner's dilemma, 130
Process market metrics, 334–35
Procter & Gamble, 164
Prodigy, 271
Productivity, marketing, 43–44
Product positioning
 customer value, 100
 differentiation, 157–62
 line positioning, 162–66
 Loctite Corporation, 153–54
 management strategies, 156–57
 new product development, 166–71
 plus-one, 162

Sears, 154–55
segment positioning strategy, 114–16
share, market, 155–56
Product(s). *See also* Brands, product;
    Differentiation, product
availability, 71
awareness, 70
bundling/unbundling, 165–66, 188–89
diversification across product-markets,
    242–43
flagship, 182
growth, product influences on market, 65–66
life cycle, 67–68
line pricing, 186–87
marketing mix, 69
organizations, product driven, 44–45
perceived benefits and value creation, 90–91
preference, 70
purchase, 71
substitutes, 129, 186–87
value creation, customer analysis and, 87–90,
    92–93
Profit impact of market-based management
assets, marketing strategies affecting, 350–53
connectivity between market orientation/cus-
    tomer satisfaction/market-based manage-
    ment/profitability, 3
customer satisfaction, 345–47
management, market-based, 357–59
marketing strategies affecting profitability,
    347–50
overwhelming customers and shareholders,
    344–45
Profit Impact of Marketing Strategies (PIMS)
    database, 279–81
return measures of profitability, 353–55
shareholder value, measures of, 355–57
Stericycle, Inc., 360
Profit(s)
accounting systems, 37–39
channels and sales systems, marketing,
    210–212
customer satisfaction, 11–15
Dell Computer, 47
elements of profitability, breaking down the,
    32–33
Fluid Life Corporation (FLC), 256

marketing strategies designed to grow prof-
    itability, 39–42
net, 350
net marketing contribution, 33–37
offensive strategic market plans, 261
penetration strategies, 321
planning, strategic market, 244
segmentation, needs-based market, 113–14
Promotion, 69, 116
Promotion pricing, 187–89, 229–30
Protect market strategies
customer retention, 284–85
follower share position, 281–83
growth, market/business, 279–80
high-share position, 280–81
niche share position, 282–84
selective market focus, 285–86
share, market, 278–79
Psychological needs, 95
Pull type communications, 225–30
Pulsing and message reinforcement, 223
Push communications, 225, 230–31

Quality, product, 158–59
Quicken, 80

Rate of entry, 63
Rate of market development, 63–64
Reference price and price strategy, 181–82
Relationship marketing, 205–6
Relative performance, 87–88
Relative price, 88–89
Reliability and service quality, 160
Reputation, brand/company, 142
Resource allocation, 299, 313, 322, 324, 328
Responsiveness and service quality, 160
Return measures of profitability, 353–55
Revenue per customer, strategies to increase, 41
Rivalry, competitive, 129
Roll-out of a marketing plan, 331

Sales. *See also* **Channels and sales systems,**
    marketing
advertising carryover effects, 227–28
advertising elasticity, 226–27
budget, marketing, 308
defensive strategic market plans, 251–52

Sales *(continued)*
   diversification across product-markets, 242–43
   Fluid Life Corporation (FLC), 256
   market-based *vs.* sales-based organizational structure, 46
   new product development, 166
   offensive strategic market plans, 250, 261
   planning, strategic market, 244
   price elasticity, 229–30
   productivity, 209
   return on, 353–55
   revenues, 33
   sales force advantage, 143, 208–9
Santa Fe Sportswear Company. *See* Performance, market-based
Scale effect, 138–39
Schmalansee, Richard, 194
Scope effect, 139
Sears, 20, 154–55
Segmentation, needs-based market, 105
   acid test, segment strategy, 116–17
   adjacent segment strategies, 119
   attractiveness, segment, 111–13
   business market needs, forces that shape, 107–8
   consumer market needs, forces that shape, 106–7
   demographic trap, 109–10
   identification, segment, 111
   large segment strategy, 118–19
   lead segments in mainstream market, 64
   marketing mix strategy, 117
   mass customization, 122
   mass market strategy, 118
   multisegment strategies, 120, 121
   niche segment strategies, 122
   penetration strategies, 318
   positioning, segment, 114–16
   price and pricing strategies, 178–79
   profitability, 113–14
   small segment strategy, 120–21
   steps in segmentation process, 110–11
   strategies, segmentation, 118–23
   Web Depot, 123
Selective market focus, 285–86, 323
Selling power, supplier, 129
Served market definition, 58–59, 76

Service(s)
   channels and sales systems, marketing, 205
   differentiation, product, 141–42, 159, 160
   perceived benefits and value creation, 91–92
   quality, product, 159
Share, market. *See also* Protect market strategies
   Blockbuster Entertainment, 212
   break-even analysis and pricing strategies, 192–93
   decomposition of a marketing plan, variance, 337–40
   defensive strategic market plans, 251–52
   distributor and market share, relationship between, 143
   Fluid Life Corporation (FLC), 256
   harvest resource strategy, 288
   marketing strategies to increase, 41
   Market Share Index, 71–72
   measuring/determining, equation for, 68
   offensive strategic market plans, 250, 261
   penetration strategies, 263–65, 319, 323
   planning, strategic market, 244
   potential and market share management, share, 72–73
   product positioning, 155–56
   Share Development Index (SDI), 73–74, 76, 264
   Share Development Tree, 69–71
Shareholder value, 344–45, 355–57, 359
Short-run benefits of a strong market orientation, 6
Simon, H., 151
Situation analysis, 300–3, 311, 317–21
Six sigma programs, 158
Skills and implementing the marketing plan, 329
Skim pricing, 189–90
Small segment strategy, 120–21
Smith, Fred, 57, 239
Solutions, developing complete, 63–64, 66
Standard Industrial Classification (SIC) code, 107
Stead, Jerry, 53
Stericycle, Inc., 297, 314, 317–24, 341, 360. *See also* Plan, building a marketing
Stericycle Marketing Plan, 317–24
Strategic market definition, 57
Strategic market planning. *See* Defensive strategic market plans; Offensive strategic market

plans; Planning, strategic market; Portfolio analysis and strategic market plans

Structure *vs.* creativity in building a marketing plan, 298

Substitute products, 129, 186–87

Sub-Zero, 122

Supplier selling power, 129

Survival and a strong market orientation, 6

Sustainers, cost-focused, 108

SWOT analysis, 303–4, 311–12, 321

Tactical marketing strategy/plan, 244, 252–55, 295, 305–6, 312–13. *See also* Implementation and performance metrics; Plan, building a marketing; Profit impact of market-based management

Tangibles and service quality, 160

Target customers, 329

Team approach, 7

Testing, new product concept, 168, 170

3M, 223–24

Timberland, 96

Time to succeed, 328

Top-down budget, 307

Total contribution, 349

Toyota, 119, 163

Trade-offs, customer, 97–100, 104

Trade press, 329

Trade promotions and customer response, 230–31

Transaction costs, 162, 208

Two-tier marketing channels, 200–201

Umbrella branding, 164–65

Unit volume vector, 74–75

Usage behaviors, shaping business/consumer market needs, 107, 108

Usage costs, 84–85

Use, restricting a market from reaching its full potential, ability to, 60

Value-added resellers (VARs), 165, 200, 203

Value creation, customer analysis and. *See also* Perceived benefits and value creation channels and sales systems, marketing, 204–7

economic benefits, 83–87

emotional benefits, 95–97

lifetime value of a customer, 16–18

price and performance, 87–90

shareholder value, 344–45, 355–57, 359

trade-offs, customer, 97–100, 104

Value map, 89–90

Value proposition and positioning strategy, 115–16

Variable costs, 34, 42, 137–39

Variable expenses, 33

Variance decomposition of a marketing plan, 337–40

Vertical *vs.* horizontal market opportunities, 57–58

Vision, market, 56–57

Volume, customer, 347–48, 351–53

Volume advantage, unit cost advantage due to, 138–39

Volvo, 131, 132, 162

Vulnerability and diversification across product-markets, 270

Wal-Mart, 136

Web Depot, 123

Welch, Jack, 3

Westinghouse, 269

Weyerhaeuser, 81, 82–83

Whirlpool, 167, 168

Xerox, 135–36

Young, Whitney, Jr., 295

Zi-Tech Acoustics, 253–55